365 Homemade Halal Recipes

(365 Homemade Halal Recipes - Volume 1)

Doris Naquin

Content

365 AWESOME HALAL RECIPES 9

1. 3 Bean Good Luck Salad With Cumin Vinaigrette 9
2. Alaskan Cod In Sweet And Sour Pepper Sauce 10
3. Amaranth Porridge With Grated Apples And Maple Syrup 10
4. Amaranth, Ricotta And Greens Pancakes 11
5. Andalusian Chickpea And Spinach Soup .. 12
6. Apple Compote 12
7. Apple Walnut Galette 13
8. Apple And Bitter Lettuces Salad 14
9. Apricot, Cherry And Almond Galette 14
10. Arugula And Corn Salad With Roasted Red Peppers And White Beans 15
11. Asian Pasta With Tofu, Shiitake Mushrooms And Broccoli 16
12. Asparagus, Green Beans And Potatoes With Green Mole Sauce 17
13. Avocado And Roasted Tomatillo Salsa 17
14. Baked Acorn Squash With Walnut Oil And Maple Syrup 18
15. Baked Beans With Sweet Potatoes And Chipotles 18
16. Baked Halibut With Tomato Caper Sauce 19
17. Baked Orzo With Tomatoes, Roasted Peppers And Zucchini 20
18. Baked Ricotta Frittata With Fresh Mint 21
19. Baked Stuffed Acorn Squash 21
20. Baked Tomatoes With Arugula Pesto 22
21. Baked And Sautéed Spaghetti Squash On A Bed Of Spinach 22
22. Balsamic Roasted Winter Squash And Wild Rice Salad 23
23. Banana Muesli Smoothie 24
24. Banana Oatmeal Almond Smoothie 25
25. Banana Wild Blueberry Smoothie With Chia Seeds 25
26. Barberry And Orange Tea 26
27. Barley And Herb Salad With Roasted Asparagus 26
28. Barley, Celery Root And Mushroom Salad With Scallion Vinaigrette 27
29. Beet Green, Rice And Ricotta Blinis 28
30. Beet Greens Bulgur With Carrots And Tomatoes 28
31. Beet Greens And Rice Gratin 29
32. Beet And Arugula Salad With Berries 30
33. Beet And Chia Pancakes 30
34. Beet, Mushroom And Beef Burgers 31
35. Berry Clafoutis 32
36. Black Quinoa, Fennel And Celery Salad 32
37. Black Eyed Pea Salad 33
38. Black Eyed Peas With Collard Greens 34
39. Blackberry Lime Smoothie With Chia Seeds And Cashews 34
40. Blender Gazpacho With Celery, Carrot, Cucumber And Red Pepper 35
41. Blood Orange, Grapefruit And Pomegranate Compote 35
42. Blueberry Kefir Smoothie With Greens 36
43. Breakfast Wheat Berries 37
44. Broccoli, Quinoa And Purslane Salad 37
45. Broiled Calf's Liver 38
46. Brown Rice With Carrots And Leeks 38
47. Brown Rice And Barley Salad With Sprouted Red Lentils And Green Beans 39
48. Brown Rice, Sesame, Spinach And Scallion Pancakes 40
49. Brown Soda Bread With Oats 40
50. Buckwheat Crêpes 41
51. Bulgur Bowl With Spinach, Mushrooms And Dukkah 42
52. Bulgur Pilaf With Dried Fruit And Nuts ... 43
53. Bulgur Salad With Greens, Barberries And Yogurt 44
54. Bulgur And Chickpea Salad With Roasted Artichokes 44
55. Bulgur And Lentil Salad 45
56. Bulgur And Walnut Kibbeh 46
57. Butternut Squash And Purple Potato Latkes 46
58. Butternut Squash And Sage Latkes 47
59. Cabbage And Carrot Noodles With Egg .. 48
60. Cabbage And Spring Onion Quiche With Caraway 49
61. Carrot, Parsnip And Potato Colcannon 50
62. Cauliflower Gratin With Goat Cheese Topping 50
63. Cauliflower, Potato And Quinoa Patties ... 51

64. Celeriac, Celery And Carrot Remoulade ... 52
65. Celeriac, Potato, Leek And Apple Soup.... 52
66. Celery And Walnut (or Hazelnut) Tzatziki53
67. Chard Stalk, Celeriac And Leek Soup........ 54
68. Chard Stalk, Chickpea, Tahini And Yogurt Dip 54
69. Chard And Sweet Corn Tacos 55
70. Cherry And Apricot Clafoutis................... 55
71. Cherry And Spring Onion Salsa 56
72. Chicken Soup With Lime And Avocado .. 56
73. Chickpeas With Baby Spinach 57
74. Chilean Cabbage And Avocado Slaw 58
75. Chipotle Gazpacho 58
76. Chopped Salad With Apples, Walnuts And Bitter Lettuces 59
77. Chunky Avocado Papaya Salsa 59
78. Cold Poached Pacific Cod With Spices..... 60
79. Cold Sesame Noodles With Sweet Peppers 60
80. Collard Greens Stuffed With Quinoa And Turkey.. 61
81. Collard Greens With Farro...................... 62
82. Cooked Tomatillo Salsa 63
83. Cornmeal And Buckwheat Blueberry Muffins 64
84. Cornmeal And Oatmeal Polenta With Tomato Sauce And Parmesan 64
85. Couscous With Tomatoes, Cauliflower, Red Peppers And Olives 65
86. Couscous With Tomatoes, Kale And Chickpeas 65
87. Couscous With Tomatoes, White Beans, Squash And Peppers 66
88. Cracked Farro Risotto (Farrotto) With Parsley And Marjoram 67
89. Creamy 'Ranch' Dressing........................... 68
90. Crispy Polenta Medallions 69
91. Cucumber Salad With Soy, Ginger And Garlic 69
92. Cucumber And Radish Salad With Yogurt And Cumin 70
93. Dill Soup.. 70
94. Dried Fruit Compote With Fresh Apple And Pear 71
95. Dried Porcini Consommé........................ 72
96. Easy Fish Stew With Mediterranean Flavors 72
97. Egg Lemon Soup With Turkey 73
98. Eggplant And Tomato Pie 74
99. Eggplant, Tomato And Chickpea Casserole 75
100. Endive Leaves With Crab Rillettes............ 76
101. Endive Salad With Blue Cheese Dressing. 76
102. Endive, Apple And Kasha Salad................ 76
103. Enfrijoladas... 77
104. Farro And Swiss Chard Salad With Grapefruit Vinaigrette..................................... 78
105. Farro Or Bulgur With Black Eyed Peas, Chard And Feta.. 79
106. Fattoush With Dukkah 79
107. Fava Bean And Asparagus Salad................ 80
108. Fennel Rice.. 80
109. Fettuccine With Brussels Sprouts, Lemon And Ricotta... 81
110. Focaccia With Cauliflower And Sage......... 82
111. Focaccia With Tomatoes And Rosemary.. 82
112. Forbidden Rice Pudding With Blueberries 83
113. Fried Green Beans, Scallions And Brussels Sprouts With Buttermilk Cornmeal Coating.......84
114. Fried Small Peppers Filled With Feta And Quinoa 85
115. Frittata With Brown Rice, Peas And Pea Shoots 85
116. Garlic Shrimp With Peas 86
117. Garlic Soup With Spinach........................87
118. Gingered Winter Fruit Ambrosia 87
119. Gluten Free Apple, Pear And Cranberry Pecan Crumble 88
120. Gluten Free Apple Almond Tart...............89
121. Gluten Free Banana Chocolate Muffins....90
122. Gluten Free Buckwheat, Poppy Seed And Blueberry Muffins 91
123. Gluten Free Chocolate Buckwheat Biscotti 91
124. Gluten Free Cornmeal Molasses Muffins .92
125. Gluten Free Cornmeal, Fig And Orange Muffins 93
126. Gluten Free Dessert Pastry........................93
127. Gluten Free Penne With Peas, Ricotta And Tarragon 94
128. Gluten Free Raisin Pistachio Biscotti 95
129. Gluten Free Spaghetti With Baby Broccoli, Mushrooms And Walnuts 95

130. Granola Muffins 96
131. Greek Baked Squash Omelet 97
132. Green Bean Salad With Lime Vinaigrette And Red Quinoa......................97
133. Green Pipian 98
134. Green Smoothie With Cucumber And Cumin 99
135. Green Smoothie With Pineapple, Arugula, Greens And Cashews......................99
136. Green Tomato Salsa Verde 99
137. Greens And Chayote Enchiladas With Salsa Verde......................100
138. Grilled Eggplant And Tomatoes With Chermoula 101
139. Grilled Goat Cheese, Roasted Pepper, And Greens Sandwich 102
140. Grilled Pizza With Grilled Red Onions And Feta 102
141. Grilled Vanilla Ginger Pineapple.............103
142. Grilled Watermelon And Feta Salad........104
143. Grits Rancheras 104
144. Herb Fritters......................105
145. Honey Spice Bread......................106
146. Italian Meat Sauce With Half The Meat..107
147. Kasha......................107
148. Korean Chilled Buckwheat Noodles With Chilled Broth And Kimchi 108
149. Lasagna With Spinach And Wild Mushrooms......................109
150. Leek, Kale And Potato Latkes 110
151. Lemon And Garlic Chicken With Spiced Spinach......................110
152. Lentil Soup With Cilantro (Lots Of It) ...111
153. Lentil And Herb Salad With Roasted Peppers And Feta......................112
154. Lentils With Smoked Trout Rilletes........113
155. Mackerel With Peas......................114
156. Mango Buttermilk Smoothie 114
157. Mango Lime Sorbet 114
158. Maple Pecan Pancakes......................115
159. Marinated Cauliflower And Carrots With Mint 115
160. Marinated Olives 116
161. Mashed Potato And Broccoli Raab Pancakes......................116
162. Mashed Potato And Cabbage Pancakes..117
163. Meal In A Bowl With Chicken, Rice Noodles And Spinach......................118
164. Mediterranean Lentil Purée......................119
165. Millet Polenta With Mushrooms And Broccoli Or Broccoli Raab......................119
166. Millet Polenta With Tomato Sauce, Eggplant And Chickpeas......................120
167. Millet And Greens Gratin......................121
168. Millet And Red Pepper Polenta 122
169. Mini Peppers Stuffed With Tuna And Olive Rillettes 123
170. Mushroom Burgers With Almonds And Spinach......................123
171. Mushroom Melt With Parsley Pesto, Kale And Arugula......................124
172. Mushroom Omelet With Chives.............125
173. Mushroom And Beef Burgers 126
174. Mushroom And Daikon Soup.................127
175. Noodle Bowl With Mushrooms, Spinach And Salmon 127
176. Northern Greek Mushroom And Onion Pie 128
177. Oatmeal And Teff With Cinnamon And Dried Fruit......................129
178. Oats With Amaranth, Chia Seeds And Blueberries......................129
179. Olive Oil Granola With Dried Apricots And Pistachios......................130
180. Omelets With Roasted Vegetables And Feta 130
181. Onion And Zucchini Frittata To Go 131
182. Orecchiette With Basil And Pistachio Pesto And Green And Yellow Beans......................131
183. Orecchiette With Fresh And Dried Beans And Tomatoes......................132
184. Orecchiette With Raw And Cooked Tomatoes......................133
185. Oven Fries 134
186. Oven Baked Millet......................134
187. Oven Steamed Cod Or Mahi Mahi In Green Tomatillo Salsa......................135
188. Pan Fried Broccoli Stems......................135
189. Pasta With Asparagus, Arugula And Ricotta 136
190. Pasta With Mushrooms And Broccoli....136
191. Pasta With Mushrooms And Gremolata 137
192. Pasta With Zucchini And Mint 138
193. Pear Clafoutis 138

194. Pear Vanilla Sorbet......................................139
195. Pear And Apple Soufflé 140
196. Pearl Couscous With Sautéed Cherry Tomatoes..140
197. Peppers Stuffed With Rice, Zucchini And Herbs 141
198. Peppers Stuffed With Farro And Smoked Cheese...142
199. Perciatelli With Broccoli, Tomatoes And Anchovies 142
200. Persimmon Spice Bread 143
201. Pesto Filled Deviled Eggs.........................144
202. Pickled Asparagus 144
203. Pickled Green Tomatoes 145
204. Pineapple Avocado Salsa 146
205. Pineapple Chia Smoothie With Herbs.....146
206. Pineapple And Millet Smoothie................147
207. Pizza Margherita 147
208. Pizza With Spring Onions And Fennel...147
209. Pizza On The Grill With Cherry Tomatoes, Mozzarella And Arugula 148
210. Polenta Or Grits With Beans And Chard 149
211. Poppy, Lemon And Sunflower Seed Pancakes..150
212. Potato Focaccia With Oyster Mushrooms 150
213. Potato And Collard Green Hash...............152
214. Potato, Green Bean And Spinach Salad..152
215. Provençal Artichoke Ragout 153
216. Provençal Onion Pizza................................154
217. Provençal Tomato And Bean Gratin.......155
218. Provençal Zucchini And Swiss Chard Tart 156
219. Publican Chicken...157
220. Pumpkin Caramel Mousse.........................157
221. Puree Of Chickpea Soup 158
222. Puree Of Shell Beans And Potato............159
223. Pureed Carrot Soup 159
224. Pureed Potato And Broccoli Soup With Parmesan Croutons....................................160
225. Puréed Trahana And Vegetable Soup 161
226. Puréed Winter Squash Soup With Ginger 162
227. Quiche With Red Peppers And Spinach.162
228. Quick Fresh Tomatillo Salsa 163
229. Quick Grilled Flanken With Chili, Sesame

And Ginger 164
230. Quick Quesadilla With Dukkah 164
231. Quinoa Bowl With Artichokes, Spring Onions And Peas 165
232. Quinoa And Carrot Kugel 166
233. Rainbow Beef.. 166
234. Raw And Cooked Tomato And Herb Salad With Couscous 167
235. Red Cabbage, Carrot And Broccoli Stem Latkes With Caraway And Sesame 168
236. Refrigerator Corn Relish 169
237. Rice Pilaf With Carrots And Parsley 169
238. Rice Pilaf With Pistachios And Almonds170
239. Risotto With Winter Squash And Collard Greens 171
240. Risotto With Asparagus And Pesto......... 172
241. Roasted Broccoli With Tahini Garlic Sauce 173
242. Roasted Carrot, Parsnip And Potato Soup 173
243. Roasted Carrots With Turmeric And Cumin 174
244. Roasted Carrots And Scallions With Thyme And Hazelnuts...................................... 175
245. Roasted Corn And Tomato Salsa 176
246. Roasted Mushroom Base 176
247. Roasted Mushroom And Gruyère Sandwich 177
248. Roasted Sweet Potato Oven Fries 178
249. Roasted Tomatillo Poblano Avocado Salsa 178
250. Roasted Winter Vegetable Medley.......... 179
251. Rose Petal And Vanilla Tea 180
252. Salmon Rillettes... 180
253. Salmon Tacos With Greens And Tomatillo Salsa 181
254. Salmon And Cucumber Tartare With Wasabi Sauce 181
255. Salmon In Fig Leaves................................ 182
256. Salsa Fresca With Kohlrabi...................... 182
257. Sautéed Apple Rings 183
258. Sautéed Spicy Carrots With Black Quinoa 183
259. Sautéed Winter Squash With Swiss Chard, Red Quinoa And Aleppo Pepper..................... 184
260. Savory Cornbread Stuffing 185
261. Savory Oatmeal Pan Bread 186

262. Savory Whole Wheat Buttermilk Scones With Rosemary And Thyme 186

263. Scallion And Celery Quiche 187

264. Seared Brussels Sprouts 188

265. Seared Red Cabbage Wedges 188

266. Shell Beans And Potato Ragout With Swiss Chard 189

267. Shredded Beet And Radish Slaw With Rice Noodles 189

268. Sicilian Cauliflower And Black Olive Gratin 190

269. Simple Pencil Cob Breakfast Grits 191

270. Simple Trahana Soup With Lemon And Olive Oil 191

271. Skordalia 192

272. Small Apricot Galettes 193

273. Smoked Sardines Rillettes 193

274. Soba Noodles With Shiitakes, Broccoli And Tofu 194

275. Soba And Herb Salad With Roasted Eggplant And Pluots 194

276. Soda Bread With Walnuts And Raisins ... 195

277. Soft Tacos With Chicken And Tomato Corn Salsa 196

278. Soft Tacos With Scrambled Tofu And Tomatoes 197

279. Soufflé Omelet With Apricot Sauce 197

280. Soy Ginger Chicken With Greens 198

281. Spaghetti Squash With Garlic, Parsley And Breadcrumbs 199

282. Spaghetti With Broccoli And Walnut/Ricotta Pesto 200

283. Spaghetti With Cauliflower, Almonds, Tomatoes And Chickpeas 200

284. Spaghetti With Roasted Cauliflower, Tomato Sauce And Olives 201

285. Spiced Green Beans And Baby Broccoli Tempura 202

286. Spiced Roasted Almonds 203

287. Spiced Tomato Ketchup 203

288. Spiced Wok Popped Popcorn 204

289. Spiced Yellow Lentils With Quinoa 204

290. Spicy Carrot And Spinach Latkes 205

291. Spicy Carrot, Parsnip And Potato Latkes 206

292. Spicy Egyptian Dukkah With Chickpea Flour 207

293. Spicy Lentil And Sweet Potato Stew With Chipotles 207

294. Spicy Quinoa Salad With Broccoli, Cilantro And Lime 208

295. Spinach Gnocchi 208

296. Spinach Soup With Coriander, Cinnamon And Allspice 209

297. Spinach With Garlic Yogurt And Walnut Dukkah 210

298. Spring Rolls With Spinach, Mushrooms, Sesame, Rice And Herbs 211

299. Spring Rolls With Tofu, Vegetables, Rice Noodles And Herbs 212

300. Stir Fried Beans With Tofu And Chiles .. 213

301. Stir Fried Rice Noodles With Beets And Beet Greens 213

302. Stir Fried Soba Noodles With Turkey And Cabbage 214

303. Stir Fried Tofu And Peppers 215

304. Stir Fried Turkey Breast With Snap Or Snow Peas And Chard 216

305. Stir Fried Rice With Amaranth Or Red Chard And Thai Basil 217

306. Stracciatella With Spinach 218

307. Strawberry Smoothie 218

308. Strawberry Soup 218

309. Stuffed Peppers With Red Rice, Chard And Feta 219

310. Stuffed Roasted Yellow Peppers Or Red Peppers In Tomato Sauce 220

311. Summer Squash Ribbons With Cherry Tomatoes And Mint/Basil Pesto 221

312. Summer Tacos With Corn, Green Beans And Tomatillo Salsa 221

313. Summer Tomato Gratin 222

314. Suvir Saran's Palak Ki Tiki (Spinach And Potato Patties) 222

315. Sweet Potato And Apple Latkes With Ginger And Sweet Spices 223

316. Sweet Potato, Quinoa, Spinach And Red Lentil Burger 224

317. Sweet Whole Wheat Focaccia With Pears And Walnuts 225

318. Sweet And Sour Stir Fried Radishes With Their Greens 226

319. Sweet And Sour Winter Squash 227

320. Sweet Potato Stew 227

321. Tacos With Summer Squash, Tomatoes

And Beans..228

322. Tacos With Roasted Potatoes, Squash And Peppers (Rajas)..228

323. Tarragon Cucumber Pickles....................229

324. Teff Polenta Croutons Or Cakes.............230

325. Teff Pancakes With Chia, Millet And Blueberries..230

326. Thanksgiving Mixed Bean Chili With Corn And Pumpkin..231

327. Three Greens Gratin...............................232

328. Tomato And Avocado Salsa....................233

329. Tostadas With Smashed Black Beans Or Vaqueros..233

330. Tuna Ceviche Or Tartare With Avocado 234

331. Tuna Mushroom Burgers.........................234

332. Turkey And Vegetable Burgers................235

333. Turkish Pumpkin Soup............................236

334. Turkish Tarator Sauce With Beets And Beet Greens..236

335. Turkish Yogurt And Spinach Dip............237

336. Two Bean And Tuna Salad.......................238

337. Uncooked Tomato And Mint Sauce With Poached Eggs..238

338. Vegetable Torta.....................................239

339. Veracruzana Vinegar Bathed Shrimp.......240

340. Warm Chickpeas And Greens With Vinaigrette..241

341. Warm Hummus.......................................242

342. West African Peanut Soup With Chicken 242

343. Wheat Berries With Broccoli.....................243

344. Wheat Berries With Spinach And Spring Onion..244

345. White Tepary Bean And Potato Purée....245

346. Whole Grain Macaroni And Cheese........245

347. Whole Wheat Almond Biscotti................246

348. Whole Wheat Apple Pecan Scones..........247

349. Whole Wheat Focaccia With Cherry Tomatoes And Olives..248

350. Whole Wheat Focaccia With Peppers And Eggplant..249

351. Whole Wheat Focaccia With Tomatoes And Fontina..250

352. Whole Wheat Mediterranean Pie Crust...251

353. Whole Grain Blueberry Buckle................252

354. Whole Grain Pasta With Mushrooms, Asparagus And Favas..253

355. Whole Wheat Buttermilk Scones With Raisins And Oatmeal..254

356. Whole Wheat Focaccia..........................255

357. Whole Wheat Seeded Loaves..................255

358. Winter Squash Puree With Tahini..........256

359. Winter Squash And Potato Gratin..........257

360. Winter Squash, Leek And Farro Gratin With Feta And Mint..257

361. Winter Tomato Quiche............................258

362. Yogurt And Bean Dressing With Cilantro And Lime..259

363. Yogurt And Bean Dressing With Thai Flavors..260

364. Yogurt Or Buttermilk Soup With Spinach And Grains..260

365. Yogurt Or Buttermilk Soup With Toasted Barley..261

INDEX 262

CONCLUSION 267

365 Awesome Halal Recipes

***

---

1. 3 Bean Good Luck Salad With Cumin Vinaigrette

Serving: 6 servings | Prep: | Cook: |Ready in: 1hours45mins

Ingredients

- For the Beans
- ¾ cup dried black beans, washed, picked over and soaked for 6 hours or overnight in 3 cups water
- ¾ cup dried red beans or kidney beans, washed, picked over and soaked for 6 hours or overnight in 3 cups water
- 2 onions, halved
- 4 garlic cloves, minced
- Salt to taste
- ¾ cup black-eyed peas, washed and picked over
- 1 bay leaf
- For the Dressing and Salad
- ¼ cup red wine vinegar or sherry vinegar
- 1 garlic clove, minced
- Salt and freshly ground pepper to taste
- 2 teaspoons lightly toasted cumin, ground
- 1 teaspoon Dijon mustard
- ½ cup broth from the beans
- ⅓ cup extra virgin olive oil
- 1 red bell pepper, diced
- ½ cup chopped cilantro

Direction

- Place a strainer over a bowl and drain the black beans. Add enough water to the soaking water to measure 6 cups. Drain the red beans and discard the soaking water. Combine the black and red beans, water, all but 1/2 onion, and 3 of the garlic cloves in a large, heavy pot and bring to a gentle boil. Reduce the heat, cover and simmer 1 hour. Add salt to taste (beans take a lot of salt) and continue to simmer for another 30 minutes, or until the beans are tender but intact. Remove and discard the onions. Set a strainer over a bowl and drain. Measure out 1/4 cup of the broth.
- Meanwhile in a separate pot combine the black-eyed peas, remaining 1/2 onion and garlic clove, the bay leaf and 3 cups water. Bring to a boil, add salt to taste, cover, reduce the heat and simmer 45 minutes, or until the beans are tender but intact. Remove and discard the bay leaf and onion. Set a strainer over a bowl and drain. Measure out 1/4 cup of the broth and add to the black and red bean broth.
- In a bowl or measuring cup, whisk together the dressing ingredients. Combine all of the beans in a large bowl and toss with the dressing. Taste and adjust salt. At this point the mixture can be refrigerated, or the salad can be served warm or at room temperature.
- Stir the peppers and cilantro into the beans and serve.

Nutrition Information

- 315: calories;
- 9 grams: monounsaturated fat;
- 39 grams: carbohydrates;
- 4 grams: sugars;
- 404 milligrams: sodium;
- 13 grams: fat;
- 2 grams: polyunsaturated fat;
- 0 grams: trans fat;
- 12 grams: protein;

2. Alaskan Cod In Sweet And Sour Pepper Sauce

Serving: Serves 4 | Prep: | Cook: | Ready in: 40mins

Ingredients

- 1 ½ pounds Alaskan cod fillets
- Salt and freshly ground pepper to taste
- 2 tablespoons extra virgin olive oil
- 1 large onion, halved and sliced across the grain
- 1 tablespoon coriander seeds
- 2 large red bell peppers, or 1 red pepper and 1 yellow pepper, sliced
- 2 garlic cloves, minced
- 2 teaspoons curry powder (optional)
- 1 14-ounce can chopped tomatoes
- 2 tablespoons mild honey, such as clover
- 4 tablespoons sherry vinegar or cider vinegar
- 2 bay leaves

Direction

- Preheat the oven to 300 degrees. Line a sheet pan with foil and oil the foil. Season the fish fillets with salt and pepper and lay on the foil. Leave at room temperature while you make the sauce.
- Heat the oil in a large skillet or casserole over medium heat and add the onion and coriander seeds. Cook, stirring often, until the onion is tender, about 5 minutes, and add the bell peppers and a generous pinch of salt. Cook, stirring often, until the peppers and onions are soft, another 8 to 10 minutes. Stir in the garlic and curry powder, if using, and stir together for a minute, until fragrant. Add the tomatoes and bay leaves and cook, stirring often, until the tomatoes cook down slightly, about 8 minutes. Stir in the honey and vinegar, salt to taste and black pepper, and simmer 5 minutes.
- Meanwhile, place a pan of just boiled water on the floor of your oven and place the baking sheet with the fish in the oven on the middle rack. Bake 10 to 15 minutes, until the fish is opaque on the surface but still slightly firm in the middle. Remove from the oven and place in the sauce. Spoon sauce over the top so that the fish is surrounded by it. Simmer for 5 minutes, until the fish is cooked through and can be pulled apart with a fork. Remove from the heat and serve, or even better, chill overnight, then gently reheat the next day.

Nutrition Information

- 313: calories;
- 9 grams: fat;
- 1097 milligrams: sodium;
- 6 grams: dietary fiber;
- 16 grams: sugars;
- 33 grams: protein;
- 1 gram: polyunsaturated fat;
- 5 grams: monounsaturated fat;
- 26 grams: carbohydrates;

3. Amaranth Porridge With Grated Apples And Maple Syrup

Serving: Serves 1 | Prep: | Cook: | Ready in: 25mins

Ingredients

- For each serving
- ¼ cup amaranth
- ½ cup water
- Pinch of salt
- ⅓ cup milk
- 1 teaspoon maple syrup
- ½ small or 1/4 large apple, grated

Direction

- Heat a small saucepan over medium-high heat and add the amaranth seeds. Shake them in the pan until they begin to smell toasty and a few seeds begin to pop, about 2 minutes. Immediately pour in the water. Do not wait too long because the line between toasted and burnt amaranth is a thin one – as soon as you smell the toasty aroma and see a few seeds popping, add the water. Add the salt, bring to a boil, reduce the heat to low and cover. Simmer 10 minutes.

- Stir in the milk and bring back to a simmer, stirring. Cover and simmer another 10 to 15 minutes, stirring occasionally, or until the amaranth is tender. Remove from heat and stir in the maple syrup. Transfer to a bowl, sprinkle the grated apple on top and serve.

4. Amaranth, Ricotta And Greens Pancakes

Serving: About 20 2 1/2- to 3-inch cakes, serving 6 | Prep: | Cook: | Ready in: 1hours15mins

Ingredients

- ½ cup amaranth
- 1 cup chicken stock or vegetable stock
- Salt to taste
- 1 large bunch chard, stemmed and washed
- 1 cup (8 ounces) ricotta cheese
- 2 eggs, beaten
- ½ cup low-fat milk (2 percent)
- 5 tablespoons grated Parmesan
- ½ cup plus 2 tablespoons whole-wheat pastry flour or white whole-wheat pastry flour
- 1 teaspoon baking powder
- ½ teaspoon salt
- 2 tablespoons extra virgin olive oil
- ½ medium onion, finely chopped (about 2/3 cup)
- 2 large garlic cloves, minced
- Freshly ground pepper
- Olive oil or butter for the pan or griddle
- Marinara sauce for serving (optional)

Direction

- Cook the amaranth. Combine with the stock and salt to taste in a medium saucepan and bring to a boil. Reduce the heat, cover and simmer 30 minutes, until all of the liquid has

been absorbed. Remove from the heat and let sit for 15 minutes or longer without disturbing.

- Steam the greens above 1 inch of boiling water for about 1 to 2 minutes, just until wilted. Remove from the heat, allow to cool and squeeze out excess water. Chop fine. You should have 1 cup chopped blanched chard.
- Heat the oil over medium heat in a medium-size skillet and add the onion. Cook, stirring, until tender, about 5 minutes. Stir in the garlic and cook, stirring, until fragrant, about 30 seconds. Add the greens, season with salt and pepper, stir together until well coated with oil, and remove from the heat.
- In a large bowl, beat together the ricotta, eggs, milk and Parmesan. Sift together the flour, baking powder and salt and whisk into the ricotta mixture. Stir in the greens, amaranth and pepper.
- Heat a griddle or a heavy nonstick skillet over medium-high heat. Brush with olive oil or butter, enough to coat the bottom, and drop the batter in by the heaped tablespoon (or use a small ladle or a 1/4-cup measuring cup, filling it only partway). The pancakes should be 2 1/2 to 3 inches in diameter. Cook for about 3 minutes, until lightly browned and risen, and turn over. Cook for another 3 minutes, until brown on the other side. The pancakes will be moist in the middle, but there should not be a raw flour taste. Remove from the heat and serve, or cool on a rack and heat later in a medium-low oven. Serve with a dollop of tomato sauce.

Nutrition Information

- 358: calories;
- 9 grams: monounsaturated fat;
- 4 grams: sugars;
- 17 grams: protein;
- 20 grams: fat;
- 7 grams: saturated fat;
- 0 grams: trans fat;
- 5 grams: dietary fiber;

- 643 milligrams: sodium;
- 2 grams: polyunsaturated fat;
- 30 grams: carbohydrates;

5. Andalusian Chickpea And Spinach Soup

Serving: 6 servings | Prep: | Cook: | Ready in: 3hours

Ingredients

- 1 cup chickpeas, washed, picked over and soaked for 4 hours or overnight in 1 quart water
- 2 tablespoons extra virgin olive oil
- 1 medium onion, chopped
- 3 garlic cloves, minced
- 1 14-ounce can chopped tomatoes with juice, or 1 pound tomatoes, peeled, seeded and chopped
- 2 teaspoons sweet paprika
- 1 pound potatoes, peeled and diced
- ¼ cup dry white wine
- Salt to taste
- Pinch of saffron
- 1 pound spinach , stemmed, washed thoroughly in 2 changes of water, and coarsely chopped
- Freshly ground pepper

Direction

- Drain the chickpeas and combine with 1 quart fresh water in a large saucepan. Bring to a boil, reduce the heat, cover and simmer 1 hour. Add salt to taste and continue to simmer until tender, 30 minutes to an hour.
- Heat the oil over medium heat in a heavy soup pot and add the onion. Cook, stirring, until tender, about 5 minutes. Add 2 of the garlic cloves and cook, stirring, until fragrant, about 30 seconds. Add the tomatoes, paprika and a generous pinch of salt and cook, stirring often, until the tomatoes cook down to a fragrant sauce, 10 to 15 minutes.

- Add the chickpeas with their liquid, the potatoes, wine, more salt to taste, pepper, and 2 cups water. Bring to a boil, reduce the heat to low and cook until the potatoes are tender, about 30 minutes.
- Stir in the remaining garlic, the saffron and the spinach and simmer another 5 minutes. Add freshly ground pepper, taste and adjust seasoning, and serve.

Nutrition Information

- 274: calories;
- 1 gram: saturated fat;
- 2 grams: polyunsaturated fat;
- 43 grams: carbohydrates;
- 665 milligrams: sodium;
- 7 grams: sugars;
- 4 grams: monounsaturated fat;
- 9 grams: dietary fiber;
- 12 grams: protein;

6. Apple Compote

Serving: Makes about 3 1/2 cups, serving 6 | Prep: | Cook: | Ready in: 30mins

Ingredients

- 3 pounds tart apples, such as pippins, Gravensteins, Macintosh, Granny Smith, Pink Lady, peeled if desired, cored and cut in chunks
- 2 tablespoons water
- 2 tablespoons turbinado sugar
- 1 tablespoon fresh lemon or lime juice
- Sweet spices if desired (cinnamon, nutmeg, allspice, cloves)

Direction

- Place apples and water in a heavy saucepan and stir over medium-high heat until the mixture is bubbling. Reduce heat to low and cover. Cook, stirring often, until the apples have cooked down but still have some texture, 15 to 20 minutes. Add sugar, lemon or lime juice, and spices, cover and simmer for another 3 to 5 minutes. Remove from heat and allow to cool, or serve warm or hot.

Nutrition Information

- 151: calories;
- 36 grams: carbohydrates;
- 7 grams: dietary fiber;
- 26 grams: sugars;
- 1 gram: protein;
- 3 milligrams: sodium;
- 0 grams: polyunsaturated fat;

7. Apple Walnut Galette

Serving: 1 9-inch galette, serving 8 | Prep: | Cook: | Ready in: 3hours

Ingredients

- 1 dessert galette pastry (1/2 recipe)
- Juice of 1/2 lemon
- 2 pounds slightly tart apples, like Braeburns, peeled, cored and cut in wedges (about 1/2 inch thick at the thickest point)
- 2 tablespoons (1 ounce) unsalted butter
- ¼ cup (50 grams) plus 1 tablespoon dark brown sugar or turbinado sugar
- 1 teaspoon vanilla extract
- ¼ cup lightly toasted walnuts, chopped
- ¾ teaspoon cinnamon
- ¼ teaspoon freshly grated nutmeg
- ¼ cup (25 grams) almond flour
- 1 egg beaten with 1 teaspoon milk, for egg wash

Direction

- Line 2 sheet pans with parchment. In a large bowl combine the lemon juice and apples and toss together.

- Heat a large, heavy frying pan over high heat and add the butter. Wait until it becomes light brown and carefully add the apples and 1/4 cup of the sugar. Do not add the apples until the pan and the butter are hot enough or they won't sear properly and retain their juice. But be careful when you add them so that the hot butter doesn't splatter. When the apples are brown on one side, add the vanilla, 1/2 teaspoon of the cinnamon and the nutmeg, flip the apples and continue to sauté until golden brown, about 5 to 7 minutes. Stir in the walnuts, then scrape out onto one of the lined sheet pans and allow to cool completely.
- Remove the pastry from the freezer and place it on the other parchment-lined baking sheet. Leave to thaw while the apples cool, but don't keep it out of the freezer for too long. It's easiest to handle if it's cold and will thaw quickly. You just want it soft enough so that you can manipulate it.
- Sprinkle the almond flour over the pastry, leaving a 2- to 3-inch border all around. Place the apples on top. Fold the edges of the dough in over the fruit, pleating the edges as you work your way around the fruit to form a free-form tart that is roughly 9 inches in diameter. Place in the freezer on the baking sheet for 45 minutes to an hour. This helps the galette maintain its shape.
- Meanwhile preheat the oven to 350 degrees. Remove the galette from the freezer. Brush the exposed edge of the pastry with the egg wash. Combine the remaining tablespoon of sugar and 1/4 teaspoon cinnamon and sprinkle over the fruit and the crust. Place in the oven and bake 1 hour, until the crust is nicely browned and the apples are sizzling. Remove from the oven and allow to cool for at least 15 minutes. Serve hot, warm or at room temperature.

Nutrition Information

- 180: calories;
- 27 grams: carbohydrates;
- 4 grams: dietary fiber;

- 18 grams: sugars;
- 8 grams: fat;
- 2 grams: protein;
- 1 gram: polyunsaturated fat;
- 19 milligrams: sodium;
- 3 grams: saturated fat;
- 0 grams: trans fat;

8. Apple And Bitter Lettuces Salad

Serving: Serves 4 to 6 | Prep: | Cook: | Ready in: 10mins

Ingredients

- For the dressing
- 1 tablespoon fresh lemon juice
- 1 tablespoon sherry vinegar
- 1 teaspoon balsamic vinegar
- Salt to taste
- 1 scant teaspoon Dijon mustard
- 1 small garlic clove, puréed
- ¼ cup extra virgin olive oil or grapeseed oil
- 2 tablespoons walnut oil
- For the salad
- 4 to 5 cups mixed bitter and pungent lettuces, such as endive, radicchio, arugula, frisee, or 3 to 4 cups bitter lettuces and 1 to 2 cups torn up milder lettuce such as bibb or romaine
- 1 large or 2 smaller tart apples, such as a Braeburn or Pink Lady, cored and cut into very small dice (1/2 to 1/4 inch)
- 1 tablespoon chopped fresh tarragon
- ¼ cup toasted cashews or broken walnuts or pecans (lightly toasted if desired)

Direction

- In a small measuring cup or bowl, whisk together lemon juice, vinegars, salt, Dijon mustard and garlic. Whisk in oils. Taste and adjust salt.
- Combine lettuces, apples, tarragon and nuts in a salad bowl. Toss with the dressing and serve.

Nutrition Information

- 153: calories;
- 0 grams: trans fat;
- 8 grams: monounsaturated fat;
- 4 grams: polyunsaturated fat;
- 6 grams: carbohydrates;
- 169 milligrams: sodium;
- 14 grams: fat;
- 2 grams: dietary fiber;
- 3 grams: sugars;
- 1 gram: protein;

9. Apricot, Cherry And Almond Galette

Serving: 8 servings | Prep: | Cook: | Ready in: 2hours30mins

Ingredients

- 1 dessert galette pastry (1/2 recipe)
- 6 ounces cherries, pitted and cut in half
- 1 pound apricots, pitted and halved or quartered, depending on the size
- 30 grams (3 tablespoons) slivered almonds
- ½ teaspoon almond extract
- 3 tablespoons raw brown sugar
- 25 grams (1/4 cup) almond powder
- ¼ teaspoon cinnamon
- 1 egg beaten with 1 teaspoon milk, for egg wash

Direction

- Remove the pastry from the freezer and place it on a baking sheet lined with parchment. Leave it to thaw while you prepare the fruit, but don't keep it out of the freezer for too long. It will thaw quickly, and it is easiest to handle if it's cold. You want it just soft enough so that you can manipulate it.
- Combine the cherries, apricots, slivered almonds, almond extract and 2 tablespoons of

the sugar in a large bowl and gently toss together.

- Sprinkle the almond powder over the pastry, leaving a 2- to 3-inch border all around. Place the fruit on top. Fold the edges of the dough in over the fruit, pleating the edges as you work your way around the fruit to form a free-form tart that is roughly 9 inches in diameter. Place in the freezer on the baking sheet for 45 minutes to an hour. This helps the galette maintain its shape.

- Meanwhile, preheat the oven to 350 degrees. Remove the galette from the freezer. Brush the exposed edge of the pastry with the egg wash. Combine the remaining tablespoon of sugar and 1/4 teaspoon cinnamon and sprinkle over the fruit and the crust. Place in the oven and bake 1 hour, until the fruit is bubbly and the juice is running out and caramelizing on the parchment. Remove from the oven and allow to cool for at least 15 minutes. Serve hot or warm or at room temperature.

Nutrition Information

- 127: calories;
- 6 grams: fat;
- 4 grams: monounsaturated fat;
- 12 grams: sugars;
- 17 milligrams: sodium;
- 0 grams: trans fat;
- 17 grams: carbohydrates;
- 3 grams: protein;
- 1 gram: polyunsaturated fat;

---

10. Arugula And Corn Salad With Roasted Red Peppers And White Beans

Serving: Serves 4 | Prep: | Cook: | Ready in: 15mins

Ingredients

- 1 ear sweet corn

- 3 cups baby or wild arugula
- 2 red bell peppers, roasted
- 1 ½ cups (1 can) cooked white beans, such as cannellini or navy beans, rinsed if using canned beans
- 1 tablespoon chopped chives
- 1 tablespoon slivered fresh basil (more to taste)
- 2 tablespoons sherry vinegar or red wine vinegar
- 1 teaspoon balsamic vinegar
- Salt to taste
- 1 small garlic clove, pureed or put through a press
- ¼ teaspoon Dijon mustard
- 5 tablespoons extra-virgin olive oil
- Freshly ground pepper to taste
- ¼ cup shaved Parmesan

Direction

- Steam corn for 4 to 5 minutes, until just tender. Remove from heat, allow to cool, and cut kernels off cob. Combine with arugula in a large bowl.

- Remove seeds and membranes from roasted peppers and cut in 2-inch strips. Place in another bowl. Add beans, chives and basil and toss together.

- Whisk together vinegars, salt, garlic, mustard, and olive oil. Set aside 3 tablespoons of the dressing and toss the rest with beans and peppers. Season to taste with salt and pepper, and allow to sit for at least 15 minutes and for up to 3 days (in the refrigerator).

- Toss remaining dressing with arugula and corn. Line salad plates or a platter with arugula and corn mixture. Top with peppers and beans. Garnish with shaved Parmesan, and serve.

Nutrition Information

- 339: calories;
- 0 grams: trans fat;
- 13 grams: monounsaturated fat;

- 2 grams: polyunsaturated fat;
- 31 grams: carbohydrates;
- 5 grams: sugars;
- 12 grams: protein;
- 20 grams: fat;
- 4 grams: saturated fat;
- 544 milligrams: sodium;
- 7 grams: dietary fiber;

11. Asian Pasta With Tofu, Shiitake Mushrooms And Broccoli

Serving: Serves 4 generously | Prep: | Cook: | Ready in: 20mins

Ingredients

- 1 pound broccoli, crowns broken or cut into small florets, stems peeled and diced
- 2 tablespoons canola oil or peanut oil
- 6 ounces shiitake mushrooms, stems removed, caps quartered
- 2 plump garlic cloves, minced
- 2 teaspoons minced fresh ginger
- 6 scallions, white and light green parts only, sliced
- ½ teaspoon hot red pepper flakes
- ½ pound firm tofu, sliced and drained on paper towels
- 1 cup chicken stock or vegetable stock
- 2 tablespoons soy sauce (more to taste)
- ½ pound buckwheat pasta (soba), udon noodles or dried rice sticks (soak rice sticks in hot water for 20 minutes)
- ¼ cup chopped cilantro
- 2 teaspoons Chinese sesame oil

Direction

- Bring a large pot of salted water to a boil. Fill a bowl with ice water. Add the broccoli to the boiling water and blanch for 1 minute. Remove to the ice water. Allow to cool, then drain and dry on paper towels. Cover the pot of water and keep hot.
- Heat a wide, heavy skillet or wok over medium-high heat and add 1 tablespoon of the oil. When it is rippling hot, add the mushrooms and sear for 5 minutes, stirring from time to time. Turn the heat to medium, add the garlic, ginger, scallions, and red pepper flakes and cook for another 30 seconds to a minute, until fragrant. Remove from the heat and transfer the contents of the pan to a bowl.
- Return the pan to medium-high heat and heat the remaining tablespoon of oil until rippling. Add the tofu and sear on both sides until it begins to color, about 1 minute per side. Add 1 teaspoon soy sauce and stir together. Return the mushroom mixture and the broccoli to the pan. Add the stock and soy sauce, bring to a simmer and turn the heat to low. Simmer uncovered for a minute or two, until the broccoli is crisp-tender, then turn off the heat.
- Meanwhile, bring the pot of water back to a boil and add the pasta. Cook soba or udon noodles until al dente, about 5 minutes. Cook softened rice noodles for 1 minute. Drain and toss with the mushrooms and the broccoli. Heat through, add the cilantro and sesame oil, toss together, and serve.

Nutrition Information

- 464: calories;
- 7 grams: monounsaturated fat;
- 8 grams: dietary fiber;
- 582 milligrams: sodium;
- 2 grams: saturated fat;
- 0 grams: trans fat;
- 6 grams: sugars;
- 60 grams: carbohydrates;
- 23 grams: protein;
- 17 grams: fat;

12. Asparagus, Green Beans And Potatoes With Green Mole Sauce

Serving: Serves 4 | Prep: | Cook: | Ready in: 50mins

Ingredients

- ½ cup hulled untoasted pumpkin seeds
- ½ pound tomatillos, husked, rinsed and coarsely chopped
- 1 serrano chile or 1/2 jalapeño (more to taste), stemmed and roughly chopped
- 3 romaine lettuce leaves, torn into pieces (about 1 1/2 cups / 1 1/2 ounces)
- ¼ small white onion, coarsely chopped, soaked for 5 minutes in cold water, drained and rinsed (optional)
- 2 garlic cloves, halved, green shoots removed
- ¼ cup loosely packed chopped cilantro, plus additional for garnish
- ½ teaspoon cumin seeds, lightly toasted and ground
- 1 ½ cups vegetable stock, garlic broth or chicken stock
- 1 tablespoon canola or extra-virgin olive oil
- Salt to taste
- ½ to ¾ pound asparagus
- ½ to ¾ pound green beans
- ¾ to 1 pound boiling potatoes or Yukon golds, cut in wedges

Direction

- Heat a heavy Dutch oven or saucepan over medium heat and add pumpkin seeds. Wait until you hear one pop, then stir constantly until they have puffed and popped, and smell toasty. They should not get any darker than golden or they will taste bitter. Transfer to a bowl or a baking sheet and allow to cool.
- Place cooled pumpkin seeds in a blender and add tomatillos, chiles, lettuce, onion, garlic, cilantro, cumin, salt, and 1/2 cup of the stock. Cover blender and blend mixture until smooth, stopping blender to stir if necessary.
- Heat oil in the Dutch oven or heavy saucepan over medium-high heat. Drizzle in a bit of the blended mixture and if it sizzles, add the rest. Cook, stirring, until mixture darkens and thickens, about 5 minutes. (Hold the lid above the pot to shield you and your stove from splatters.) Add remaining stock, bring to a simmer, reduce heat to medium-low and simmer uncovered, stirring often, until sauce is thick and creamy, 15 to 20 minutes. Season to taste with salt. You should have about 2 cups.
- Steam potato wedges above 1 inch boiling water for 10 to 15 minutes, until tender. Steam asparagus and green beans for 5 minutes, or blanch for the same amount of time in salted boiling water. Transfer to a bowl of cold water, drain and drain again on a kitchen towel.
- Arrange the vegetables on a platter or plates and spoon mole sauce over, or heat through in the sauce, in the saucepan. Serve with rice or corn tortillas if desired.

Nutrition Information

- 289: calories;
- 2 grams: saturated fat;
- 0 grams: trans fat;
- 6 grams: monounsaturated fat;
- 4 grams: polyunsaturated fat;
- 13 grams: protein;
- 34 grams: carbohydrates;
- 8 grams: sugars;
- 979 milligrams: sodium;

13. Avocado And Roasted Tomatillo Salsa

Serving: About 2 cups, serving 6 to 8 | Prep: | Cook: | Ready in: 25mins

Ingredients

- 1 pound tomatillos, husked

- 1 to 2 serrano chiles (to taste), stems removed
- 1 medium garlic clove, unpeeled
- 1 slice white or red onion
- ½ cup chopped cilantro, with stems
- 1 medium avocado
- Salt to taste

Direction

- Heat a heavy cast-iron skillet or griddle over medium-high heat. Place tomatillos in pan and toast until charred on 1 side, about 10 minutes for a medium or large tomatillo. The color in the middle should be fading from pale green to olive. Turn tomatillos over and continue to grill until charred on the other side, about 10 minutes, but not for so long that they burst. Transfer to a bowl and allow to cool.
- Place chile(s), garlic clove and onion slice in skillet and toast, turning often, until chile is lightly charred and garlic is charred in spots and softened. The onion should be lightly colored on both sides but not charred black (that will make it bitter). Remove from heat. Peel the garlic and transfer, with the onion and chiles, to a blender. Add tomatillos and any liquid that may have accumulated in the bowl.
- Add remaining ingredients to blender and blend until smooth. Taste, adjust seasoning, and serve.

Nutrition Information

- 61: calories;
- 4 grams: fat;
- 1 gram: protein;
- 3 grams: sugars;
- 6 grams: carbohydrates;
- 202 milligrams: sodium;

14. Baked Acorn Squash With Walnut Oil And Maple Syrup

Serving: Makes four large servings or eight medium servings | Prep: | Cook: | Ready in: 1hours

Ingredients

- 2 acorn squash
- 2 tablespoons maple syrup
- 2 tablespoons walnut oil
- Freshly ground nutmeg
- Ground walnuts

Direction

- Preheat the oven to 350 degrees. Place the squash on a baking sheet and bake for 20 minutes, until soft enough to easily cut in half. Cut in half, and scoop out the seeds and membranes.
- Cover a baking sheet with foil. Stir the maple syrup and walnut oil together in a bowl, then brush over the cut surfaces of the squash. Sprinkle with a very small amount of ground nutmeg. Place in the oven and bake 1 hour, brushing every 10 minutes with more oil and maple syrup. When the squash is tender, brush once more, then spoon a tablespoonful of finely chopped walnuts into each cavity and return to the oven for 5 to 10 minutes, until the walnuts are toasty. Remove from the heat. Serve hot or warm.

15. Baked Beans With Sweet Potatoes And Chipotles

Serving: 6 servings | Prep: | Cook: | Ready in: 3hours

Ingredients

- 1 pound red beans, San Franciscano beans, or pintos, washed, picked over for stones, and soaked in 2 quarts water for 4 hours or overnight

- 1 bay leaf
- 2 tablespoons extra virgin olive oil
- 1 yellow or red onion, chopped
- Salt to taste
- 2 to 4 garlic cloves (to taste), minced
- ¼ cup tomato paste
- 2 tablespoons honey or agave nectar
- 2 chipotles in adobo, seeded and minced
- 2 large sweet potatoes (1 1/2 to 2 pounds), peeled and cut in large dice

Direction

- Place beans and soaking water in an ovenproof casserole. Add bay leaf and bring to a gentle boil over medium heat. Reduce heat to low, cover and simmer 1 hour. Check beans at regular intervals to make sure they are submerged, and add water as necessary.
- Meanwhile, heat oven to 300 degrees . Heat 1 tablespoon of the oil in a heavy skillet and add onion. Cook, stirring often, until tender, about 5 minutes. Add a generous pinch of salt and the garlic and cook, stirring, until garlic is fragrant, 30 seconds to a minute. Stir onion and garlic into beans, along with salt to taste, tomato paste, honey or agave nectar, and chipotles, and stir together. Add sweet potatoes and bring back to a simmer, drizzle with remaining olive oil, and place in oven.
- Bake 1 to 1 1/2 hours, until beans are thoroughly soft and sweet potatoes are beginning to fall apart, checking and stirring from time to time to make sure that beans are submerged. Either add liquid or push them down into the simmering broth if necessary. Remove from heat and serve hot or warm.

Nutrition Information

- 190: calories;
- 644 milligrams: sodium;
- 6 grams: dietary fiber;
- 14 grams: sugars;
- 1 gram: polyunsaturated fat;
- 3 grams: monounsaturated fat;
- 36 grams: carbohydrates;

- 4 grams: protein;
- 5 grams: fat;

16. Baked Halibut With Tomato Caper Sauce

Serving: Serves 6 | Prep: | Cook: |Ready in: 1hours

Ingredients

- For the tomato caper sauce
- 1 tablespoon extra virgin olive oil
- ½ medium onion, finely chopped
- 4 plump garlic cloves, minced or mashed in a mortar and pestle
- ¼ cup capers, drained, rinsed and finely chopped or mashed with the garlic in a mortar and pestle
- 2 pounds tomatoes, peeled, seeded and finely chopped, or 1 28-ounce can diced tomatoes with juice
- Salt, preferably kosher salt
- freshly ground pepper to taste
- Pinch of sugar
- 1 teaspoon chopped fresh thyme leaves
- 1 tablespoon slivered fresh basil leaves
- For the baked halibut
- 1 recipe tomato-caper sauce, above
- 6 6-ounce halibut fillets (Choose Pacific halibut over Atlantic halibut. According to the Environmental Defense Fund and the Blue Ocean Institute, Pacific halibut fisheries have been properly managed, but they are overfished in the Atlantic.)
- Salt, preferably kosher salt
- freshly ground pepper
- 1 tablespoon extra-virgin olive oil
- 6 lemon slices

Direction

- Heat the olive oil in a large, heavy skillet over medium heat, and add the onion. Cook, stirring often, until tender, three to five minutes, and add the garlic and the capers.

Cook, stirring, for three to five minutes, until the onion has softened thoroughly and the mixture is fragrant. Add the tomatoes, salt, pepper and a pinch of sugar. Stir in the thyme, bring to a simmer and cook, stirring often, for 15 to 20 minutes, until the sauce is thick and fragrant. Taste and adjust seasonings. Serve hot or cold.

- Make the sauce as directed and keep warm.
- Preheat the oven to 450 degrees. Oil a baking dish large enough for the fish to lie flat. Season the fish with salt and pepper, and arrange in the baking dish. Drizzle the olive oil over the fillets, and place a round of lemon on each one. Cover the dish tightly with foil, and place in the oven. Bake 15 minutes. Check the fish; if you can cut into it with a fork, it is done. If it doesn't yield, (halibut fillets tend to be thick can take time to cook), cover and return to the oven for five minutes. Remove from the oven, and check again. Remove the lemon slices from the fish.
- Place a spoonful of sauce on each plate, and place a piece of fish partially on top. Spoon some of the liquid from the baking dish over the fish. If you wish, top the fish with another spoonful of sauce, garnish with basil leaves and serve.

Nutrition Information

- 254: calories;
- 1 gram: polyunsaturated fat;
- 4 grams: monounsaturated fat;
- 15 grams: carbohydrates;
- 6 grams: sugars;
- 34 grams: protein;
- 984 milligrams: sodium;
- 8 grams: fat;

17. Baked Orzo With Tomatoes, Roasted Peppers And Zucchini

Serving: Serves six | Prep: | Cook: |Ready in: 1hours

Ingredients

- ½ pound orzo (about 1 1/8 cups)
- Salt to taste
- 1 large red pepper, roasted and diced
- 3 tablespoons extra virgin olive oil
- 2 medium zucchini, sliced about 1/4 inch thick
- Freshly ground pepper to taste
- 1 pound tomatoes, peeled, seeded and diced; or 1 14-ounce can diced tomatoes, with juice
- 1 or 2 plump garlic cloves (to taste), minced
- 2 ounces freshly grated Parmesan or 2 ounces crumbled goat cheese (1/2 cup, tightly packed)

Direction

- Bring a large pot of generously salted water to a boil, and add the orzo. Cook eight minutes, or until it is cooked through but still firm to the bite. Drain and transfer to a large bowl. Toss with the diced roasted pepper and 1 tablespoon of the olive oil.
- Preheat the oven to 375 degrees. Oil a 2-quart baking dish. Heat another tablespoon of olive oil over medium-high heat in a large, wide skillet. Add the zucchini and cook — stirring and turning over the slices, or tossing them in the pan — until just cooked through and lightly colored, about five minutes. Scrape into the bowl with the orzo.
- Return the pan to the heat, add the final tablespoon of oil and the garlic. Cook just until fragrant, 20 to 30 seconds, and add the tomatoes and salt to taste. Cook, stirring from time to time, until the tomatoes have cooked down slightly and smell fragrant. Taste and adjust seasoning. Scrape into the bowl with the orzo, add the Parmesan or goat cheese, and mix everything together. Add freshly ground pepper to taste, and adjust salt. Transfer to the baking dish.

- Bake 30 to 40 minutes, until the top is just beginning to color. Serve hot or warm.

Nutrition Information

- 192: calories;
- 1 gram: polyunsaturated fat;
- 6 grams: protein;
- 2 grams: saturated fat;
- 10 grams: fat;
- 5 grams: sugars;
- 22 grams: carbohydrates;
- 3 grams: dietary fiber;
- 478 milligrams: sodium;

18. Baked Ricotta Frittata With Fresh Mint

Serving: Serves six | Prep: | Cook: | Ready in: 30mins

Ingredients

- 2 tablespoons extra virgin olive oil
- 6 large or extra large eggs
- Salt
- freshly ground pepper to taste
- 1 cup fresh ricotta
- 3 tablespoons chopped fresh mint
- 1 garlic clove, minced or mashed in a mortar and pestle

Direction

- Preheat the oven to 350 degrees. Place the oil in a 2-quart baking dish or a 9-inch cast iron skillet. Rub the oil over the sides of the pan, and place in the oven. Meanwhile, whisk the eggs in a large bowl. Whisk in the salt (about 1/2 teaspoon), pepper, ricotta, mint and garlic. Remove the baking dish from the oven and scrape in the egg mixture. Return to the oven, and bake 30 minutes or until lightly colored on the top and set.

- Remove from the heat, and allow to sit for 10 minutes or longer before serving. Serve hot, or allow to cool and serve at room temperature.

Nutrition Information

- 195: calories;
- 12 grams: protein;
- 245 milligrams: sodium;
- 15 grams: fat;
- 6 grams: saturated fat;
- 0 grams: sugars;
- 7 grams: monounsaturated fat;
- 2 grams: carbohydrates;

19. Baked Stuffed Acorn Squash

Serving: 8 substantial main dish servings, 12 to 16 smaller servings | Prep: | Cook: | Ready in: 2hours

Ingredients

- 4 large or 6 smaller acorn squash
- 3 tablespoons extra virgin olive oil, plus additional for basting
- 1 medium onion, finely chopped
- 1 red pepper, diced
- 1 28-ounce can chopped tomatoes with juice, pulsed to a coarse purée in a food processor
- 2 tablespoons tomato paste
- 2 tablespoons mild honey, maple syrup or pomegranate molasses
- 2 tablespoons red wine vinegar, sherry vinegar or apple cider vinegar
- Salt to taste
- ½ teaspoon cayenne
- 3 cups cooked pintos, black beans or red beans, or 2 cans, drained and rinsed
- 1 cup corn kernels
- ⅔ cup breadcrumbs
- 2 ounces / 1/2 cup Gruyère, grated

Direction

- Heat oven to 375 degrees. Place squash on a baking sheet and bake 20 minutes, until soft enough to easily cut in half. Wait until cool enough to handle (about 15 minutes), then cut in half (stem to tip) and scoop out seeds and membranes.
- Meanwhile, heat 2 tablespoons of olive oil over medium heat in a large skillet and add onion. Cook, stirring often, until it begins to soften, about 3 minutes. Add red pepper and a generous pinch of salt and cook, stirring, until tender, about 5 minutes. Add tomatoes and tomato paste and cook, stirring often, until tomatoes have cooked down slightly, about 5 minutes. Add honey, maple syrup or pomegranate molasses, vinegar, salt and cayenne, and bring to a simmer. Simmer 8 to 10 minutes, until thick and fragrant. Taste and adjust seasonings. Stir in beans and corn and simmer another 5 minutes.
- Oil 1 or 2 baking dishes or a sheet pan that will accommodate all the squash. Season cavities and cut sides of the squash with salt and pepper and brush with olive oil or melted butter. Fill with bean mixture. Mix together bread crumbs, Gruyère and remaining olive oil and sprinkle over the filling. Brush exposed edges of squash with oil. Place in the baking dish or on baking sheet and cover tightly with foil. Bake large squash for 45 minutes, check smaller squash after 30 minutes. The flesh should be easy to penetrate with the tip of a knife. Uncover and return to oven for 5 to 10 minutes, or until breadcrumbs and cheese are lightly browned. Serve hot or warm.

Nutrition Information

- 513: calories;
- 10 grams: fat;
- 5 grams: monounsaturated fat;
- 90 grams: carbohydrates;
- 11 grams: sugars;
- 1088 milligrams: sodium;
- 3 grams: saturated fat;

- 2 grams: polyunsaturated fat;
- 18 grams: dietary fiber;
- 23 grams: protein;

20. Baked Tomatoes With Arugula Pesto

Serving: Serves six | Prep: | Cook: | Ready in: 20mins

Ingredients

- 6 medium or large ripe, firm tomatoes
- Salt
- freshly ground pepper to taste
- 6 tablespoons arugula pesto (1/2 recipe)

Direction

- Preheat the oven to 425 degrees. Oil a baking dish that will snugly accommodate the tomatoes. Core the tomatoes, and season with salt and pepper. Place a spoonful of pesto into each core.
- Place in the oven and bake for 20 minutes, until the surface of the pesto is just beginning to color. Remove from the heat. Serve warm.

Nutrition Information

- 80: calories;
- 327 milligrams: sodium;
- 6 grams: carbohydrates;
- 1 gram: saturated fat;
- 0 grams: polyunsaturated fat;
- 2 grams: protein;
- 3 grams: sugars;

21. Baked And Sautéed Spaghetti Squash On A Bed Of Spinach

Serving: Serves 6 | Prep: | Cook: | Ready in: 2hours

Ingredients

- 1 spaghetti squash, about 3 pounds
- 3 tablespoons extra virgin olive oil
- 2 plump garlic cloves, minced
- Salt
- 1 12-ounce bag (or box) baby spinach, rinsed
- 2 tablespoons bread crumbs
- Lots of freshly ground pepper
- 1 teaspoon sumac (optional)
- ¼ cup freshly grated Parmesan (more to taste)
- ¼ cup chopped walnuts (more to taste)
- 1 tablespoon walnut oil

Direction

- Heat oven to 375 degrees. Pierce spaghetti squash in several places with a sharp knife. Cover a baking sheet with foil and place squash on top. Bake 1 to 1 1/2 hours, until squash is soft and easy to cut into with a knife. Remove from oven and allow to cool until you can handle it, then cut in half lengthwise and allow to cool some more. Scoop out seeds and discard. Scoop out flesh and place in a bowl. Run a fork through to separate the spaghetti-like strands.
- Heat 1 tablespoon olive oil over medium-high heat in a heavy 12-inch skillet. Add half the garlic and as soon as it begins to sizzle and smell fragrant add spinach. It should wilt quickly in the liquid left on leaves after washing. Add salt to taste and toss in pan (tongs are a good tool for this) until all spinach has wilted, 2 to 3 minutes. Place a strainer or colander in the sink and drain spinach. Allow to drain while you sauté spaghetti squash.
- Wipe skillet and heat again over medium-high heat. Add remaining olive oil and breadcrumbs. When breadcrumbs are crisp, after about 1 minute, stir in remaining garlic, stir for a few seconds, until fragrant, and add spaghetti squash and salt to taste. Toss together over medium-high heat until the squash is infused with oil and breadcrumbs are beginning to color, 5 to 8 minutes. Add sumac if using and lots of freshly ground

pepper. Taste and adjust seasoning. Remove from heat.
- Arrange spinach on a platter. Top with squash. Sprinkle Parmesan and walnuts over squash and drizzle on walnut oil. Serve hot.

Nutrition Information

- 206: calories;
- 5 grams: sugars;
- 17 grams: carbohydrates;
- 4 grams: dietary fiber;
- 712 milligrams: sodium;
- 15 grams: fat;
- 2 grams: saturated fat;
- 6 grams: protein;

22. Balsamic Roasted Winter Squash And Wild Rice Salad

Serving: 6 servings | Prep: | Cook: | Ready in: 2hours

Ingredients

- 1 cup wild rice
- 3 ½ cups water or stock (chicken or vegetable)
- Salt to taste
- 2 pounds kabocha or butternut squash, peeled and cut in small dice (about 3 cups peeled and diced, weighing 1 1/2 to 1 3/4 pounds)
- Salt to taste
- 1 tablespoon balsamic vinegar
- 3 tablespoons extra virgin olive oil
- 2 tablespoons fresh lemon juice (more to taste)
- 1 garlic clove, minced or puréed
- 1 teaspoon Dijon mustard
- 3 tablespoons walnut oil, or substitute extra virgin olive oil
- ½ cup chopped fresh herbs, like parsley, chives, tarragon
- ½ cup diced celery
- 1 5- or 6-ounce bag baby arugula or spinach

Direction

- Rinse the wild rice. Bring the water or stock to a boil in a medium saucepan, add salt to taste and the rice. Bring back to a boil, reduce the heat, cover and simmer 45 minutes, until the rice is tender and has begun to splay. Drain through a strainer, return to the pot and cover the pot with a clean dishtowel. Return the lid to the pot and let sit for 10 minutes
- Meanwhile, preheat the oven to 425 degrees. Line a baking sheet with foil. Place the squash in a bowl or directly on the baking sheet and toss with salt to taste, the balsamic vinegar and 1 tablespoon of the olive oil. Spread on the baking sheet in an even layer and make sure to tip all of the liquid remaining in the bowl over the squash. Roast for 20 to 30 minutes, stirring every 10 minutes so that the squash browns evenly. The squash should be tender all the way through. Remove from the heat
- In a small bowl or measuring cup, whisk together the lemon juice, garlic, salt to taste and mustard. Whisk in the remaining olive oil and the walnut oil
- Combine the wild rice, squash, herbs and celery in a large bowl. Toss with the dressing. Add salt and pepper to taste. Line a platter, individual plates or a wide salad bowl with the baby spinach or arugula. Top with the salad and serve

Nutrition Information

- 309: calories;
- 14 grams: fat;
- 0 grams: trans fat;
- 6 grams: dietary fiber;
- 5 grams: sugars;
- 8 grams: protein;
- 924 milligrams: sodium;
- 2 grams: polyunsaturated fat;
- 10 grams: monounsaturated fat;
- 42 grams: carbohydrates;

23. Banana Muesli Smoothie

Serving: 1 serving | Prep: | Cook: |Ready in:

Ingredients

- ¼ cup muesli
- 3 tablespoons low-fat milk or water
- 1 tablespoon soaked chia seeds (1 teaspoon dry unsoaked)
- 1 small banana (4 ounces without the skin)
- 1 heaped teaspoon almond butter (I prefer toasted unsalted)
- 1 teaspoon honey
- 1 cup yogurt, milk, almond or rice beverage, coconut water or soy milk
- 1 or 2 ice cubes (optional)

Direction

- The night before, place the muesli in a small bowl or ramekin and cover with 3 tablespoons milk or water. Refrigerate overnight. To soak the chia seeds, place in a jar or bowl and add 4 tablespoons water for every tablespoon of chia seeds. Place in the refrigerator for several hours or overnight. The seeds and water will be become gelatinous. The measure of 1 tablespoon includes the seeds and the gelatinous liquid that enrobes them after soaking.
- Scoop up a tablespoon of seeds with the gooey liquid and place in a blender (don't worry, your smoothie won't have this consistency). AddPlace the soaked muesli along with any liquid remaining in the bowl in a blender. Add the remaining ingredients and blend until smooth.

Nutrition Information

- 338: calories;
- 63 grams: carbohydrates;
- 325 milligrams: sodium;
- 9 grams: fat;
- 2 grams: saturated fat;
- 3 grams: monounsaturated fat;

- 4 grams: polyunsaturated fat;
- 0 grams: trans fat;
- 11 grams: dietary fiber;
- 34 grams: sugars;
- 10 grams: protein;

24. Banana Oatmeal Almond Smoothie

Serving: 1 generous serving | Prep: | Cook: | Ready in:

Ingredients

- 2 tablespoons rolled oats
- 2 to 3 tablespoons hot or boiling water (enough to just cover the oats)
- 1 cup unsweetened almond milk, or 1/3 cup light coconut milk and 2/3 cup almond milk
- ½ teaspoon vanilla
- 1 frozen banana, sliced
- 1 tablespoon almond butter
- 1 teaspoon agave nectar
- 1 tablespoon soaked chia seeds (1 teaspoon dry unsoaked; see note)

Direction

- Combine the rolled oats and hot or boiling water in a small bowl or ramekin and leave until the oatmeal is soft, about 15 minutes.
- Place all of the ingredients (including the soaked oatmeal) in a blender and blend at high speed for 1 minute. Serve at once.

Nutrition Information

- 382: calories;
- 18 grams: fat;
- 12 grams: dietary fiber;
- 290 milligrams: sodium;
- 3 grams: saturated fat;
- 0 grams: trans fat;
- 17 grams: monounsaturated fat;
- 10 grams: protein;

- 51 grams: carbohydrates;
- 20 grams: sugars;

25. Banana Wild Blueberry Smoothie With Chia Seeds

Serving: 1 serving | Prep: | Cook: | Ready in:

Ingredients

- 1 tablespoon soaked chia seeds (1 teaspoon dry unsoaked)
- 1 small banana (about 4 ounces without the skin)
- ½ cup frozen organic wild blueberries
- 1 cup buttermilk
- 1 teaspoon honey

Direction

- To soak the chia seeds, place in a jar or bowl and add 4 tablespoons water for every tablespoon of chia seeds. Place in the refrigerator for several hours or overnight. The seeds and water will be become gelatinous.
- Scoop up a tablespoon of seeds with the gooey liquid and place in a blender (don't worry, your smoothie won't have this consistency). Add the remaining ingredients and blend for 1 full minute at high speed.

Nutrition Information

- 307: calories;
- 2 grams: saturated fat;
- 1 gram: monounsaturated fat;
- 471 milligrams: sodium;
- 10 grams: dietary fiber;
- 30 grams: sugars;
- 11 grams: protein;
- 6 grams: fat;
- 0 grams: trans fat;
- 3 grams: polyunsaturated fat;
- 55 grams: carbohydrates;

26. Barberry And Orange Tea

Serving: Serves 2 | Prep: | Cook: |Ready in: 30mins

Ingredients

- 20 grams dried barberries (2 heaped tablespoons)
- 3 strips orange zest
- 1 or 2 slices orange
- 2 cloves
- 2 ½ cups boiling water
- 2 teaspoons honey

Direction

- Place the dried barberries in a teapot or pyrex measuring cup. Add the orange zest, orange slices and cloves. Pour on the boiling water. Stir in the honey. Cover and allow the mixture to steep for 15 to 30 minutes. Strain and reheat gently if desired but do not boil.

Nutrition Information

- 51: calories;
- 0 grams: protein;
- 14 grams: carbohydrates;
- 1 gram: dietary fiber;
- 12 grams: sugars;
- 13 milligrams: sodium;

27. Barley And Herb Salad With Roasted Asparagus

Serving: Serves 4 as a main dish salad, 6 as a side | Prep: | Cook: |Ready in: 1hours

Ingredients

- 1 cup barley
- 3 cups water
- Salt, preferably kosher salt, to taste
- 1 pound thick-stemmed asparagus
- 2 tablespoons extra- virgin olive oil
- Freshly ground pepper to taste
- ½ cup chopped fresh herbs, such as parsley, marjoram, chives, tarragon and thyme
- For the vinaigrette
- 1 ½ tablespoons fresh lemon juice
- 1 tablespoon sherry vinegar
- Salt to taste
- 1 teaspoon lemon zest
- 1 small garlic clove, puréed
- ½ teaspoon dry mustard or 1 teaspoon Dijon mustard
- 6 tablespoons extra- virgin olive oil
- Lemon wedges or sliced lemon for garnish (optional)

Direction

- Heat a 3- quart saucepan over medium-high heat and add barley. Toast in the pan, shaking pan or stirring grains until they begin to smell a little bit like popcorn. Add water and bring to a boil. Add salt to taste (I suggest 1/2 to 3/4 teaspoon for 1 cup barley), reduce heat, cover and simmer 45 to 50 minutes, until barley is tender (it will always be chewy). Drain off any liquid remaining in the pot through a strainer (set it over a bowl if you think you might want to use the barley water in a stock or risotto – it'll keep for a day in the refrigerator). Shake strainer and return barley to the pot. Cover pot with a clean dishtowel and return the lid. Allow barley to sit for 10 to 15 minutes.
- Meanwhile, roast asparagus and make dressing. Preheat oven to 425 degrees F. Line a baking sheet with parchment. Snap off woody ends of the asparagus and place on parchment-lined baking sheet. Add olive oil and salt and pepper to taste and toss together until all of the asparagus is coated with oil (I do this with my hands). Make sure that asparagus is in one layer on the baking sheet in the pan and place in oven. Roast for about 12 minutes, or until tender and beginning to

shrivel. It should be browned in spots. Remove from heat.
- Whisk together lemon juice, vinegar, salt, lemon zest, garlic, and mustard. Whisk in olive oil.
- Transfer cooked barley to a large bowl. Add herbs and vinaigrette and toss together until barley is evenly coated with dressing. Arrange on a platter or on plates. Lay stalks of roasted asparagus on over the top, and serve.

Nutrition Information

- 449: calories;
- 895 milligrams: sodium;
- 29 grams: fat;
- 0 grams: trans fat;
- 20 grams: monounsaturated fat;
- 43 grams: carbohydrates;
- 3 grams: sugars;
- 4 grams: polyunsaturated fat;
- 12 grams: dietary fiber;
- 10 grams: protein;

28. Barley, Celery Root And Mushroom Salad With Scallion Vinaigrette

Serving: 4 to 6 servings. | Prep: | Cook: |Ready in: 1hours30mins

Ingredients

- 1 cup pearl barley
- 1 large celery root, peeled and cut into 1/2-inch cubes (about 3 cups)
- ½ cup plus 1 tablespoon extra virgin olive oil
- 2 tablespoons plus 1 teaspoon salt, more as needed
- Black pepper, to taste
- 1 pound mixed mushrooms, like cremini, oyster and hedgehog, cut into bite-size pieces
- 1 tablespoon cider vinegar, more as needed
- 3 scallions, finely chopped
- 1 tablespoon chopped celery leaves
- ⅓ cup celery stalk, finely diced
- ¾ cup parsley leaves.

Direction

- Preheat oven to 350 degrees. Spread the barley grains on a rimmed baking sheet and toast until fragrant and golden, 20 minutes.
- Increase oven temperature to 400 degrees. On a rimmed baking sheet, toss the celery root with 2 tablespoons oil, .25 teaspoon salt and pepper. On a separate baking sheet, toss the mushrooms with .25 cup oil, .5 teaspoon salt and pepper. Roast both, tossing occasionally, until golden and tender, 15 to 20 minutes for the mushrooms, and 30 to 40 minutes for the celery root. Transfer to a large bowl.
- Meanwhile, in a large pot, bring 10 cups water and 2 tablespoons salt to a boil. Add the barley and simmer until tender, 45 to 50 minutes; drain. Add to the mushrooms and celery root.
- In a small bowl, whisk the vinegar, scallions, celery leaves, .25 teaspoon salt and pepper. Whisk in 3 tablespoons oil. Toss the vinaigrette and diced celery stalk into the salad. Coarsely chop .25 cup parsley leaves and add to the salad. Toss in the remaining whole leaves, tearing larger leaves into smaller pieces. Taste and adjust seasonings, if necessary. Serve warm or at room temperature.

Nutrition Information

- 389: calories;
- 23 grams: fat;
- 3 grams: polyunsaturated fat;
- 15 grams: monounsaturated fat;
- 7 grams: dietary fiber;
- 35 grams: carbohydrates;
- 2 grams: sugars;
- 13 grams: protein;
- 528 milligrams: sodium;

29. Beet Green, Rice And Ricotta Blinis

Serving: 24 about 2 1/2-inch cakes, serving 6 to 8 | Prep: | Cook: | Ready in: 20mins

Ingredients

- ¾ pound beet greens, or a mix of beet greens and other greens, such as chard or mustard greens, washed, stemmed and coarsely chopped (6 cups tightly packed)
- 1 cup (8 ounces) ricotta cheese
- 2 eggs, beaten
- ½ cup low-fat milk (2 percent)
- 5 tablespoons grated Parmesan
- ½ cup whole-wheat pastry flour or white whole-wheat pastry flour
- 1 teaspoon baking powder
- ½ teaspoon salt
- 1 cup cooked brown or white rice, preferably medium- or short-grain
- 2 tablespoons finely chopped chives
- 2 teaspoons finely chopped marjoram
- Freshly ground pepper
- Olive oil for the pan or griddle
- Marinara sauce for serving (optional)

Direction

- Steam the greens above an inch of boiling water for 1 to 2 minutes, just until wilted. Remove from the heat, allow to cool and squeeze out excess water. Chop fine.
- In a large bowl, beat together the ricotta, eggs, milk and Parmesan. Sift together the flour, baking powder and salt and whisk into the ricotta mixture. Stir in the greens, rice, herbs and pepper. The mixture will be thick.
- Heat a griddle or a heavy nonstick skillet over medium-high heat. Brush with olive oil, enough to coat the bottom, and drop the batter in by the heaped tablespoon. Cook for about 3 minutes, until dark brown and nicely risen, and turn over. Cook for another 2 to 3 minutes, until brown on the other side. The

pancakes will be moist in the middle, but there should not be a raw flour taste. Remove from the heat and serve, or cool on a rack and heat later in a medium-low oven. Serve with a dollop of tomato sauce.

Nutrition Information

- 249: calories;
- 1 gram: polyunsaturated fat;
- 29 grams: carbohydrates;
- 329 milligrams: sodium;
- 2 grams: sugars;
- 12 grams: protein;
- 10 grams: fat;
- 5 grams: saturated fat;
- 0 grams: trans fat;
- 4 grams: monounsaturated fat;
- 3 grams: dietary fiber;

30. Beet Greens Bulgur With Carrots And Tomatoes

Serving: Serves 6 | Prep: | Cook: | Ready in: 1hours

Ingredients

- 2 generous bunches beet greens (1 to 1 1/2 pounds)
- ¼ cup extra virgin olive oil
- 1 medium onion, chopped
- 1 large or 2 medium carrots, peeled and cut in small dice (1 to 1 1/2 cups)
- 2 garlic cloves, minced
- 1 teaspoon sweet paprika
- Salt and freshly ground black pepper to taste
- 1 14.5-ounce can chopped tomatoes, or 1 1/2 cups chopped fresh tomatoes
- 1 cup coarse bulgur
- 2 cups water
- ¼ cup chopped fresh parsley
- ¼ cup chopped fresh dill
- Juice of 1 to 2 lemons

Direction

- Stem beet greens (discard stems), wash greens well in 2 changes of water, and coarsely chop. You should have about 6 cups chopped greens.
- Heat 3 tablespoons olive oil over medium heat in a deep, lidded skillet or a wide, lidded saucepan. Add onion and carrots and cook, stirring often, until tender, about 5 minutes. Add garlic and stir until fragrant, about 30 seconds. Add beet greens and cook, stirring, until they are coated with oil and wilted, about 2 minutes. Season to taste with salt and pepper. Add paprika and tomatoes and cook, stirring often, for another 5 minutes, until tomatoes have begun to cook down and soften a bit. Taste and adjust seasoning.
- Add bulgur and stir to coat with tomato mixture. Add water, more salt to taste, parsley and dill and bring to a boil. Cover, reduce heat to low and simmer 20 to 25 minutes until water has been absorbed.
- Remove from heat, uncover and quickly stir in lemon juice. Place a towel across the top of the pan. Return lid and let sit for 10 minutes. Serve hot, with the remaining olive oil drizzled over the top.

Nutrition Information

- 213: calories;
- 1 gram: polyunsaturated fat;
- 9 grams: dietary fiber;
- 4 grams: sugars;
- 750 milligrams: sodium;
- 10 grams: fat;
- 7 grams: monounsaturated fat;
- 30 grams: carbohydrates;
- 6 grams: protein;

31. Beet Greens And Rice Gratin

Serving: 4 to 6 servings. | Prep: | Cook: |Ready in: 1hours15mins

Ingredients

- 1 generous bunch beet greens, stemmed and washed
- 2 tablespoons extra virgin olive oil
- 1 medium onion, chopped
- 2 large garlic cloves, minced
- Salt to taste
- 1 teaspoon fresh thyme leaves or 1/2 teaspoon dried thyme
- 3 eggs
- ½ cup low-fat milk (2 percent)
- Freshly ground pepper
- 1 cup cooked brown rice, arborio rice or Calrose rice
- 2 ounces Gruyère cheese, grated (1/2 cup, tightly packed)
- 2 tablespoons freshly grated Parmesan
- ¼ cup bread crumbs (optional)

Direction

- Preheat the oven to 375 degrees. Oil a 2-quart gratin dish with olive oil. Either blanch the beet greens for 1 minute in a large pot of generously salted boiling water, or steam over an inch of boiling water for 2 to 5 minutes, until wilted and tender. Rinse with cold water, squeeze out water and chop medium-fine. Set aside.
- Heat 1 tablespoon of the oil over medium heat in a large, heavy skillet and add the onion. Cook, stirring, until tender, about 5 minutes, and add the garlic and a generous pinch of salt. Cook, stirring, until the garlic is fragrant, about 30 seconds. Stir in the cooked greens and the thyme and toss together. Season to taste with salt and pepper. Remove from the heat.
- In a large bowl, beat together the eggs and milk. Add 1/2 teaspoon salt and freshly ground pepper to taste. Stir in the greens mixture, the rice and the cheeses and mix

together well. Scrape into the oiled baking dish. Sprinkle the bread crumbs over the top. Drizzle on the remaining tablespoon of oil.

- Bake 35 to 40 minutes, until sizzling and lightly browned on the top and sides. Remove from the heat and allow to sit for at least 10 minutes before serving.

Nutrition Information

- 269: calories;
- 0 grams: trans fat;
- 2 grams: sugars;
- 11 grams: protein;
- 4 grams: saturated fat;
- 6 grams: monounsaturated fat;
- 1 gram: dietary fiber;
- 31 grams: carbohydrates;
- 308 milligrams: sodium;

32. Beet And Arugula Salad With Berries

Serving: Serves 6 to 8 | Prep: | Cook: | Ready in: 15mins

Ingredients

- For the dressing
- 1 tablespoon plus 2 teaspoons sherry vinegar
- 1 teaspoon balsamic vinegar
- Salt to taste
- ½ teaspoon Dijon mustard
- 4 tablespoons extra- virgin olive oil
- 1 tablespoon walnut oil
- For the salad
- 3 medium-size beets, roasted
- 1 bunch or 6-ounce bag arugula, preferably wild arugula (about 6 cups)
- ⅔ cup blueberries, blackberries or a combination
- 3 tablespoons broken walnuts
- 1-2 tablespoons chopped fresh tarragon

Direction

- Whisk together vinegars, salt, Dijon mustard, olive oil and walnut oil.
- Peel beets and slice in half-moons or wedges. Place in a salad bowl and toss with 2 tablespoons of the dressing.
- Add remaining salad ingredients and remaining dressing, toss well and serve.

Nutrition Information

- 116: calories;
- 0 grams: trans fat;
- 2 grams: protein;
- 10 grams: fat;
- 1 gram: saturated fat;
- 6 grams: monounsaturated fat;
- 3 grams: sugars;
- 5 grams: carbohydrates;
- 170 milligrams: sodium;

33. Beet And Chia Pancakes

Serving: About 15 pancakes | Prep: | Cook: | Ready in: 1hours30mins

Ingredients

- 1 large or 2 medium beets (enough for 1/2 cup puréed roasted beets)
- 125 grams (1 cup) whole wheat flour or teff flour (or a combination)
- 60 grams (1/2 cup) unbleached all-purpose flour
- 10 grams (2 teaspoons) baking powder
- 5 grams (1 teaspoon) baking soda
- 2 grams (rounded 1/4 teaspoon) salt
- 1 tablespoon sugar, honey, or agave syrup (optional)
- 2 eggs
- 5 grams (1 teaspoon) vanilla
- 1 ½ cups buttermilk or 1 cup yogurt + 1/2 cup milk
- 35 grams (3 tablespoons) chia seeds

- 3 tablespoons sunflower, grapeseed or canola oil

Direction

- Preheat the oven to 425 degrees. Cut the greens away from the beets, leaving about 1/4 inch of stems. Scrub the beets and place in a baking dish (or lidded ovenproof casserole). Add 1/2 inch water to the dish. Cover tightly. Place in the oven and roast medium beets (4 to 6 ounces) for 50 minutes, large beets (8 ounces) 60 minutes, or until very soft and easily penetrated with the tip of a knife. Remove from the oven and allow to cool in the covered baking dish. Cut away the ends and slip off the skins. Purée in a food processor fitted with the steel blade until smooth. Measure out 1/2 cup. Freeze any extra.
- Sift together the flours, baking powder, baking soda, salt, and sugar (if using sugar). In a medium-size bowl, beat together the eggs, buttermilk or yogurt and milk, oil, vanilla, beet purée and honey or agave nectar (if using). Quickly whisk in the flour mixture and fold in the chia seeds.
- Heat a large skillet or griddle over medium-high heat and brush with butter or oil. Drop the pancakes by the scant 1/4 cup onto the hot pan or griddle. Cook until bubbles break through and turn the pancakes. They will be quite moist so make sure to wait long enough so that they don't fall apart when you turn them. Cook for 1 to 2 minutes on the other side, until lightly browned. Remove to a rack. Serve with maple syrup and butter.

Nutrition Information

- 101: calories;
- 2 grams: sugars;
- 12 grams: carbohydrates;
- 4 grams: protein;
- 203 milligrams: sodium;
- 5 grams: fat;
- 1 gram: saturated fat;
- 0 grams: trans fat;

34. Beet, Mushroom And Beef Burgers

Serving: Serves 4 | Prep: | Cook: | Ready in: 20mins

Ingredients

- ¼ pound peeled roasted beets (1 medium)
- ½ pound roasted mushroom mix
- ½ pound lean ground beef
- 1 tablespoon minced chives
- 1 shallot minced
- 1 teaspoon fresh lemon juice (more or less to taste)
- Salt
- freshly ground black pepper
- Olive oil for cooking (no more than 1 tablespoon)
- 1 tablespoon finely chopped mint

Direction

- Grate beet on large holes of a grater.
- . In a large bowl mix together all of the ingredients except the oil for cooking until well combined. Shape into 4 patties. I like to pile the mixture into a 3-inch ring and pull the ring away, then when I place the patties in the hot pan I press them down with the back of my spatula so they are about 1 inch thick.
- Heat a heavy skillet over medium-high heat and add a small amount of olive oil, just enough to coat pan. Cook patties for 4 minutes on each side. Remove from pan and serve. You can use a bun or not (I think they are fine without). Baby arugula, mizuna or spicy micro-greens make a very nice accompaniment.

Nutrition Information

- 201: calories;
- 14 grams: fat;

- 7 grams: monounsaturated fat;
- 8 grams: carbohydrates;
- 2 grams: dietary fiber;
- 378 milligrams: sodium;
- 1 gram: polyunsaturated fat;
- 4 grams: sugars;
- 12 grams: protein;
- 5 grams: saturated fat;

35. Berry Clafoutis

Serving: 8 servings | Prep: | Cook: |Ready in: 1hours15mins

Ingredients

- 3 cups/450 grams mixed blueberries and blackberries (or use just one type), rinsed and drained on paper towels
- 2 tablespoons kirsch, eau de vie de myrtille or crème de cassis (optional)
- 7 tablespoons/105 grams sugar, preferably organic
- About 1/3 cup/40 grams unbleached all-purpose flour
- About 1/3 cup/35 grams almond flour
- 3 extra-large eggs (165 grams)
- 1 vanilla bean, scraped, or 1 teaspoon vanilla extract
- Pinch of salt
- About 2/3 cup/165 grams low-fat yogurt or kefir

Direction

- Toss berries in a medium bowl with the kirsch, eau de vie or crème de cassis and 2 tablespoons of the sugar, and let sit for 30 minutes. Meanwhile, sift together all-purpose flour and almond flour.
- Heat oven to 375 degrees. Butter a 9- or 10-inch ceramic tart pan or clafoutis dish.
- In a medium bowl, beat eggs with remaining sugar, seeds from the vanilla bean or vanilla, and salt. Place a strainer over the bowl and

drain berries, allowing all of the liquid from the berries to run into the egg and sugar mixture. Whisk to combine. Arrange drained berries in the buttered baking dish.
- Beat the sifted flours into the egg mixture and whisk until smooth. Add yogurt or kefir and combine well. Pour over fruit, scraping out all of the batter with a rubber spatula.
- Bake for 35 minutes, or until the top is browned and the clafoutis is firm and puffed. Press gently on the top in the middle to see if it's firm. If it isn't, return to the oven for 5 minutes. Remove from the oven and cool on a rack. Serve warm or at room temperature.

Nutrition Information

- 192: calories;
- 0 grams: trans fat;
- 33 grams: carbohydrates;
- 23 grams: sugars;
- 6 grams: protein;
- 78 milligrams: sodium;
- 5 grams: dietary fiber;
- 1 gram: polyunsaturated fat;

36. Black Quinoa, Fennel And Celery Salad

Serving: Serves 4 | Prep: | Cook: |Ready in: 5mins

Ingredients

- 1 medium-size fennel bulb (about 10 ounces), quartered, cored and very thinly sliced
- 1 long or 2 shorter celery sticks, very thinly sliced
- 2 cups cooked black quinoa (about 3/4 cup uncooked)
- ¼ cup chopped flat-leaf parsley
- 2 tablespoons chopped chives
- 2 tablespoons freshly squeezed lemon juice
- 1 small garlic clove, puréed
- Salt and freshly ground pepper to taste

- 5 tablespoons extra virgin olive oil

Direction

- In a salad bowl, combine the sliced fennel and celery, the quinoa, parsley and chives.
- In a small bowl or measuring cup, whisk together the lemon juice, garlic, salt, pepper and olive oil. Toss with the salad and serve.

Nutrition Information

- 289: calories;
- 19 grams: fat;
- 3 grams: polyunsaturated fat;
- 13 grams: monounsaturated fat;
- 27 grams: carbohydrates;
- 5 grams: protein;
- 4 grams: sugars;
- 474 milligrams: sodium;

37. Black Eyed Pea Salad

Serving: 4 servings | Prep: | Cook: | Ready in: 2hours

Ingredients

- 1 cup black-eyed peas, rinsed and picked over
- 3 large garlic cloves, 2 of them crushed and left in the skin, 1 of them minced
- ½ onion, intact
- 1 bay leaf
- Salt to taste
- 2 medium tomatoes, in season only, diced
- 1 medium fennel bulb (about 1/2 pound), trimmed, quartered, cored and sliced very thin across the grain
- 1 tablespoon fresh lemon juice
- 2 tablespoons red wine vinegar or cider vinegar
- 3 tablespoons extra virgin olive oil
- 1 teaspoon cumin seeds, lightly toasted and ground
- Freshly ground black pepper to taste
- ⅓ cup chopped flat-leaf parsley
- ⅓ cup chopped fresh dill
- ⅓ cup chopped chives
- 2 ounces feta, crumbled

Direction

- Place the black-eyed peas, whole crushed garlic cloves, halved onion and bay leaf in a large, heavy saucepan and add enough water to cover by 2 inches. Bring to a boil, add salt to taste, reduce the heat, cover and simmer until tender but intact, about 45 minutes. Remove from the heat, remove the lid and allow the black-eyed peas to cool for 30 minutes. Remove and discard the onion. Remove the garlic cloves, squeeze the cooked garlic out of the skins and back into the black-eyed peas, and drain through a strainer set over a bowl.
- Transfer the black-eyed peas to a large bowl. Whisk together the lemon juice, vinegar, minced garlic, cumin, salt, pepper and olive oil. Toss with the beans. Add the remaining ingredients except the feta and toss together. If you want a bit more liquid with the beans, add back some of the broth (I found the dressing to be sufficient). Marinate in the refrigerator for at least 30 minutes before serving. Sprinkle the feta over the top and serve.

Nutrition Information

- 210: calories;
- 1 gram: polyunsaturated fat;
- 5 grams: protein;
- 6 grams: sugars;
- 512 milligrams: sodium;
- 14 grams: fat;
- 4 grams: saturated fat;
- 8 grams: monounsaturated fat;
- 18 grams: carbohydrates;

38. Black Eyed Peas With Collard Greens

Serving: Serves six | Prep: | Cook: |Ready in: 1hours30mins

Ingredients

- ½ pound black-eyed peas, rinsed
- 3 tablespoons extra virgin olive oil
- 1 large onion, chopped
- 3 large garlic cloves, minced
- 1 bay leaf
- Salt to taste
- 1 large bunch collard greens (1 1/2 to 2 pounds), stemmed, washed well and chopped or cut in ribbons
- 2 tablespoons tomato paste dissolved in 1/2 cup water
- ¼ to ½ cup chopped fresh dill (to taste)
- Freshly ground pepper to taste
- For topping (optional): crumbled feta or fresh lemon juice

Direction

- Place the black-eyed peas in a large saucepan, cover with water by two inches, bring to a boil and then drain. Combine with half the onion and one of the garlic cloves in the saucepan. Add water to cover by two inches, and bring back to a simmer. Add the bay leaf, and reduce the heat. Add salt to taste, cover and simmer 30 minutes, until the beans are just tender. Drain through a strainer set over a bowl.
- Meanwhile, preheat the oven to 350 degrees. In a large, ovenproof lidded skillet or Dutch oven, heat 2 tablespoons of the olive oil over medium heat and add the remaining onion. Cook, stirring, until tender, about five minutes, and add the remaining garlic. Stir together for 30 seconds to a minute, until fragrant. A handful at a time, stir in the greens. As the greens wilt, stir in another handful, until all the greens have been added and have collapsed in the pan. Add the dissolved tomato paste and stir together. Add salt to taste. Add the beans and enough cooking liquid to barely cover everything, cover and place in the oven for 30 minutes, until the collards are tender and the beans very soft.
- Uncover the pot, and add a bit of liquid if the beans are dry. Stir in the remaining tablespoon of olive oil and the dill, cover and continue to simmer for another 10 minutes. Add salt and freshly ground pepper to taste. Serve warm or hot. If you wish, top with crumbled feta or a squeeze of lemon.

Nutrition Information

- 156: calories;
- 491 milligrams: sodium;
- 8 grams: dietary fiber;
- 1 gram: polyunsaturated fat;
- 5 grams: monounsaturated fat;
- 19 grams: carbohydrates;
- 3 grams: sugars;
- 6 grams: protein;

39. Blackberry Lime Smoothie With Chia Seeds And Cashews

Serving: 1 serving | Prep: | Cook: |Ready in:

Ingredients

- 1 tablespoon soaked chia seeds (1 teaspoon dry unsoaked)
- 1 heaped tablespoon cashews (1/2 ounce), soaked overnight in water and drained
- 1 heaped cup blackberries (about 5 ounces)
- ¾ cup limeade (see below)
- 1 tablespoons geranium syrup (see below) or 1 teaspoon rose water
- 2 ice cubes
- Limeade
- ½ cup water
- ½ cup sugar
- 1 to 1 ¼ cups fresh lime juice (to taste)

- 4 to 5 cups water, to taste (or for a variation, sparkling water)

Direction

- To make the limeade, combine 1/2½ cup water and 1/2½ cup sugar in a saucepan and bring to a boil. Turn down the heat and simmer until the sugar dissolves. Remove from the heat and allow to cool, then combine with the lime juice and additional 4 to 5 cups water.
- For To make geranium syrup, make the syrup as directed above, and when you take it off the heat, pour 1/2½ cup over 1 sprig rose geranium and allow to steep for 30 minutes. Remove the rose geranium sprig from the syrup.
- To soak the chia seeds, place in a jar or bowl and add 4 tablespoons water for every tablespoon of chia seeds. Place in the refrigerator for several hours or overnight. The seeds and water will be become gelatinous. Soak the cashews overnight and drain.
- Scoop up a tablespoon of seeds with the gooey liquid and place in a blender (don't worry, your smoothie won't have this consistency). Add the remaining ingredients and blend for 1 full minute at high speed. Strain through a medium-mesh strainer and serve.

40. Blender Gazpacho With Celery, Carrot, Cucumber And Red Pepper

Serving: Serves 6 | Prep: | Cook: | Ready in: 10mins

Ingredients

- 2 slices red or white onion
- ¾ pound cucumber (such as 1 long European), peeled and coarsely chopped
- 1 ½ pounds ripe tomatoes, quartered
- 1 medium carrot, peeled and coarsely chopped
- 2 sticks celery, coarsely chopped

- 1 medium size red pepper, coarsely chopped
- 2 large garlic cloves, halved, green germs removed
- 2 tablespoons sherry vinegar, plus a little extra for the onion
- 2 tablespoons extra virgin olive oil
- Salt to taste
- 1 cup ice water
- Chopped fresh tarragon or slivered fresh basil leaves for garnish

Direction

- Put the onion slices in a bowl, cover with cold water and add a few drops of vinegar. Let sit for 5 minutes while you prepare the remaining ingredients. Drain and rinse with cold water. Cut in half or into smaller pieces.
- Working in 2 batches, blend all of the ingredients except the tarragon or basil leaves in a blender for 2 minutes or longer, until smooth and frothy. Transfer to a bowl or container (a metal bowl is the most efficient for chilling) and chill for at least 2 hours before eating. Garnish each bowl or glass with chopped fresh tarragon or slivered basil leaves.

Nutrition Information

- 96: calories;
- 3 grams: dietary fiber;
- 12 grams: carbohydrates;
- 7 grams: sugars;
- 2 grams: protein;
- 679 milligrams: sodium;
- 5 grams: fat;
- 1 gram: polyunsaturated fat;

41. Blood Orange, Grapefruit And Pomegranate Compote

Serving: 6 servings | Prep: | Cook: | Ready in: 45mins

Ingredients

- 2 pounds blood oranges (they are small, so this is usually around 8 or 9)
- 2 ruby red grapefruit
- 80 grams (6 tablespoons) sugar, preferably organic
- 2 tablespoons water
- 1 tablespoon agave nectar
- 2 tablespoons port wine
- ½ teaspoon vanilla
- ⅓ cup pomegranate seeds

Direction

- Set aside two oranges and a grapefruit half. Remove peel and pith from remaining oranges and grapefruit. Cut away both ends of the fruit so that it sits flat on your cutting board (it helps to use one with a canal around the edges so you can pour off the juice). Using a chef's knife, utility knife or a paring knife, cut skin and pith completely away from the fruit, following the natural curve of the fruit from top to bottom. Slice peeled fruit into rounds. Cut the grapefruit rounds into thirds or quarters and combine with the sliced oranges in a serving bowl. Pour accumulated juice into a separate, small bowl. Squeeze the juice from the remaining two oranges and grapefruit half (you need about 3/4 cup), and add to the small bowl. Peel and slice any remaining grapefruit and add to the bowl with the fruit. Set aside fruit while you make caramel syrup.
- Stir vanilla and port into the citrus juice. In a medium saucepan, combine sugar, water and agave nectar. With a wet pastry brush, brush down sides of pan to dislodge any stray sugar granules. Over medium heat, bring mixture to a boil, continuing to brush down any errant sugar crystals. Cover pan, turn heat down to medium-low and set timer for 4 minutes. Uncover and cook until the caramel is golden to amber. Swirl pan if necessary to distribute the darkening caramel, but do not stir. Bubbles should be breaking on the surface. Insert a candy thermometer and as soon as the caramel reaches 310 to 325 degrees (it will be a deep

golden color), remove from heat and allow bubbles to subside.
- Carefully add juice-port mixture to the sugar mixture, standing away from pan to avoid splashes. Heat through over medium heat stirring with a heat-proof spatula. The caramel may seize on the spatula; just continue to stir and heat until the caramel has melted again and the juice and caramel come together. (The caramel is very hot so resist temptation to taste it.) Remove from heat and allow to cool, then pour over fruit. Toss gently. Sprinkle pomegranate seeds on top. Serve at room temperature or chilled.

Nutrition Information

- 184: calories;
- 37 grams: sugars;
- 2 grams: protein;
- 1 milligram: sodium;
- 0 grams: polyunsaturated fat;
- 45 grams: carbohydrates;
- 6 grams: dietary fiber;

42. Blueberry Kefir Smoothie With Greens

Serving: 1 generous serving | Prep: | Cook: | Ready in: 2mins

Ingredients

- 1 cup plain kefir or yogurt
- 1 cup frozen wild blueberries
- 1 banana (frozen or not)
- 1 teaspoon honey
- ½ teaspoon chia seeds
- ½ cup, tightly packed, mixed baby greens, such as kale, red chard, and spinach

Direction

- Place all of the ingredients in a blender and blend at high speed for 1 minute or until smooth. Serve at once.

Nutrition Information

- 368: calories;
- 9 grams: fat;
- 5 grams: saturated fat;
- 2 grams: monounsaturated fat;
- 1 gram: polyunsaturated fat;
- 31 grams: sugars;
- 131 milligrams: sodium;
- 0 grams: trans fat;
- 65 grams: carbohydrates;
- 10 grams: dietary fiber;
- 11 grams: protein;

43. Breakfast Wheat Berries

Serving: Serves 4 to 6 | Prep: | Cook: | Ready in: 1hours30mins

Ingredients

- 1 cup wheat berries
- 5 cups water
- Salt to taste
- ¼ cup honey, agave syrup or brown sugar, or more to taste
- ½ to 1 teaspoon rose water, to taste
- 1 teaspoon ground anise or fennel seeds
- ¾ teaspoon ground cinnamon
- ⅛ teaspoon freshly grated nutmeg
- ½ cup raisins or other chopped dried fruit of choice
- ⅓ cup chopped walnuts, almonds, hazelnuts, or a mixture for garnish
- 2 cups plain low-fat yogurt (optional)
- Pomegranate seeds for garnish (optional)

Direction

- The night before, combine wheat berries, 1 quart of the water and salt and bring to a boil in a saucepan. Reduce heat, cover and simmer 1 hour. Remove from heat, stir in the honey, agave syrup or sugar, rose water, anise or fennel seeds, cinnamon, nutmeg and raisins or dried fruit. Cover and leave overnight (or for 5 to 6 hours).
- In the morning, add remaining cup of water to the wheat berries and bring to a simmer. Cook 30 to 45 minutes, stirring often, until berries are soft and splayed at one end. There should be some liquid surrounding the wheat berries (add more water if necessary). Taste and add more sweetener if desired.
- Serve on their own with some of the liquid in the saucepan (stir in some milk if desired), or spoon about 1/3 cup yogurt into bowls and top with a generous spoonful of the berries, with some of the sweet broth. Top with a handful of chopped nuts and a few pomegranate seeds if desired.

Nutrition Information

- 170: calories;
- 5 grams: dietary fiber;
- 17 grams: sugars;
- 3 grams: protein;
- 591 milligrams: sodium;
- 1 gram: fat;
- 0 grams: polyunsaturated fat;
- 41 grams: carbohydrates;

44. Broccoli, Quinoa And Purslane Salad

Serving: Serves 4 to 6 | Prep: | Cook: | Ready in: 15mins

Ingredients

- ½ pound broccoli crowns (about 2 large), sliced very thin
- 2 tablespoons fresh lemon juice

- 1 tablespoon sherry vinegar
- Salt to taste
- 1 garlic clove, puréed
- Freshly ground pepper to taste
- 6 tablespoons extra virgin olive oil
- ¼ pound purslane, thick stems trimmed, or mâche
- 1 ½ cups cooked quinoa
- 2 tablespoons finely chopped tarragon
- 1 ½ cups wild or baby arugula

Direction

- Place the sliced broccoli and all the little bits of florets that remain on your cutting board after you slice it in a large bowl.
- Whisk together the lemon juice, vinegar, salt, garlic, pepper and olive oil and toss with the broccoli. Let marinate for about 10 minutes while you prepare the remaining ingredients.
- Add the purslane or mâche, the quinoa and the tarragon to the bowl and toss together.
- Line plates or a platter with the arugula, top with the salad, and serve.

Nutrition Information

- 197: calories;
- 2 grams: dietary fiber;
- 10 grams: monounsaturated fat;
- 14 grams: carbohydrates;
- 1 gram: sugars;
- 4 grams: protein;
- 295 milligrams: sodium;
- 15 grams: fat;

45. Broiled Calf's Liver

Serving: 2 servings | Prep: | Cook: | Ready in: 30mins

Ingredients

- 8 ounces sliced bacon
- 2 tablespoons olive oil

- 4 medium sweet onions, halved root-to-stem and thinly sliced
- ½ teaspoon paprika
- 1 pound calf's liver, sliced in half horizontally
- Salt
- freshly ground black pepper

Direction

- Preheat a broiler. In a large skillet over medium heat, sauté bacon, turning as needed, until crispy. Transfer to paper towels to drain. Discard excess bacon fat but do not wash pan.
- Return pan to medium heat. Add oil, onions and paprika. Sauté until onions are very soft and beginning to brown, 15 to 20 minutes. Toward the end of cooking, season liver with salt and pepper to taste, and broil as desired, 1 1/2 to 2 minutes a side for a medium (lightly pink) center.
- To serve, remove onions from heat and season with salt to taste. Place a slice of liver on each of two serving plates. Smother with onions and top with bacon. Serve hot.

46. Brown Rice With Carrots And Leeks

Serving: Serves four | Prep: | Cook: | Ready in: 1hours

Ingredients

- 2 tablespoons extra virgin olive oil
- 1 pound leeks, white and light green parts only, trimmed, cut in half lengthwise, washed thoroughly and cut in 1/2-inch slices
- ½ pound carrots, peeled and sliced
- 2 garlic cloves, halved, green shoots removed and thinly sliced
- 1 cup brown rice (short- or long-grain)
- Salt to taste
- 2 ½ cups water
- 2 to 3 tablespoons freshly squeezed lemon juice, to taste

Direction

- Heat the olive oil over a medium-sized, heavy skillet or saucepan, and add the leeks and carrots. Cook, stirring, until the leeks are tender and translucent and the carrots have softened slightly, about five minutes. Add the garlic and salt to taste. Cook, stirring, until the garlic smells fragrant, about a minute. Add the rice and about 1/2 teaspoon salt, and stir to coat the grains with olive oil. Add the water, and bring to a boil. Reduce the heat, cover and simmer over low heat until the rice is tender, about 45 minutes. Remove from the heat, and do not remove the cover for 10 minutes. Then stir in the lemon juice, and taste and adjust salt. Serve hot or warm.

Nutrition Information

- 328: calories;
- 890 milligrams: sodium;
- 9 grams: fat;
- 1 gram: polyunsaturated fat;
- 5 grams: dietary fiber;
- 59 grams: carbohydrates;
- 7 grams: sugars;
- 6 grams: protein;

47. Brown Rice And Barley Salad With Sprouted Red Lentils And Green Beans

Serving: Serves 6 | Prep: | Cook: | Ready in:

Ingredients

- For the grains
- ⅓ cup barley
- Salt to taste
- ½ cup brown rice (short or long -grain)
- 2 tablespoons fresh lemon juice
- For the dressing
- 1 tablespoon mayonnaise
- ¼ cup plain yogurt
- 1 teaspoon curry powder
- ½ teaspoon lightly toasted cumin seeds, ground
- ¼ teaspoon mild chili powder
- 2 tablespoons lemon juice
- Salt to taste
- ¼ cup grapeseed oil
- For the salad
- 2 tablespoons split red lentils, soaked for 2 hours or longer in water to cover and drained (1/4 cup soaked)
- 1 cup diced European or Japanese cucumber
- 3 ounces green beans, blanched for 4 minutes and cut in 1-inch lengths (about 1/2 cup)
- 1 small green pepper, either sweet or hot, cut in small dice
- ¼ cup raisins or finely diced plums or pluots
- 2 tablespoons chopped chives
- ¼ cup chopped cilantro
- 2 teaspoons nigella seeds

Direction

- To cook barley, bring 1 quart water to a boil in a medium-size saucepan, add salt to taste and barley. Boil like pasta for 40 to 50 minutes, until tender (some stores now sell par-boiled barley, which takes 15 to 20 minutes – not the 10 minutes that the package says to cook it). Turn off heat, drain, return barley to the pot, cover pot with a towel and return lid. Let sit for 10 minutes or longer.
- While barley is cooking, cook rice in another saucepan. Combine with 1 cup and plus 2 tablespoons water and salt to taste and bring to a boil. Reduce heat, cover and simmer over low heat for 30 to 40 minutes, until water has been absorbed by the rice. Turn off heat, cover pot with a dish towel and return lid. Let sit for 10 minutes or longer.
- Transfer cooked barley and rice to a bowl (you should have 2 1/2 to 3 cups cooked grains) and toss with 2 tablespoons fresh lemon juice. Allow to cool if desired.
- Make dressing. In a bowl or jar, whisk or shake together mayonnaise, yogurt, curry

powder, ground cumin, chili powder, lemon juice, salt, and grapeseed oil. The mixture should be creamy. Taste and adjust salt.

- Combine all of the salad ingredients except the nigella seeds and toss with dressing. Transfer to a platter, a salad bowl or individual plates. Sprinkle nigella seeds over each serving.

Nutrition Information

- 249: calories;
- 13 grams: fat;
- 4 grams: dietary fiber;
- 2 grams: monounsaturated fat;
- 8 grams: polyunsaturated fat;
- 31 grams: carbohydrates;
- 6 grams: sugars;
- 5 grams: protein;
- 266 milligrams: sodium;

48. Brown Rice, Sesame, Spinach And Scallion Pancakes

Serving: 16 pancakes | Prep: | Cook: | Ready in: 30mins

Ingredients

- 1 ½ cups (200 grams) whole-wheat flour or whole-wheat pastry flour
- 2 teaspoons baking powder
- 1 teaspoon baking soda
- ½ teaspoon salt
- ¼ teaspoon turmeric
- 2 tablespoons (30 grams) toasted sesame seeds or black sesame seeds
- 2 eggs
- 1 cup buttermilk
- 1 cup milk
- 2 tablespoons canola oil
- 1 ½ cups (300 grams) cooked brown rice
- 1 bunch scallions, sliced
- 6 ounces spinach leaves (baby spinach or stemmed bunch spinach)

- 2 ounces (1/2 cup) crumbled feta

Direction

- Sift together the flour, baking powder, baking soda, salt and turmeric. Stir in the sesame seeds
- In a separate bowl, beat the eggs and whisk in the buttermilk, milk and canola oil. Quickly whisk in the flour mixture and fold in the brown rice and scallions
- Steam the spinach over 1 inch of boiling water for 2 minutes, or just until wilted. Rinse with cold water, squeeze out excess water and chop. Stir into the pancake batter, along with the feta
- Heat a griddle or a large skillet, either nonstick or seasoned cast iron, over medium-high heat. Brush with butter or oil. Use a 1/4-cup ladle or cup measure to drop 3 to 4 tablespoons of batter per pancake onto your heated pan or griddle. Cook until they are brown on the edges and bubbles break through, 3 to 4 minutes, then carefully slide a spatula underneath and flip them over. Cook on the other side until pancakes are nicely browned. Serve hot

Nutrition Information

- 127: calories;
- 5 grams: protein;
- 1 gram: polyunsaturated fat;
- 0 grams: trans fat;
- 2 grams: sugars;
- 17 grams: carbohydrates;
- 216 milligrams: sodium;

49. Brown Soda Bread With Oats

Serving: 1 loaf, about 12 slices | Prep: | Cook: | Ready in: 1hours

Ingredients

- Soft butter for the bread pan
- 125 grams (approximately 1 cup) whole-wheat flour
- 62 grams (approximately 1/2 cup) unbleached all-purpose or bread flour
- 25 grams (2 rounded tablespoons) steel-cut oats, either regular or quick-cooking
- 40 grams (approximately 1/3 cup) rolled oats
- 8 grams (approximately 2 teaspoons, tightly packed) brown sugar
- 3.5 grams (1/2 teaspoon) salt
- 10 grams (2 teaspoons) baking soda, sifted
- 290 grams (approximately 1 1/4 cups) buttermilk

Direction

- Preheat oven to 350 degrees. Butter an 8 1/2 x 4 1/2 x 2 1/2-inch bread pan.
- In a large bowl, mix together flours, steel-cut oats, rolled oats, brown sugar, salt and sifted baking soda. Mix well with your hands.
- Make a well in the center of flour mixture. Pour in buttermilk. Working from the center of the bowl in concentric clockwise circles, with fingers outstretched, stir buttermilk into flour mixture. (You can use a rubber spatula instead if you don't like getting dough on your hands.) This should take about a half a minute at most. Dough will be quite moist. Use a rubber spatula to scrape into bread pan and smooth out the dough to fill pan evenly (the pan will be filled only about halfway.)
- Place in the oven and bake 40 minutes, until dark brown and a tester inserted comes out clean. Remove from pan and cool on a rack.

Nutrition Information

- 182: calories;
- 549 milligrams: sodium;
- 3 grams: dietary fiber;
- 1 gram: polyunsaturated fat;
- 0 grams: trans fat;
- 33 grams: carbohydrates;
- 4 grams: sugars;

- 7 grams: protein;

50. Buckwheat Crêpes

Serving: About 12 8-inch crêpes | Prep: | Cook: | Ready in: 2hours15mins

Ingredients

- 1 cup low-fat (2 percent) milk
- ⅓ cup water
- 3 large eggs
- ½ teaspoon salt
- ⅔ cup buckwheat flour
- ½ cup unbleached white flour
- 3 tablespoons canola oil
- For the buckwheat crêpes with spinach and egg
- 6 ounces baby spinach
- Salt, preferably kosher salt
- freshly ground pepper to taste
- 2 buckwheat crêpes, above
- 2 eggs, poached or fried for four minutes
- 2 tablespoons grated Gruyère cheese

Direction

- Place the milk, water, eggs and salt in a blender. Cover the blender, and turn on at low speed. Add the flours, then the canola oil, and increase the speed to high. Blend for one minute. Transfer to a bowl, cover and refrigerate for one to two hours.
- Place a seasoned 7- or 8-inch crêpe pan over medium heat. Brush with butter or oil, and when the pan is hot, remove from the heat and ladle in about 3 tablespoons batter. Tilt or swirl the pan to distribute the batter evenly, and return to the heat. Cook for about one minute, until you can easily loosen the edges with a spatula. Turn and cook on the other side for 30 seconds. Turn onto a plate. Continue until all of the batter is used.
- Bring a large pot of generously salted water to a boil, and add the spinach. Blanch for 20

seconds, and transfer to a bowl of ice water. Drain and squeeze dry. Chop and season with salt and pepper.

- Heat the crêpes in a dry skillet over medium heat (or use the skillet you used to fry your eggs). Top with a spoonful of spinach, and top the spinach with the egg, setting the egg to one side so you can fold the crêpe over. Sprinkle the cheese over the top, fold the crêpe over, and transfer to a plate with a spatula. Serve hot.

Nutrition Information

- 146: calories;
- 15 grams: carbohydrates;
- 6 grams: protein;
- 198 milligrams: sodium;
- 7 grams: fat;
- 2 grams: sugars;
- 0 grams: trans fat;
- 3 grams: monounsaturated fat;

---

51. Bulgur Bowl With Spinach, Mushrooms And Dukkah

Serving: Serves 4 | Prep: | Cook: | Ready in: 1hours30mins

Ingredients

- For the Dukkah
- ¼ cup lightly toasted unsalted peanuts or almonds
- ¼ cup lightly toasted sesame seeds
- 2 tablespoons coriander seeds
- 1 tablespoon cumin seeds
- 2 teaspoons nigella seeds
- 1 teaspoon ground sumac
- ½ teaspoon salt (or to taste)
- For the Bulgur and Vegetables
- 1 cup coarse bulgur (#3)
- 2 cups water or stock (chicken or vegetable)
- Salt to taste

- 2 tablespoons extra virgin olive oil, plus additional if desired for drizzling
- ½ red onion, thinly sliced across the grain
- 1 pound white, cremini or wild mushrooms, trimmed and quartered
- 2 to 4 garlic cloves (to taste), minced
- 2 tablespoons dry white wine (optional)
- Freshly ground pepper
- 1 ½ pounds bunch spinach, stemmed and washed, or 12 ounces baby spinach, washed
- 1 cup cooked chickpeas
- 1 to 2 tablespoons chopped fresh dill

Direction

- Bring 2 cups water to a boil in a medium saucepan. Add the bulgur and salt to taste, reduce the heat, cover and simmer 15 to 20 minutes, until the water is absorbed. Remove from the heat, uncover and place a clean dish towel over the pan, then replace the lid. Allow to sit undisturbed for 10 minutes or longer. Alternatively, reconstitute the bulgur just by placing it in a bowl, mixing with salt to taste, and pouring on 1 1/2 cups boiling water or stock. Cover and let sit for 30 minutes, until the bulgur is tender and the liquid has been absorbed. Transfer to a strainer and press out excess water. Set aside.
- To make the dukkah, chop the nuts very fine. Mix with the toasted sesame seeds in a bowl. In a dry skillet lightly toast the coriander seeds just until fragrant and immediately transfer to a spice mill and allow to cool completely. In the same skillet toast the cumin seeds just until fragrant and transfer to the spice mill. Allow to cool. When the spices have cooled, grind and add to the nuts and sesame seeds. Add the nigella seeds, sumac and salt and mix together.
- In a large, heavy skillet heat 1 tablespoon of the olive oil over medium heat and add the red onion and a pinch of salt. Cook, stirring often, until the onion is very tender and lightly colored, about 8 minutes. Remove from the heat and set aside.

- Add the mushrooms to the skillet and turn up the heat to medium high. Cook, stirring or tossing in the pan, until the mushrooms begin to sweat, about 3 minutes. Season with salt and pepper and continue to cook, stirring, until just tender and moist, another couple of minutes. Add the remaining olive oil and the garlic, stir together for about 30 seconds, until fragrant, and stir in the wine. Cook, stirring and scraping the bottom of the pan with a wooden spoon, until the liquid in the pan has evaporated, and add the spinach and salt to taste. Cook, tossing the spinach in the pan with tongs, until the spinach has wilted, which shouldn't take much longer than a couple of minutes. Add the dill and stir everything together.
- Combine the bulgur and chickpeas and heat through, either on top of the stove or in the microwave. Spoon into wide bowls and top with the mushrooms and spinach. Arrange the red onions on top and if desired add a drizzle of olive oil. Sprinkle each serving with about 2 to 3 teaspoons dukkah and serve.

Nutrition Information

- 410: calories;
- 61 grams: carbohydrates;
- 20 grams: protein;
- 1215 milligrams: sodium;
- 13 grams: fat;
- 2 grams: saturated fat;
- 5 grams: sugars;

52. Bulgur Pilaf With Dried Fruit And Nuts

Serving: Serves six | Prep: | Cook: | Ready in: 40mins

Ingredients

- 2 ounces dried apricots (about 1/3 cup)
- 2 ounces prunes (about 1/3 cup), pitted
- 1 cup coarse bulgur (#3)
- 2 tablespoons unsalted butter
- ½ teaspoon salt, or to taste
- ¼ cup dark or golden raisins (or use half raisins, half-dried cranberries)
- ¼ cup blanched almonds, lightly toasted
- 2 tablespoons pine nuts, lightly toasted
- Plain Greek-style yogurt for serving

Direction

- Place the apricots and prunes in a bowl, cover with water and soak overnight or for several hours. Place a strainer over a bowl, and drain the dried fruit. Cut in thin slices.
- Measure out 2 cups of the soaking water (or add enough water to make 2 cups), and bring to a simmer. Meanwhile, melt the butter in a saucepan over medium heat. Add the bulgur, and stir constantly for a few minutes until the bulgur smells toasty. Add the salt, dried fruit and water, and bring to a boil. Boil for five minutes, then reduce the heat and simmer gently for eight to 10 minutes until the water has been absorbed. Remove from the heat, cover with a clean dish towel and place a lid over the towel. Allow the bulgur to sit for 15 minutes.
- Spoon the bulgur into a serving dish, top with the nuts and serve with plain yogurt on the side.

Nutrition Information

- 229: calories;
- 9 grams: fat;
- 4 grams: dietary fiber;
- 5 grams: protein;
- 134 milligrams: sodium;
- 3 grams: saturated fat;
- 0 grams: trans fat;
- 2 grams: polyunsaturated fat;
- 35 grams: carbohydrates;
- 8 grams: sugars;

53. Bulgur Salad With Greens, Barberries And Yogurt

Serving: Serves 4 to 6 | Prep: | Cook: |Ready in: 1hours

Ingredients

- 2 cups water
- Salt to taste
- 1 cup medium bulgur
- 1 generous bunch Swiss chard, about 1 pound
- ⅓ cup extra virgin olive oil
- 1 garlic clove, minced
- Freshly ground pepper
- 2 tablespoons chopped fresh tarragon
- 1 to 2 tablespoons (to taste) chopped fresh mint
- 1 teaspoon za'atar
- ½ teaspoon ground allspice
- 2 to 3 tablespoons barberries or chopped dried cranberries or cherries (to taste)
- 3 tablespoons fresh lemon juice
- 1 cup drained yogurt or thick Greek style yogurt
- 1-2 additional garlic cloves

Direction

- Bring 2 cups water to a boil in a medium saucepan. Add the bulgur and salt to taste, reduce the heat, cover and simmer 20 minutes, or until the water is absorbed. Remove from the heat, uncover and place a clean dishtowel over the pan, then replace the lid. Allow to sit undisturbed for 10 minutes. Uncover and place on a baking sheet or in a wide bowl to cool.
- Meanwhile, strip the chard leaves from the stems (retain the stems if they're wide and meaty) and wash well in 2 changes of water. Steam above 1 inch of boiling water for about 2 minutes, until wilted; alternatively, blanch for about 1 minute in salted boiling water. Transfer to a bowl of cold water, then drain and squeeze out excess water, taking the chard up by the handful. Chop fine.
- Dice the chard stems. Measure out 1 cup. Heat 1 tablespoon of the olive oil over medium heat in a medium skillet and add the chard stems. Cook, stirring, for about 3 minutes, just until crisp-tender. Add 1 minced garlic clove, stir for about 30 seconds, until fragrant, and remove from the heat.
- Combine the bulgur, chopped chard, chard stems, chopped tarragon and mint, za'atar, allspice and barberries in a large bowl. Whisk together the lemon juice, salt and pepper to taste, and olive oil. Toss with the bulgur mixture. Transfer to a platter or a wide salad bowl.
- Pound the remaining garlic to a paste with a pinch of salt in a mortar and pestle. Stir into the yogurt. Spoon on top of the salad and serve.

Nutrition Information

- 259: calories;
- 15 grams: fat;
- 9 grams: monounsaturated fat;
- 26 grams: carbohydrates;
- 5 grams: sugars;
- 8 grams: protein;
- 589 milligrams: sodium;
- 3 grams: saturated fat;
- 2 grams: polyunsaturated fat;

54. Bulgur And Chickpea Salad With Roasted Artichokes

Serving: serves 4 | Prep: | Cook: |Ready in: 50mins

Ingredients

- For the artichokes
- 4 medium-size or 2 large artichokes , trimmed
- 1 lemon, cut in half
- 3 tablespoons extra virgin olive oil
- Salt and freshly ground pepper
- For the salad

- 1 cup medium (No. #2) bulgur
- Salt, preferably kosher salt, to taste
- 2 cups water
- ¼ cup fresh lemon juice
- 1 to 2 garlic cloves, minced
- 1 teaspoon Dijon mustard
- ⅓ cup extra- virgin olive oil
- ¼ cup finely chopped parsley, or (more to taste)
- 2 tablespoons chopped chives or green onions
- 2 tablespoons finely chopped fresh mint
- 1 15-ounce can chick peas, drained and rinsed

Direction

- Preheat oven to 400 degrees. Trim artichokes and cut medium artichokes into quarters, cut large ones into 6ths or 8ths, rubbing cut surfaces with lemon and placing the pieces in a bowl of water acidulated with lemon juice as you work.
- Drain artichokes and dry as thoroughly as you can with paper towels. Line a sheet pan with parchment paper and toss artichoke wedges with the olive oil and salt and pepper to taste. Take care to coat all cut surfaces with olive oil.
- Place in oven and roast for 30 to 40 minutes, turning artichokes every 10 minutes, until the hearts are tender and edges of the leaves are browned, even charred.
- Meanwhile, make bulgur salad. Place bulgur in a bowl with salt to taste (I use 1/2 to 3/4 teaspoon kosher salt) and pour on 2 cups hot or boiling water. Allow to sit for 20 to 25 minutes, until most of water is absorbed. Drain and press against strainer to remove excess water.
- While bulgur is soaking, make dressing. Mix together lemon juice, garlic, mustard, and salt to taste. Whisk in olive oil. Toss with bulgur in a bowl. Add remaining ingredients, toss together, taste and adjust seasonings.
- Spoon bulgur salad onto a platter or onto plates. Garnish with artichoke wedges, and serve.

Nutrition Information

- 523: calories;
- 30 grams: fat;
- 4 grams: polyunsaturated fat;
- 59 grams: carbohydrates;
- 18 grams: dietary fiber;
- 6 grams: sugars;
- 14 grams: protein;
- 0 grams: trans fat;
- 21 grams: monounsaturated fat;
- 1147 milligrams: sodium;

55. Bulgur And Lentil Salad

Serving: Serves six | Prep: | Cook: | Ready in: 45mins

Ingredients

- 1 cup green or beluga lentils, rinsed and picked over
- 1 small onion, cut in half
- 2 garlic cloves, slightly crushed
- 1 bay leaf
- Salt to taste
- 1 cup fine or medium bulgur
- 4 scallions, thinly sliced (more to taste)
- 4 to 6 radishes, thinly sliced
- 1 cup finely chopped parsley
- 2 to 4 tablespoons finely chopped fresh mint
- ⅓ cup fresh lemon juice
- 1 teaspoon cumin seeds, lightly toasted and ground
- ½ cup extra virgin olive oil

Direction

- Combine the lentils, onion, garlic and bay leaf in a saucepan, and add 2 to 3 cups water, enough to cover by an inch or two. Bring to a gentle boil, add salt to taste, reduce the heat, cover and simmer 25 minutes until tender but intact. Remove from the heat. Remove and discard the onion, garlic cloves and bay leaf. Drain.

- Meanwhile, place the bulgur in a medium bowl, and add salt to taste. Cover with 2 cups hot or boiling water, and allow to sit for 20 to 25 minutes until most of the water is absorbed. Drain through a strainer and squeeze out the water.
- Combine the lentils, bulgur, scallions, radishes, parsley and mint in a large bowl or salad bowl. Whisk together the lemon juice, cumin, salt and pepper to taste, and the olive oil. Toss with the salad, and serve.

Nutrition Information

- 372: calories;
- 43 grams: carbohydrates;
- 12 grams: protein;
- 309 milligrams: sodium;
- 19 grams: fat;
- 3 grams: saturated fat;
- 13 grams: monounsaturated fat;
- 2 grams: sugars;
- 8 grams: dietary fiber;

56. Bulgur And Walnut Kibbeh

Serving: About 24 kibbeh, serving six to eight as an appetizer | Prep: | Cook: | Ready in: 40mins

Ingredients

- ¾ cup fine bulgur
- 2 garlic cloves, halved, green shoots removed
- Salt to taste
- ½ cup walnuts, lightly toasted and finely chopped
- 2 tablespoons extra virgin olive oil
- ¼ cup finely chopped flat-leaf parsley
- 2 tablespoons finely chopped fresh mint
- Freshly ground pepper to taste
- ¾ teaspoon ground cinnamon
- 2 tablespoons fresh lemon juice
- Small romaine lettuce leaves (or larger ones, cut into 2- or 3-inch pieces)

Direction

- Place the bulgur in a bowl, add salt to taste and pour on boiling water to cover by 1/2 inch. Let sit for one hour, then drain and squeeze out excess water.
- Place the garlic in a mortar and pestle with a generous pinch of salt, and mash to a paste. Stir into the bulgur. Add the walnuts, olive oil, parsley, mint, pepper, cinnamon and 1 tablespoon plus 1 teaspoon of the lemon juice. Moisten your hands and knead the mixture for a couple of minutes, then allow to sit for 15 to 30 minutes.
- With moistened fingers, form the bulgur mixture into bite-size balls, and press an indentation into the middle of each ball. Place on a lettuce leaf, sprinkle with lemon juice and serve. Guests can use the lettuce leaves as a sort of wrap to eat with the kibbeh.

Nutrition Information

- 90: calories;
- 1 gram: polyunsaturated fat;
- 3 grams: monounsaturated fat;
- 11 grams: carbohydrates;
- 2 grams: protein;
- 0 grams: sugars;
- 62 milligrams: sodium;
- 5 grams: fat;

57. Butternut Squash And Purple Potato Latkes

Serving: About 20 to 24 latkes, serving 6 | Prep: | Cook: | Ready in: 15mins

Ingredients

- ½ medium onion, grated
- 3 cups grated butternut squash (1 small squash)
- 3 cups grated purple potatoes

- 3 tablespoons chopped or slivered fresh sage (more to taste)
- Salt and freshly ground pepper
- 1 teaspoon baking powder
- 3 tablespoons oat bran
- ¼ cup all-purpose flour or cornstarch
- 2 eggs, beaten
- About 1/4 cup canola, grape seed or rice bran oil

Direction

- Preheat the oven to 300 degrees. Place a rack over a sheet pan.
- Place the grated onion in a strainer set over a bowl while you prepare the other ingredients. Then wrap in a dishtowel and squeeze out excess water, or just take up by the handful to squeeze out excess water. Place in a large bowl and add the squash, potatoes, sage, baking powder, salt and pepper, oat bran, and flour or cornstarch. Add the eggs and stir together.
- Begin heating a large heavy skillet over medium-high heat. Add 2 to 3 tablespoons of the oil and when it is hot, take up heaped tablespoons of the latke mixture, press the mixture against the spoon to extract liquid (or squeeze in your hands), and place in the pan. Press down with the back of the spatula to flatten. Repeat with more spoonfuls, being careful not to crowd the pan. In my 10-inch pan I can cook 4 at a time without crowding; my 12-inch pan will accommodate 5. Cook on one side until golden brown, about 3 minutes. Slide the spatula underneath and flip the latkes over. Cook on the other side until golden brown, another 2 to 3 minutes. Transfer to the rack set over a baking sheet and place in the oven to keep warm. The mixture will continue to release liquid, which will accumulate in the bottom of the bowl. Stir from time to time, and remember to squeeze the heaped tablespoons of the mix before you add them to the pan.
- Serve hot topped with low-fat sour cream, Greek style yogurt or crème fraiche.

Nutrition Information

- 224: calories;
- 4 grams: polyunsaturated fat;
- 29 grams: carbohydrates;
- 11 grams: fat;
- 3 grams: saturated fat;
- 0 grams: trans fat;
- 5 grams: protein;
- 1 gram: sugars;
- 407 milligrams: sodium;

58. Butternut Squash And Sage Latkes

Serving: About 25 latkes, serving 6 | Prep: | Cook: | Ready in: 45mins

Ingredients

- ½ medium onion, grated
- 6 cups grated butternut squash (1 3-pound squash)
- ¼ cup chopped or slivered fresh sage (more to taste)
- 1 teaspoon baking powder
- Salt and freshly ground pepper
- 3 tablespoons oat bran
- ¼ cup all-purpose flour
- 2 eggs, beaten
- About 1/4 cup canola, grape seed or rice bran oil

Direction

- Place the grated onion in a strainer set over a bowl while you prepare the other ingredients. Then wrap in a dishtowel and squeeze out excess water, or just take up by the handful to squeeze out excess water. Place in a large bowl and add the squash, sage, baking powder, salt and pepper, oat bran, and flour. Taste and adjust salt. Add the eggs and stir together.
- Begin heating a large heavy skillet over medium heat. Heat the oven to 300 degrees.

Line a sheet pan with parchment. Place a rack over another sheet pan. Take a 1/4 cup measuring cup and fill with 3 tablespoons of the mixture. Reverse onto the parchment-lined baking sheet. Repeat with the remaining latke mix. You should have enough to make about 30 latkes.

- Add the oil to the pan and when it is hot (hold your hand a few inches above – you should feel the heat), use a spatula to transfer a ball of latke mixture to the pan. Press down with the spatula to flatten. Repeat with more mounds. In my 10-inch pan I can cook 3 or 4 at a time without crowding; my 12-inch pan will accommodate 4 or 5. Cook on one side until golden brown, 4 to 5 minutes. Slide the spatula underneath and flip the latkes over. Cook on the other side until golden brown, another 3 to 4 minutes. Transfer to the rack set over a baking sheet and place in the oven to keep warm.
- Serve hot topped with low-fat sour cream, Greek style yogurt or crème fraîche.

Nutrition Information

- 252: calories;
- 12 grams: fat;
- 0 grams: trans fat;
- 4 grams: polyunsaturated fat;
- 37 grams: carbohydrates;
- 638 milligrams: sodium;
- 3 grams: saturated fat;
- 8 grams: dietary fiber;
- 6 grams: protein;

59. Cabbage And Carrot Noodles With Egg

Serving: 4 to 6 servings | Prep: | Cook: | Ready in: 45mins

Ingredients

- 8 ounces rice noodles or glass noodles
- ½ cup chicken or vegetable stock
- 2 tablespoons soy sauce
- 2 teaspoons rice vinegar
- ½ teaspoon sugar
- 2 tablespoons peanut oil, rice bran oil or canola oil
- 2 large eggs, beaten
- Salt to taste
- 1 to 2 green chilies, like jalapeño or serrano, minced
- 2 plump garlic cloves, minced
- 1 tablespoon minced ginger
- 4 cups thinly sliced green cabbage
- 2 cups shredded carrots
- 1 cup chopped cilantro leaves and stems
- ⅛ teaspoon freshly ground pepper

Direction

- Place the noodles in a bowl and cover with warm water. Let sit for 20 minutes, until pliable. Drain in a colander and cut into 6-inch lengths with kitchen scissors. Set aside
- Mix together the broth, soy sauce, rice vinegar and sugar in a small bowl
- Heat a 14-inch flat-bottomed wok or 12-inch steel skillet over high heat until a drop of water evaporates within a second or two when added to the pan. Meanwhile, beat 1 of the eggs in a bowl and add salt to taste. Swirl 1 teaspoon of the oil into the wok and add the egg, using a rubber spatula to scrape out every last bit. Tilt the wok to spread the egg into a pancake and cook until set, 30 seconds to a minute. Using a metal spatula, flip over the egg pancake and brown it for about 5 seconds, then transfer to a cutting board. Allow to cool and cut into 2-inch-long by 1/4-inch-wide slices. Repeat with the other egg
- Add the remaining oil to the wok, swirl the pan, then add the garlic, ginger and chili and stir-fry for no more than 10 seconds. Add the cabbage and carrots and stir-fry 1 to 2 minutes, then add the noodles, the broth mixture and salt to taste. Turn the heat down to medium and stir-fry for about 2 minutes, until the

noodles are just tender and the broth has evaporated. Sprinkle with salt and pepper, add the eggs and cilantro, and stir-fry for another 30 seconds to a minute. Serve

Nutrition Information

- 248: calories;
- 7 grams: protein;
- 1 gram: saturated fat;
- 2 grams: polyunsaturated fat;
- 454 milligrams: sodium;
- 3 grams: dietary fiber;
- 40 grams: carbohydrates;
- 5 grams: sugars;
- 0 grams: trans fat;

60. Cabbage And Spring Onion Quiche With Caraway

Serving: Serves 6 generously | Prep: | Cook: | Ready in: 1hours15mins

Ingredients

- 2 tablespoons extra-virgin olive oil
- 1 cup chopped spring onion
- ½ medium cabbage (1 pound), cored and shredded (about 5 cups shredded cabbage)
- Salt to taste
- ½ teaspoon caraway seeds
- 2 egg yolks
- 2 whole eggs
- 1 (9-inch) whole wheat pâte brisée pie crust fully baked and cooled
- ½ teaspoon salt
- Freshly ground pepper
- ⅔ cup milk
- 3 ounces Gruyère, grated, or 1 ounce Parmesan and 2 ounces Gruyère, grated (3/4 cup grated cheese)

Direction

- Preheat oven to 350 degrees.
- Heat olive oil over medium heat in a large, heavy skillet and add onions. Cook, stirring often, until tender, about 5 minutes. Add a generous pinch of salt and continue to cook 3 to 5 minutes, until beginning to color. Add cabbage and cook, stirring often, until cabbage wilts, about 5 minutes. Add another pinch of salt and caraway seeds and continue to cook for another 5 to 10 minutes, until cabbage is sweet, cooked down, lightly colored and very tender. Taste, adjust salt, and add freshly ground pepper. Remove from heat.
- Beat together egg yolks and eggs in a medium bowl. Set tart pan on a baking sheet to allow for easy handling. Using a pastry brush, lightly brush the bottom of the crust with some of the beaten egg and place in the oven for 5 minutes. (The egg seals the crust so that it won't become soggy when it comes into contact with the custard.)
- Add salt (I use 1/2 teaspoon), pepper, and milk to remaining eggs and whisk together.
- Spread cabbage and onion in an even layer in the crust. Sprinkle cheese evenly on top. Very slowly pour in the egg custard over the filling. If your tart pan has low edges, you may not need all of it to fill the quiche, and you want to keep the custard from spilling over. Place quiche, on baking sheet, in oven and bake for 30 to 35 minutes, until set and just beginning to color on top. Remove from oven and allow to sit for at least 10 minutes before serving.

Nutrition Information

- 381: calories;
- 474 milligrams: sodium;
- 25 grams: fat;
- 3 grams: dietary fiber;
- 0 grams: trans fat;
- 11 grams: monounsaturated fat;
- 26 grams: carbohydrates;
- 4 grams: sugars;
- 13 grams: protein;
- 10 grams: saturated fat;

61. Carrot, Parsnip And Potato Colcannon

Serving: Serves 6 | Prep: | Cook: | Ready in: 45mins

Ingredients

- 10 ounces Yukon gold potatoes, scrubbed
- 1 pound carrots, peeled, quartered, and cut into 3-inch lengths
- 1 pound parsnips, peeled, quartered, cored and cut into 3-inch lengths
- Salt to taste
- 1 tablespoon extra virgin olive oil
- 1 medium leek, white and light green parts only, cleaned and chopped
- 2 to 3 tablespoons unsalted butter (to taste)
- ¾ cup milk
- Freshly ground pepper
- 1 tablespoons chopped fresh dill or chervil (optional)

Direction

- Place potatoes, carrots, and parsnips in a saucepan and cover by an inch with water. Add salt to taste, bring to a boil, reduce heat to medium-low and cover partially. Simmer until tender, 25 to 30 minutes. Drain, return to pot and cover pot tightly. Leave to steam in covered pot for 5 minutes. Peel potatoes.
- Meanwhile, heat olive oil over medium heat in a heavy skillet and add leek. Cook, stirring often, until it begins to wilt, about 3 minutes. Add salt to taste and continue to cook, stirring, until very tender, 3 to 5 more minutes. Remove from heat.
- Mash vegetables with a potato masher or in a standing mixer fitted with the paddle, or put through a food mill. Combine milk and butter and heat until butter melts. Gradually add to purée, stirring or beating on low speed. Stir in leeks and mix until well blended. Season to taste with salt and pepper. Put through the

fine or medium blade of a food mill, or press through a medium-mess strainer. Garnish if desired with dill or chervil. Serve hot.

Nutrition Information

- 216: calories;
- 9 grams: fat;
- 4 grams: protein;
- 1 gram: polyunsaturated fat;
- 3 grams: monounsaturated fat;
- 33 grams: carbohydrates;
- 7 grams: dietary fiber;
- 10 grams: sugars;
- 588 milligrams: sodium;
- 0 grams: trans fat;

62. Cauliflower Gratin With Goat Cheese Topping

Serving: Serves 4 | Prep: | Cook: | Ready in: 30mins

Ingredients

- 1 large or 2 smaller cauliflowers (about 2 pounds), broken into florets
- 3 tablespoons extra virgin olive oil
- Salt
- freshly ground pepper
- 6 ounces fresh goat cheese
- 1 plump garlic clove, halved, green shoot removed
- 5 tablespoons low-fat milk
- 1 teaspoon chopped fresh thyme leaves or 1/2 teaspoon dried thyme
- ¼ cup dry, fine breadcrumbs

Direction

- Preheat the oven to 450 degrees. Oil a two-quart gratin dish with olive oil.
- Place the cauliflower in a steaming basket above one inch of boiling water. Cover and steam for one minute. Lift the lid and allow

steam to escape for 15 seconds, then cover again and steam for six to eight minutes, until the cauliflower is tender. Remove from the heat and refresh with cold water. Drain on paper towels, then transfer to the gratin dish.

- Season the cauliflower generously with salt and pepper, then toss with 2 tablespoons of the olive oil and half of the thyme. Spread in an even layer.
- Place the garlic in a mortar and pestle with a quarter-teaspoon salt, and mash to a paste. Combine with the goat cheese and milk in a food processor fitted with the steel blade, and blend until smooth. Add the remaining thyme and freshly ground pepper to taste, and pulse together. Spread this mixture over the cauliflower in an even layer.
- Just before baking, sprinkle on the breadcrumbs and drizzle on the remaining tablespoon of olive oil. Bake 15 to 20 minutes, until the top is lightly browned and the dish is sizzling. Serve at once.

Nutrition Information

- 263: calories;
- 1 gram: polyunsaturated fat;
- 2 grams: dietary fiber;
- 3 grams: sugars;
- 714 milligrams: sodium;
- 8 grams: saturated fat;
- 10 grams: monounsaturated fat;
- 11 grams: protein;
- 20 grams: fat;

63. Cauliflower, Potato And Quinoa Patties

Serving: 9 to 12 patties, depending on size | Prep: | Cook: | Ready in: 1hours

Ingredients

- 3 cups finely minced cauliflower (about 12 ounces, or 1/2 medium cauliflower)
- salt to taste
- 1 ½ pounds potatoes, scrubbed, peeled if desired and quartered
- ½ cup chopped cilantro
- 2 teaspoons toasted cumin seeds, lightly crushed in a mortar and pestle
- 2 teaspoons nigella seeds
- 1 teaspoon garam masala
- ½ teaspoon Aleppo pepper or mild chili powder
- Freshly ground black pepper to taste
- ½ cup cooked black quinoa
- 1 cup mixed black and white sesame seeds
- ¼ cup grapeseed oil
- Sriracha sauce for serving

Direction

- Steam potatoes over 1 inch of boiling water until tender, 15 to 20 minutes. Transfer to a bowl and mash with a fork. The skins will break up in the mash.
- Line steamer with cheesecloth and place cauliflower on cheesecloth so the small pieces don't fall through. Steam 5 to 6 minutes, until very tender. Remove from heat and stir into potatoes. Add remaining ingredients except sesame seeds and oil. Season generously with salt, combine well, taste and adjust seasonings.
- Place sesame seeds in a wide bowl. Scoop out about 1/3 cup of cauliflower-potato mixture and roll into a ball (moisten your hands to prevent sticking). Roll in the seeds, then gently flatten into a patty shape. Place on a plate or sheet pan and continue to shape all of the patties. If you have time, refrigerate for 1 hour or longer (I have made these with no problem without refrigerating first).
- When you are ready to cook, place a rack over a sheet pan and cover the rack with paper towels. Heat 2 tablespoons oil in a large, heavy nonstick frying pan over high heat. When pan is hot, swirl to coat with oil. Turn heat down to medium. Place 3 to 5 patties in the pan (do not crowd), and cook until well browned on one

side, 3 to 4 minutes. Turn and brown for 3 to 4 more minutes. Remove to rack. Heat remaining oil in the pan and cook remaining patties. Remove paper towels from underneath patties and keep them warm in a low oven until ready to serve. Serve topped with Sriracha, with a salad on the side.

Nutrition Information

- 262: calories;
- 25 grams: carbohydrates;
- 6 grams: dietary fiber;
- 7 grams: protein;
- 383 milligrams: sodium;
- 17 grams: fat;
- 2 grams: sugars;
- 5 grams: monounsaturated fat;
- 9 grams: polyunsaturated fat;

64. Celeriac, Celery And Carrot Remoulade

Serving: Serves 6 | Prep: | Cook: | Ready in: 30mins

Ingredients

- 1 medium celeriac, about 3/4 pound without stalks, peeled and grated (about 4 cups)
- 6 ounces carrots, peeled and grated (about 2 cups)
- 4 ounces celery, thinly sliced (about 1 1/8 cups)
- Salt
- 2 tablespoons chopped chives
- 2 tablespoons chopped parsley
- ¼ cup crème fraîche
- 2 tablespoons mayonnaise
- 2 tablespoons grapeseed oil
- ¼ cup Greek yogurt
- 2 tablespoons lemon juice
- 1 ½ to 2 tablespoons Dijon mustard, to taste
- Freshly ground black pepper

Direction

- Place celeriac, carrots and celery in a bowl or colander and salt generously. Toss and leave for 30 minutes. Taking mixture up by the handful, squeeze out excess water and transfer to a bowl. Add chives and parsley and toss together.
- Whisk together crème fraîche, mayonnaise, grapeseed oil, yogurt, lemon juice and mustard. Season to taste with salt and pepper. Add to the vegetables and toss together. Serve right away or for even better results, refrigerate for an hour or so before serving.

Nutrition Information

- 165: calories;
- 3 grams: protein;
- 14 grams: carbohydrates;
- 480 milligrams: sodium;
- 4 grams: sugars;
- 11 grams: fat;
- 0 grams: trans fat;
- 2 grams: monounsaturated fat;
- 6 grams: polyunsaturated fat;

65. Celeriac, Potato, Leek And Apple Soup

Serving: 16 to 18 demitasse servings or 8 bowls | Prep: | Cook: | Ready in: 1hours30mins

Ingredients

- 1 tablespoon extra virgin olive oil
- 1 medium onion, chopped
- 2 leeks, white and light green part only, halved lengthwise, cleaned and sliced or chopped
- Salt to taste
- 2 pounds celeriac, peeled and diced (retain tops for bouquet garni and garnish)
- 1 large russet potato (about 3/4 pound), peeled and diced

- 2 granny smith or braeburn apples, cored, peeled and diced
- 2 quarts water, chicken stock, or vegetable stock
- A bouquet garni made with a bay leaf and a couple of sprigs each thyme and parsley, and a stem or two of the celery from the celery root, if still attached
- Freshly ground pepper to taste
- Garnish
- Slivered celery leaves for garnish

Direction

- Heat the olive oil in a large, heavy soup pot over medium heat and add the onion, leeks and a pinch of salt. Cook, stirring, until tender, about 5 minutes. Add the celeriac and a generous pinch of salt, cover partially and cook for another 5 minutes, stirring often, until the celeriac has begun to soften. Add the potatoes, apples, water or stock, salt to taste, and the bouquet garni. Bring to a boil, reduce the heat, cover and simmer 1 hour, or until the vegetables are very tender and the soup is fragrant. Remove and discard the bouquet garni.
- Blend the soup in batches in a blender (cover the top with a towel and hold it down to avoid hot splashes), or through a food mill fitted with the fine blade. The soup should be very smooth. Strain if desired. Return to the pot. Stir and taste. Adjust salt, add freshly ground pepper, and heat through. Serve in small bowls or espresso cups, garnished with thin slivers of celery leaves.

Nutrition Information

- 174: calories;
- 4 grams: fat;
- 2 grams: monounsaturated fat;
- 0 grams: polyunsaturated fat;
- 5 grams: dietary fiber;
- 12 grams: sugars;
- 3 grams: protein;
- 1 gram: saturated fat;

- 34 grams: carbohydrates;
- 1681 milligrams: sodium;

66. Celery And Walnut (or Hazelnut) Tzatziki

Serving: Serves 4 | Prep: | Cook: |Ready in: 30mins

Ingredients

- 2 cups very thinly sliced celery (about 1/2 pound celery stalks)
- Salt
- 1 medium garlic clove (more to taste)
- 1 ¼ cups Greek yogurt (more to taste)
- ⅓ cup (1 ounce) finely chopped walnuts or hazelnuts
- 2 tablespoons walnut oil or toasted hazelnut oil
- Freshly ground black pepper
- Chopped fresh dill (optional)

Direction

- Place celery in a colander and salt generously. Toss in colander and let sit in the sink for 15 to 30 minutes. Press celery against colander to extract water and transfer to a bowl.
- Purée garlic in a mortar and pestle. Combine with yogurt, nuts and nut oil and stir into celery. Combine well. Add ground black pepper, taste and adjust salt. Transfer to a serving bowl or to individual plates. Garnish with chopped fresh dill if desired, and serve.

Nutrition Information

- 195: calories;
- 16 grams: fat;
- 4 grams: sugars;
- 2 grams: monounsaturated fat;
- 8 grams: protein;
- 6 grams: carbohydrates;
- 1 gram: dietary fiber;

- 362 milligrams: sodium;

67. Chard Stalk, Celeriac And Leek Soup

Serving: Serves 4 | Prep: | Cook: | Ready in: 1hours

Ingredients

- 2 tablespoons extra virgin olive oil
- ¾ pound leeks (2 large), white and light green parts only, cleaned and chopped (about 2 cups)
- Salt to taste
- ¾ pound Swiss chard stems, diced (about 2 1/2 cups)
- ¾ pound celeriac, peeled and diced (about 2 cups
- 1 large yellow or russet potato (10 to 12 ounces), peeled and diced (about 1 1/2 cups)
- 5 to 6 cups water or stock (chicken or vegetable)
- Freshly ground pepper
- Chopped fresh parsley or celery leaves for garnish

Direction

- Heat olive oil over medium heat in a soup pot or Dutch oven and add leeks. Cook, stirring, until tender but not colored, about 5 minutes. Add a generous pinch of salt and add chard stems, celeriac, potato and water or stock. Stir together and bring to a boil. Add salt to taste (I use about 1 teaspoon per quart of water to start when making soup).
- Reduce heat to low, cover and simmer 45 minutes.
- Using a hand blender, or in batches in a regular blender, purée the soup. If using a regular blender, cover top of jar with a towel pulled down tight, rather than airtight with the lid. Return to pot and heat through, stirring. Season with salt and pepper. If desired, thin out with a little more water or

stock. Garnish each serving with chopped parsley or celery leaves.

Nutrition Information

- 164: calories;
- 1262 milligrams: sodium;
- 7 grams: fat;
- 1 gram: polyunsaturated fat;
- 5 grams: monounsaturated fat;
- 24 grams: carbohydrates;
- 4 grams: sugars;
- 3 grams: protein;

68. Chard Stalk, Chickpea, Tahini And Yogurt Dip

Serving: Makes about 3 cups, serving 10 to 12 | Prep: | Cook: | Ready in: 35mins

Ingredients

- ½ pound Swiss chard stalks, sliced (about 2 1/2 cups)
- Salt to taste
- 2 to 4 garlic cloves (to taste), peeled, green shoots removed
- 1 can chickpeas (or 1 1/2 cups cooked chickpeas), drained and rinsed
- ⅓ cup sesame tahini, stirred if the oil has separated
- ½ cup plain Greek yogurt or drained plain yogurt (low-fat or whole)
- ¼ cup freshly squeezed lemon juice, to taste
- ½ teaspoon lightly toasted cumin seeds, ground
- 2 tablespoons extra-virgin olive oil

Direction

- Steam chard stalks over 1 inch water until tender when pierced with a fork, 15 to 20 minutes. Drain well in a strainer for 10 minutes. Place in a food processor fitted with the steel blade, along with chickpeas. Purée, stopping the machine from time to time to scrape down the sides.

- In a mortar, mash garlic with 1/2 teaspoon salt until you have a smooth paste. Add to chard stalks and chickpeas. Process until smooth. Add tahini, yogurt and cumin and process until smooth. With machine running, add lemon juice, olive oil and salt to taste. Stop machine, taste and adjust seasonings.
- Transfer dip to a wide bowl. It will probably be runny but will thicken. Serve with pita and/or crudités.

Nutrition Information

- 107: calories;
- 1 gram: sugars;
- 3 grams: monounsaturated fat;
- 2 grams: dietary fiber;
- 8 grams: carbohydrates;
- 4 grams: protein;
- 167 milligrams: sodium;
- 7 grams: fat;

69. Chard And Sweet Corn Tacos

Serving: 8 tacos, serving 4 | Prep: | Cook: | Ready in: 15mins

Ingredients

- 1 generous bunch Swiss chard (about 3/4 pound)
- Salt to taste
- 1 medium white, red or yellow onion, sliced
- 3 large garlic cloves, minced
- Kernels from 2 ears sweet corn
- Freshly ground pepper
- 8 warm corn tortillas
- ½ cup crumbled queso fresco or feta (but not too salty a feta)
- Salsa of your choice

Direction

- Bring a large pot of water to a boil while you stem chard and wash leaves in 2 rinses of water. Rinse stalks and dice them if they are wide and not stringy.
- When water in pot comes to a boil, salt generously and add chard leaves. Blanch for a minute, then transfer to a bowl of cold water and drain. Take chard up by the handful and squeeze out excess water, then cut into 1/2-inch wide strips. Set aside.
- Heat oil over medium heat in a large, heavy skillet and add onion. Cook, stirring often, until onions are tender and beginning to color, about 8 minutes, and add a generous pinch of salt, the garlic, diced chard stalks and corn kernels. Continue to cook, stirring often, until corn is just tender, about 4 minutes. Stir in chard and cook, stirring, for another minute or two, until ingredients are combined nicely and chard is tender but still bright. Season to taste with salt and pepper. Remove from heat.
- Heat tortillas. Top with vegetables, a sprinkling of cheese and a spoonful of salsa.

70. Cherry And Apricot Clafoutis

Serving: 8 servings. | Prep: | Cook: | Ready in: 1hours30mins

Ingredients

- ¾ pound ripe cherries, stemmed and pitted
- ¾ pound ripe apricots, halved and pitted
- 2 tablespoons Kirsch
- 6 tablespoons sugar
- ⅓ cup (40 grams) unbleached all-purpose flour
- ⅓ cup (35 grams) almond flour
- 3 eggs
- 1 vanilla bean, scraped, or 1 teaspoon vanilla
- Pinch of salt
- ⅔ cup low-fat yogurt

Direction

- Toss the cherries and apricots with the Kirsch and 2 tablespoons of the sugar, and let sit for 30 minutes. Drain over a bowl. Sift together the all-purpose flour and almond flour.
- Preheat the oven to 375 degrees. Butter a 9- or 10-inch ceramic tart pan or clafoutis dish. Arrange the drained cherries and apricots in the dish.
- In a medium bowl, beat the eggs with the remaining sugar and the seeds from the vanilla bean or vanilla. Add the salt and the liquid from the cherries and apricots and combine well. Slowly beat in the sifted flours and whisk until smooth. Add the yogurt and combine well. Pour over the fruit, scraping out all of the batter with a rubber spatula.
- Bake in the preheated oven for 40 minutes, until the top is browned and the clafoutis is firm and puffed. Press gently on the top in the middle to see if it's firm. If it isn't, return to the oven for 5 minutes.
- Remove from the oven and cool on a rack. Serve warm or at room temperature.

Nutrition Information

- 172: calories;
- 21 grams: sugars;
- 6 grams: protein;
- 1 gram: monounsaturated fat;
- 2 grams: dietary fiber;
- 74 milligrams: sodium;
- 4 grams: fat;
- 0 grams: polyunsaturated fat;
- 27 grams: carbohydrates;

71. Cherry And Spring Onion Salsa

Serving: 4 to 8 servings | Prep: | Cook: |Ready in: 15mins

Ingredients

- 1 small red spring onion bulb and greens
- 3 tablespoons lemon juice, or more to taste
- 1 ½ cups pitted cherries, or about 8 ounces
- 1 teaspoon finely chopped chives
- 1 tablespoon finely chopped parsley
- 1 small jalapeño, seeded and finely chopped
- 5 tablespoons extra virgin olive oil
- ½ teaspoon kosher salt

Direction

- Finely dice spring onion bulb and greens. Place 3 tablespoons diced bulb and 1 tablespoon greens in a small bowl and pour lemon juice over them. Set aside for 10 minutes to macerate.
- Halve the cherries and slice into slivers. Place cherries, herbs, jalapeño, olive oil and salt in a medium-size bowl and stir to combine.
- Add onion and greens, taste and add more salt and lemon juice if needed.
- Let the salsa sit for at least 5 minutes to meld flavors.

Nutrition Information

- 124: calories;
- 131 milligrams: sodium;
- 11 grams: fat;
- 1 gram: dietary fiber;
- 6 grams: carbohydrates;
- 0 grams: protein;
- 2 grams: saturated fat;
- 8 grams: monounsaturated fat;
- 5 grams: sugars;

72. Chicken Soup With Lime And Avocado

Serving: Serves four | Prep: | Cook: |Ready in: 30mins

Ingredients

- 2 quarts chicken stock, preferably homemade, or 1 quart commercial chicken broth and 1 quart water
- 1 medium onion, finely chopped
- 1 garlic clove, minced
- 1 serrano or jalapeño chile, seeded if desired and minced
- 1 pound tomatoes, peeled, seeded and diced, or 1 (14-ounce) can, drained
- 1 cup shredded cooked chicken breast
- ¼ cup chopped cilantro
- 1 to 2 tablespoons freshly squeezed lime juice (to taste), plus thin slices of lime for garnish
- 1 avocado, cut in small dice or thinly sliced
- Corn tortilla crisps for garnish

Direction

- Bring the chicken stock to a simmer, add the onion, garlic and chile, and simmer 15 minutes.
- Add the tomatoes, and simmer for another five minutes. Taste and adjust salt, then stir in the chicken breast and chopped cilantro. Cover and let sit for five minutes. Add the lime juice.
- Divide the avocado between four soup bowls. Ladle in the soup, place a slice of lime on each bowl, and serve with crisp corn tortillas.

Nutrition Information

- 342: calories;
- 3 grams: saturated fat;
- 2 grams: polyunsaturated fat;
- 28 grams: carbohydrates;
- 5 grams: dietary fiber;
- 15 grams: fat;
- 8 grams: monounsaturated fat;
- 12 grams: sugars;
- 25 grams: protein;
- 732 milligrams: sodium;

73. Chickpeas With Baby Spinach

Serving: Serves three | Prep: | Cook: | Ready in: 30mins

Ingredients

- 1 tablespoon olive oil
- 1 medium onion, chopped
- 2 garlic cloves, minced
- 1 teaspoon cumin seeds, lightly toasted and ground
- Salt, preferably kosher salt
- Freshly ground black pepper, to taste
- 1 tablespoon tomato paste
- 1 (15-ounce) can chickpeas, drained and rinsed
- 1 cup chicken or vegetable stock, or water
- Cayenne, to taste
- 1 (6-ounce) bag baby spinach

Direction

- Heat the olive oil in a large, heavy saucepan over medium heat and add the onion. Cook, stirring, until tender, about five minutes. Add the garlic, cumin, tomato paste and 1/2 teaspoon salt. Cook, stirring for one to two minutes, until fragrant and the tomato paste has turned a darker color. Add the chickpeas, the stock or water, and the cayenne, and bring to a simmer. Cover, reduce the heat, and simmer 10 minutes.
- Stir in the spinach, a handful at a time, stirring until each addition of spinach wilts. Add salt to taste and simmer uncovered, stirring often, for five minutes. Add lots of freshly ground pepper, taste and adjust salt and cayenne, and serve.

Nutrition Information

- 306: calories;
- 2 grams: polyunsaturated fat;
- 764 milligrams: sodium;
- 1 gram: saturated fat;
- 5 grams: monounsaturated fat;
- 43 grams: carbohydrates;
- 12 grams: dietary fiber;

- 9 grams: sugars;
- 15 grams: protein;
- 10 grams: fat;

- 4 grams: dietary fiber;
- 163 milligrams: sodium;
- 7 grams: fat;
- 1 gram: protein;
- 5 grams: monounsaturated fat;

74. Chilean Cabbage And Avocado Slaw

Serving: Serves 4 | Prep: | Cook: | Ready in: 15mins

Ingredients

- ½ large cabbage, cored and finely shredded (about 1 pound cabbage, which produces 5 cups shredded cabbage)
- Salt to taste
- 4 to 5 tablespoons fresh lemon juice (more to taste)
- 1 large or 1 1/2 medium-size ripe avocados
- Freshly ground pepper (optional)

Direction

- Place shredded cabbage in a large bowl or colander and salt generously. Tossand rub the salt into cabbage with your hands. Let sit for 1 hour or longer (refrigerate if longer than 1 hour). If cabbage tastes too salty, rinse, then squeeze out excess moisture and transfer to a dry bowl.
- Toss cabbage with half the lemon juice.
- Mash avocados in a mortar and pestle, or in a bowl using a fork, potato masher or a whisk. Add salt to taste and remaining lemon juice and mix until smooth. Scrape into the bowl with cabbage and stir together until shredded cabbage is thoroughly coated with mashed avocado. Taste and adjust salt. Add pepper if desired. If mixture isn't creamy, add more avocado.

Nutrition Information

- 85: calories;
- 6 grams: carbohydrates;

75. Chipotle Gazpacho

Serving: Serves 4 | Prep: | Cook: | Ready in: 10mins

Ingredients

- 2 slices red or white onion
- 2 pounds ripe tomatoes
- 2 to 3 garlic cloves, to taste
- ¼ cup extra virgin olive oil
- 1 to 2 tablespoons sherry vinegar or wine vinegar (to taste), plus a little extra for the onion
- 1 to 2 canned chipotles in adobo (to taste)
- ½ to 1 cup ice water, depending on how thick you want your soup to be
- Salt to taste
- For serving
- 1 avocado, cut in small dice
- ½ cup cucumber, cut in fine dice
- Torn or slivered fresh basil or chopped cilantro

Direction

- Put the onion slices in a bowl, cover with cold water and add a few drops of vinegar. Let sit for 5 minutes while you prepare the remaining ingredients. Drain and rinse with cold water. Cut in half or into smaller pieces.
- Combine the tomatoes, garlic, onion, olive oil, vinegar, chipotle, water and salt in a blender and blend until smooth. Strain through a medium strainer into a bowl. Taste and adjust salt. Thin out as desired with ice water. Chill for several hours.
- Ladle the cold soup into bowls and garnish with a spoonful each diced avocado and diced cucumber (seasoned with salt if desired).

Sprinkle with cilantro or basil (or both) and serve.

Nutrition Information

- 269: calories;
- 987 milligrams: sodium;
- 3 grams: polyunsaturated fat;
- 19 grams: carbohydrates;
- 7 grams: dietary fiber;
- 21 grams: fat;
- 15 grams: monounsaturated fat;
- 9 grams: sugars;
- 4 grams: protein;

76. Chopped Salad With Apples, Walnuts And Bitter Lettuces

Serving: 6 to 8 servings | Prep: | Cook: | Ready in: 20mins

Ingredients

- For the dressing
- 1 tablespoon sherry vinegar or champagne vinegar
- 1 teaspoon balsamic vinegar
- 1 tablespoon freshly squeezed lemon juice
- 1 small garlic clove, green shoot removed, puréed (optional)
- 2 teaspoons Dijon mustard
- Salt and freshly ground pepper to taste
- 2 tablespoons walnut oil
- 5 tablespoons extra virgin olive oil
- For the salad
- 4 to 5 cups chopped bitter lettuces such as radicchio, endive or escarole
- 2 crisp, tart, juicy apples, cut in small dice (1/4 inch)
- ½ cup chopped walnuts
- ½ cup crumbled blue cheese or feta
- ¼ cup chopped fresh parsley or a mix of parsley, chives and tarragon

Direction

- In a small bowl or measuring cup, whisk together vinegars, lemon juice, garlic, mustard, salt and pepper. Whisk in walnut oil and olive oil.
- Combine all of the salad ingredients in a large bowl. Toss with dressing until well coated, and serve.

Nutrition Information

- 215: calories;
- 19 grams: fat;
- 0 grams: trans fat;
- 8 grams: monounsaturated fat;
- 5 grams: sugars;
- 240 milligrams: sodium;
- 4 grams: protein;
- 7 grams: polyunsaturated fat;
- 9 grams: carbohydrates;
- 2 grams: dietary fiber;

77. Chunky Avocado Papaya Salsa

Serving: Serves 6 to 8 | Prep: | Cook: | Ready in: 20mins

Ingredients

- 2 medium-size ripe Hass avocados, halved, pitted and cut in small dice
- 1 small ripe papaya, halved, seeded, peeled and cut in small dice (about 2 cups dice)
- 1 tart apple, unpeeled, or Asian pear, peeled if desired, cored and cut in small dice
- ¼ cup freshly squeezed lime juice
- 1 fresh red or green serrano chile, seeded and thinly sliced or minced, or more to taste
- ¼ cup chopped cilantro
- 2 tablespoons chopped fresh mint
- ½ small red onion, diced small, soaked for 5 minutes in water to cover, drained and rinsed (optional)
- Salt to taste

Direction

- Combine diced avocados and papaya in a medium bowl. Add remaining ingredients and toss together. Season to taste with salt. Serve as a salad or a salsa.

Nutrition Information

- 105: calories;
- 7 grams: fat;
- 1 gram: protein;
- 5 grams: dietary fiber;
- 11 grams: carbohydrates;
- 4 grams: sugars;
- 241 milligrams: sodium;

78. Cold Poached Pacific Cod With Spices

Serving: Serves 4 | Prep: | Cook: | Ready in: 45mins

Ingredients

- 1 ½ pounds Pacific cod fillets
- Salt and freshly ground pepper
- 1 teaspoon sweet paprika
- ½ teaspoon ground cinnamon
- ¼ teaspoon ground allspice
- ½ teaspoon ground caraway
- ⅛ to ¼ teaspoon cayenne (to taste)
- 2 tablespoons extra-virgin olive oil
- 2 onions, sliced thin
- 4 garlic cloves, minced or puréed
- 2 ½ cups vinegar court-bouillon (recipe follows; more as needed)
- 3 to 4 tablespoons fresh lemon juice
- 2 tablespoons chopped fresh parsley
- 2 tablespoons chopped cilantro
- Vinegar Court-Bouillon
- 1 quart water
- ½ cup quality red wine vinegar or sherry vinegar
- 1 onion, sliced

- 2 leeks, cleaned and sliced
- 1 carrot, sliced
- 1 stalk celery, sliced
- 2 whole garlic cloves, peeled
- A bouquet garni made with 1 sprig each parsley and thyme, and a bay leaf
- 6 peppercorns
- Salt to taste

Direction

-
-

Nutrition Information

- 313: calories;
- 6 grams: sugars;
- 33 grams: protein;
- 1 gram: polyunsaturated fat;
- 5 grams: monounsaturated fat;
- 19 grams: carbohydrates;
- 4 grams: dietary fiber;
- 1741 milligrams: sodium;
- 8 grams: fat;

79. Cold Sesame Noodles With Sweet Peppers

Serving: Serves 6 | Prep: | Cook: | Ready in: 15mins

Ingredients

- For the dressing
- 3 tablespoons tahini (a runny variety if possible, available in Middle Eastern markets)
- 1 tablespoon soy sauce
- 2 tablespoons seasoned rice wine vinegar
- 1 to 2 teaspoons hot red pepper oil (to taste)
- Pinch of cayenne (optional)
- 2 teaspoons finely minced fresh ginger or 1 teaspoon ginger juice (see below)
- Salt and freshly ground pepper to taste
- 1 tablespoon sesame oil

- ¼ cup vegetable or chicken broth or water (more to taste)
- For the salad
- ¾ pound udon or soba noodles
- 1 tablespoon dark sesame oil
- 1 yellow or red pepper, cut in thin 2-inch strips
- 1 Persian cucumber or 1/3 European cucumber, cut in 2-inch julienne
- 1 medium-size ripe tomato, diced
- 1 cup chopped cilantro
- ¼ cup chopped chives or scallions
- 1 tablespoon black sesame seeds

Direction

- For ginger juice, grate a 1-inch piece of ginger. Wrap in a piece of cheesecloth, twist both ends of the cheesecloth and, holding the package over a bowl, wring out so that the juice is squeezed through the cheesecloth into the bowl.
- In a bowl or measuring cup, whisk together all of the ingredients for the dressing. Taste and adjust seasoning. You can make it spicier if desired.
- Cook the noodles. I like to cook wheat udon and soba the Japanese way. Bring 3 or 4 quarts of water to a boil in a large pot. Add the noodles gradually, so that the water remains at a boil, and stir once with a long-handled spoon or pasta fork so that they don't stick together. Wait for the water to come back up to a rolling boil — it will bubble up, so don't fill the pot all the way — and add 1 cup of cold water. Allow the water to come back to a rolling boil, and add another cup of cold water. Allow the water to come to a boil one more time, and add a third cup of water. When the water comes to a boil again, the noodles should be cooked through. Drain and toss with 1 tablespoon sesame oil.
- Combine the noodles, pepper, cucumber, tomato, cilantro, chives or scallions and black sesame seeds in a large bowl. Toss with the dressing and serve. The salad can also be refrigerated for a few hours before serving. In

this case add half the cilantro now and the rest just before serving.

Nutrition Information

- 314: calories;
- 4 grams: polyunsaturated fat;
- 48 grams: carbohydrates;
- 610 milligrams: sodium;
- 11 grams: protein;
- 2 grams: sugars;
- 0 grams: trans fat;

80. Collard Greens Stuffed With Quinoa And Turkey

Serving: About 1 dozen stuffed leaves | Prep: | Cook: | Ready in: 1hours30mins

Ingredients

- 12 large collard greens
- Salt
- ¼ cup extra virgin olive oil
- 1 onion, finely chopped
- 2 to 3 garlic cloves (to taste), minced
- 1 (14-ounce) can chopped tomatoes
- 1 teaspoon sugar
- 2 tablespoons to 1/4 cup currants (optional)
- ½ teaspoon cinnamon
- ¼ teaspoon freshly ground allspice berries
- 1 ½ cups cooked quinoa
- ½ to ¾ cup shredded turkey
- ¼ cup chopped fresh parsley
- 3 tablespoons chopped fresh mint
- Freshly ground pepper
- ½ to 1 cup water (as needed)
- Juice of 1 large lemon
- 1 tablespoon tomato paste
- Salt to taste

Direction

- Fill a bowl with cold water. Bring a large pot of water to a boil while you carefully remove the thick, tough stems from collard greens, trying to keep leaves intact. Break them off about 1 to 2 inches into the leaf, where they become less ropey. When water in pot comes to a boil, salt generously and add collard leaves, in batches. Blanch 2 minutes and transfer to cold water. Drain, gently squeeze out excess water and set aside on paper towels.
- Heat 2 tablespoons of oil over medium heat in a large lidded skillet and add onion. Cook, stirring, until tender, about 5 minutes. Add garlic and a generous pinch of salt and cook, stirring, until garlic is fragrant, 30 seconds to a minute. Add tomatoes with juice, sugar, currants, cinnamon, allspice, and salt to taste. Cook, stirring often, until tomatoes have cooked down and mixture is fragrant, 10 to 15 minutes. Remove from heat.
- In a large bowl combine quinoa, turkey, mint and parsley. Add tomato mixture and stir together. Season to taste with salt and pepper.
- Oil a wide, deep, lidded sauté pan or saucepan with olive oil. To fill leaves, place one on your work surface, vein side up with stem end nearest to you. The leaf may have a big space in the middle where you stemmed it; if it does, pull the two sides of the leaf in toward each other and overlap them slightly. Place 2 level tablespoons of filling on bottom center of each leaf, leaving a margin of about 3/4 inch below. Fold bottom up and over, fold sides over, then roll up tightly, tucking in the sides as you go. Place seam side down in pan, crowding the pan with snug layers. Drizzle on remaining 2 tablespoons of olive oil.
- Whisk together 1/2 cup water, tomato paste and lemon juice. Season with salt if desired. Pour over stuffed collard greens. The rolls should be just submerged. Add more water if necessary. Cover stuffed leaves with a round of parchment or wax paper, and place a plate or small lid over the paper to weight them during cooking. Bring to a simmer, cover and simmer over low heat for 30 to 45 minutes.

Leaves should be just tender. Remove from heat and carefully remove rolls from pot with a slotted spoon or tongs. Serve warm or cold, with juice from pan spooned over if desired.

Nutrition Information

- 110: calories;
- 348 milligrams: sodium;
- 1 gram: polyunsaturated fat;
- 4 grams: dietary fiber;
- 11 grams: carbohydrates;
- 2 grams: sugars;
- 5 grams: protein;
- 6 grams: fat;
- 0 grams: trans fat;

81. Collard Greens With Farro

Serving: Serves six | Prep: | Cook: | Ready in: 1hours10mins

Ingredients

- 1 large bunch collard greens (about 1 1/2 pounds), stemmed, leaves washed
- Salt to taste
- 2 tablespoons extra virgin olive oil
- ½ medium onion, chopped
- 2 large garlic cloves, minced
- 1 teaspoon chopped fresh rosemary
- 1 ½ cups farro
- ½ cup dry white wine
- 2 quarts chicken stock, vegetable stock, or water, or 1 quart each
- ¼ cup finely chopped flat-leaf parsley
- Crumbled feta for serving

Direction

- Bring a large pot of water to a boil. Fill a bowl with ice water. When the water comes to a boil, salt generously and add the collard greens. Blanch for four minutes, and transfer to the ice water with a slotted spoon or skimmer. Drain and squeeze out extra water. Cut the greens into ribbons about _-inch wide.

- Heat the olive oil over medium heat in a wide, heavy saucepan or Dutch oven, and add the onion. Cook, stirring, until tender, about five minutes. Add a generous pinch of salt, the garlic and the rosemary, and continue to cook for another minute, until the garlic is fragrant. Stir in the farro, and mix for a couple of minutes. Add the white wine, and stir until it has reduced by half. Add the stock and/or water and salt, and bring to a boil. Reduce the heat, stir in the collard greens, cover and simmer 45 minutes, or until the farro is tender. Drain any water remaining, and return the mixture to the pan. Taste and adjust seasonings. Sprinkle a little feta over each serving if desired.

Nutrition Information

- 361: calories;
- 18 grams: protein;
- 1195 milligrams: sodium;
- 10 grams: fat;
- 2 grams: polyunsaturated fat;
- 5 grams: monounsaturated fat;
- 50 grams: carbohydrates;
- 9 grams: sugars;

82. Cooked Tomatillo Salsa

Serving: 2 cups | Prep: | Cook: | Ready in: 40mins

Ingredients

- 1 pound fresh tomatillos, husked and rinsed, or 2 13-ounce cans, drained
- 2 or 3 jalapeño or serrano chiles, stemmed, seeded for a milder salsa
- ¼ cup chopped white onion, soaked for 5 minutes in cold water, then drained and rinsed
- 2 large garlic cloves, peeled
- ½ cup chopped cilantro
- 1 tablespoon grapeseed oil, sunflower oil or canola oil
- 2 cups chicken stock or vegetable stock
- Salt to taste (1/2 to 1 teaspoon)

Direction

- Place the tomatillos in a saucepan, cover with water and bring to a boil. Reduce the heat and simmer for 8 to 10 minutes, flipping them over halfway through, until softened and olive green. Drain and place in a blender. Add the chiles, chopped onion, garlic, salt, and cilantro sprigs. Blend until smooth.
- Heat the oil in a large, heavy saucepan or skillet over medium-high heat until it ripples. Drizzle in a drop of tomatillo purée to test the heat. If it makes a lot of noise and sputters immediately, the oil is hot enough. Add the tomatillo purée, and stir constantly until it thickens and begins to stick to the pan, about 5 minutes. When you run your spoon down the middle of the pan it should leave a canal. Stir in the stock, bring to a simmer, and simmer 10 to 15 minutes, stirring often. The sauce should coat the front and back of your spoon. Taste and adjust seasoning. Remove from the heat. Serve warm or at room temperature.

Nutrition Information

- 119: calories;
- 3 grams: dietary fiber;
- 13 grams: carbohydrates;
- 7 grams: sugars;
- 5 grams: protein;
- 597 milligrams: sodium;
- 6 grams: fat;
- 1 gram: monounsaturated fat;

Ingredients

- 1 ⅓ cups couscous, preferably whole wheat
- 1 to 2 tablespoons extra virgin olive oil
- 2 garlic cloves, minced
- Pinch of red pepper flakes
- 1 can (28-ounce) tomatoes, with juice, pulsed a few times in a food processor or mini processor
- Pinch of sugar
- Salt to taste
- 1 can chickpeas, drained and rinsed
- 1 bunch (about 3/4 pound) black kale, stemmed and washed thoroughly
- ¼ to ½ cup chopped cilantro (optional)

Direction

- Begin heating a saucepan full of water for the kale. Put the couscous in a bowl, add salt to taste, and if desired, 1 tablespoon of the olive oil. Stir or rub between your fingers to distribute the oil (with the oil the couscous is a little fluffier, but you can omit this step). Cover with ½ inch of warm water or stock, if you have some. Let sit while you prepare the tomato sauce. Stir every once in a while to fluff.
- Heat the remaining tablespoon of oil over medium heat in a wide skillet or saucepan and add the garlic and red pepper flakes. As soon as the garlic begins to smell fragrant (30 seconds to 1 minute), add the tomatoes, sugar, and salt and bring to a simmer. Cook, stirring often, until thick and fragrant, about 15 minutes. Remove from the heat, taste and adjust seasoning.
- By now the water in the pot will be boiling. Add salt to taste and the kale. Blanch for 3 to 4 minutes, until tender but still bright. Using a skimmer, transfer to a bowl of cold water. Drain and squeeze out excess water. Chop medium-fine and stir into the tomato sauce, along with the chickpeas and cilantro. Keep warm.
- Cover the couscous bowl with plastic wrap, pierce in a few places and microwave for 2

minutes at full power. Remove from the microwave carefully, as the bowl will be hot. Carefully remove the plastic and fluff. Cover again and return to the microwave for 1 minute. Serve the couscous topped with the tomato and kale sauce.

Nutrition Information

- 454: calories;
- 21 grams: dietary fiber;
- 12 grams: sugars;
- 19 grams: protein;
- 2 grams: polyunsaturated fat;
- 80 grams: carbohydrates;
- 1 gram: saturated fat;
- 4 grams: monounsaturated fat;
- 1052 milligrams: sodium;
- 10 grams: fat;

---

87. Couscous With Tomatoes, White Beans, Squash And Peppers

Serving: 6 to 8 servings | Prep: | Cook: |Ready in: 3hours30mins

Ingredients

- 2 tablespoons extra virgin olive oil
- 1 large onion, chopped
- 2 to 4 large garlic cloves (to taste), minced
- Salt to taste
- 1 ½ teaspoons paprika
- ½ teaspoon cayenne (more to taste)
- 1 pound ripe tomatoes, peeled, seeded and chopped, or 1 14-ounce can, with juice
- 2 cups dried white beans, soaked in 2 quarts water for 6 hours or overnight and drained
- A bouquet garni consisting of 3 sprigs each parsley and cilantro
- 2 to 3 teaspoons harissa (more to taste), plus additional for serving

- 1 pound bell peppers (red, green, yellow or mixed), seeded and cut in large dice
- 2 Anaheim peppers, seeded and diced
- 2 serranos or 1 to 2 jalapeños (more to taste), seeded and chopped
- 1 pound summer squash, sliced or cut in large dice
- 2 to 4 tablespoons chopped parsley, mint or cilantro, or a combination
- 2 to 2 ⅔ cups couscous (1/3 cup per serving)

Direction

- Heat 1 tablespoon of the olive oil in a large, heavy soup pot or Dutch oven over medium heat and add the onion. Cook, stirring, until onion is tender, about 5 minutes, and stir in the garlic, the spices and salt to taste. Stir together for about 30 seconds, until the mixture is fragrant, and add the tomatoes. Cook, stirring often, until the tomatoes have cooked down slightly, 5 to 10 minutes. Stir in the beans, 2 quarts water and the bouquet garni. Bring to a gentle boil, reduce the heat, cover and simmer 1 hour.
- Add the harissa, sweet and hot peppers, squash and salt to taste. Bring back to a simmer and simmer 45 minutes to an hour, until the beans are tender. Stir in the chopped fresh herbs and simmer another 5 minutes. Taste and adjust salt. Remove a cup of the broth for seasoning the couscous. The stew should be spicy and flavorful.
- Reconstituting and steaming the couscous: In a large microwave-safe bowl, combine the couscous and salt to taste. Drizzle the remaining olive oil over the couscous and add the cup of broth you removed from the stew. Stir well, or moisten your fingers and rub the couscous with them to evenly distribute the oil and broth. Add enough water to cover by 1/2 inch and let sit for 20 minutes, or until all of the liquid is absorbed. Stir every 5 minutes with a wooden spoon or rub the couscous between your moistened thumbs and fingers, so that the couscous doesn't lump. The couscous will now be fairly soft; fluff it with a fork or with your hands. The traditional way to finish reconstituting the couscous is to place it above the simmering stew for 45 minutes. I find, however, that steaming it in a microwave results in perfectly fluffy couscous. Cover the bowl tightly with plastic and pierce the plastic with the tip of a paring knife. Heat at 100 percent power for 3 minutes. Remove from the microwave carefully and allow it to sit for 1 minute. Carefully remove the plastic and fluff with forks or a spoon. Cover again with plastic and microwave for 2 to 3 more minutes. Be very careful when you remove the plastic, as the couscous will be steamy. You can reconstitute the couscous a day ahead and reheat in the microwave shortly before serving.
- Reheat the stew and the couscous. Serve the couscous in wide bowls or mound onto plates and top with the stew. Pass more harissa at the table.

Nutrition Information

- 442: calories;
- 21 grams: protein;
- 3 grams: monounsaturated fat;
- 81 grams: carbohydrates;
- 14 grams: dietary fiber;
- 8 grams: sugars;
- 5 grams: fat;
- 1 gram: polyunsaturated fat;
- 725 milligrams: sodium;

88. Cracked Farro Risotto (Farrotto) With Parsley And Marjoram

Serving: Serves 4 | Prep: | Cook: | Ready in: 40mins

Ingredients

- 1 cup (7 ounces) farro
- 2 cups boiling water

- 7 cups chicken, vegetable or garlic stock or broth
- 2 tablespoons extra virgin olive oil
- 2 shallots, minced, or 1/2 cup finely chopped onion
- 2 garlic cloves, minced
- ½ cup dry white wine
- Salt to taste
- Freshly ground pepper to taste
- ¼ cup minced flat leaf parsley
- 1 to 2 tablespoons chopped fresh marjoram
- ¼ to ½ cup freshly grated Parmesan

Direction

- Several hours or the day before you plan on serving the farrotto, place farro in a bowl and pour on 2 cups boiling water. Let sit for 3 hours, or refrigerate overnight.
- Drain farro and place in a food processor fitted with steel blade. Pulse 5 to 10 times. Scrape down sides of bowl and pulse again 5 to 10 times. Some, but not all of the farro should be broken. Scrape into a bowl.
- Put your stock or broth into a saucepan and bring it to a simmer on the stove, with a ladle nearby or in the pot. Make sure that it is well seasoned.
- Heat oil in a wide, heavy skillet or saucepan over medium heat. Add shallots or onion and cook gently until just tender, 3 to 5 minutes. Add garlic and cook, stirring, until fragrant, about 30 seconds. Add farro and stir over medium heat until grains dry out a bit and begin to crackle. Add wine and cook, stirring, until wine is no longer visible in pan.
- Stir in enough of the simmering stock or broth to just cover the farro. The stock should bubble slowly. Cook, stirring often, until it is just about absorbed. Add another ladleful or two of the stock and continue to cook in this fashion, not too fast and not too slowly, adding more stock when the farro is almost dry and stirring often, until mixture is creamy and farro is tender, about 25 minutes. Taste, adjust salt, and add pepper.
- Add another ladleful or two of stock to the pan. Stir in the parsley, marjoram and Parmesan, and remove from heat. The mixture should be creamy. Serve right away in wide soup bowls or on plates.

Nutrition Information

- 475: calories;
- 13 grams: sugars;
- 1561 milligrams: sodium;
- 4 grams: saturated fat;
- 2 grams: polyunsaturated fat;
- 58 grams: carbohydrates;
- 16 grams: fat;
- 8 grams: monounsaturated fat;
- 7 grams: dietary fiber;
- 23 grams: protein;

89. Creamy 'Ranch' Dressing

Serving: 1 cup, about 6 to 8 servings | Prep: | Cook: | Ready in: 5mins

Ingredients

- 1 small garlic clove, halved, green shoot removed
- ½ cup cooked white beans, drained and rinsed if using canned beans
- ½ cup whole milk or 2 percent Greek yogurt or regular yogurt
- 1 ice cube, if using Greek yogurt
- 1 tablespoon fresh lemon juice
- Salt to taste
- 1 tablespoon extra-virgin olive oil
- 1 teaspoon minced chives
- 1 teaspoon each minced tarragon and dill (optional)

Direction

- Process garlic in a food processor fitted with a steel blade until the minced garlic is adhering to sides. Stop processor and scrape down. Add beans, yogurt and ice cube and process until smooth. With the machine running, add lemon juice, salt, and olive oil and process until smooth. Taste and adjust seasoning.

- Scrape into a bowl and stir in chives, tarragon and dill. Serve as a dip or use with crisp salads (it's a bit too thick for delicate lettuces like spring mixes).

Nutrition Information

- 65: calories;
- 4 grams: fat;
- 1 gram: dietary fiber;
- 0 grams: polyunsaturated fat;
- 5 grams: carbohydrates;
- 2 grams: sugars;
- 3 grams: protein;
- 143 milligrams: sodium;

90. Crispy Polenta Medallions

Serving: Serves 8 to 12 as an hors d'oeuvre | Prep: | Cook: | Ready in: 50mins

Ingredients

- 1 recipe Soft Anson Mills Polenta
- 2 to 3 tablespoons olive oil, as needed
- Toppings
- Blue cheese or gorgonzola (about 1 ounce)
- Romesco Sauce (about 1/4 cup)
- Marinara Sauce (about 1/4 cup)
- Green Pipian (about 1/4 cup)

Direction

- Cover a baking sheet with plastic or lightly oil a baking dish. Make polenta and when done, pour onto plastic or into lightly oiled baking dish. Spread to a thickness of about 1/3 inch using an offset spatula. If you are using a baking dish and can't spread the polenta that thin, you can always slice the rounds after

they are cut to make thinner medallions. Cover with plastic and allow to stiffen completely, preferably in the refrigerator overnight.

- Cut the stiff polenta into 1 1/2 to 2-inch rounds with a cookie cutter. If the rounds are thick, cut crosswise into 1/3 inch thick rounds.
- Heat 2 tablespoons olive oil over medium-high heat in a heavy nonstick or cast iron skillet. The polenta should sizzle as soon as you place the medallion in the oil. Cook the rounds in batches until nicely browned on each side, about 3 minutes per side. Turn them carefully with a spatula, and do not crowd the pan. Drain on paper towels. Transfer to a platter while warm and place a pinch – about 1/4 teaspoon – of blue cheese on each round. It should soften and melt a little bit on the hot surface of the polenta. Or top with small dollops of the other toppings of your choice. Serve warm (they are also good when they cool down).

91. Cucumber Salad With Soy, Ginger And Garlic

Serving: Serves 4 | Prep: | Cook: | Ready in: 20mins

Ingredients

- 2 large thin-skinned cucumbers (about 1 1/2 pounds), thinly sliced
- Salt, to taste
- 3 tablespoons seasoned rice vinegar
- 1 tablespoon soy sauce
- 1 teaspoon sugar
- 1 small garlic clove, minced, or granulated garlic or garlic flakes to taste
- 1 teaspoon minced fresh ginger
- ⅛ teaspoon ground cayenne, plus more to taste
- Freshly ground pepper
- 2 tablespoons dark sesame oil
- 3 tablespoons sunflower oil or grapeseed oil

- 1 bunch scallions, white and light green parts, very thinly sliced
- 2 tablespoons chopped cilantro

Direction

- Sprinkle the cucumbers with a generous amount of salt and let sit in a colander in the sink for 15 minutes. Rinse and dry on a kitchen towel. Transfer to a salad bowl.
- Whisk together the vinegar, soy sauce, sugar, garlic, ginger, cayenne, and pepper. Whisk in the sesame oil and the sunflower or grapeseed oil. Toss with the cucumbers, scallions, and cilantro. Chill until ready to serve.

Nutrition Information

- 196: calories;
- 2 grams: protein;
- 7 grams: polyunsaturated fat;
- 10 grams: carbohydrates;
- 5 grams: sugars;
- 546 milligrams: sodium;
- 17 grams: fat;

92. Cucumber And Radish Salad With Yogurt And Cumin

Serving: Serves 4 | Prep: | Cook: | Ready in: 30mins

Ingredients

- ¾ pound cucumbers, peeled if the skin is thick, preferably seedless (Japanese, Persian or hothouse)
- Salt to taste
- 1 medium-size bunch radishes (about 5 ounces), trimmed and sliced very thin
- ½ to ¾ teaspoon black sesame seeds or nigella seeds (to taste)
- ½ teaspoon cumin seeds, lightly toasted and ground

- ⅛ to ¼ teaspoon freshly ground black pepper (to taste)
- ⅛ teaspoon turmeric
- ½ teaspoon curry powder
- ⅓ cup thick Greek style yogurt
- 1 small garlic clove, puréed
- 1 tablespoon fresh lemon juice
- Chopped chives for garnish

Direction

- Cut the cucumbers in half and using a teaspoon, scoop out seeds if necessary. Slice paper-thin. Toss with a generous amount of salt and place in a colander over a bowl or in the sink for 10 minutes. Place in a bowl of cold water and swish them around, then salt again and let sit for another 10 minutes. Rinse and drain on a clean kitchen towel. Transfer to a salad bowl and add the radishes and sesame seeds or nigella seeds.
- In a small bowl stir the cumin, pepper, turmeric and curry powder into the yogurt. Whisk in the garlic and lemon juice. Add salt to taste. Toss with the cucumbers and radishes, garnish with chopped chives and serve, or refrigerate until ready to serve.

Nutrition Information

- 46: calories;
- 2 grams: fat;
- 1 gram: dietary fiber;
- 0 grams: polyunsaturated fat;
- 6 grams: carbohydrates;
- 3 grams: protein;
- 348 milligrams: sodium;

93. Dill Soup

Serving: Serves four | Prep: | Cook: | Ready in: 1hours20mins

Ingredients

70

- 1 tablespoon extra virgin olive oil
- 1 small onion, chopped
- 1 leek, white and light green parts only, cut in half lengthwise, cleaned and sliced
- Salt, preferably kosher salt, to taste
- 1 large or 2 medium carrots (about 1/4 pound), sliced
- 1 rib celery, sliced
- 2 large garlic cloves, sliced
- 1 to 1 ¼ pounds russet potatoes, peeled and diced
- 1 quart water, chicken stock or vegetable stock
- A bouquet garni made with a bay leaf, 1 sprig of parsley and 1 sprig of dill
- ¼ cup finely chopped fresh dill
- ½ cup plain low-fat yogurt, plus additional for garnish
- ½ teaspoon cornstarch
- Garlic croutons
- small dill sprigs for garnish if serving hot
- Thinly sliced cucumbers if serving cold

Direction

- Heat the olive oil in a large, heavy soup pot over medium heat, and add the onion and leeks. Cook, stirring, until they begin to soften, about three minutes, and add 1/2 teaspoon salt, the carrot and the celery. Cook, stirring, for five minutes, and add the garlic. Stir together for about a minute, until fragrant, and add the potatoes, water, salt and the bouquet garni. Bring to a boil, reduce the heat and simmer for one hour. Remove the bouquet garni.
- Puree the soup in an immersion blender, or blend 1 1/2 cups at a time in a blender, covering the top tightly with a towel to avoid splashes. If you want a smoother consistency, put the soup through a medium strainer.
- Stir together the yogurt, cornstarch and dill, and stir into the soup. Heat through. Add a generous amount of freshly ground pepper, taste and adjust salt. Serve hot, garnished with garlic croutons and small dill sprigs; or chill and serve cold, garnished with a dollop of

yogurt, thinly sliced cucumbers and small dill sprigs.

Nutrition Information

- 170: calories;
- 32 grams: carbohydrates;
- 3 grams: dietary fiber;
- 1074 milligrams: sodium;
- 4 grams: protein;
- 1 gram: saturated fat;
- 2 grams: monounsaturated fat;
- 0 grams: polyunsaturated fat;

94. Dried Fruit Compote With Fresh Apple And Pear

Serving: Serves 6 to 8 | Prep: | Cook: | Ready in: 10mins

Ingredients

- 2 cups mixed dried fruit, such as raisins (several types), apples, pears, peaches, cranberries, chopped apricots (about 1/2 pound)
- 2 ½ cups water
- 3 tablespoons mild honey, such as clover (more to taste)
- 1 cinnamon stick
- 1 teaspoon vanilla extract
- 2 strips orange zest
- 1 strip lemon zest
- 1 firm but ripe pear, peeled, cored and diced (optional)
- 1 apple, preferably a slightly tart variety like Pink Lady, peeled, cored and diced (optional)
- Whipped cream or plain yogurt for serving, if desired

Direction

- Cut large pieces of dried fruit into smaller pieces.

- Combine all of the ingredients in a saucepan and bring to a boil. Reduce heat, cover and simmer 5 minutes. Turn off heat and allow fruit to steep for 30 minutes or longer. Remove cinnamon stick and orange and lemon zest. Serve topped with whipped cream or yogurt if desired, or stir into your morning yogurt.

Nutrition Information

- 39: calories;
- 10 grams: carbohydrates;
- 2 grams: dietary fiber;
- 8 grams: sugars;
- 4 milligrams: sodium;
- 0 grams: protein;

95. Dried Porcini Consommé

Serving: Makes enough for 10 to 12 shots or 4 to 6 bowls. | Prep: | Cook: | Ready in: 1hours30mins

Ingredients

- 1 ounce dried porcini mushrooms (about 1 cup, approximately)
- 2 cups boiling water
- ¼ pound fresh white mushrooms, cleaned
- 1 quart chicken or vegetable stock
- 2 large garlic cloves, sliced thin
- 1 tablespoon soy sauce
- Salt and freshly ground pepper
- A few drops fresh lemon juice
- 1 tablespoon chopped fresh chives

Direction

- Place the dried porcinis in a bowl or a pyrex measuring cup and cover with 2 cups boiling water. Let sit for 30 minutes. Meanwhile, wipe the fresh mushrooms, trim away the bottoms if they are sandy, break off the stems and set them aside. Set aside half of the caps in a separate bowl and slice the rest.

- Line a strainer with cheesecloth and set it over a bowl. Drain the porcinis through the cheesecloth-lined strainer. Squeeze over the strainer to extract as much flavorful liquid as possible and set aside the broth. Rinse the reconstituted mushrooms in several changes of water. Measure the mushroom soaking water and add enough water to make 4 cups.
- In a soup pot or a large saucepan, combine the mushroom soaking liquid, the chicken or vegetable stock, the soaked porcinis, fresh mushroom stems and sliced caps, garlic, and salt to taste, and bring to a simmer. Cover and simmer over very low heat for 30 minutes. Strain the soup and return to the saucepan. Add salt and freshly ground pepper to taste, and the soy sauce.
- Slice the fresh mushroom caps you set aside paper-thin and toss with a couple of drops of lemon juice. Ladle the soup into bowls or espresso cups, garnish with a couple of slices of mushroom and a sprinkling of chives, and serve.

Nutrition Information

- 44: calories;
- 1 gram: dietary fiber;
- 0 grams: polyunsaturated fat;
- 6 grams: carbohydrates;
- 2 grams: sugars;
- 3 grams: protein;
- 339 milligrams: sodium;

96. Easy Fish Stew With Mediterranean Flavors

Serving: Serves four | Prep: | Cook: | Ready in: 1hours15mins

Ingredients

- 4 large garlic cloves, cut in half, green shoots removed

- 4 anchovy fillets, soaked in water for 4 minutes, drained and rinsed
- 2 tablespoons extra virgin olive oil
- 1 large onion, chopped
- 1 celery rib, chopped
- 1 medium carrot, chopped
- Salt, preferably kosher salt, to taste
- 1 (28-ounce) can chopped tomatoes, with liquid
- 1 quart water
- 1 pound small new potatoes, scrubbed and quartered or sliced
- A bouquet garni made with a bay leaf, a strip of orange zest, a couple of sprigs each thyme and parsley, and a dried red chile if desired, tied together with a string
- Freshly ground pepper
- 1 to 1 ½ pounds firm white-fleshed fish such as halibut, tilapia, Pacific cod or black cod, cut in 2-inch pieces

Direction

- Place the garlic cloves and 1/4 teaspoon salt in a mortar and pestle, and mash to a paste. Add the anchovy fillets and mash with the garlic. Set aside.
- Heat the olive oil over medium heat in a large, heavy soup pot or Dutch oven, and add the onion, celery and carrot with 1/2 teaspoon salt. Cook, stirring, until the onion is tender, about five minutes. Add the pureed garlic and anchovy. Cook, stirring, until the mixture is very fragrant, about one minute, and then add the tomatoes. Cook, stirring often, until the tomatoes have cooked down a bit and the mixture smells aromatic, about 10 to 15 minutes. Add the water, potatoes, salt (to taste) and the bouquet garni. Bring to a simmer. Turn the heat to low, cover partially and simmer 30 minutes. Taste, adjust salt and add pepper to taste. Remove the bouquet garni.
- Season the fish with salt and pepper, and stir into the soup. The soup should not be boiling. Simmer five to 10 minutes (depending on the thickness of the fillets) or just until it flakes

easily when poked. Remove from the heat, stir in the parsley, taste once more, adjust seasonings and serve.

Nutrition Information

- 352: calories;
- 1793 milligrams: sodium;
- 10 grams: fat;
- 2 grams: polyunsaturated fat;
- 6 grams: monounsaturated fat;
- 35 grams: carbohydrates;
- 8 grams: sugars;
- 33 grams: protein;

97. Egg Lemon Soup With Turkey

Serving: 6 servings | Prep: | Cook: | Ready in: 15mins

Ingredients

- 2 quarts well-seasoned turkey stock, garlic broth or vegetable stock
- 1 broccoli crown, cut or broken into small florets
- 2 cups chopped shredded turkey
- 1 tablespoon extra-virgin olive oil
- Salt and pepper
- 3 egg yolks
- ¼ cup freshly squeezed lemon juice (more to taste)
- 2 tablespoons chopped fresh parsley
- 1 ½ cups warm cooked rice

Direction

- Bring stock to a simmer over medium heat. Add broccoli and simmer 3 to 5 minutes, until just tender. Stir in turkey and olive oil and turn heat to low. Season with salt and pepper.
- In a medium bowl, whisk egg yolks until creamy. Whisk in lemon juice.
- Making sure soup is not boiling, slowly whisk a couple of ladles of hot soup into egg yolks,

whisking constantly. Turn off heat under soup and stir in tempered egg-lemon mixture. Stir in parsley. Taste and adjust salt and pepper.

- Distribute rice among six bowls. Ladle soup into bowls and serve.

Nutrition Information

- 177: calories;
- 15 grams: carbohydrates;
- 13 grams: protein;
- 1013 milligrams: sodium;
- 1 gram: sugars;
- 0 grams: trans fat;
- 3 grams: monounsaturated fat;
- 7 grams: fat;
- 2 grams: saturated fat;

98. Eggplant And Tomato Pie

Serving: 1 pie, serving 6 generously | Prep: | Cook: | Ready in: 2hours

Ingredients

- 1 Whole Wheat Yeasted Olive Oil Crust (1/2 recipe)
- 1 ½ pounds eggplant (2 medium)
- Salt and freshly ground pepper
- 2 eggs
- ⅓ cup milk
- 1 ½ cups marinara sauce
- 2 teaspoons fresh thyme leaves
- 2 ounces Gruyère, grated (1/2 cup)
- 1 ounce Parmesan, grated (1/4 cup)
- 2 medium-size fresh tomatoes, in season, sliced
- 2 tablespoons extra virgin olive oil

Direction

- Line a lightly oiled 9- or 10-inch tart pan with the dough. Using a fork, pierce at regular

intervals to allow for even baking. Refrigerate or freeze until ready to prebake and fill.

- Heat the oven to 450 degrees Fahrenheit. Slice the eggplant about 1/3 inch thick and toss with salt to taste and 1 tablespoon olive oil. Line 1 to 2 baking sheets (as needed) with foil and brush the foil with olive oil. Lay the eggplant slices on the foil in 1 layer. Roast in the hot oven for 15 to 20 minutes, until the slices are soft when pierced with a knife and browned in spots. Remove from the oven and carefully fold the foil up over the eggplant slices (be careful not to burn yourself!). Crimp the edges of the foil and allow the eggplant to steam for another 15 to 20 minutes. It should now be completely cooked. Turn the oven down to 350 degrees.

- Beat together the eggs in a medium bowl. Set the tart pan on a baking sheet to allow for easy handling. Using a pastry brush lightly brush the bottom of the crust with the beaten egg and place in the oven for 10 minutes. Remove from the oven and set aside.

- Whisk the milk into the eggs. Add salt (I usually use about 1/2 teaspoon) and pepper. Spread 1/4 cup tomato sauce over the bottom of the crust. Top with a layer of eggplant slices. Season with salt and pepper. Spoon one third of the remaining sauce over the eggplant and sprinkle with thyme, Parmesan, and half of the Gruyère. Repeat the layers one or two more times, depending on the size of your eggplant slices, ending with the Gruyère. Pour on the egg and milk mixture. It should seep down into the layers; if it looks like it's moving and going to overflow the crust, use a fork to create some holes so it does seep down. Arrange the sliced tomatoes on top and sprinkle any remaining thyme over the tomatoes. Drizzle on 1 tablespoon of olive oil. Place in the oven and bake for 40 to 45 minutes, until set and bubbling and browned on the top and edges. Remove from the heat and allow to sit for at least 10 minutes before serving. Serve hot, warm, or room temperature.

Nutrition Information

- 203: calories;
- 12 grams: fat;
- 6 grams: monounsaturated fat;
- 1 gram: polyunsaturated fat;
- 15 grams: carbohydrates;
- 5 grams: dietary fiber;
- 10 grams: protein;
- 4 grams: saturated fat;
- 0 grams: trans fat;
- 628 milligrams: sodium;

99. Eggplant, Tomato And Chickpea Casserole

Serving: 4 to 6 servings | Prep: | Cook: | Ready in: 2hours

Ingredients

- 1 large eggplant or 2 medium (1 pound), peeled if desired, cut in half lengthwise, then sliced about 1/2 inch thick
- Salt to taste
- 3 tablespoons extra virgin olive oil
- 1 large onion, sliced thin across the grain
- 2 to 4 garlic cloves (to taste), minced
- 1 (28-ounce) can chopped tomatoes
- 2 tablespoons tomato paste
- Pinch of sugar
- ⅛ teaspoon cinnamon
- 1 sprig basil
- 1 (15-ounce) can chickpeas, drained
- 3 tablespoons chopped flat-leaf parsley (optional)

Direction

- Preheat the oven to 450 degrees. Line a baking sheet with aluminum foil, and brush the foil with olive oil. Place the eggplant slices on the foil, sprinkle with salt and brush each slice lightly with oil. Place in the oven for 15 minutes or until lightly browned. Remove from the heat, and carefully fold the foil in half over the eggplant. Crimp the edges together, so that the eggplant is sealed inside the foil and will continue to steam and soften. Leave for at least 15 minutes.
- Meanwhile, make the tomato sauce. Heat 2 tablespoons olive oil in a large, heavy skillet over medium heat. Add the onion. Cook, stirring often, until tender, about five minutes, and add the garlic and a generous pinch of salt. Cook, stirring, until the garlic is fragrant, about a minute. Add the tomatoes, tomato paste, sugar, cinnamon, basil and salt to taste. Bring to a simmer, and simmer uncovered, stirring often, for 20 to 25 minutes, until the sauce is thick and fragrant. Add freshly ground pepper, then taste and adjust salt. Remove the basil sprig, and stir in the drained chickpeas.
- Preheat the oven to 350 degrees. Oil a 2-quart baking dish or gratin. Cover the bottom with thin layer of tomato sauce, and make a layer of half the eggplant. Spoon half the remaining sauce over the eggplant, and repeat the layers.
- Bake 30 minutes, until bubbling. Remove from the heat, and allow to cool for at least 10 to 15 minutes. Sprinkle on the parsley before serving.

Nutrition Information

- 212: calories;
- 1 gram: saturated fat;
- 2 grams: polyunsaturated fat;
- 28 grams: carbohydrates;
- 10 grams: sugars;
- 7 grams: protein;
- 739 milligrams: sodium;
- 9 grams: fat;
- 5 grams: monounsaturated fat;

100. Endive Leaves With Crab Rillettes

Serving: Serves 6 to 8 | Prep: | Cook: | Ready in: 20mins

Ingredients

- 8 ounces lump crabmeat
- 2 tablespoons extra virgin olive oil
- 2 tablespoons plain Greek yogurt
- 2 tablespoons crème fraîche (or omit and use 4 tablespoons yogurt)
- 1 to 2 tablespoons fresh lime juice (to taste)
- 1 to 2 tablespoons minced chives (to taste)
- 1 to 2 tablespoons finely chopped mint (to taste)
- 1 serrano pepper, finely chopped
- Salt to taste
- 4 endives

Direction

- Drain crabmeat and place in a medium bowl. Mash with a fork. Add olive oil, yogurt and crème fraîche and mash together until mixture is spreadable. Add lime juice, chives, mint and chile and work in. Season to taste with salt. You should have about 1 1/3 cups.
- Break off endive leaves at the base. The easiest way to do this is to cut base away, break off a round of leaves, then keep slicing away the base so that the leaves will easily break off at the bottom. Spoon crab rillettes onto leaves and arrange on a platter. Serve at once, or refrigerate until ready to serve.

Nutrition Information

- 70: calories;
- 0 grams: sugars;
- 3 grams: monounsaturated fat;
- 2 grams: carbohydrates;
- 6 grams: protein;
- 166 milligrams: sodium;
- 5 grams: fat;
- 1 gram: dietary fiber;

101. Endive Salad With Blue Cheese Dressing

Serving: 4 servings | Prep: | Cook: | Ready in: 15mins

Ingredients

- 1 small garlic clove, finely minced or puréed
- ½ cup plain yogurt, thinned out with a little milk if thick
- 2 tablespoons extra virgin olive oil
- Salt and freshly ground black pepper to taste
- 2 ounces good quality blue cheese or Roquefort, at room temperature, crumbled (about 1/2 cup)
- ½ teaspoon Dijon mustard
- 4 large or 6 medium endives
- Minced chives
- 1 apple, cut in very small (1/4 inch or smaller) dice and tossed with lemon juice for garnish

Direction

- Whisk together garlic and yogurt in a medium bowl. Add olive oil, salt and pepper and whisk together. Add blue cheese or Roquefort and Dijon mustard and whisk together until mixture is fairly smooth, with a few lumps of cheese.
- Trim away the very end of the endives and cut lengthwise into quarters. Arrange on a platter or on individual plates and spoon on dressing. Top with chives and finely diced apple, and serve.

102. Endive, Apple And Kasha Salad

Serving: Serves 6 | Prep: | Cook: | Ready in: 20mins

Ingredients

- 1 good-size crisp apple, cored and cut into small dice
- 1 tablespoon fresh lime or lemon juice
- 4 Belgian endives, sliced
- 1 cup cooked kasha
- ⅓ cup broken walnuts
- 1 ounce Gruyère, cut in small dice
- 1 to 2 tablespoons chopped fresh parsley (to taste)
- 2 tablespoons fresh lemon or lime juice
- 1 to 2 teaspoons honey or agave nectar (to taste)
- Salt to taste
- freshly ground pepper to taste
- 1 teaspoon Dijon mustard
- 2 tablespoons walnut oil
- ¼ cup extra virgin olive oil

Direction

- In a large salad bowl, toss together apple and lime or lemon juice. Add endives, kasha, walnuts, Gruyère and parsley.
- In a small bowl or measuring cup whisk together lemon juice, honey or agave, salt, pepper, Dijon mustard, walnut oil and olive oil. Toss with salad and serve.

Nutrition Information

- 274: calories;
- 17 grams: fat;
- 3 grams: saturated fat;
- 0 grams: trans fat;
- 8 grams: monounsaturated fat;
- 5 grams: protein;
- 29 grams: carbohydrates;
- 289 milligrams: sodium;

103.   Enfrijoladas

Serving: Serves 4 | Prep: | Cook: | Ready in: 2hours30mins

Ingredients

- ½ pound (1 1/8 cups) black beans, washed, picked over and soaked for 4 to 6 hours or overnight in 1 quart water
- 1 onion, cut in half
- 2 plump garlic cloves, minced
- 1 to 2 sprigs epazote or 2 tablespoons chopped cilantro, plus additional for garnish (optional)
- 1 to 2 teaspoons ground cumin, to taste
- ½ to 1 teaspoon ground mild chili powder (more to taste)
- Salt to taste
- 12 corn tortillas
- ¼ cup chopped walnuts (optional)

Direction

- In a large soup pot or Dutch oven combine the black beans with their soaking water (they should be submerged by at least 1 1/2 inches of water; add if necessary), one half of the onion, and half the garlic and bring to a boil. Reduce the heat, cover and simmer gently for 1 hour. Add the remaining garlic, epazote or cilantro if using, cumin, chili powder, and salt to taste and simmer for another hour, until the beans are very soft and the broth thick, soupy and aromatic. Remove from the heat. Remove and discard the onion.
- Using an immersion blender or a food processor fitted with the steel blade coarsely puree the beans. The mixture should retain some texture and the consistency should be thick and creamy. Heat through, stirring the bottom of the pot so the beans don't stick. Taste and adjust salt. Keep warm.
- Slice the remaining onion half crosswise into thin half-moons and cover with cold water while you assemble the enfrijoladas. Heat the corn tortillas: either wrap them in a damp dish towel and heat them, 4 at a time, in the microwave for about 30 seconds at 100 percent power, or wrap in a dish towel and steam for 1 minute, then let rest for 5 minutes.
- Assemble the enfrijoladas just before serving them. Spoon about 1/2 cup of the hot, thick beans over the bottom of a large lightly oiled

baking dish or serving platter. Using tongs, dip a softened tortilla into the beans and flip over to coat both sides with black beans. Remove from the beans and place on the baking dish or platter (this is messy; have the serving dish right next to the pot.) Fold into quarters. Use the tongs to do this, and if you find that the tortilla tears too much, then just coat one side with the black beans, transfer to the baking dish and spoon some of the black beans over the other side, then fold into quarters. Continue with the remaining tortillas, arranging the quartered bean-coated tortillas in overlapping rows. When all of the tortillas are in the dish, spoon the remaining black bean sauce over the top. Drain and rinse the onions, dry briefly on paper towels and sprinkle over the bean sauce. Garnish with cilantro and chopped walnuts if desired and serve at once.

Nutrition Information

- 369: calories;
- 3 grams: sugars;
- 1 gram: polyunsaturated fat;
- 72 grams: carbohydrates;
- 14 grams: dietary fiber;
- 17 grams: protein;
- 378 milligrams: sodium;

---

104. Farro And Swiss Chard Salad With Grapefruit Vinaigrette

Serving: 4 servings | Prep: | Cook: | Ready in: 15mins

Ingredients

- 1 tablespoon extra virgin olive oil
- ½ cup diced chard stems
- 1 garlic clove, minced
- 1 cup coarsely chopped blanched or steamed chard leaves (about 1/2 pound uncooked) (see note)
- Salt and freshly ground pepper to taste
- 2 cups cooked farro
- 1 ounce broken walnuts (about 3 tablespoons)
- 2 tablespoons chopped parsley
- ½ cup grapefruit vinaigrette

Direction

- Heat the olive oil over medium heat in a medium size skillet and add the chard stems. Cook, stirring often, until the stems are crisp-tender, 3 to 4 minutes. Add the garlic and continue to cook, stirring, for another 30 seconds to a minute, until the garlic is fragrant. Stir in the chopped blanched or steamed Swiss chard leaves, add salt and pepper to taste, and stir the mixture until the chard is coated with oil, 30 seconds to a minute. Remove from the heat and transfer to a large bowl.
- Add the farro, walnuts and parsley to the bowl. When ready to serve, toss with the dressing. Arrange on a platter or in a serving bowl.

Nutrition Information

- 333: calories;
- 1 gram: sugars;
- 7 grams: protein;
- 4 grams: saturated fat;
- 10 grams: polyunsaturated fat;
- 28 grams: carbohydrates;
- 5 grams: dietary fiber;
- 23 grams: fat;
- 8 grams: monounsaturated fat;
- 357 milligrams: sodium;

105. Farro Or Bulgur With Black Eyed Peas, Chard And Feta

Serving: Serves 6 | Prep: | Cook: | Ready in: 1hours

Ingredients

- 1 pound black-eyed peas
- 2 tablespoons extra virgin olive oil
- 1 large onion, chopped
- 3 large garlic cloves, minced
- 1 to 2 serrano peppers, minced (optional)
- 1 bay leaf
- Salt to taste
- 1 bunch Swiss chard (about 1 pound), stemmed, leaves washed in two changes of water, stems diced if wide and fleshy, discarded if thin and stringy
- ¼ cup chopped fresh dill or cilantro
- Freshly ground pepper to taste
- 3 cups cooked farro or bulgur
- 1 red pepper, cut in small dice, for topping
- 2 ounces feta, crumbled

Direction

- Rinse the beans and pick over to check for stones. Heat 1 tablespoon of the oil over medium heat in a large, heavy soup pot or Dutch oven and add the onion. Cook, stirring, until tender, about 5 minutes, and add half the garlic and the chiles. Cook, stirring, until fragrant, 30 seconds to a minute, and add the black-eyed peas, 2 quarts water and the bay leaf. Bring to a boil, reduce the heat to low, and skim off any foam that rises. Cover and simmer 30 minutes.
- Add salt to taste and the remaining garlic. A handful at a time, stir in the chard. As the greens wilt, stir in another handful, until all the greens have been added. Bring back to a simmer, cover and simmer over low heat for 15 to 20 minutes, or until the greens and beans are tender.
- Stir in the remaining tablespoon of olive oil and the dill or cilantro, cover and continue to simmer for another 5 minutes. Add salt and freshly ground pepper to taste.
- Spoon farro or bulgur into bowls or onto plates. Top with the beans. Top the beans with diced red pepper and crumbled feta, and serve.

Nutrition Information

- 287: calories;
- 8 grams: fat;
- 2 grams: saturated fat;
- 1 gram: polyunsaturated fat;
- 11 grams: protein;
- 677 milligrams: sodium;
- 4 grams: monounsaturated fat;
- 47 grams: carbohydrates;
- 10 grams: dietary fiber;
- 5 grams: sugars;

106. Fattoush With Dukkah

Serving: 6 to 8 generous servings | Prep: | Cook: | Ready in: 10mins

Ingredients

- 3 stale or lightly toasted pita breads, preferably whole-wheat
- ¼ cup fresh lemon juice
- Salt to taste
- 6 tablespoons extra virgin olive oil
- Freshly ground black pepper to taste
- 1 pound tomatoes, coarsely chopped
- 1 European cucumber or 3 Persian cucumbers, cut in half lengthwise, then into half-moon slices
- 6 scallions, white and light green parts, sliced
- ½ cup chopped fresh flat-leaf parsley
- 1 romaine lettuce heart (the lighter inner leaves), washed, dried, cut crosswise in 1-inch-wide pieces
- 2 to 4 tablespoons hazelnut and herb dukkah, to taste

Direction

- Break the pita into pieces.
- Combine the lemon juice, salt, olive oil and pepper in a small bowl.
- Toss the salad ingredients together in a large bowl. Just before serving, add the dressing and toss together. Crumble in the pita bread and toss again. Taste, adjust seasonings and serve.

Nutrition Information

- 175: calories;
- 16 grams: carbohydrates;
- 354 milligrams: sodium;
- 2 grams: polyunsaturated fat;
- 8 grams: monounsaturated fat;
- 3 grams: sugars;
- 12 grams: fat;
- 0 grams: trans fat;
- 4 grams: protein;

107.   Fava Bean And Asparagus Salad

Serving: 4 servings. | Prep: | Cook: |Ready in: 45mins

Ingredients

- 2 pounds fava beans, shelled and skinned
- 1 pound trimmed asparagus, preferably fat spears
- 2 tablespoons chopped fresh mint, dill or tarragon
- 2 tablespoons minced chives
- 1 to 2 teaspoons lemon zest (to taste)
- 1 tablespoon fresh lemon juice
- 2 tablespoons red or white wine vinegar or sherry vinegar
- Salt to taste
- 1 small garlic clove, minced or puréed, or 2 tablespoons minced shallots
- 3 tablespoons extra virgin olive oil

- 2 tablespoons low-fat plain yogurt
- 1 ounce Parmesan, shaved
- 1 15-ounce can chickpeas, drained and rinsed

Direction

- Blanch and skin the fava beans and place them in a bowl. Use the blanching water to blanch the asparagus, or steam the asparagus if you prefer. If blanching, bring the water in the pot to a boil, salt generously and add the asparagus spears. Blanch 1 to 4 minutes, depending on how thick the asparagus is; fat spears (recommended) will take up to 4 minutes, but thin ones are ready in 1 minute. You can steam the asparagus over 1 inch boiling water for the same amount of time if you prefer. Transfer the lightly cooked asparagus to a bowl of cold water, then drain and dry on paper towels. Cut into 1-inch lengths. Add to the bowl with the fava beans. Add the herbs, and the chickpeas if using.
- Combine the lemon zest and juice, vinegar, garlic or shallots, and salt to taste in a bowl. Whisk in the oil and yogurt. Toss with the favas and asparagus. Add the shaved Parmesan, toss again and serve, or allow to marinate for 30 minutes, then serve.

Nutrition Information

- 507: calories;
- 27 grams: dietary fiber;
- 29 grams: sugars;
- 1168 milligrams: sodium;
- 3 grams: polyunsaturated fat;
- 72 grams: carbohydrates;
- 31 grams: protein;
- 17 grams: fat;
- 9 grams: monounsaturated fat;

108.   Fennel Rice

Serving: Serves 6 | Prep: | Cook: |Ready in: 1hours

Ingredients

- ¼ cup extra virgin olive oil
- 1 medium onion, chopped
- 2 garlic cloves, minced
- 1 pound fennel (2 medium bulbs), trimmed, cored and diced small
- Salt to taste
- 1 cup long grain rice, such as basmati, rinsed, or coarse bulgur
- 2 ½ cups water
- ¼ cup chopped fresh parsley
- ¼ cup chopped fresh dill
- Freshly ground pepper

Direction

- Heat 3 tablespoons olive oil over medium heat in a deep, lidded skillet or a wide, lidded saucepan. Add onion and cook, stirring often, until tender, about 5 minutes. Add garlic and stir until fragrant, about 30 seconds. Stir in fennel, add a generous pinch of salt, and cook, stirring often, until fennel has wilted and softened, about 8 minutes. Stir in rice or bulgur and stir to coat with olive oil.
- Add water, salt, pepper, parsley and dill and bring to a boil. Reduce heat to low, cover and simmer 20 to 30 minutes, until rice or bulgur is soft and liquid absorbed. Remove from heat, uncover and place a towel across the top of the pan. Return lid and let sit for 10 minutes. Serve hot, with the remaining olive oil drizzled over the top.

Nutrition Information

- 195: calories;
- 7 grams: monounsaturated fat;
- 26 grams: carbohydrates;
- 6 grams: dietary fiber;
- 4 grams: protein;
- 539 milligrams: sodium;
- 10 grams: fat;
- 1 gram: polyunsaturated fat;

---

109. Fettuccine With Brussels Sprouts, Lemon And Ricotta

Serving: Serves 4 | Prep: | Cook: | Ready in: 20mins

Ingredients

- ¾ pound Brussels sprouts (about 16)
- 2 tablespoons extra virgin olive oil
- Salt and freshly ground pepper to taste
- ½ cup ricotta
- 1 garlic clove, mashed with a pinch of salt in a mortar and pestle or put through a press
- 2 teaspoons finely grated or chopped lemon zest (I use a microplane for this)
- 2 tablespoons minced chives or parsley, or a combination
- 1 ounce Parmesan, grated (1/4 cup)
- 12 ounces fettuccine

Direction

- Begin heating water for pasta.
- Trim bottoms of Brussels sprouts and quarter lengthwise or slice. Heat oil over high heat in a large, heavy skillet and add Brussels sprouts. Sear for about a minute without stirring, then turn the heat to medium-high, add salt and pepper to taste and stir or toss in the pan until tender and the edges are seared light brown, about 5 minutes. Some of the leaves will detach and get black, but don't worry, you can discard them. Remove from heat and transfer to a bowl or plate.
- When water comes to a boil, salt generously and add pasta. While pasta is cooking, mix together ricotta, garlic, lemon zest and chives (or parsley and chives) in a large bowl. Season to taste with salt and pepper.
- When pasta is cooked al dente (see timing instructions on package but check a minute before indicated time), remove 1/4 cup of the pasta water. Mix 2 to 4 tablespoons with ricotta. It should have the consistency of cream. Add a little more water if it doesn't. Drain the pasta and toss with Brussels sprouts,

ricotta mixture and Parmesan. If pasta seems dry, toss with a little more of the cooking water or another tablespoon of olive oil. Serve at once.

Nutrition Information

- 497: calories;
- 7 grams: monounsaturated fat;
- 73 grams: carbohydrates;
- 6 grams: dietary fiber;
- 4 grams: sugars;
- 14 grams: fat;
- 5 grams: saturated fat;
- 1 gram: polyunsaturated fat;
- 20 grams: protein;
- 509 milligrams: sodium;

110. Focaccia With Cauliflower And Sage

Serving: 12 to 15 servings | Prep: | Cook: | Ready in: 1hours15mins

Ingredients

- 1 recipe Whole-Wheat Focaccia
- 1 pound cauliflower (1 small head or 1/2 large), cut into florets, stems trimmed
- Salt and freshly ground pepper to taste
- 2 tablespoons extra virgin olive oil
- 30 to 40 fresh sage leaves (depending on the size)

Direction

- Mix up the focaccia dough as directed and set in a warm spot to rise.
- Meanwhile, bring a large pot of water to a boil and salt generously. Add the cauliflower and blanch for 2 minutes. Transfer to a bowl of cold water, then drain and pat dry. Cut the florets into small pieces and toss in a large

bowl with 2 tablespoons olive oil and salt and freshly ground pepper.

- When the focaccia dough has risen, shape as directed into 1 large focaccia or 2 smaller focacce. Cover with a damp cloth and let rise in a warm spot for 30 minutes while you preheat the oven to 425 degrees, preferably with a baking stone in it.
- Dimple the dough with your fingertips and arrange the sage leaves, then the cauliflower on top. Drizzle with olive oil. Bake, setting the pan on top of the baking stone (if using), for 25 minutes, until the bread is deep golden brown and the cauliflower lightly colored in spots. Let rest for at least 10 minutes before serving, or allow to cool completely.

Nutrition Information

- 98: calories;
- 2 grams: dietary fiber;
- 154 milligrams: sodium;
- 4 grams: fat;
- 1 gram: sugars;
- 3 grams: protein;
- 12 grams: carbohydrates;

111. Focaccia With Tomatoes And Rosemary

Serving: 12 to 15 servings | Prep: | Cook: | Ready in: 2hours45mins

Ingredients

- 2 teaspoons (8 grams) active dry yeast
- 1 teaspoon (5 grams) sugar
- 1 ½ cups lukewarm water
- 2 tablespoons (25 grams) olive oil, plus an additional 2 tablespoons (25 grams) for drizzling
- 250 grams (approximately 2 cups) whole-wheat flour

- 200 to 220 grams (approximately 1 2/3 to 1 3/4 cups) unbleached all-purpose flour or bread flour, plus additional as needed for kneading
- 1 ¾ teaspoons (13 grams) salt
- ¾ pound Roma tomatoes
- Coarse salt and freshly ground pepper to taste
- 1 to 2 tablespoons chopped fresh rosemary (to taste)

Direction

- In the bowl of a standing mixer, or in a large bowl, dissolve the yeast and sugar in the water. Add the olive oil, whole-wheat flour, 200 grams of the all-purpose flour and salt and mix together briefly using the paddle attachment. Change to the dough hook and beat for 8 to 10 minutes at medium speed, adding flour as necessary. The dough should eventually form a ball around the dough hook and slap against the sides of the bowl as the mixer turns; it will be sticky. Remove from the bowl, flour your hands and knead for a minute on a lightly floured surface, and shape into a ball.
- If kneading the dough by hand, dissolve the yeast in the water with the sugar as directed. Stir in the olive oil, whole-wheat flour, salt and all-purpose flour by the half-cup, until the dough can be scraped out onto a floured work surface. Knead, adding flour as necessary, for 10 minutes, until the dough is elastic and smooth. Shape into a ball.
- Clean and dry your bowl and oil lightly with olive oil. Place the dough in it, rounded side down first, then rounded side up. Cover tightly with plastic and let rise in a warm spot for 1 1/2 to 2 hours, or in the refrigerator for 4 to 8 hours, until doubled.
- Punch down the dough. Cover with lightly oiled plastic and let the dough rest for 15 minutes.
- Preheat the oven to 425 degrees, preferably with a baking stone in it. Line a sheet pan with parchment and oil generously. Roll or press out the dough into a rectangle the size of the sheet pan or just slightly smaller. To do this

efficiently, roll or press out the dough, stop and wait 5 minutes for the gluten to relax, then roll or press out again, and repeat until the dough reaches the right size. Cover with a damp towel and let rest for 30 minutes. Just before baking, use your fingertips to dimple the dough all over.
- Cut the tomatoes into rounds and place on top of the focaccia. Sprinkle with coarse salt and the rosemary. Drizzle a tablespoon or two of olive oil over all.
- Bake, setting the pan on top of the baking stone (if using), for 20 to 25 minutes, until the bread is deep golden brown. Let rest for at least 10 minutes before serving, or allow to cool completely.

Nutrition Information

- 124: calories;
- 0 grams: polyunsaturated fat;
- 26 grams: carbohydrates;
- 3 grams: dietary fiber;
- 4 grams: protein;
- 195 milligrams: sodium;
- 1 gram: sugars;

| 112. | Forbidden Rice Pudding With Blueberries |

Serving: Serves six | Prep: | Cook: | Ready in: 3hours

Ingredients

- ½ cup Forbidden rice (Chinese black rice)
- 1 cup water
- ¼ teaspoon salt
- 1 cup low-fat milk or rice beverage
- 1 cup unsweetened low-fat coconut milk
- ¼ cup mild honey
- 1 teaspoon vanilla extract
- 1 cup blueberries

Direction

- Combine the rice, water and salt in a saucepan, and bring to a boil. Reduce the heat, cover and simmer 35 to 40 minutes, until all of the water is absorbed.
- Add the milk, coconut milk and honey to the rice, and stir together. Bring to a boil, stirring, then reduce the heat and simmer, stirring often, for five to 10 minutes, until creamy. Add the vanilla and blueberries, and continue to simmer for another five minutes.
- Scrape into a bowl or into individual serving dishes. Cover and chill for at least two hours before serving.

Nutrition Information

- 163: calories;
- 4 grams: fat;
- 0 grams: polyunsaturated fat;
- 17 grams: sugars;
- 3 grams: protein;
- 126 milligrams: sodium;
- 2 grams: saturated fat;
- 30 grams: carbohydrates;
- 1 gram: dietary fiber;

113. Fried Green Beans, Scallions And Brussels Sprouts With Buttermilk Cornmeal Coating

Serving: Serves 8 | Prep: | Cook: | Ready in: 30mins

Ingredients

- ½ cup cornstarch
- 2 tablespoons fine polenta or cornmeal
- ½ teaspoon salt, plus additional for sprinkling
- ½ teaspoon baking powder
- 1 cup less 2 tablespoons buttermilk or yogurt thinned with milk
- 3 tablespoons cold sparkling water
- ½ pound green beans
- ½ pound brussels sprouts
- 2 bunches scallions
- Canola or grapeseed oil for frying

Direction

- Combine cornstarch, polenta or cornmeal, salt and baking powder in a bowl and whisk together. Add buttermilk and sparkling water and whisk together until mixture is blended and has the consistency of thick cream.
- Top and tail beans. Trim brussels sprouts and quarter. Trim root end off the scallions and cut away dark green ends.
- Pour oil into a wok or wide saucepan to a depth of 3 inches and heat over medium-high heat to 360 to 375 degrees. Set up a sheet pan with a rack on it next to the pan. Cover rack with a few layers of paper towels. Have a spider or deep fry skimmer handy for removing vegetables from the oil.
- Using tongs, dip vegetables into batter a few at a time, making sure to coat thoroughly. Transfer to hot oil and fry until golden brown, which should not take more than a couple of minutes. Flip over halfway through with the spider to make sure the coating is evenly fried. It is important not to crowd pan and to let oil come back up to temperature between batches.
- Using the spider, remove vegetables from oil, allowing excess oil to drip back into pan, and drain on towel-covered rack. Sprinkle with salt right away if desired. Allow to cool slightly and serve.

Nutrition Information

- 207: calories;
- 3 grams: dietary fiber;
- 2 grams: protein;
- 41 milligrams: sodium;
- 16 grams: carbohydrates;
- 0 grams: trans fat;
- 10 grams: monounsaturated fat;
- 4 grams: polyunsaturated fat;
- 1 gram: saturated fat;

114. Fried Small Peppers Filled With Feta And Quinoa

Serving: 8 servings as an hors d'oeuvre or 4 as a side dish | Prep: | Cook: |Ready in: 30mins

Ingredients

- 8 small sweet peppers, either baby bell or Italian peppers, about 1 pound
- 1 egg yolk
- 3 ounces feta, crumbled (about 3/4 cup)
- ½ cup cooked quinoa or bulgur
- 2 tablespoons finely chopped fresh parsley or mint
- Freshly ground pepper
- 2 tablespoons unbleached all-purpose flour
- 2 to 3 tablespoons sunflower or grapeseed oil, as needed

Direction

- Roast the peppers over a flame or under the broiler until charred. Place in a bowl, cover tightly and allow to cool. Remove the skins and wipe the surface with paper towels.
- With the tip of a paring knife, make a lengthwise slit down the middle of each pepper and carefully pull out the seeds and membranes and remove the stems and seed pods at the top. Open the peppers up on your work surface.
- In a medium bowl beat together the egg yolk and the feta until amalgamated. Add the quinoa or the bulgur and the chopped herbs and stir together. Season with pepper (there's plenty of salt in the feta). Place a spoonful of filling down the middle of each pepper and fold the sides in over the filling, overlapping the edges.
- Heat the oil over medium heat in a wide skillet. Place the flour on a plate. Lightly dredge the peppers in the flour. Fry the peppers gently until nicely browned, 3 to 4 minutes on each side. Use tongs to turn them.

Drain on paper towels. Serve hot, warm or room temperature.

Nutrition Information

- 126: calories;
- 8 grams: fat;
- 3 grams: sugars;
- 2 grams: dietary fiber;
- 10 grams: carbohydrates;
- 4 grams: protein;
- 135 milligrams: sodium;

115. Frittata With Brown Rice, Peas And Pea Shoots

Serving: 6 servings. | Prep: | Cook: |Ready in: 1hours

Ingredients

- 1 pound fresh peas, shelled (about 3/4 cup)
- 6 ounces pea shoots (1/2 big bunch), curly tendrils removed and discarded
- 2 tablespoons extra virgin olive oil
- 1 bunch young spring onions or scallions, cleaned and finely chopped (about 1/2 cup)
- Salt and freshly ground pepper
- 2 tablespoons chopped fresh tarragon
- 1 tablespoon chopped chives
- 1 tablespoon chopped fresh parsley
- 1 cup cooked brown rice, long-grain or short-grain (may substitute cooked basmati or jasmine rice)
- 7 eggs
- 2 tablespoons milk

Direction

- Steam the peas over an inch of boiling water for 4 minutes, until just tender. Transfer to a bowl. Add the pea shoots to the steamer and steam 2 to 3 minutes, until just wilted. Remove from the heat and allow to cool until you can handle them. Do not discard the steaming water; pour it into a measuring cup. Squeeze out excess water from the pea shoots and chop medium-fine. You should have about 1 cup chopped leaves and tender stems.

- Heat 1 tablespoon of the olive oil over medium heat in a medium skillet and add the chopped spring onion or scallions. Cook, stirring, until wilted, about 3 minutes. Stir in the pea shoots and stir together for about a minute. Season to taste with salt and pepper. Add the peas, tarragon and parsley and about 1/4 cup of the steaming water, turn up the heat and cook, stirring, until the liquid has evaporated. Remove from the heat.
- Beat the eggs in a large bowl. Add about 1/2 teaspoon salt (or to taste), freshly ground pepper, and the milk. Stir in the rice, chives and pea mixture and combine well.
- Heat the remaining oil in a 10-inch, preferably nonstick pan over medium-high heat until a drop of egg sizzles and sets within seconds of being added to the pan. Stir the frittata mixture and add it to the pan, scraping in every last bit with a rubber spatula. Shake the pan gently, tilting it slightly with one hand while lifting up the edges of the frittata with the spatula in your other hand, to let the eggs run underneath during the first few minutes of cooking. Once a few layers of egg have cooked during the first couple of minutes of cooking, turn the heat down to low, cover the pan and cook over low heat for 10 minutes, shaking the pan gently every once in a while. From time to time remove the lid and loosen the bottom of the frittata with a wooden spatula, tilting the pan, so that the bottom doesn't burn. The eggs should be just about set; cook a few minutes longer if they're not.
- Meanwhile, heat the broiler. Uncover the pan and place under the broiler, not too close to the heat, for 1 to 3 minutes, watching very carefully to make sure the top doesn't burn (at most, it should brown very slightly and puff under the broiler). Remove from the heat, shake the pan to make sure the frittata isn't sticking and allow it to cool for at least 5 minutes and for up to 15. Loosen the edges

with a wooden or plastic spatula. Carefully slide from the pan onto a large round platter. Cut into wedges and serve hot or warm or at room temperature.

Nutrition Information

- 178: calories;
- 3 grams: dietary fiber;
- 347 milligrams: sodium;
- 2 grams: sugars;
- 0 grams: trans fat;
- 5 grams: monounsaturated fat;
- 13 grams: carbohydrates;
- 9 grams: protein;
- 10 grams: fat;

| 116. | Garlic Shrimp With Peas |

Serving: 6 servings | Prep: | Cook: | Ready in: 45mins

Ingredients

- 1 ½ pounds medium shrimp with shells, shelled and deveined; retain shells
- Salt to taste
- 1 ½ pounds fresh English peas, shelled (1 1/4 to 1 1/2 cups depending on size)
- 3 tablespoons extra-virgin olive oil
- 1 head green garlic or 6 garlic cloves, minced
- ¼ to ½ teaspoon red chile flakes, to taste
- ⅓ cup finely chopped cilantro
- ⅓ cup finely chopped parsley
- Cooked rice for serving, optional

Direction

- Place shrimp shells in a medium saucepan, add 1 quart water and salt to taste. Bring to a boil. Skim off foam, reduce heat, cover partly and simmer 30 minutes. Strain broth into a bowl and discard shells. Return broth to saucepan.

- Meanwhile, sprinkle shrimp with salt, toss and let sit for 15 minutes.
- Return broth to a boil and add peas. Boil 2 minutes, until just wrinkled and slightly tender. Scoop out with a skimmer or slotted spoon and set aside. Measure out 1/2 cup broth and set aside.
- Heat oil over medium heat in a wide heavy skillet. Add garlic and chile flakes. Cook, stirring, until garlic is fragrant and beginning to color, about 1 minute. Turn heat to medium-high and add shrimp. Cook, stirring, until shrimp turns pink, about 2 minutes. Add peas, cilantro and parsley and continue to toss in the pan for another minute. Stir in 1/2 cup broth and heat through while stirring to deglaze pan. Remove from heat, taste and adjust seasoning. Serve.

Nutrition Information

- 246: calories;
- 8 grams: fat;
- 20 grams: carbohydrates;
- 22 grams: protein;
- 651 milligrams: sodium;
- 1 gram: polyunsaturated fat;
- 0 grams: trans fat;
- 5 grams: monounsaturated fat;
- 6 grams: dietary fiber;
- 7 grams: sugars;

117.   Garlic Soup With Spinach

Serving: Serves 4 | Prep: | Cook: | Ready in: 30mins

Ingredients

- 1 ½ quarts chicken stock, turkey stock, vegetable stock, or water
- A bouquet garni made with a bay leaf and a couple of sprigs each thyme and parsley
- Salt and freshly ground pepper to taste
- 2 to 3 large garlic cloves (to taste), minced

- ½ cup elbow macaroni
- 2 eggs
- 1 6-ounce bag baby spinach, or 12 ounces of bunch spinach, stemmed, washed, dried and coarsely chopped
- ¼ cup freshly grated Parmesan (1 ounce)

Direction

- Place the stock or water in a large saucepan or soup pot with the bouquet garni. Season to taste with salt and freshly ground pepper. Bring to a simmer and add the garlic. Cover and simmer 15 minutes. Add the pasta and simmer 5 minutes, until cooked al dente. Remove the bouquet garni.
- Beat the eggs in a bowl and stir in 1/3 cup of stock, making sure that it is not boiling, and the cheese.
- Stir the spinach into the simmering stock and simmer for 1 minute. Drizzle in the egg mixture, scraping all of it in with a rubber spatula. Turn off the heat and stir very slowly with the spatula, paddling it back and forth until the eggs have set. Taste, adjust seasoning, and serve at once.

Nutrition Information

- 255: calories;
- 0 grams: trans fat;
- 26 grams: carbohydrates;
- 18 grams: protein;
- 1043 milligrams: sodium;
- 9 grams: fat;
- 3 grams: monounsaturated fat;
- 1 gram: polyunsaturated fat;
- 2 grams: dietary fiber;
- 6 grams: sugars;

118.   Gingered Winter Fruit Ambrosia

Serving: Serves 6 to 8 | Prep: | Cook: | Ready in: 1hours

Ingredients

- ¼ cup fresh lime juice
- 2 tablespoons mild honey or agave nectar
- 2 teaspoons finely minced or grated fresh ginger
- 2 pink grapefruit
- 2 ripe but firm pears
- ½ pound red grapes, cut in half
- 6 dates, pitted and halved or quartered
- Seeds from 1 small pomegranate
- 1 tablespoon chia seeds (more to taste)
- 2 to 3 tablespoons finely grated coconut (to taste)

Direction

- Whisk together the lime juice, honey or agave nectar and ginger in a small bowl.
- Cut away the peel and white pith from the grapefruit. The easiest way to do this is to cut the ends off, then stand on one end and cut away strips of skin and pith at the same time. Hold the grapefruit over your serving bowl and cut the sections away from the membranes that separate them. Place in the bowl.
- Peel, core and dice the pears. Add to the grapefruit. Add the grapes, dates, pomegranate seeds and chia seeds. Stir the lime-ginger marinade and toss with the fruit. Chill for 30 minutes or longer and toss again.
- Sprinkle the coconut over the top and serve.

Nutrition Information

- 154: calories;
- 2 milligrams: sodium;
- 1 gram: saturated fat;
- 0 grams: polyunsaturated fat;
- 38 grams: carbohydrates;
- 5 grams: dietary fiber;
- 29 grams: sugars;
- 2 grams: protein;

119.   Gluten Free Apple, Pear And Cranberry Pecan Crumble

Serving: 8 servings | Prep: | Cook: | Ready in: 1hours

Ingredients

- For the Topping
- 1 ¼ cups / 125 grams rolled oats
- ½ cup / 70 grams quinoa flour or millet flour (grind quinoa or millet in a spice mill to make the flour)
- ⅓ cup / 63 grams raw brown (turbinado) sugar
- ½ teaspoon freshly grated nutmeg
- ⅛ to ¼ teaspoon salt (to taste)
- 3 ounces (6 tablespoons) cold unsalted butter, cut into 1/2-inch pieces
- ¼ cup / 30 grams pecans
- 1 teaspoon lemon zest
- For the crumble
- 2 pounds / 900 grams / 4 large apples, peeled and cut in approximately 1/2-inch dice (see note)
- 2 tablespoons / 60 grams unsalted butter
- 2 tablespoons / 30 grams raw brown (turbinado) sugar
- 2 tablespoons fresh lemon juice
- 1 teaspoon vanilla extract
- ½ teaspoon cinnamon
- ¼ teaspoon nutmeg
- 1 large ripe but firm pear, peeled, cored and diced
- 1 cup / 60 grams dried cranberries

Direction

- Make crumble topping first. Preheat oven to 350 degrees. Cover a baking sheet with parchment. Place oats, quinoa flour, sugar, salt and nutmeg in a food processor fitted with steel blade and pulse several times to combine. Add the butter and pulse until the butter is evenly distributed throughout the grain mix. The mixture should have a crumbly consistency. You can also combine ingredients in a standing mixer fitted with the paddle and mix at low speed until mixture has a crumbly consistency.

- Spread topping over parchment-covered baking sheet in an even layer. Place in oven and bake 10 minutes. Rotate pan, stir mixture, and bake another 10 minutes, until nicely browned. Remove from heat and allow to cool. Stir in pecans and lemon zest.
- Turn oven up to 375 degrees. Butter a 2-quart baking dish. Cook apples in 2 batches. Heat half the butter over medium-high heat in a large heavy skillet until it foams and foam subsides. Add apples and wait until they begin to sizzle, then add half the sugar and cook, stirring and tossing in the pan, until apples just begin to caramelize, about 10 minutes. Transfer to a bowl and repeat with remaining butter, apples and sugar. When second batch has caramelized, add first batch back into pan, then add lemon juice, vanilla extract, cinnamon and nutmeg and stir together for another minute. Stir in diced pear and dried cranberries and stir everything together. Remove from heat and scrape into buttered baking dish.
- Spread crumble topping over apple mixture in an even layer. Place in oven and bake 30 minutes, until bubbling and top is nicely browned. Allow to cool for at least 10 minutes before serving.

Nutrition Information

- 392: calories;
- 4 grams: protein;
- 10 grams: saturated fat;
- 54 grams: carbohydrates;
- 1 gram: trans fat;
- 6 grams: dietary fiber;
- 2 grams: polyunsaturated fat;
- 31 grams: sugars;
- 61 milligrams: sodium;
- 19 grams: fat;

---

120.   Gluten Free Apple Almond Tart

Serving: 8 to 10 servings | Prep: | Cook: | Ready in: 1hours

Ingredients

- 3 large apples, preferably Braeburn or Fuji, peeled, cored, and cut in 1/2 inch dice (500 grams diced cored apples)
- 1 tablespoon freshly squeezed lemon juice or lime juice
- 1 tablespoon unsalted butter
- ¼ cup turbinado sugar, also known as sugar in the raw (50 grams)
- 1 ½ teaspoons vanilla
- ½ teaspoon cinnamon
- ¼ teaspoon nutmeg
- ¼ cup egg whites (60 grams)
- 2 tablespoons sugar, preferably organic white or brown sugar (30 grams)
- ½ cup slivered almonds (50 grams)
- 1 9-inch gluten-free dessert pastry shell (or other pastry of your choice), fully baked

Direction

- Preheat the oven to 350 degrees. Toss the apples with the lemon juice in a medium bowl. Line a sheet pan with parchment.
- Heat a large frying pan over high heat and add the butter. Wait until it stops foaming and is becoming light brown, and add the diced apples, turbinado sugar, vanilla, cinnamon and nutmeg. Spread the apples in a layer and cook without moving them for a couple of minutes, then turn the heat to medium-high and sauté, moving the apples around in the pan, until golden brown, about 5 to 7 minutes. Scrape out onto the lined sheet pan and allow to cool completely.
- Spread the cooled apples evenly over the pre-baked tart shell.
- Make the almond topping. Beat the egg whites lightly in a bowl, just until slightly foamy.

Whisk in the sugar and stir in the almonds. Spread evenly over the apples.

- Place the tart on a sheet pan and bake in the preheated oven for 30 minutes, or until the crust and topping are golden brown. Remove from the oven and cool on a rack.

Nutrition Information

- 178: calories;
- 25 grams: carbohydrates;
- 15 grams: sugars;
- 94 milligrams: sodium;
- 8 grams: fat;
- 2 grams: protein;
- 0 grams: trans fat;
- 4 grams: monounsaturated fat;

121. Gluten Free Banana Chocolate Muffins

Serving: 16 muffins (1/3 cup capacity) | Prep: | Cook: | Ready in: 45mins

Ingredients

- 75 grams (approximately 1/2 cup) buckwheat flour
- 75 grams (approximately 3/4 cup) almond powder (also known as almond flour)
- 140 grams (approximately 1 cup) whole grain or all-purpose gluten free flour mix
- 32 grams (approximately 6 tablespoons) dark cocoa powder
- 10 grams (2 teaspoons) baking powder
- 5 grams (1 teaspoon) baking soda
- 3 ½ grams (rounded 1/2 teaspoon) salt
- 100 grams (approximately 1/2 cup) raw brown sugar or packed light brown sugar
- 2 eggs
- 75 grams (1/3 cup) canola or grape seed oil
- 120 grams (1/2 cup) plain low-fat yogurt or buttermilk
- 5 grams (1 teaspoon) vanilla extract
- 330 grams ripe bananas (peeled weight), about 3 medium, mashed (1 1/4 cups)
- 115 grams (about 2/3 cup) semi-sweet or bittersweet chocolate chips or chopped bittersweet chocolate

Direction

- Preheat the oven to 350 degrees. Oil or butter muffin tins. Sift the dry ingredients into a large bowl. Pour in any bits that remain in the sifter.
- In another large bowl or in the bowl of a standing mixer fitted with the whip attachment beat together the oil and sugar until creamy. Beat in the eggs and beat until incorporated, then beat in the yogurt or buttermilk, the vanilla and the mashed bananas. Add the dry ingredients and mix at low speed or whisk gently until combined. If using a mixer, scrape down the sides of the bowl and the beaters. Fold in the chocolate chips.
- Using a spoon or ice cream scoop, fill muffin cups to the top. Place in the oven and bake 30 minutes, until a muffin springs back lightly when touched. Remove from the heat and if the muffins come out of the tins easily, remove from the tins and place on a rack. I like these best served warm, but if they don't release easily allow them to cool, then remove from the tins.

Nutrition Information

- 205: calories;
- 163 milligrams: sodium;
- 11 grams: fat;
- 0 grams: trans fat;
- 4 grams: protein;
- 27 grams: carbohydrates;
- 2 grams: monounsaturated fat;
- 3 grams: dietary fiber;
- 13 grams: sugars;

122. Gluten Free Buckwheat, Poppy Seed And Blueberry Muffins

Serving: 12 muffins (1/3 cup muffin tins) | Prep: | Cook: | Ready in: 45mins

Ingredients

- 180 grams (1 1/4 cups, approximately) buckwheat flour
- 100 grams (3/4 cup, approximately) gluten-free all-purpose flour mix or whole grain gluten-free mix
- 10 grams (2 teaspoons) baking powder
- 5 grams (1 teaspoon) baking soda
- 3 ½ grams (1/2 rounded teaspoon) salt
- 2 eggs
- 125 grams (1/3 cup) honey
- 360 grams (1 1/2 cups) buttermilk
- 75 grams (1/3 cup) canola or grape seed oil
- 5 grams (1 teaspoon) vanilla extract
- 170 grams (6 ounces/1 cup) blueberries
- 10 grams (1 tablespoon) poppy seeds (more to taste)

Direction

- Preheat the oven to 375 degrees with the rack adjusted to the middle. Oil or butter muffin tins. Sift together the flours, baking powder, baking soda and salt into a medium bowl. Add any grainy bits remaining in the sifter to the bowl.
- In a separate bowl beat together the eggs, honey, buttermilk, oil and vanilla extract. Whisk in the dry ingredients and mix until well combined. Do not beat for too long; a few lumps are fine but make sure there is no flour sitting at the bottom of the bowl. Fold in the blueberries and poppy seeds.
- Using a spoon or ice cream scoop, fill muffin cups to the top. Place in the oven and bake 25 to 30 minutes, until lightly browned and well risen. Remove from the heat and if the muffins come out of the tins easily, remove from the tins and allow to cool on a rack. If they don't

release easily, allow to cool and then remove from the tins.

Nutrition Information

- 200: calories;
- 29 grams: carbohydrates;
- 3 grams: dietary fiber;
- 8 grams: fat;
- 1 gram: saturated fat;
- 0 grams: trans fat;
- 2 grams: monounsaturated fat;
- 5 grams: protein;
- 12 grams: sugars;
- 249 milligrams: sodium;

123. Gluten Free Chocolate Buckwheat Biscotti

Serving: 3 1/2 to 4 dozen biscotti | Prep: | Cook: | Ready in: 2hours

Ingredients

- 88 grams (approximately 3/4 cup) buckwheat flour
- 37 grams (approximately scant 1/3 cup) cornstarch (or omit cornstarch and use 125 grams total buckwheat flour)
- 120 grams (approximately 1 cup) almond flour
- 60 grams (approximately 1/2 cup) unsweetened cocoa
- 10 grams (2 teaspoons) instant espresso powder or coffee extract
- 10 grams (2 teaspoons) baking powder
- 4 grams (1/2 teaspoon) salt
- 55 grams (2 ounces) unsalted butter
- 125 grams (approximately 2/3 cup, tightly packed) organic brown sugar
- 110 grams (2 large) eggs
- 10 grams (2 teaspoons) vanilla extract
- 100 grams (1 cup) walnuts, chopped

Direction

- Preheat the oven to 300 degrees. Line a baking sheet with parchment. In a medium bowl, mix together the buckwheat flour, cornstarch (if using), almond flour, cocoa, instant espresso powder (if using), baking powder and salt.
- In the bowl of an electric mixer cream the butter and sugar for 2 minutes on medium speed. Scrape down the sides of the bowl and the beater with a rubber spatula and add the eggs, coffee extract (if using) and vanilla extract. Beat together for 1 to 2 minutes, until well blended. Scrape down the sides of the bowl and the beater. Add the flour mixture and beat at low speed until well blended. Add the walnuts and beat at low speed until mixed evenly through the dough.
- Divide the dough and shape 2 wide, flat logs, about 10 inches long by 3 inches wide by 3/4 inch high. Make sure they are at least 2 inches apart on the baking sheet. Place in the oven on the middle rack and bake 40 to 45 minutes, until dry, beginning to crack in the middle, and firm. Remove from the oven and allow to cool for 20 minutes or longer.
- Place the logs on a cutting board and carefully cut into 1/2-inch thick slices. Place on two parchment-covered baking sheets and bake one sheet at a time in the middle of the oven until the slices are dry, 30 to 35 minutes. Remove from the oven and allow to cool.

Nutrition Information

- 66: calories;
- 4 grams: fat;
- 1 gram: dietary fiber;
- 0 grams: trans fat;
- 7 grams: carbohydrates;
- 3 grams: sugars;
- 2 grams: protein;
- 37 milligrams: sodium;

124. Gluten Free Cornmeal Molasses Muffins

Serving: 12 muffins (1/3 cup tins) | Prep: | Cook: | Ready in: 45mins

Ingredients

- 140 grams (approximately 1 cup) cornmeal
- 140 grams (approximately 1 cup) whole grain gluten-free mix or all-purpose gluten-free mix
- 35 grams (approximately 1/4 cup) soy flour or additional all-purpose gluten-free mix
- 2 7/10 grams (1 teaspoon) ground ginger
- 10 grams (2 teaspoons) baking powder
- 5 grams (1 teaspoon) baking soda
- 3 ½ grams (rounded 1/2 teaspoon) salt
- 2 eggs
- 240 grams (1 cup) plain low-fat yogurt or buttermilk
- 175 grams (1/2 cup) blackstrap molasses
- 5 grams (1 teaspoon) vanilla
- 75 grams (1/3 cup) canola or grape seed oil
- Optional
- 75 grams (1/2 cup) raisins (optional)

Direction

- Preheat the oven to 375 degrees with a rack in the middle. Oil or butter muffin tins. Sift together the cornmeal, gluten-free flour mix, soy flour, ginger, baking powder, baking soda and salt into a medium bowl. Pour in any grainy bits that remain in the sifter.
- In a separate large bowl whisk the eggs with the buttermilk, molasses, vanilla and oil. Quickly whisk in the cornmeal mixture. Fold in the raisins.
- Using a spoon or ice cream scoop, fill muffin cups to the top. Place in the oven and bake 25 to 30 minutes, until lightly browned and well risen. Remove from the heat and if the muffins come out of the tins easily, remove from the tins and allow to cool on a rack. If they don't release easily, allow to cool and then remove from the tins.

Nutrition Information

- 179: calories;
- 8 grams: fat;
- 5 grams: polyunsaturated fat;
- 23 grams: carbohydrates;
- 13 grams: sugars;
- 211 milligrams: sodium;
- 1 gram: dietary fiber;
- 0 grams: trans fat;
- 2 grams: monounsaturated fat;
- 4 grams: protein;

125.   Gluten Free Cornmeal, Fig And Orange Muffins

Serving: 12 muffins (1/3 cup tins) | Prep: | Cook: | Ready in: 45mins

Ingredients

- 125 grams (scant cup) figs, chopped
- 145 grams (approximately 1/2 cup) freshly squeezed orange juice
- 140 grams (approximately 1 cup) cornmeal
- 140 grams (approximately 1 cup) gluten-free whole grain mix made with rice flour and the starch of your choice
- 5 ½ grams salt (3/4 teaspoon)
- 15 grams baking powder (1 tablespoon)
- 2 ½ grams baking soda (1/2 teaspoon)
- 2 eggs
- 300 grams buttermilk (1 1/4 cups)
- 50 grams mild honey, such as clover (2 tablespoons)
- 60 grams canola or grape seed oil (1/4 cup)

Direction

- Place the figs in a bowl and pour in the orange juice. Let steep for 1 hour. Drain and weigh or measure out 60 grams (1/4 cup) of the orange juice and add it to the buttermilk. Set aside the rest for another purpose.

- Preheat the oven to 375 degrees. Oil or butter muffin tins. Sift together the cornmeal, gluten free flour mix, salt, baking powder and baking soda into a medium bowl. Pour in any grainy bits that remain in the sifter.
- In a separate large bowl whisk the eggs with the buttermilk, orange juice, honey, and oil. Quickly whisk in the flour and cornmeal mixture. Fold in the figs.
- Using a spoon or ice cream scoop, fill muffin cups to the top. Place in the oven and bake 25 to 30 minutes, until lightly browned and well risen. Remove from the heat and if the muffins come out of the tins easily, remove from the tins and allow to cool on a rack. If they don't release easily, allow to cool and then remove from the tins.

Nutrition Information

- 173: calories;
- 204 milligrams: sodium;
- 6 grams: fat;
- 1 gram: dietary fiber;
- 0 grams: trans fat;
- 3 grams: protein;
- 28 grams: carbohydrates;
- 7 grams: sugars;

126.   Gluten Free Dessert Pastry

Serving: 2 9-inch crusts | Prep: | Cook: | Ready in: 30mins

Ingredients

- 160 grams (approximately 1 1/4 cups) corn flour or finely ground cornmeal
- 150 grams (approximately 1 1/3 cups) oat flour (make sure it is from a gluten-free facility)
- 168 grams (6 ounces) butter, preferably French style Plugrà

- 4 grams (1/2 teaspoon) fine sea salt
- 50 grams (approximately 1/4 rounded cup) sugar
- 40 grams (approximately 1/3 rounded cup) almond flour
- 9 grams (approximately 2 teaspoons) vanilla extract
- 63 grams egg (approximately 1 extra large plus 2 teaspoons), beaten

Direction

- Sift together the corn flour and the oat flour. In a stand mixer fitted with the paddle attachment, or in a bowl with a rubber spatula, cream the butter and salt on medium speed for about 1 minute, taking care not to whip. Scrape down the sides of the bowl and the paddle with a rubber spatula and add the sugar. Combine with the butter at low speed. Scrape down the sides of the bowl and the paddle.
- Add the almond flour and vanilla extract and combine at low speed.
- Gradually add the egg and one fourth of the flour mixture. Beat at low speed until just incorporated. Stop the machine and scrape down the bowl and the paddle.
- Gradually add the remaining flour and mix just until the dough comes together.
- Scrape the dough out of the bowl, weigh it and divide it into 2 equal pieces. Place each piece between sheets of plastic wrap and gently roll out to a 10-1/2 inch circle. Place on a sheet pan and refrigerate for 1 hour or (preferably) longer.
- Very lightly butter a 9-inch tart pan or pie dish (depending on the recipe you'll be using this for). You should not be able to see the butter. Remove one sheet of dough from the refrigerator, and if it is very stiff set it out for about 5 minutes, until it's pliable. Ease the dough into 9-inch tart pan or pie dish. If the dough cracks, just pinch the cracked edges together. You do not have to worry with gluten-free dough about over working and

stiffening the pastry, but try not to press the dough thinner in some places than in others.

| 127. | Gluten Free Penne With Peas, Ricotta And Tarragon |

Serving: 4 servings | Prep: | Cook: | Ready in: 10mins

Ingredients

- Salt to taste
- ¾ pound gluten-free penne, such as quinoa and rice
- 2 cups frozen peas, thawed
- 1 garlic clove, mashed with a pinch of salt in a mortar and pestle or put through a press
- ½ cup fresh ricotta
- 2 tablespoons minced tarragon
- Freshly ground pepper to taste
- ¼ cup grated Parmesan

Direction

- Bring a large pot of water to a boil and salt generously. Add pasta and peas. While pasta is cooking, mix together garlic, ricotta and tarragon in a large bowl. Season to taste with salt and pepper.
- When the pasta is cooked al dente, remove 1/4 cup of the pasta water and mix 2 to 4 tablespoons of it with the ricotta. It should have the consistency of cream. Add a little more water if it doesn't. Drain pasta and peas and toss with ricotta mixture and Parmesan. Serve at once.

Nutrition Information

- 451: calories;
- 3 grams: polyunsaturated fat;
- 66 grams: carbohydrates;
- 9 grams: dietary fiber;
- 22 grams: protein;
- 447 milligrams: sodium;

- 11 grams: fat;
- 4 grams: sugars;

---

128. Gluten Free Raisin Pistachio Biscotti

Serving: 3 1/2 to 4 dozen biscotti | Prep: | Cook: | Ready in: 2hours30mins

Ingredients

- 120 grams (approximately 2/3 cup) golden raisins
- 125 grams (approximately 1 cup) millet meal or fine cornmeal
- 60 grams (approximately 1/2 cup) cornstarch
- 150 grams (approximately 1 1/4 cups) almond flour
- 10 grams (approximately 2 teaspoons) baking powder
- 1 gram (approximately 1/4 teaspoon) salt
- 55 grams (2 ounces) butter, at room temperature
- 125 grams (approximately 2/3 cup, tightly packed) organic brown sugar
- 110 grams eggs (2 large)
- 5 grams (1 teaspoon) vanilla extract
- 2 grams (1/2 teaspoon) almond extract
- 100 grams (approximately 3/4 cup) chopped lightly toasted pistachios

Direction

- Place the raisins in a bowl and cover with warm water (or see variation below). Let sit for 10 minutes, then drain and set the raisins on paper towels.
- Preheat the oven to 300 degrees. Line a baking sheet with parchment. In a medium bowl, mix together the millet flour or cornmeal, cornstarch, almond flour, baking powder and salt.
- In the bowl of an electric mixer cream the butter and sugar for 2 minutes on medium speed. Scrape down the sides of the bowl and

the beater with a rubber spatula and add the eggs, vanilla extract and almond extract. Beat together for 1 to 2 minutes, until well blended. Scrape down the sides of the bowl and the beater. Add the flour mixture and beat at low speed until well blended. Add the pistachios and raisins and beat at low speed until mixed evenly through the dough.

- Divide the dough and shape into 2 wide, flat logs, about 10 inches long by 3 inches wide by 3/4 inch high. Make sure they are at least 2 inches apart on the baking sheet. Place in the oven on the middle rack and bake 50 minutes, until dry, beginning to crack in the middle, and firm. Remove from the oven and allow to cool for 30 minutes or longer.
- Place the logs on a cutting board and carefully cut into 1/2-inch thick slices. Place on two parchment-covered baking sheets and bake one sheet at a time in the middle of the oven for 10 minutes. Turn over and bake for another 10 to 15 minutes, until the slices are dry and lightly browned.

Nutrition Information

- 79: calories;
- 31 milligrams: sodium;
- 4 grams: fat;
- 1 gram: dietary fiber;
- 0 grams: polyunsaturated fat;
- 10 grams: carbohydrates;
- 5 grams: sugars;
- 2 grams: protein;

---

129. Gluten Free Spaghetti With Baby Broccoli, Mushrooms And Walnuts

Serving: Serves 4 | Prep: | Cook: | Ready in: 30mins

Ingredients

- 2 garlic cloves, minced

- ¼ to ½ teaspoon red pepper flakes (to taste)
- 1 teaspoon fresh thyme or 1/2 teaspoon dried
- ¼ cup chopped walnuts
- ¼ cup chopped flat-leaf parsley
- ¾ pound gluten-free spaghetti, such as quinoa or quinoa, amaranth and rice
- Freshly grated Parmesan

Direction

- Begin heating a large pot of water. Trim the very bottoms away from baby broccoli and slice stalks. Keep sliced stalks and florets separate. Fill a bowl with cold water.
- When the water comes to a boil add salt to taste, drop in broccoli stalks and set the timer for 4 minutes. After 2 minutes add florets and blanch for 2 minutes. Using a Chinese skimmer, a strainer or a slotted spoon, transfer all of the baby broccoli to the cold water, then drain. Set aside in a bowl.
- Heat 1 tablespoon of the olive oil over medium-high heat in a large, heavy skillet or a wide, heavy saucepan and add mushrooms. Don't stir for 30 seconds to a minute so that mushrooms sear, then stir and cook, stirring often, until they have begun to soften and sweat, about 3 minutes. Add garlic and red pepper flakes. Cook, stirring, until fragrant, 30 seconds to a minute, until garlic is fragrant, and add thyme, walnuts and salt and pepper to taste. Continue to cook until mushrooms are tender, fragrant and juicy, another 3 to 5 minutes. Stir in broccoli and parsley, add salt and pepper to taste, and cook, stirring, for another minute. Remove from heat, taste and adjust seasoning. Keep warm.
- Bring water in pot back to a boil and add pasta. Cook al dente, using timing instructions on the package as a guide but checking pasta a minute before the time indicated is up. When pasta is ready, use a ladle to transfer 1/4 to 1/2 cup of the pasta cooking water to pan with the broccoli and mushrooms. Drain pasta and toss at once with broccoli and mushroom mixture and the remaining tablespoon of olive oil. Serve hot, passing Parmesan at the table.

Serving: 12 muffins | Prep: | Cook: | Ready in: 1hours30mins

Ingredients

- 1 cup granola
- ½ cup low-fat milk
- 1 cup golden raisins
- 1 cup whole wheat flour
- 2 teaspoons baking powder
- ½ teaspoon baking soda
- ¼ teaspoon salt
- 2 large or extra large eggs
- ¼ cup mild honey, such as clover
- ½ cup buttermilk or plain low-fat yogurt
- ¼ cup canola oil
- 1 teaspoon vanilla extract

Direction

- Preheat the oven to 375ºF with a rack in the middle. Oil 12 muffin cups. Combine the granola and milk in a bowl and let sit for 30 minutes. Meanwhile, cover the raisins with hot water and soak for 15 minutes. Drain and dry on paper towels.
- Sift together whole wheat flour, baking powder, baking soda, and salt.
- In medium bowl, beat together the eggs, honey, buttermilk or yogurt, canola oil and vanilla. Quickly whisk in the flour, then fold in the granola and raisins. Combine well
- Spoon into muffin cups, filling each about 3/4 full. Bake 20 to 25 minutes, until lightly browned. Cool in the tins for 10 minutes, then unmold and cool on a rack.

Nutrition Information

- 207: calories;
- 8 grams: fat;

- 1 gram: saturated fat;
- 3 grams: polyunsaturated fat;
- 2 grams: dietary fiber;
- 174 milligrams: sodium;
- 0 grams: trans fat;
- 4 grams: monounsaturated fat;
- 30 grams: carbohydrates;
- 16 grams: sugars;
- 5 grams: protein;

131. Greek Baked Squash Omelet

Serving: Serves six to eight | Prep: | Cook: | Ready in: 1hours

Ingredients

- 2 tablespoons extra virgin olive oil
- 1 leek, white and light green parts, cleaned and chopped
- 2 garlic cloves, minced
- ¾ pound winter squash or zucchini, cut in 1/4- to 1/3-inch dice
- Salt
- freshly ground pepper to taste
- ¼ cup chopped fresh dill
- 2 tablespoons chopped fresh mint
- 8 eggs
- ½ cup drained yogurt or thick Greek-style yogurt
- ¼ cup freshly grated Parmesan cheese

Direction

- Preheat the oven to 350 degrees.
- Heat 1 tablespoon of the oil over medium heat in a large, heavy skillet. Add the leek and cook, stirring, until tender, about three minutes. Add the garlic, stir together until fragrant, about 30 seconds, and add the squash. Cook, stirring, until tender, 10 to 12 minutes for winter squash, about 8 minutes for zucchini. Season to taste with salt and pepper.

Stir in the dill and the mint. Remove from the heat.
- Place the remaining tablespoon of oil in a 2-quart casserole or in a 9-inch cast iron skillet, brush the sides of the pan with the oil and place in the oven. Meanwhile, whisk the eggs in a large bowl. Season with salt and freshly ground pepper to taste. Whisk in the yogurt and the Parmesan. Stir in the squash or zucchini mixture.
- Remove the baking dish from the oven and scrape in the egg mixture. Place in the oven, and bake 30 minutes or until puffed and lightly colored. Allow to cool for at least 10 minutes before serving. Serve hot, warm or at room temperature.

Nutrition Information

- 145: calories;
- 3 grams: saturated fat;
- 1 gram: dietary fiber;
- 2 grams: sugars;
- 289 milligrams: sodium;
- 9 grams: protein;
- 7 grams: carbohydrates;
- 0 grams: trans fat;
- 4 grams: monounsaturated fat;

132. Green Bean Salad With Lime Vinaigrette And Red Quinoa

Serving: Serves 4 | Prep: | Cook: | Ready in: 20mins

Ingredients

- ¾ pound green beans, trimmed
- 2 to 4 tablespoons chopped red or white onion
- ¼ cup chopped toasted almonds (30 grams)
- 1 green or red serrano or Thai chile pepper, minced (more to taste)
- ¼ cup chopped cilantro

- 1 tablespoon minced chives
- 2 tablespoons fresh lime juice
- Salt to taste
- ¼ cup extra-virgin olive oil
- 1 cup cooked red quinoa
- 1 hard-boiled egg, finely chopped

Direction

- Fill a medium saucepan with water and bring to a boil. Add salt to taste and green beans. Boil 4 to 5 minutes, until crisp-tender. Transfer to a bowl of cold water, then drain and drain again on a kitchen towel. Cut in 2-inch lengths.
- Meanwhile, soak onion in cold water for 5 minutes. Drain, rinse, and drain again on paper towels.
- In a salad bowl, combine green beans, onion, almonds, chile, cilantro, and chives.
- Combine lime juice, salt, and olive oil in a small bowl or measuring cup and whisk together. Toss with beans. Add quinoa and toss again. Sprinkle chopped egg on top, and serve.

Nutrition Information

- 270: calories;
- 20 grams: carbohydrates;
- 7 grams: protein;
- 443 milligrams: sodium;
- 19 grams: fat;
- 3 grams: saturated fat;
- 11 grams: monounsaturated fat;
- 5 grams: sugars;

---

133. Green Pipian

Serving: Makes about 1 3/4 cups | Prep: | Cook: | Ready in: 40mins

Ingredients

- ½ cup hulled untoasted pumpkin seeds

- ½ pound tomatillos, husked, rinsed, and coarsely chopped, or 2 13-ounce cans, drained
- 1 serrano chile or 1/2 jalapeño (more to taste), stemmed and roughly chopped
- 3 romaine lettuce leaves, torn into pieces
- ¼ small white onion, coarsely chopped, soaked for 5 minutes in cold water, drained and rinsed
- 2 garlic cloves, halved, green shoots removed
- ¼ cup loosely packed chopped cilantro
- 1 ½ cups chicken stock
- 1 tablespoon canola or extra virgin olive oil
- Salt, preferably kosher salt, to taste

Direction

- Heat a heavy Dutch oven or saucepan over medium heat and add the pumpkin seeds. Wait until you hear one pop, then stir constantly until they have puffed and popped, and smell toasty. They should not get any darker than golden or they will taste bitter. Transfer to a bowl and allow to cool.
- Place the cooled pumpkin seeds in a blender and add the tomatillos, chiles, lettuce, onion, garlic, cilantro, and 1/2 cup of the chicken stock. Cover the blender and blend the mixture until smooth, stopping the blender to stir if necessary.
- Heat the oil in the Dutch oven or heavy saucepan over medium-high heat. Drizzle in a bit of the pumpkin seed mixture and if it sizzles, add the rest. Cook, stirring, until the mixture darkens and thickens, 8 to 10 minutes. It will splutter, so be careful. Hold the lid of the pot above the pot to shield you and your stove from the splutters. Add the remaining chicken stock, bring to a simmer, reduce the heat to medium-low and simmer uncovered, stirring often, until the sauce is thick and creamy, 15 to 20 minutes. Season to taste with salt. For a silkier sauce, blend again in batches.

Nutrition Information

- 176: calories;
- 2 grams: dietary fiber;

- 0 grams: trans fat;
- 9 grams: carbohydrates;
- 416 milligrams: sodium;
- 13 grams: fat;
- 6 grams: monounsaturated fat;
- 4 grams: sugars;
- 8 grams: protein;

---

134. Green Smoothie With Cucumber And Cumin

Serving: 1 generous serving | Prep: | Cook: | Ready in: 2mins

Ingredients

- 1 cup kefir
- ½ cup chopped celery
- 1 cup chopped cucumber (seedless) (about 5 ounces)
- 2 tablespoons chopped flat-leaf parsley
- 1 tablespoon fresh mint leaves
- ½ cup, tightly packed, greens such as kale, chard, spinach
- 1 quarter-size slice ginger, peeled
- ½ teaspoon chia seeds
- ½ teaspoon lightly toasted cumin seeds
- 2 teaspoons fresh lemon juice
- Pinch of cayenne (more to taste)

Direction

- Place all of the ingredients in a blender and blend at high speed for 1 minute. Serve.

Nutrition Information

- 248: calories;
- 5 grams: dietary fiber;
- 0 grams: trans fat;
- 3 grams: monounsaturated fat;
- 31 grams: carbohydrates;
- 15 grams: sugars;
- 10 grams: fat;

- 183 milligrams: sodium;
- 1 gram: polyunsaturated fat;
- 12 grams: protein;

---

135. Green Smoothie With Pineapple, Arugula, Greens And Cashews

Serving: 1 generous serving | Prep: | Cook: | Ready in: 2mins

Ingredients

- ¼ pineapple, peeled, cored and cut into chunks (about 6 ounces peeled and cored pineapple)
- ¾ cup freshly squeezed orange juice (or the juice that accumulates after cutting up the pineapple mixed with enough orange juice to make 3/4 cup)
- 2 tablespoons raw cashews (about 3/4 ounce)
- ½ teaspoon chia seeds
- ¼ cup, tightly packed, arugula (about 1/4 ounce)
- ¾ cup, tightly packed (or 3 handfuls – about 1 1/2 ounces) mixed baby greens
- 1 quarter-size slice ginger, peeled
- 2 or 3 ice cubes

Direction

- Place all of the ingredients in a blender and blend for 1 minute, or until smooth.

---

136. Green Tomato Salsa Verde

Serving: About 1 3/4 cups (more if thinned with water) | Prep: | Cook: | Ready in: 45mins

Ingredients

- 1 pound green tomatoes
- 2 to 3 jalapeño or serrano peppers (more to taste)
- ½ medium onion, preferably a white onion, chopped, soaked for five minutes in cold water, drained, rinsed and drained again on paper towels
- Salt to taste
- ½ cup roughly chopped cilantro
- ¼ to ½ cup water, as needed (optional)

Direction

- Preheat the broiler. Line a baking sheet with foil. Place the green tomatoes on the baking sheet, stem-side down, and place under the broiler about 2 inches from the heat. Broil two to five minutes, until charred. Using tongs, turn the tomatoes over, and grill on the other side for two to five minutes, until blackened. Remove from the heat. When cool enough to handle, core the tomatoes and remove the charred skin. Quarter and place in a blender or a food processor fitted with a steel blade (I prefer the blender).
- Add the remaining ingredients, except the water, to the blender or food processor, and blend to a coarse or a smooth puree (to your taste). Transfer to a bowl, taste and adjust seasonings, and thin out with water if desired. Allow to stand for 30 minutes or longer before serving to allow the flavors to develop. You may wish to thin out after it stands.

Nutrition Information

- 39: calories;
- 0 grams: polyunsaturated fat;
- 9 grams: carbohydrates;
- 2 grams: protein;
- 6 grams: sugars;
- 358 milligrams: sodium;

137.   Greens And Chayote Enchiladas With Salsa Verde

Serving: 6 to 8 servings | Prep: | Cook: |Ready in: 2hours

Ingredients

- 1 pound Swiss or rainbow chard, or a combination
- 2 medium-size chayote or summer squash (about 1 1/4 pounds), cut in small dice (4 cups diced)
- 1 pound fresh tomatillos, husked and rinsed
- 2 jalapeño or 2 to 3 serrano chiles, stemmed
- ½ white onion, coarsely chopped
- Salt to taste
- 4 large peeled garlic cloves; 2 whole and 2 minced
- 12 cilantro sprigs, plus chopped cilantro for garnish
- 1 tablespoon canola or grapeseed oil, plus 1/3 cup for frying
- 2 ½ cups chicken or vegetable stock
- 2 tablespoons extra-virgin olive oil
- 1 teaspoon Mexican oregano
- Black pepper
- 18 corn tortillas
- About 1/2 cup crumbled queso fresco or feta

Direction

- Strip chard leaves from stems and wash in 2 changes of water. Rinse stems and cut in small dice if wide, or, if thin, slice crosswise 1/4 inch thick. Set aside stems with chayote in one bowl and leaves in another.
- Make the salsa verde: Combine tomatillos, jalapeños and onion in a medium saucepan; cover with water and bring to a boil. Reduce heat and simmer 10 minutes, until tomatillos have gone from pale green to olive and have softened. Using a slotted spoon, transfer tomatillos, onion and one of the jalapeños to a blender. Do not drain water from pot. Let vegetables cool in blender while you blanch greens and chayote.

- Add more water to the pot so it is about 2/3 full. Return to a boil, salt generously, and add leaves. Blanch until tender, 1 to 2 minutes. Transfer leaves to a bowl of cold water to quickly shock, then drain and dry. Chop coarsely and set aside.
- Return water to a simmer and add chayote and chard stems. Simmer 5 minutes, or until just tender. Drain through a colander and again on paper towels.
- Add whole garlic cloves and cilantro sprigs to ingredients in blender and blend until smooth. Taste for heat and add remaining jalapeño if desired.
- Heat 1 tablespoon canola oil in a large, heavy saucepan over medium-high heat. When hot, add tomatillo purée and partly cover to protect from splattering. Cook, stirring often, until it thickens and begins to stick to the pan, about 5 minutes.
- Stir in stock, add salt to taste, and bring to a simmer. Cook uncovered for 20 minutes, stirring often, until sauce is thick and coats the front and back of a spoon. Taste and adjust seasoning.
- Heat olive oil in medium skillet over medium heat and add minced garlic. When fragrant, after about 30 seconds, stir in oregano, blanched leaves, stems and chayote. Cook, stirring for about 3 minutes, until tender, fragrant and coated with oil. Season with salt and pepper. Stir in 1 cup salsa verde and set aside.
- Prepare the tortillas: Heat 1/3 cup canola oil in a medium skillet over medium heat, until oil bubbles around the edges of a tortilla when you dip it into the pan. Place a platter covered with paper towels next to pan. Using tongs, slide tortillas, one at a time, into hot oil. As soon as tortilla begins to puff, about 10 to 15 seconds, flip over and leave another 10 to 15 seconds. Immediately remove from pan and drain on paper towels. Cover with foil to keep warm.
- One by one, quickly dip tortillas into the remaining warm salsa verde, lay on serving platter, and top with about 1/4 cup filling.

Roll up tortilla and place seam side down on platter. When all tortillas have been filled, pour remaining salsa verde on top, sprinkle with cilantro and queso fresco and serve.

Nutrition Information

- 341: calories;
- 0 grams: trans fat;
- 6 grams: sugars;
- 9 grams: protein;
- 37 grams: carbohydrates;
- 7 grams: dietary fiber;
- 762 milligrams: sodium;
- 3 grams: saturated fat;
- 19 grams: fat;

138. Grilled Eggplant And Tomatoes With Chermoula

Serving: Serves 4 | Prep: | Cook: | Ready in: 15mins

Ingredients

- 1 recipe chermoula (see recipe)
- 2 long Asian-style eggplants
- 4 medium tomatoes, halved
- 2 to 4 tablespoons olive oil, as needed

Direction

- Prepare a hot grill. Cut the eggplants in half lengthwise, sprinkle with salt and brush on both sides with olive oil. Cut the tomatoes in half, sprinkle with salt and toss with 1 tablespoon olive oil. Grill the eggplant on both sides until soft and charred. Grill the tomatoes on the cut side until grill marks appear, turn and grill briefly on the other side.
- Transfer the grilled vegetables to a platter. Spoon chermoula over the top. Serve hot or at room temperature.

Nutrition Information

- 275: calories;
- 3 grams: saturated fat;
- 7 grams: monounsaturated fat;
- 23 grams: carbohydrates;
- 13 grams: sugars;
- 297 milligrams: sodium;
- 20 grams: fat;
- 1 gram: polyunsaturated fat;
- 10 grams: dietary fiber;
- 5 grams: protein;

---

139.   Grilled Goat Cheese, Roasted Pepper, And Greens Sandwich

Serving: 1 serving | Prep: | Cook: | Ready in: 30mins

Ingredients

- 1 red pepper, roasted (you'll need only half of it for 1 sandwich)
- Salt and freshly ground pepper to taste
- 1 trimmed artichoke heart, quartered if small, sliced about 1/2 inch thick if large and tossed with 1 tablespoon extra-virgin olive oil and salt and pepper to taste (optional)
- 1 tablespoon chopped blanched greens, such as beet greens, chard, or spinach
- 1 ounce goat cheese (about 1/4 cup)
- 2 slices whole-grain country bread
- 1 ½ teaspoons extra-virgin olive oil
- 1 clove garlic (optional)

Direction

- Dice roasted red pepper small and toss with salt, pepper and a teaspoon of olive oil. Measure out 1/4 cup, tightly packed.
- If including artichoke hearts in the mix, preheat oven or toaster oven to 425 degrees. Cover a baking sheet with parchment and spread the artichoke hearts over the pan in a single layer. Roast for 10 minutes and turn

over the pieces. Return to oven and roast for another 10 minutes, until browned and tender. Remove from heat and cut in small dice.
- Mash goat cheese in a bowl and add peppers, chopped greens, and diced roasted artichoke hearts if using. Mash together.
- If desired, rub 1 slice of bread with a cut clove of garlic, then purée garlic and stir into the goat cheese mixture. Spread goat cheese mixture over the bread. Top with the other slice of bread (rub it with garlic if desired) and press down firmly. Drizzle remaining olive oil over top slice of bread.
- Toast in toaster oven 3 to 4 minutes, until cheese has melted. Remove from oven, press down firmly, cut in half and serve.

Nutrition Information

- 372: calories;
- 8 grams: sugars;
- 0 grams: trans fat;
- 36 grams: carbohydrates;
- 16 grams: protein;
- 539 milligrams: sodium;
- 18 grams: fat;
- 7 grams: monounsaturated fat;
- 2 grams: polyunsaturated fat;
- 5 grams: dietary fiber;

---

140.   Grilled Pizza With Grilled Red Onions And Feta

Serving: 3 10-inch pizzas | Prep: | Cook: | Ready in: 30mins

Ingredients

- 2 to 3 medium red onions, cut in half lengthwise and thinly sliced across the grain
- Extra virgin olive oil
- Salt and freshly ground pepper
- 3 10-inch pizza crusts (1 recipe)

102

- ¾ cup marinara sauce made with fresh or canned tomatoes
- 1 tablespoon (or more, to taste) fresh thyme leaves
- 3 ounces crumbled feta

Direction

- Prepare a hot grill. Place the onions in a bowl and toss with 1 tablespoon of the olive oil and salt and pepper to taste. Place a perforated grill pan on the grill and let it get hot, then add the onions and cook, tossing in the pan or stirring with tongs, for about 3 to 5 minutes, just until they soften slightly and begin to char. Remove from the grill and return the onions to the bowl.
- Oil the hot grill rack with olive oil, either by brushing with a grill brush or by dipping a folded wad of paper towels in olive oil and using tongs to rub the rack with it. Place a round of dough on a lightly dusted baker's peel or rimless baking sheet. Slide the pizza dough from the peel or baking sheet onto the grill rack. If the dough has just come from the freezer and is easy to handle, you can just place it on the rack without bothering with the peel. Close the lid of the grill – the vents should be closed —-- and set the timer for 2 minutes.
- Lift up the grill lid. The surface of the dough should display some big air bubbles. Using tongs, lift the dough to see if it is evenly browning on the bottom. Rotate the dough to assure even browning. Keep it on the grill, moving it around as necessary, until it is nicely browned, with grill marks. Watch closely so that it doesn't burn. When it is nicely browned on the bottom (it may be blackened in spots), use tongs or a spatula to slide the dough onto the baking sheet or peel, and remove from the grill. Cover the grill again.
- Make sure that there is still some flour on the peel or baking sheet and flip the dough over so that the uncooked side is now on the bottom. Brush the top lightly with oil, then top

with a thin layer of tomato sauce (no more than 1/4¼ cup) and a layer of grilled sliced onions. Sprinkle with thyme and feta, and drizzle on a little more olive oil. Slide the pizza back onto the grill. If using a gas grill, reduce the heat to medium-high. Close the lid and cook for 2 to 3 more minutes, until the bottom is brown. Open the grill and check the pizza. The top should be hot and the bottom nicely browned. If the bottom is getting too dark but the pizza still needs a little more time, move it to a cooler part of the grill and close the top. Use a spatula or tongs to remove the pizza to a cutting board. Cut into wedges and serve. Repeat with the other two crusts.

Nutrition Information

- 794: calories;
- 127 grams: carbohydrates;
- 10 grams: dietary fiber;
- 8 grams: sugars;
- 1731 milligrams: sodium;
- 20 grams: fat;
- 7 grams: monounsaturated fat;
- 4 grams: polyunsaturated fat;
- 26 grams: protein;

---

141. Grilled Vanilla Ginger Pineapple

Serving: Serves 4 | Prep: | Cook: | Ready in: 25mins

Ingredients

- 1 large ripe pineapple
- 1 teaspoon vanilla extract
- ¼ cup ginger palm sugar syrup or honey
- Pinch of cayenne
- 1 tablespoon grape seed oil or canola oil
- Fresh mint for garnish

Direction

- Cut ends off pineapple. Quarter lengthwise, peel and core.
- Prepare a hot or medium-hot grill. (If you are using the grill after cooking meat or fish, allow residue to burn off and scrape away with a spatula.) Stir together vanilla extract, ginger palm sugar syrup or honey, and cayenne.
- Brush pineapple wedges lightly with butter or oil and place on grill. Cook for 6 to 8 minutes per side, basting with the syrup, until you see grill marks and the pineapple is lightly colored. Remove to a platter or to plates and brush on remaining syrup or honey. Garnish with fresh mint, and serve warm.
-

Nutrition Information

- 238: calories;
- 0 grams: saturated fat;
- 1 gram: monounsaturated fat;
- 2 grams: protein;
- 54 grams: carbohydrates;
- 28 grams: sugars;
- 17 milligrams: sodium;
- 4 grams: dietary fiber;

142. Grilled Watermelon And Feta Salad

Serving: Serves 4 | Prep: | Cook: |Ready in: 10mins

Ingredients

- 1 small red onion, sliced
- 3 large or 4 smaller 1-inch-thick slices watermelon
- 3 tablespoons extra-virgin olive oil
- 2 tablespoons sherry vinegar
- Salt to taste
- 2 tablespoons chopped fresh mint
- 2 ounces feta cheese, crumbled
- ¼ to ½ teaspoon Aleppo pepper or mild chili powder (to taste)

Direction

- Place sliced onion in a bowl and cover with water and 1 teaspoon of the vinegar. Soak 5 minutes, then drain and rinse. Drain on paper towels.
- Prepare a medium-hot grill. Use 1 tablespoon of the olive oil to brush the watermelon slices lightly. Grill for about 3 minutes per side, or until charred. Remove from heat and dice. Transfer, with juice, to a large salad bowl.
- Add onions and remaining ingredients and toss together. Let sit for a few minutes or for up to an hour before serving. Toss again just before serving.
-

143. Grits Rancheras

Serving: Serves 4 | Prep: | Cook: |Ready in: 1hours

Ingredients

- 1 cup Anson Mills Colonial Coarse Pencil Cob Grits
- Filtered or spring water
- 1 large can (28-ounce) chopped tomatoes with juice, or in season, 1 1/2 pounds fresh ripe tomatoes
- 2 to 3 serrano or jalapeño chiles, seeded for a milder sauce, and chopped
- 2 garlic cloves, peeled, halved, green shoots removed
- ½ small onion, chopped
- 1 to 2 tablespoons grapeseed oil
- Salt to taste
- 2 tablespoons butter
- 4 eggs
- Chopped cilantro for garnish

Direction

- Place grits in a heavy, medium saucepan. Add 2 cups spring or filtered water and stir once. Allow grits to settle a full minute, then tilt pan and, using a fine tea strainer or fine skimmer, skim off and discard chaff and hulls. Cover and allow grits to soak overnight at room temperature.

- If using fresh tomatoes, preheat broiler and line a baking sheet with foil. Place tomatoes on foil and roast under broiler for 4 to 5 minutes, until blackened and soft. Turn over and roast on other side until blackened and soft, 3 to 4 more minutes. Remove from heat and when you can handle them, core and skin. Place tomatoes (fresh or canned), chiles, garlic, and onion in a blender and purée, retaining a bit of texture.

- Heat 1 tablespoon grapeseed oil over high heat in a large, heavy skillet or saucepan until a drop of purée sizzles when it hits the pan. Add tomato purée and cook, stirring, for about10 minutes, until sauce thickens, darkens, and leaves a canal when you run a spoon down the middle of the pan. Season to taste with salt and remove from heat. Keep warm while you cook grits and fry eggs (you can also make the salsa while the grits are cooking, but I like to focus my attention on the grits).

- Heat 2 cups water in a small saucepan to a bare simmer and keep hot. Set saucepan with grits over medium heat. Bring to a simmer, stirring constantly with a wooden spoon, until the first starch takes hold (the mixture will begin to thicken and you will no longer have to stir constantly). Reduce heat to lowest possible setting. The grits should not be bubbling, they should be sighing, or breathing like somebody in a deep, comfortable sleep, rising up lazily in one big bubble, then falling as the bubble bursts. Watch carefully and each time they are thick enough to hold a spoon upright, stir in about 1/4 cup of the hot water. Stir in the salt after the first 10 minutes of gentle cooking. It should take about 25 minutes for the grits to be tender and creamy and by this time you should have added 3/4 to 1 cup water (perhaps a little more) in 3 or 4 additions.

- Just before grits are done, fry eggs over medium-high heat, preferably in a nonstick skillet that is lightly coated with oil (use as much of the remaining tablespoon of grapeseed oil as you need to). The yolks should still be runny and the whites set; this takes about 4 minutes.

- When grits are done – tender, creamy but not mushy, and able to hold their shape on a spoon – stir in butter vigorously, add pepper, taste (carefully – don't burn your tongue after all that care) and adjust salt. If they have stiffened up stir in some more hot water. Spoon onto plates and make a depression in the center with the back of a spoon. Spoon salsa ranchera into the depression and top with an egg. Season egg with salt and pepper if desired, garnish with cilantro, and serve. You may have some ranchera sauce left over but if you only use a small can of tomatoes you might not have enough.

Nutrition Information

- 318: calories;
- 16 grams: fat;
- 0 grams: trans fat;
- 35 grams: carbohydrates;
- 9 grams: protein;
- 6 grams: saturated fat;
- 4 grams: monounsaturated fat;
- 5 grams: polyunsaturated fat;
- 3 grams: dietary fiber;
- 2 grams: sugars;
- 374 milligrams: sodium;

---

144.   Herb Fritters

Serving: Serves 6 to 8 | Prep: | Cook: | Ready in: 2hours30mins

Ingredients

- ½ cup whole wheat flour
- ¼ cup unbleached all-purpose flour
- ½ teaspoon baking powder

- Rounded 1/2 teaspoon salt
- 1 egg, separated
- 1 tablespoon extra virgin olive oil
- ¾ cup sparkling water
- 1 ½ cups finely chopped fresh herbs or a mix of herbs and greens (such as spinach or chard)

Direction

- Mix together flours, baking powder and salt in a large bowl. Make a well in the center and add egg yolk and oil. Beat egg yolk and oil together, add sparkling water and mix in flour. Whisk until smooth. Cover with plastic and let sit for 2 hours.
- Beat egg white to stiff but not dry peaks and fold into batter. Fold in finely chopped herbs and greens.
- Pour oil into a wok or wide saucepan to a depth of 3 inches and heat over medium-high heat to 360 to 375 degrees. Set up a sheet pan with a rack on it next to pan. Cover rack with a few layers of paper towels. Have a spider or deep fry skimmer handy for removing fritters from oil.
- . Scoop up the batter by the tablespoon and carefully drop into the hot oil. You should be able to fry about 5 at a time. After a few seconds flip the fritters over, then fry until golden brown, about 2 minutes, flipping over again halfway through. Remove from oil with a spider or deep-fry skimmer and drain on the towel-covered rack. Allow to cool slightly, and serve.

Nutrition Information

- 64: calories;
- 1 gram: dietary fiber;
- 9 grams: carbohydrates;
- 108 milligrams: sodium;
- 2 grams: protein;
- 0 grams: sugars;

145.   Honey Spice Bread

Serving: About 40 mini-cakes or 1 small loaf, serving 12. | Prep: | Cook: |Ready in: 1hours

Ingredients

- 175 grams (1/2 cup) honey
- 20 grams (2 tablespoons) brown sugar
- 62 grams (1/2 cup) whole wheat flour
- 62 grams (1/2 cup) rye flour
- 5 grams (1 teaspoon) baking powder
- 1 teaspoon ground anise
- ¼ teaspoon freshly ground pepper
- ½ teaspoon freshly grated nutmeg
- ½ teaspoon ground cinnamon
- ¼ teaspoon ground ginger
- ¼ teaspoon ground cloves
- 2 grams (1/4 teaspoon) salt
- 55 grams (1 extra large) egg
- 50 grams (3 tablespoons) milk

Direction

- Preheat the oven to 350 degrees. Butter a small (8 x 4-inch or smaller) bread pan and dust lightly with flour. Line with parchment if desired. Alternatively, use buttered and floured mini-muffin molds or silicone mini muffin molds.
- Place the honey and sugar in a small saucepan, insert a thermometer and heat to 158 degrees while stirring with a rubber spatula.
- Sift together the whole wheat flour, rye flour, baking powder, spices and salt and transfer them to the bowl of your mixer.
- In a small bowl whisk together the milk and whole eggs. Turn the mixer on low and slowly add the milk and egg mixture. Stop the mixer and, using a rubber spatula or a plastic bowl scraper, scrape up any flour sticking to the bottom of the bowl. Add the warm honey mixture and mix on medium speed until incorporated. Scrape into the bread pan or spoon about 1 to 2 teaspoons into each mini-mold, filling them 3/4 full.

- Bake mini-cakes for 15 to 20 minutes, loaves for 40 to 45 minutes, until deep brown and a tester comes out clean. Remove from the heat, unmold and cool on a rack. If making a loaf, for best results, once cool wrap tightly in plastic and allow the cake to rest for a day.

Nutrition Information

- 29: calories;
- 4 grams: sugars;
- 1 gram: protein;
- 25 milligrams: sodium;
- 0 grams: dietary fiber;
- 7 grams: carbohydrates;

146. Italian Meat Sauce With Half The Meat

Serving: 3 cups, or enough for 9 pasta servings | Prep: | Cook: | Ready in: 35mins

Ingredients

- 1 tablespoon extra virgin olive oil
- ½ yellow or red onion, finely chopped
- 2 plump garlic cloves, minced
- ¼ pound ground beef or veal
- Pinch of ground cinnamon
- Salt to taste
- freshly ground black pepper to taste
- ¼ pound (about 2/3 cups) roasted mushroom mix
- 1 28-ounce can plus 1 14.5-ounce can chopped tomatoes in juice, pulsed in a food processor
- ¼ teaspoon sugar
- 1 teaspoon oregano
- 1 teaspoon fresh thyme leaves or 1/2 teaspoon dried thyme

Direction

- In a large, deep skillet or casserole heat olive oil over medium heat and add onion. Cook, stirring often, until tender, about 5 minutes, and add garlic. Cook, stirring, until fragrant, about 30 seconds, and turn heat up to medium-high. Add ground beef or veal and brown for about 5 minutes, stirring. Add cinnamon and season to taste with salt and pepper.
- Stir in roasted mushroom mix, tomatoes, sugar, oregano and thyme. Season with salt and pepper and bring to a rapid bubble over medium-high heat. Turn heat down to medium, cover partially if sauce is spluttering too much, and simmer, stirring often, until thick and fragrant, 15 to 20 minutes. Taste and adjust seasonings. Serve with pasta, figuring on 1/3 cup per 3-ounce serving.

Nutrition Information

- 113: calories;
- 2 grams: saturated fat;
- 1 gram: polyunsaturated fat;
- 5 grams: dietary fiber;
- 6 grams: protein;
- 590 milligrams: sodium;
- 7 grams: fat;
- 0 grams: trans fat;
- 3 grams: monounsaturated fat;
- 10 grams: carbohydrates;

147. Kasha

Serving: 4 servings | Prep: | Cook: | Ready in: 30mins

Ingredients

- 2 cups water
- Salt to taste (I used 3/4 teaspoon)
- 1 tablespoon unsalted butter
- 1 cup toasted buckwheat groats (kasha), preferably medium-cut (cracked)
- 1 egg

Direction

- Combine water, salt, and butter in a small saucepan and bring to a boil. Once it reaches the boil turn off heat and cover.
- Meanwhile, beat egg in a medium bowl and add kasha. Mix together until grains are thoroughly and evenly coated.
- Transfer to a medium-size, wide, heavy saucepan (I use Analon nonstick), place over high heat and stir egg-coated kasha constantly until grains are dry, smell toasty, and no egg is visible, 2 to 3 minutes. Add just-boiled water, turn heat to very low, cover and simmer 10 to 12 minutes for cracked kasha, 30 minutes for whole kasha, or until all of the liquid is absorbed. Remove from heat.
- Remove lid from pan, place clean dish towel over pan (not touching the grains), and cover tightly. Let sit undisturbed for 10 to 15 minutes. Fluff and serve.

Nutrition Information

- 183: calories;
- 0 grams: sugars;
- 1 gram: polyunsaturated fat;
- 31 grams: carbohydrates;
- 4 grams: dietary fiber;
- 5 grams: fat;
- 2 grams: saturated fat;
- 6 grams: protein;
- 404 milligrams: sodium;

148. Korean Chilled Buckwheat Noodles With Chilled Broth And Kimchi

Serving: Serves 4 | Prep: | Cook: | Ready in: 40mins

Ingredients

- For the broth
- 6 dried shiitake mushrooms or a small handful of dried porcinis or other dried mushrooms
- 1 bunch scallions, sliced, or 1/2 cup chopped chives
- 1 4- to 6-inch stick of kombu
- 1 medium carrot, sliced thin
- A handful of mushroom stems, or a couple of dried shiitakes
- 5 cups water
- Soy sauce to taste
- Salt and sugar to taste
- For the soup
- 9 ounces soba noodles (1 package imported)
- 2 tablespoons dark sesame oil
- 1 cup, tightly packed, cabbage kimchi, cut in thin strips (more to taste; we love it)
- 6 ounces firm tofu, cut in small cubes
- 1 bunch scallions, cut lengthwise into threads
- ½ European cucumber (about 6 ounces), cut into fine 4-inch long julienne
- ½ Asian pear or firm, ripe plum or pluot, peeled (pear only), seeded and cut into 2- or 3-inch long julienne
- 2 hardboiled eggs, cut into quarters
- 2 tablespoons seasoned rice vinegar
- Korean chili powder to taste (optional)
- Chopped cilantro or sprigs for garnish

Direction

- Make the broth. Combine all the ingredients for the broth except the salt and sugar in a saucepan and bring to a simmer. Cover and simmer 20 minutes. Strain. Season to taste with salt and sugar if desired. Place in the refrigerator until cold.
- Cook the soba noodles. Drain well and toss with 1 tablespoon of the sesame oil. Place in the refrigerator and chill while you prepare the other ingredients.
- Toss the kimchi with the remaining sesame oil and refrigerate. Chill all of the other ingredients.
- Divide the noodles among 4 wide bowls. Arrange the tofu, pear or plum and vegetables on top of and around the noodles and top with wedges of boiled egg. Stir the vinegar into the cold broth. Taste and adjust salt and sugar. Ladle into the bowls. Garnish with Korean

chili powder and cilantro if desired, and serve. Guests should stir the mixture so that the kimchi flavors the broth and noodles.

Nutrition Information

- 18: calories;
- 3 grams: carbohydrates;
- 93 milligrams: sodium;
- 1 gram: protein;
- 0 grams: sugars;

---

149. Lasagna With Spinach And Wild Mushrooms

Serving: 6 servings | Prep: | Cook: | Ready in: 1hours30mins

Ingredients

- 1 pound spinach, stemmed and washed in 2 changes water if using bunch spinach, rinsed if using bagged baby spinach
- Salt
- 2 tablespoons extra virgin olive oil, plus additional for oiling baking dish
- ½ pound wild mushrooms, such as oyster mushrooms or maitakes, torn or cut into smaller slices if large or in clumps
- 2 garlic cloves, minced
- 1 teaspoon fresh thyme leaves
- 8 ounces ricotta cheese
- 1 egg
- 1 tablespoon water
- Pinch of nutmeg
- Salt and freshly ground pepper
- 2 ⅓ to 2 ½ cups marinara sauce (more to taste)
- 7 to 8 ounces no-boil lasagna (depends on the size and shape of your dish)
- 4 ounces (1 cup) freshly grated Parmesan

Direction

- Heat a large frying pan over high heat and add the wet spinach. Wilt in the water left on the leaves, stirring until all of the spinach has collapsed in the pan. Transfer to a bowl of cold water, then drain and squeeze out excess water, taking up spinach by the handful. Chop fine and season with a little bit of salt. Set aside. (Alternatively, blanch for 20 seconds in salted boiling water).
- Clean and dry skillet and heat 1 tablespoon olive oil over high heat. Add mushrooms. Let sear without moving for about 30 seconds, then toss and stir in the pan until they begin to sweat, 2 to 3 minutes. Turn heat to medium and add minced garlic and thyme. Season with salt and pepper and continue to cook over medium heat until mushrooms are soft, 3 to 5 more minutes. Taste and adjust seasoning. Remove from heat.
- Heat oven to 350 degrees. Lightly oil a rectangular baking dish. Blend ricotta cheese with egg, water, nutmeg, and salt and pepper to taste. Stir in spinach.
- Spread a small spoonful of marinara sauce in a thin layer over the bottom of the baking dish. Top with a layer of lasagna noodles. Top the noodles with a thin layer of ricotta. Spoon on a few dollops then spread it with an offset or rubber spatula. Top ricotta with half the mushrooms, then top with a layer of marinara sauce and a layer of Parmesan. Repeat layers, then add a final layer of lasagna noodles topped with marinara sauce and Parmesan. Drizzle on remaining olive oil.
- Cover baking dish tightly with foil and place in the oven. Bake 40 minutes, until noodles are tender and mixture is bubbling. Remove from heat and allow to sit for 5 to 10 minutes before serving.

Nutrition Information

- 408: calories;
- 22 grams: protein;
- 817 milligrams: sodium;
- 18 grams: fat;

- 8 grams: sugars;
- 0 grams: trans fat;
- 2 grams: polyunsaturated fat;
- 42 grams: carbohydrates;
- 6 grams: dietary fiber;
- 7 grams: monounsaturated fat;

150. Leek, Kale And Potato Latkes

Serving: Makes 2 to 2 1/2 dozen, serving 6 | Prep: | Cook: | Ready in: 30mins

Ingredients

- 5 cups, tightly packed, grated potatoes (use a starchy potato like Idaho or Yukon gold)
- 2 large leeks, halved lengthwise, cleaned and sliced very thin
- ½ pound kale, stemmed, washed, dried and finely chopped or cut in thin slivers (about 3 cups, tightly packed)
- 1 teaspoon baking powder
- Salt and freshly ground pepper to taste
- 2 teaspoons cumin seeds, lightly toasted and coarsely ground
- ¼ cup chopped chives
- ¼ cup all-purpose flour or cornstarch
- 2 eggs, beaten
- About 1/4 cup canola, grape seed or rice bran oil

Direction

- Preheat the oven to 300 degrees. Meanwhile, place a rack over a sheet pan.
- In a large bowl mix together the potatoes, leeks, kale, baking powder, salt and pepper, cumin, chives, and flour or cornstarch. Add the eggs stir together.
- Begin heating a large heavy skillet over medium-high heat. Add 2 to 3 tablespoons of the oil and when it is hot, take up heaped tablespoons of the latke mixture, press the mixture against the spoon to extract liquid (or

squeeze in your hands), and place in the pan. Press down with the back of the spatula to flatten. Repeat with more spoonfuls, being careful not to crowd the pan. In my 10-inch pan I can cook 4 at a time without crowding; my 12-inch pan will accommodate 5. Cook on one side until golden brown, about 3 minutes. Slide the spatula underneath and flip the latkes over. Cook on the other side until golden brown, another 2 to 3 minutes. Transfer to the rack set over a baking sheet and place in the oven to keep warm. The mixture will continue to release liquid, which will accumulate in the bottom of the bowl. Stir from time to time, and remember to squeeze the heaped tablespoons of the mix before you add them to the pan.
- Serve hot topped with low-fat sour cream, Greek yogurt or crème fraiche, or other toppings of your choice such as salsa, chutney or yogurt blended with cilantro, mint, and garlic.

Nutrition Information

- 58: calories;
- 3 grams: fat;
- 1 gram: sugars;
- 0 grams: trans fat;
- 8 grams: carbohydrates;
- 2 grams: protein;
- 120 milligrams: sodium;

151. Lemon And Garlic Chicken With Spiced Spinach

Serving: Serves 4 | Prep: | Cook: | Ready in: 30mins

Ingredients

- 2 boneless skinless chicken breasts (most weigh 8 to 10 ounces)
- 2 tablespoons extra-virgin olive oil
- 3 tablespoons fresh lemon juice

- 2 garlic cloves, minced or pureed
- 1 teaspoon chopped fresh rosemary
- 1 generous bunch spinach, stemmed and washed well in 2 changes water, or 2 6-ounce bags baby spinach, washed
- 2 allspice berries, lightly toasted and ground
- ½ teaspoon coriander seeds or cumin seeds, lightly toasted and ground
- ¼ teaspoon ground cinnamon
- Salt to taste
- Freshly ground pepper
- 2 tablespoons all-purpose flour or a gluten-free flour such as rice flour or corn flour
- 2 tablespoons grapeseed, sunflower or canola oil

Direction

- Stir together the olive oil, lemon juice, garlic, rosemary, and salt and pepper in a large bowl. Cut each chicken breast into 2 equal pieces (3 if they are 12 ounces or more) and place in the bowl. Stir together and refrigerate 15 to 30 minutes.
- Combine ground allspice, coriander or cumin, and cinnamon in a small bowl or ramekin and set aside.
- Remove chicken from the marinade and pat dry (discard marinade). Place two sheets of plastic wrap (1 large sheet if you have extra-wide wrap) on your work surface, overlapping slightly, to make 1 wide sheet, and brush lightly with olive oil. Place a piece of chicken in the middle of plastic sheet and brush lightly with oil. Cover the chicken with another wide layer of plastic wrap. Working from the center to the outside, pound chicken breast with the flat side of a meat tenderizer until about 1/4 inch thick. (Don't pound too hard or you'll tear the meat. If that happens it won't be the end of the world, you'll just have a few pieces to cook.) Repeat with the remaining chicken breast pieces.
- Season pounded chicken breasts with salt and pepper on one side only. Dredge lightly in the flour (you won't use all of it).

- Turn oven on low. Heat a wide, heavy skillet over high heat and add the oil. When oil is hot, place one or two pieces of chicken in the pan – however many will fit without crowding the pan. Cook for for 1 1/2 minutes until bottom is browned in spots. Turn over and brown on other side, about 1 1/2 minutes. (Do not overcook or chicken will be dry.) Transfer to a platter or sheet pan and keep warm in the oven. If there is more than a tablespoon of fat in the pan, pour some (but not all) of it off into a jar or bowl.
- Turn burner heat down to medium. Add ground spices to the pan and when they begin to sizzle add spinach and salt and pepper to taste. Cook, stirring with a wooden spoon and deglazing the bottom of the pan with the liquid that comes off the spinach, until spinach wilts, 2 to 3 minutes. Remove to a platter or to plates and serve with the chicken.

Nutrition Information

- 333: calories;
- 10 grams: carbohydrates;
- 3 grams: dietary fiber;
- 591 milligrams: sodium;
- 2 grams: saturated fat;
- 0 grams: trans fat;
- 18 grams: fat;
- 1 gram: sugars;
- 34 grams: protein;

---

152. Lentil Soup With Cilantro (Lots Of It)

Serving: Serves four | Prep: | Cook: | Ready in: 1hours

Ingredients

- 1 tablespoon extra virgin olive oil
- 2 garlic cloves, minced
- 1 ¼ teaspoons cumin seeds, lightly toasted and ground

- Pinch of cayenne
- ½ pound brown lentils (about 1 1/8 cups), picked over and rinsed
- 1 small onion, cut in half
- 1 bay leaf
- 1 ½ quarts water
- Salt, preferably kosher salt, to taste
- Freshly ground pepper
- 1 cup chopped cilantro (from 1 large bunch)
- Plain low-fat yogurt for garnish

Direction

- Heat the oil in a large, heavy soup pot over medium heat, and add the garlic. Stir until fragrant, about a minute, and stir in the cumin and cayenne. Add the lentils, onion, bay leaf, water and salt. Bring to a boil, reduce the heat and simmer 40 minutes, until the lentils are tender and the broth aromatic. Add pepper, taste and adjust salt. Remove the halved onion and the bay leaf.
- Coarsely puree the soup in an immersion blender or food mill. Alternatively, puree half the soup in blender, 1 1/2 cups at time, being careful to cover the top of the blender with a towel to avoid hot splashes, then stir back into the soup. Heat through.
- Chop the cilantro, discarding the stems. Stir into the soup just before serving. Taste, adjust seasoning and serve, topping each bowl with a dollop of yogurt.

Nutrition Information

- 237: calories;
- 4 grams: fat;
- 38 grams: carbohydrates;
- 7 grams: dietary fiber;
- 2 grams: sugars;
- 1017 milligrams: sodium;
- 1 gram: polyunsaturated fat;
- 3 grams: monounsaturated fat;
- 14 grams: protein;

---

153. Lentil And Herb Salad With Roasted Peppers And Feta

Serving: Serves 6 generously | Prep: | Cook: | Ready in: 40mins

Ingredients

- 2 cups / 14 ounces green, brown or black lentils, rinsed and picked over6 cups water
- 1 small or 1/2 large onion, cut in half
- 3 to 4 garlic cloves (to taste), minced
- 1 bay leaf
- Salt to taste
- ¼ cup red wine vinegar or sherry vinegar
- ⅓ cup extra virgin olive oil
- ¼ cup broth from the lentils
- 2 roasted red peppers peeled, seeded sliced in 2-inch long julienne
- 1 cup chopped fresh herbs, such as parsley, chives, mint, dill, oregano (any combination)
- Freshly ground pepper
- 3 ounces feta, crumbled

Direction

- In a medium size pot, combine lentils, water, onion, bay leaf and 2 of the garlic cloves. Bring to a gentle boil over medium-high heat. Add salt to taste, cover, reduce heat to low and simmer 25 minutes, until lentils are cooked through but still have some texture. They should not be mushy. Taste and adjust salt. Using tongs, remove onion and bay leaf.
- Meanwhile, in a small bowl or measuring cup, mix together vinegar, remaining garlic, salt to taste, and olive oil. Set aside.
- Place a strainer over a bowl and carefully drain lentils. Transfer lentils to a bowl. Measure out 1/4 cup of the broth and whisk it into the dressing, then toss dressing with the lentils. Stir in roasted pepper strips and allow to cool if desired. Taste and adjust salt. Shortly before serving stir in fresh herbs, pepper, and feta.

Nutrition Information

- 433: calories;
- 9 grams: dietary fiber;
- 412 milligrams: sodium;
- 2 grams: polyunsaturated fat;
- 53 grams: carbohydrates;
- 5 grams: sugars;
- 21 grams: protein;
- 16 grams: fat;
- 4 grams: saturated fat;
- 10 grams: monounsaturated fat;

154. Lentils With Smoked Trout Rilletes

Serving: Serves 6 | Prep: | Cook: | Ready in: 45mins

Ingredients

- For the lentils
- 2 cups / 14 ounces lentils (green, brown, or black), rinsed and picked over
- 1 ½ quarts water
- 1 onion, cut in half
- 1 bay leaf
- 2 garlic cloves, crushed
- Pinch of cayenne, or 1 dried cayenne pepper (optional)
- Salt
- Freshly ground pepper
- For the rillettes
- 7 to 8 ounces smoked trout fillets, skin and bones removed
- 2 tablespoons extra virgin olive oil
- 2 tablespoons unsalted butter, at room temperature (may substitute Greek yogurt)
- 4 to 6 tablespoons plain Greek yogurt (depending on whether or not you use butter)
- 1 to 2 tablespoons fresh lemon juice (to taste)
- 1 to 2 tablespoons minced chives (to taste)
- Freshly ground pepper

Direction

- In a medium size pot, combine lentils, water, onion, bay leaf, garlic and optional cayenne. Bring to a gentle boil over medium-high heat. Add salt, cover, reduce heat to low and simmer 30 to 40 minutes, until lentils are cooked through but still have some texture. They should not be mushy but they shouldn't be crunchy either. Taste and adjust salt. Add pepper. Using tongs, remove and discard onion and bay leaf.
- While lentils are simmering make rillettes. In a medium bowl, break up trout with your fingers or with a fork. In a small bowl, mix together olive oil and butter until well amalgamated. Mash trout with a fork, then work in olive oil and butter, and yogurt. Make sure to mash well and to distribute butter, olive oil and yogurt evenly through the mixture. Work in lemon juice and stir in minced chives and pepper. Refrigerate if not using right away. Remove from refrigerator 30 minutes before serving.
- Spoon warm lentils onto plates or wide bowls. To form quenelles, dip a soup spoon into warm water and scoop up a spoonful of trout mixture. With another soup spoon, round the top of the mound, then ease off on top of the lentils. Repeat with another spoonful and serve.

Nutrition Information

- 358: calories;
- 9 grams: fat;
- 0 grams: trans fat;
- 1 gram: polyunsaturated fat;
- 25 grams: protein;
- 912 milligrams: sodium;
- 2 grams: saturated fat;
- 4 grams: monounsaturated fat;
- 47 grams: carbohydrates;
- 8 grams: dietary fiber;
- 3 grams: sugars;

155. Mackerel With Peas

Serving: 4 servings | Prep: | Cook: |Ready in: 30mins

Ingredients

- 2 tablespoons olive oil
- 1 onion, chopped
- 2 cloves garlic, minced
- 3 or 4 thyme sprigs
- 1 large or 2 medium tomatoes, chopped
- Salt
- pepper
- 2 cups or more shelled peas, fresh or frozen
- 4 medium-sized mackerel, about 3/4 to 1 pound each, cleaned
- ½ cup white wine or water
- Crusty bread for serving

Direction

- Put oil in a broad skillet over medium heat; add onion, garlic and thyme. When onion turns golden, add tomato and some salt and pepper. Turn heat to high; when tomato breaks down, add 1/2 cup of water or white wine.
- When liquid returns to a boil, lower heat and add peas and mackerel. Cover and cook for 10 to 15 minutes, or until mackerel is done (a thin knife pierces thickest part of fish with little resistance).
- Put mackerel on a serving plate, covered with peas and sauce; serve with bread.

Nutrition Information

- 982: calories;
- 1331 milligrams: sodium;
- 14 grams: polyunsaturated fat;
- 5 grams: dietary fiber;
- 27 grams: monounsaturated fat;
- 18 grams: carbohydrates;
- 7 grams: sugars;
- 79 grams: protein;
- 62 grams: fat;

156. Mango Buttermilk Smoothie

Serving: One 16-ounce or two 8-ounce servings | Prep: | Cook: |Ready in: 5mins

Ingredients

- 1 heaped cup fresh or frozen ripe mango
- 1 cup buttermilk
- 1 teaspoon honey
- ½ medium size ripe banana
- 4 frozen strawberries
- 2 or 3 ice cubes

Direction

- Combine all of the ingredients in a blender, and blend at high speed until smooth.

157. Mango Lime Sorbet

Serving: 1 quart, serving 5 to 6 | Prep: | Cook: |Ready in: 35mins

Ingredients

- ½ cup/100 grams sugar
- 4 cups/750 grams diced mango (3 to 4 large mangos)
- ⅔ cup/150 grams fresh lime juice (about 6 limes)
- 2 tablespoons/50 grams corn syrup

Direction

- Combine 1/2 cup water and sugar in a small saucepan and stir. Bring to a simmer and simmer until sugar has dissolved. Remove from heat.
- Combine all ingredients in a blender and purée until completely smooth. Transfer to a bowl or container and chill overnight in refrigerator.

- (Chill a 1-quart container in the freezer while you spin the sorbet.) Remove bowl from refrigerator and blend the mango purée again for 1 to 2 minutes in a blender or with an immersion blender. Add to ice cream maker and spin for about 25 minutes. Transfer to chilled container and freeze for 2 hours or longer to pack.
- Once frozen solid, allow to soften in refrigerator for 30 minutes before serving.

Nutrition Information

- 169: calories;
- 1 gram: protein;
- 0 grams: polyunsaturated fat;
- 44 grams: carbohydrates;
- 2 grams: dietary fiber;
- 41 grams: sugars;
- 7 milligrams: sodium;

158. Maple Pecan Pancakes

Serving: 15 pancakes | Prep: | Cook: | Ready in: 35mins

Ingredients

- 1 cup (140 grams) whole-wheat flour
- ½ cup (60 grams) almond flour
- 2 teaspoons baking powder
- 1 teaspoon baking soda
- ¼ teaspoon salt
- 2 eggs
- 1 tablespoon maple syrup
- 1 ½ cups buttermilk
- 2 tablespoons canola oil
- 1 teaspoon vanilla extract
- ½ cup (60 grams) chopped pecans
- ½ cup dried cranberries
- Butter or oil as needed for cooking

Direction

- Sift together the flours, baking powder, baking soda and salt
- In a medium bowl, whisk the eggs. Whisk in the maple syrup, buttermilk, canola oil and vanilla. Quickly whisk in the flour mix. Fold in the pecans and the cranberries. Do not overwork the batter
- Heat a griddle or a large skillet, either nonstick or seasoned cast iron, over medium-high heat. Brush with butter or oil. Use a 1/4-cup ladle or cup measure to drop 3 to 4 tablespoons of batter per pancake onto your heated pan or griddle. When bubbles break through the pancakes, carefully slide a spatula under them (they are delicate), flip them over and cook for another minute, until they are brown on the other side. Serve right away, or allow to cool and wrap individual servings in plastic, then place in a freezer bag and freeze

Nutrition Information

- 140: calories;
- 0 grams: trans fat;
- 188 milligrams: sodium;
- 4 grams: protein;
- 8 grams: fat;
- 1 gram: saturated fat;
- 3 grams: monounsaturated fat;
- 2 grams: dietary fiber;
- 14 grams: carbohydrates;
- 5 grams: sugars;

159. Marinated Cauliflower And Carrots With Mint

Serving: 8 to 10 servings as a starter or side | Prep: | Cook: | Ready in: 15mins

Ingredients

- 1 pound carrots, peeled, quartered, or if fat, cut into sixths at fat ends, then into 2-inch lengths

- 1 pound cauliflower (1 small head, 1/2 to 3/4 of a large head), cut or broken into small florets
- Salt and freshly ground black pepper
- ¼ cup sherry vinegar or champagne vinegar
- ¼ cup extra virgin olive oil
- 2 to 4 tablespoons chopped fresh mint (to taste)

Direction

- Place carrots and cauliflower in a steamer above 1 inch of boiling water, cover and steam 5 to 8 minutes, until both vegetables are tender but not too soft. Drain and transfer to a bowl. Add salt and pepper, and toss with vinegar and olive oil. Allow to cool slightly, then toss with mint. Serve warm or at room temperature. If serving warm, just before serving heat in a pan over medium heat, preferably before adding mint.

Nutrition Information

- 75: calories;
- 6 grams: carbohydrates;
- 1 gram: protein;
- 4 grams: monounsaturated fat;
- 2 grams: dietary fiber;
- 3 grams: sugars;
- 198 milligrams: sodium;

160.   Marinated Olives

Serving: 2 cups, serving 12 | Prep: | Cook: |Ready in: 5mins

Ingredients

- ¼ cup extra virgin olive oil
- 2 tablespoons red wine vinegar
- 5 bay leaves
- 2 large garlic cloves, peeled, green shoots removed, thinly sliced

- Strips of rind from 1 lemon (preferably organic)
- 1 tablespoon fresh thyme leaves, coarsely chopped
- 1 teaspoon chopped fresh rosemary
- ½ teaspoon fennel seeds
- 2 cups imported olives (black, green or a mix) (about 3/4 pound)

Direction

- Combine the olive oil, vinegar, bay leaves and garlic in a small saucepan and heat just until warm over low heat. Remove from the heat and stir in the lemon rind, thyme, rosemary and fennel seeds.
- Place the olives in a wide mouthed jar and pour in the olive oil mixture. Shake the jar to coat the olives. Refrigerate for two hours or for up to two weeks. Shake the jar a few times a day to redistribute the seasonings.

161.   Mashed Potato And Broccoli Raab Pancakes

Serving: Makes 2 to 2 1/2 dozen small pancakes, serving 6 | Prep: | Cook: |Ready in: 15mins

Ingredients

- 2 ½ cups mashed potatoes (about 1 pound 2 ounces potatoes, peeled, cut in chunks and steamed until tender, then mashed with a potato masher or a fork)
- 1 ½ cups finely chopped steamed or blanched broccoli raab
- ¼ cup chopped chives
- 1 teaspoon baking powder
- Salt and freshly ground pepper to taste
- ⅓ to ½ cup freshly grated Parmesan, to taste
- 3 heaped tablespoons all-purpose flour
- 2 eggs
- 3 to 4 tablespoons sunflower oil, grapeseed oil or canola oil for frying

Direction

- In a large bowl, mix together the mashed potatoes, finely chopped broccoli raab, chives, baking powder, salt, pepper, Parmesan and flour. Beat the eggs and stir in.
- Begin heating a large heavy skillet over medium heat. Heat the oven to 300 degrees. Add 2 tablespoons of the oil and when it is hot carefully scoop up heaped tablespoons of the potato mixture and use a spoon or spatula to ease them out of the spoon into the pan. Gently flatten the mounds slightly with the back of a spoon or a spatula but don't worry if this is hard to do – if they stick -- because when you flip them over you can flatten them into pancakes. Brown on the first side – about 2 or 3 minutes – and using a spatula, flip the potato and broccoli raab mounds over and gently push them down so that they will be shaped like pancakes. Brown on the other side and remove to a baking sheet. Continue with the remaining potato mixture, adding oil to the pan as necessary.

Nutrition Information

- 51: calories;
- 111 milligrams: sodium;
- 3 grams: fat;
- 1 gram: polyunsaturated fat;
- 0 grams: sugars;
- 4 grams: carbohydrates;
- 2 grams: protein;

---

162.   Mashed Potato And Cabbage Pancakes

Serving: Makes about 2 to 2 1/2 dozen small pancakes, serving 6 | Prep: | Cook: | Ready in: 30mins

Ingredients

- 2 cups finely chopped steamed cabbage (about 1 pound cabbage)
- 2 ½ cups mashed potatoes (about 1 pound 2 ounces potatoes, peeled, cut in chunks and steamed until tender – about 20 minutes – then mashed with a potato masher or a fork)
- ½ cup chopped chives
- 1 tablespoon chopped fresh marjoram (optional)
- 1 teaspoon baking powder
- Salt and freshly ground pepper to taste
- ¼ cup all-purpose flour
- 2 eggs
- 3 to 4 tablespoons sunflower oil, grapeseed oil or canola oil for frying

Direction

- To prepare the cabbage, remove the outer leaves and quarter a small head or 1/2 of a larger head. Core and place in a steamer above 1 inch of boiling water. Steam 10 to 15 minutes, until tender when pierced with a knife or skewer. Remove from the heat and allow to cool, then squeeze out water, and chop fine. Mix with the potatoes in a large bowl. Add the chives, baking powder, marjoram if using, salt, pepper, and flour. Beat the eggs and stir in.
- Begin heating a large heavy skillet over medium heat. Heat the oven to 300 degrees. Add 2 tablespoons of the oil and when it is hot carefully scoop up heaped tablespoons of the potato mixture and use a spoon or spatula to ease them out of the spoon into the pan. Gently flatten the mounds slightly with the back of a spoon or a spatula but don't worry if this is hard to do – if they stick -- because when you flip them over you can flatten them into pancakes. Brown on the first side – about 2 or 3 minutes – and using a spatula, flip the mounds over and gently push them down so that they will be shaped like pancakes. Brown on the other side and remove to a baking sheet. Continue with the remaining potato mixture, adding oil to the pan as necessary.

Nutrition Information

- 49: calories;
- 3 grams: fat;
- 0 grams: trans fat;
- 1 gram: protein;
- 5 grams: carbohydrates;
- 108 milligrams: sodium;

163.   Meal In A Bowl With Chicken, Rice Noodles And Spinach

Serving: Serves 4 to 6 (you'll have some chicken left over) | Prep: | Cook: |Ready in: 1hours30mins

Ingredients

- 1 smallish chicken, about 3 to 3 1/2 pounds, cut up and skinned, or the equivalent of chicken pieces, skinned
- 1 onion, quartered
- 1 piece ginger root, about 2 inches long, peeled and sliced
- 4 garlic cloves, peeled
- 1 teaspoon peppercorns
- Salt to taste
- 2 tablespoons Vietnamese or Thai fish sauce (you can substitute soy sauce if you don't have fish sauce)
- ½ pound dried rice noodles (rice sticks)
- 1 5- or 6-ounce bag baby spinach
- 1 cup chopped cilantro
- 2 limes, cut into wedges

Direction

- If possible, do this step a day ahead: Combine the chicken and 3 quarts water in a large, heavy soup pot and bring to a simmer. Skim off foam and add the onion, ginger root, garlic cloves, peppercorns and 1 teaspoon salt. Reduce the heat, cover partially, and simmer 40 minutes. Skim occasionally. Remove the chicken pieces from the broth and allow to cool. Line a strainer with cheesecloth and strain the broth into a bowl. When the chicken is cool enough to handle, shred and refrigerate in a covered container until ready to serve the soup. Refrigerate the broth for at least 3 hours or, preferably, overnight. Lift off the fat from the surface and discard.
- About 30 minutes before you wish to serve the meal, remove the chicken and broth from the refrigerator. Bring the broth to a simmer and add the fish sauce (or soy sauce) and salt to taste. Taste and adjust seasonings. Place the rice noodles in a bowl and cover with hot water. Let sit for 20 minutes, then drain.
- Bring a large pot of water to a boil. Add the noodles and cook just until tender, 30 seconds to a minute. Drain and rinse with cold water. Set aside.
- Just before serving, add the spinach to the simmering soup. To serve the soup, distribute the noodles among 4 to 6 large bowls. Top with shredded chicken and a handful of chopped cilantro. Ladle the simmering broth, with some of the spinach, into each bowl over the chicken and noodles. Serve at once, passing the limes for guests to squeeze on as they wish.

Nutrition Information

- 495: calories;
- 663 milligrams: sodium;
- 7 grams: saturated fat;
- 5 grams: polyunsaturated fat;
- 2 grams: sugars;
- 10 grams: monounsaturated fat;
- 37 grams: carbohydrates;
- 32 grams: protein;
- 23 grams: fat;
- 0 grams: trans fat;

164. Mediterranean Lentil Purée

Serving: | Prep: | Cook: | Ready in: 1hours15mins

Ingredients

- ¼ cup olive oil
- 1 large garlic clove, minced or pureed
- ½ teaspoon freshly ground cumin seeds
- ½ teaspoon freshly ground coriander seeds
- ⅛ teaspoon freshly ground cardamom seeds
- ¼ teaspoon ground fenugreek seeds
- ¾ cup brown or green lentils, washed and picked over
- Salt and freshly ground pepper to taste
- 1 tablespoon plain low-fat yogurt (more to taste) or additional liquid from the lentils for a vegan version
- Chopped cilantro for garnish (optional)

Direction

- Combine 2 tablespoons of the olive oil and the garlic in a small frying pan or saucepan over medium heat. When the garlic begins to sizzle, add the spices. Stir together for about 30 seconds, then remove from the heat and set aside.
- Place the lentils in a medium saucepan, cover by 1 to 2 inches with water, add a bay leaf, and bring to a boil. Add salt to taste, reduce the heat and cook until tender, 40 to 50 minutes. Remove the bay leaf. Taste and adjust salt. Place a strainer over a bowl and drain the lentils. Transfer to a food processor fitted with the steel blade.
- Purée the lentils along with the garlic and spices. With the machine running add the additional olive oil. Thin out as desired with the broth from the lentils. The purée should be very smooth; if it is dry or pasty, add more yogurt, broth, or olive oil. Taste and adjust salt. If desired add a few drops of lemon juice. Transfer to a bowl and sprinkle the cilantro over the top if desired, or spread directly on croutons or pita triangles.

Nutrition Information

- 174: calories;
- 9 grams: fat;
- 1 gram: sugars;
- 7 grams: protein;
- 17 grams: carbohydrates;
- 3 grams: dietary fiber;
- 85 milligrams: sodium;

165. Millet Polenta With Mushrooms And Broccoli Or Broccoli Raab

Serving: Serves 6 | Prep: | Cook: | Ready in: 1hours30mins

Ingredients

- ½ ounce (1/2 cup) dried mushrooms, like porcinis
- 1 cup millet
- Salt to taste
- 4 cups water or vegetable stock
- 1 tablespoon unsalted butter
- 6 ounces fresh shiitake mushrooms, stems removed, caps sliced
- 1 pound white or cremini mushrooms, wiped if gritty and cut in thick slices
- 2 tablespoons extra-virgin olive oil
- Salt and freshly ground pepper
- 2 shallots, minced
- 2 garlic cloves, minced
- 1 teaspoon chopped fresh thyme
- 1 teaspoon chopped fresh rosemary
- 2 teaspoons soy sauce
- ¼ cup dry white wine, such as Sauvignon blanc (optional)
- 1 tablespoon chopped fresh parsley
- 1 to 2 ounces Parmesan, grated (1/4 to 1/2 cup) (optional)

- 1 bunch broccoli or broccoli rabe, broken into florets or coarsely chopped and steamed until tender, about 5 minutes

Direction

- Place the dried mushrooms in a pyrex measuring cup or a bowl and pour on 1 cup boiling water. Let soak 20 minutes, while you prepare the other ingredients. Place a strainer over a bowl, line it with cheesecloth or paper towels, and drain the dried mushrooms. Squeeze the mushrooms over the strainer then rinse, away from the bowl with the soaking liquid, until they are free of sand. Squeeze dry over the strainer and set aside. If very large, chop coarsely. Set aside the broth.
- Preheat the oven to 350 degrees. While the dried mushrooms are soaking, start the millet polenta. Heat a 10-inch cast iron skillet over medium-high heat and add the millet. Toast, stirring or shaking the pan, until the grains begin to pop and smell sort of like popcorn. Add the water or stock and salt (up to 1 teaspoon, to taste). Transfer the pan to the hot oven. After 25 minutes, give the millet a stir and then bake for another 20 to 25 minutes. There should still be some liquid in the pan. Stir in the butter and bake for another 5 to 10 minutes, until the millet is thick and no more water or stock is visible in the pan.
- While the millet is in the oven cook the mushrooms. Heat a large, heavy frying pan over medium-high heat and add 1 tablespoon of the olive oil. When the oil is hot (you can feel the heat when you hold your hand above the pan), add the shiitakes and the fresh mushrooms. Don't stir for 30 seconds to a minute, then cook, stirring or tossing in the pan, for a few minutes, until they begin to soften and sweat. Add the remaining oil, turn the heat to medium, and add the shallots, garlic, thyme and rosemary. Stir together, add salt to taste and freshly ground pepper to taste, and cook, stirring often, for another couple of minutes, until the shallots and garlic have softened and the mixture is fragrant. Add

the chopped dried mushrooms, the soy sauce and wine and cook, stirring often and scraping the bottom of the pan, until the wine has evaporated. Add the broth from the dried mushrooms, turn up the heat and cook, stirring, until it has reduced by about a third. The mushrooms should be moist. Stir in the parsley, taste, adjust seasonings, and remove from the heat.
- When the polenta is done, remove it from the oven and if desired, stir in the Parmesan. Spoon onto plates or wide bowls, make a depression in the middle with the back of your spoon and top with the mushrooms. Arrange steamed broccoli or broccoli rabe next to the mushrooms or on top, and serve.

Nutrition Information

- 248: calories;
- 2 grams: saturated fat;
- 0 grams: trans fat;
- 7 grams: dietary fiber;
- 9 grams: fat;
- 4 grams: sugars;
- 1 gram: polyunsaturated fat;
- 37 grams: carbohydrates;
- 10 grams: protein;
- 925 milligrams: sodium;

---

166. Millet Polenta With Tomato Sauce, Eggplant And Chickpeas

Serving: Serves 6 | Prep: | Cook: | Ready in: 2hours30mins

Ingredients

- 1 pound eggplant
- 2 tablespoons extra virgin olive oil (plus additional for oiling the foil)
- Salt and freshly ground pepper to taste
- 1 cup millet

- 4 cups water or vegetable stock
- 1 tablespoon unsalted butter
- 1 can (28-ounce) tomatoes, with juice
- 2 garlic cloves, minced
- 1 to 2 teaspoons fresh thyme leaves (to taste), plus additional for garnish
- Pinch of sugar
- Salt to taste
- 1 can chickpeas, drained and rinsed
- Optional: 1/2 cup freshly grated Parmesan

Direction

- Roast the eggplant. Cut it into 3/4-inch cubes and toss with 1 tablespoon of the olive oil and salt and pepper to taste. Preheat the oven to 450 degrees. Line a baking sheet with foil and brush the foil with olive oil. Lay the eggplant on the foil in a single layer. Roast in the hot oven for 15 to 20 minutes, until the cubes are soft when pierced with a knife and browned in spots. They'll look dry on the surface but when you pierce them with a knife you should be able to see that the flesh is soft. Remove from the oven and carefully fold the foil up over the eggplant slices (be careful not to burn yourself!). Crimp the edges of the foil so that the eggplant is hermetically sealed in a big foil packet, and allow the eggplant to steam for another 15 to 20 minutes. Turn the oven down to 350 degrees.
- Begin the polenta. Heat a 10-inch cast iron skillet over medium-high heat and add the millet. Toast, stirring or shaking the pan, until the grains begin to pop and smell sort of like popcorn. Add the water or stock and salt (up to 1 teaspoon, to taste). Transfer the pan to the hot oven. After 25 minutes give the millet a stir and bake for another 20 to 25 minutes. There should still be some liquid in the pan. Stir in the butter and bake for another 5 to 10 minutes, until the millet is thick and no more water or stock is visible in the pan.
- While the millet is in the oven make the tomato sauce. Pulse the tomatoes in a food processor so that you have a nice puréed texture. Heat the remaining tablespoon of olive oil over medium heat in a wide nonstick skillet or saucepan and add the garlic and thyme. As soon as it begins to smell fragrant (1/2 to 1 minute), add the tomatoes, sugar, eggplant, and salt, stir and turn up the heat. When the tomatoes begin to bubble, turn the heat to medium-low and cook, partially covered and stirring often, until thick and fragrant, about 20 minutes. Stir in the chickpeas and heat through. Remove from the heat, taste and adjust seasonings.
- When the polenta is done, remove it from the oven and if desired, stir in the Parmesan. Spoon onto plates or wide bowls, make a depression in the middle with the back of your spoon and top with the tomato, eggplant and chickpeas mixture. Garnish with more fresh thyme and Parmesan, and a drizzle of olive oil if desired, and serve.

Nutrition Information

- 328: calories;
- 2 grams: polyunsaturated fat;
- 0 grams: trans fat;
- 51 grams: carbohydrates;
- 9 grams: sugars;
- 10 grams: fat;
- 4 grams: monounsaturated fat;
- 13 grams: dietary fiber;
- 11 grams: protein;
- 1099 milligrams: sodium;

167. Millet And Greens Gratin

Serving: 4 to 6 servings | Prep: | Cook: | Ready in: 1hours10mins

Ingredients

- 1 generous bunch beet greens
- Salt to taste
- 2 tablespoons extra virgin olive oil
- ½ medium onion, finely chopped

- 2 large garlic cloves, minced
- 1 teaspoon chopped fresh thyme
- 1 teaspoon chopped fresh rosemary
- 2 eggs plus 1 egg yolk
- ½ cup low-fat milk
- 1 to 1 ¼ cups cooked millet
- 3 ounces Gruyère cheese, grated (3/4 cup)

Direction

- Stem the greens and wash the leaves in 2 changes of water. To blanch the greens, bring a large pot of water to a rolling boil, salt generously and add the greens. Blanch for 1 minute or until tender. Alternatively, steam the greens over 1 inch of boiling water for about 2 minutes, until tender. Transfer to a bowl of cold water and drain. Taking the greens up by the handful, squeeze hard to expel excess water. Chop medium-fine. You should have about 11/4 cups.
- Preheat the oven to 375 degrees. Oil a 2-quart gratin or baking dish. Heat 1 tablespoon of the oil in a heavy skillet over medium heat and add the onion. Cook, stirring often, until tender, about 5 minutes. Add a generous pinch of salt and the garlic and cook, stirring, until the garlic is fragrant, 30 seconds to a minute. Add the herbs, beet greens, and salt and pepper to taste, and stir and toss in the pan for about a minute, until the mixture is nicely infused with the oil, garlic and herbs. Remove from the heat.
- In a large bowl, beat together the eggs, egg yolk and milk. Add salt to taste (about 1/2 teaspoon), pepper, the millet, the greens and the cheese and stir together until the mixture is well blended. Scrape into the oiled baking dish. Drizzle the remaining tablespoon of olive oil on top.
- Bake in the preheated oven for 35 minutes, or until it is sizzling and set, and the top is just beginning to color. Remove from the oven and allow to sit for 10 minutes or longer before serving.

Nutrition Information

- 194: calories;
- 1 gram: dietary fiber;
- 2 grams: sugars;
- 10 grams: protein;
- 280 milligrams: sodium;
- 12 grams: fat;
- 5 grams: saturated fat;
- 0 grams: trans fat;
- 6 grams: monounsaturated fat;
- 11 grams: carbohydrates;

168.   Millet And Red Pepper Polenta

Serving: Serves 6 | Prep: | Cook: | Ready in: 1hours

Ingredients

- 2 red bell peppers, roasted
- 1 cup millet
- 4 cups water (or stock)
- 1 teaspoon salt
- 1 tablespoon butter (more to taste)
- ⅓ cup freshly grated Parmesan
- Freshly ground pepper

Direction

- Preheat oven to 350 degrees. Peel, seed and dice roasted peppers. Season with a little salt if desired and set aside.
- Heat a 10-inch cast iron skillet over medium-high heat and add millet. Toast, stirring or shaking the pan, until grains begin to pop and smell toasty, sort of like popcorn. Add water or stock and salt.
- Transfer pan to the preheated oven. Set timer for 25 minutes. When it goes off, stir in peppers. Bake for another 20 minutes. Stir in butter and if there is any liquid remaining in the pan, bake for another 5 to 10 minutes, until millet is thick and no more water or stock is visible in the pan. Remove from oven and stir

in Parmesan. Serve right away or allow to cool in the pan, or spread in a small sheet pan, baking dish, or cake pan if desired. When it is solid, cut into squares, slices or rounds, which you can grill, fry, or layer in a gratin.

Nutrition Information

- 182: calories;
- 6 grams: protein;
- 0 grams: trans fat;
- 1 gram: polyunsaturated fat;
- 4 grams: dietary fiber;
- 2 grams: sugars;
- 484 milligrams: sodium;
- 5 grams: fat;
- 3 grams: saturated fat;
- 27 grams: carbohydrates;

---

169. Mini Peppers Stuffed With Tuna And Olive Rillettes

Serving: Serves 6 | Prep: | Cook: | Ready in: 30mins

Ingredients

- 1 pound mini bell peppers (usually 2 bags)
- 2 ounces / about 1/3 cup imported black olives, pitted
- 1 plump garlic clove, peeled, green shoot removed
- 1 tablespoon capers, rinsed
- 1 can olive oil-packed tuna, drained
- 1 teaspoon Dijon mustard
- 2 tablespoons extra virgin olive oil
- 2 tablespoons Greek yogurt
- 2 to 3 teaspoons fresh lemon juice (more to taste)
- 1 teaspoon finely chopped fresh rosemary
- 1 teaspoon thyme leaves, chopped

Direction

- Heat oven to 425 degrees. Line a sheet pan with foil. Place peppers on baking sheet and roast very small peppers (less than 2 inches long) for 8 to 10 minutes, larger peppers for 15 minutes, turning them over halfway through. They should be soft but only charred in a few spots. Remove from oven and allow to cool.
- Meanwhile, in a mini-chop or in a mortar and pestle, pulse or grind olives, garlic and capers to a paste.
- In a bowl, mash tuna with a fork and work in olive mixture, mustard, olive oil, yogurt, lemon juice, rosemary and thyme.
- When peppers have cooled, slice off ends just below shoulders. Carefully remove any seeds and membranes. The peppers should be intact, but sometimes they split down one side. Cut large peppers in half lengthwise. Spoon tuna rillettes into peppers and arrange on a plate or platter. Serve at once, or chill until 30 minutes before serving. Bring to room temperature before serving so that the rillettes are soft.

Nutrition Information

- 188: calories;
- 2 grams: dietary fiber;
- 0 grams: trans fat;
- 6 grams: carbohydrates;
- 3 grams: sugars;
- 17 grams: protein;
- 341 milligrams: sodium;
- 11 grams: fat;

---

170. Mushroom Burgers With Almonds And Spinach

Serving: 4 to 6 patties, depending on the size | Prep: | Cook: | Ready in: 3hours

Ingredients

- ¼ cup fine bulgur
- ½ cup roasted almonds

- 2 tablespoons extra virgin olive oil
- 1 pound fresh mushrooms, trimmed and quartered
- 2 large garlic cloves, green shoots removed, minced
- 1 teaspoon fresh thyme leaves
- Salt
- freshly ground pepper to taste
- 2 tablespoons dry white wine (optional)
- 1 6-ounce bag baby spinach, rinsed, or a 12-ounce bunch of spinach, stemmed and washed
- 1 egg, beaten (optional)
- Whole grain buns and condiments of your choice

Direction

- Place the bulgur in a bowl with a little salt if desired. Cover with ½ cup hot water and leave for 20 to 25 minutes, until most of the water has been absorbed and the bulgur is soft. Drain through a strainer and squeeze out the water.
- Meanwhile, in a food processor fitted with the steel blade, grind the almonds coarsely.
- Heat 1 tablespoon of the olive oil in a large, heavy skillet over medium-high heat and add the mushrooms. When they begin to soften and sweat, turn the heat to medium and cook, stirring often, for 5 minutes, until the mushrooms have softened. Add the garlic, thyme, salt, pepper and white wine, and continue to cook, stirring, until there is no more liquid in the pan, about 5 minutes. Remove from the heat, transfer to the food processor and process until very finely chopped.
- Return the pan to the heat and add the spinach, a handful at a time. Cook just until it wilts and remove from the heat. Transfer to a strainer and, with the back of a spoon, press out excess water. Add spinach to the food processor and process with the mushrooms and almonds until the ingredients are well blended. Scrape the mixture into a bowl, stir in the bulgur and egg (if using), and season to

taste with salt and pepper. Form into patties. If there is time, cover and chill for 1 to 2 hours.
- Heat the remaining oil in a large, heavy skillet or on a griddle over medium heat, and brown the patties for 3 minutes on each side, being very careful when you turn them over. Don't worry if they fall apart; just patch them together. An offset spatula works well for turning them, and when you remove the patties from the pan, it helps if you place the bottom bun over the patty, slide the spatula underneath the patty and, with your hand on the bun, flip it over. Serve with the condiments of your choice.

Nutrition Information

- 155: calories;
- 11 grams: carbohydrates;
- 1 gram: saturated fat;
- 7 grams: monounsaturated fat;
- 4 grams: dietary fiber;
- 6 grams: protein;
- 0 grams: trans fat;
- 2 grams: sugars;
- 298 milligrams: sodium;

---

171.   Mushroom Melt With Parsley Pesto, Kale And Arugula

Serving: | Prep: | Cook: | Ready in: 10mins

Ingredients

- 2 slices whole wheat country bread or 1 5-inch square focaccia, sliced in half laterally
- 1 heaped tablespoon parsley pesto (see recipe)
- ¼ cup sautéed mushrooms (see below)
- ¾ ounce Gruyère cheese, cut in thin slices (I use a cheese slicer)
- 2 to 3 tablespoons blanched kale
- ½ ounce baby arugula or wild arugula tossed with 1/2 teaspoon vinaigrette

Direction

- Spread the bottom slice of bread with parsley pesto. Top with the sautéed mushrooms and top the mushrooms with the kale. Lay the cheese over the kale. Place both slices of bread in a toaster oven and toast until the cheese melts, about 3 minutes. Remove from the toaster oven, top the melted cheese with the arugula, place the top slice of bread on top, press down hard, cut the sandwich in half, and serve.

Nutrition Information

- 110: calories;
- 5 grams: protein;
- 1 gram: sugars;
- 2 grams: monounsaturated fat;
- 0 grams: polyunsaturated fat;
- 11 grams: carbohydrates;
- 255 milligrams: sodium;

172.   Mushroom Omelet With Chives

Serving: 2 servings | Prep: | Cook: |Ready in: 15mins

Ingredients

- For the mushroom omelet with chives
- 2 tablespoons plus 1 teaspoon extra-virgin olive oil
- 1 shallot, minced
- ¼ pound white or cremini mushrooms, rinsed briefly and wiped dry
- Salt
- freshly ground pepper to taste
- 1 to 2 garlic cloves (to taste), minced
- 2 teaspoons minced flat-leaf parsley
- 4 eggs
- 1 tablespoon minced chives
- 2 teaspoons low-fat milk
- 3 tablespoons grated Gruyère cheese

Direction

- Trim off the ends of the mushrooms, and cut into thick slices. Heat a large, heavy frying pan over medium-high heat, and add 1 tablespoon of the olive oil. Add the shallot, and cook, stirring, until it begins to soften, two or three minutes. Add the mushrooms, and cook, stirring or tossing in the pan, for a few minutes, until they begin to soften and sweat. Add salt to taste and the garlic, and cook, stirring often, until the mushrooms are tender, about five minutes. Stir in the parsley, season to taste with salt and pepper, and remove from the heat.

- If making individual omelets: Heat an 8-inch nonstick omelet pan over medium-high heat. Break 2 eggs into a bowl, and beat with a fork or a whisk until frothy. Add salt and freshly ground pepper to taste, and 2 teaspoons milk. Whisk in half the chives. Add 2 teaspoons of the olive oil to the pan. When the pan feels hot as you hold your hand above it, pour in the eggs, scraping every last bit into the pan. Tilt the pan to distribute the eggs evenly over the surface. Tilt it slightly again, and gently shake with one hand while lifting up the edges of the omelet with the spatula in your other hand so as to let the eggs run underneath during the first few minutes of cooking. Spread half the mushrooms down the middle of the eggs. Top with half the cheese. As soon as the eggs are set on the bottom (the top will still be runny), jerk the pan quickly away from you then back towards you so that the omelet folds over on itself. Shake in the pan for another minute if you don't like the omelet soft on the inside; for a moist omelet, tilt the pan at once and roll out onto a plate. Keep warm in a low oven while you repeat with the remaining eggs and herbs, and serve.

- If making 1 large omelet, heat a 10-inch nonstick pan over medium-high heat. Beat all 4 eggs in a bowl with the milk, salt and pepper, and the chives. Heat the remaining tablespoon of olive oil in the pan, and follow the instructions for the 2-egg omelet, pouring all of the eggs into the pan. The eggs will take longer to set, and you may want to flip the omelet in the pan again after it's rolled, if the middle seems too runny. Roll the finished omelet onto a platter, or cut in half in the pan, and serve.

- Add 2 teaspoons of the olive oil to the pan. When the pan feels hot as you hold your hand above it, pour in the eggs, scraping every last bit into the pan. Tilt the pan to distribute the eggs evenly over the surface. Tilt it slightly again, and gently shake with one hand while lifting up the edges of the omelet with the spatula in your other hand so as to let the eggs run underneath during the first few minutes of cooking.
- Spread half the mushrooms down the middle of the eggs. Top with half the cheese. As soon as the eggs are set on the bottom (the top will still be runny), jerk the pan quickly away from you then back towards you so that the omelet folds over on itself. Shake in the pan for another minute if you don't like the omelet soft on the inside; for a moist omelet, tilt the pan at once and roll out onto a plate. Keep warm in a low oven while you repeat with the remaining eggs and herbs, and serve.

Nutrition Information

- 388: calories;
- 509 milligrams: sodium;
- 0 grams: trans fat;
- 17 grams: monounsaturated fat;
- 4 grams: sugars;
- 2 grams: dietary fiber;
- 19 grams: protein;
- 31 grams: fat;
- 9 grams: saturated fat;
- 10 grams: carbohydrates;

---

173.   **Mushroom And Beef Burgers**

Serving: Eight 4.5-ounce patties or six 6-ounce patties | Prep: | Cook: | Ready in: 50mins

Ingredients

- 1 pound lean ground beef
- 1 pound roasted mushroom base
- ½ cup finely chopped onion
- Salt and freshly ground pepper to taste
- ½ teaspoon Worcestershire sauce
- ½ cup chopped fresh parsley or a mix of parsley, mint, cilantro and dill
- 1 egg
- Canola or grapeseed oil for the pan (1 to 2 tablespoons)
- Hamburger buns (preferably whole wheat), lettuce, sliced tomatoes, and the usual burger fixings

Direction

- In a large bowl, mix together the beef, roasted mushroom base, onion, salt, pepper, Worcestershire sauce, herbs, and egg. Form 6 to 8 patties and place them on a plate or a lightly oiled sheet pan. Refrigerate for 30 minutes.
- Preheat the oven to 425 degrees. Line a sheet pan with parchment. Heat 1 or 2 large, heavy skillets over medium-high heat and add enough oil to lightly coat the bottom (about 1 tablespoon). When the pans are hot, add the patties and cook for 4 minutes on each side. Transfer to the parchment-lined sheet pan and place in the oven for 5 minutes. Remove from the oven, let sit for a couple of minutes, and serve.

Nutrition Information

- 237: calories;
- 7 grams: monounsaturated fat;
- 3 grams: carbohydrates;
- 15 grams: protein;

- 351 milligrams: sodium;
- 18 grams: fat;
- 6 grams: saturated fat;
- 1 gram: dietary fiber;
- 2 grams: sugars;

---

174.   Mushroom And Daikon Soup

Serving: 4 servings | Prep: | Cook: | Ready in: 30mins

Ingredients

- 3 dried shiitake mushrooms
- 4 dried porcini mushrooms
- 1 tablespoon vegetable oil
- ½ small onion, thinly sliced
- 1 clove garlic, finely chopped
- ¼ cup Shaoxing wine or dry sherry
- 1 piece kombu, rinsed (optional)
- 8 ounces mixed fresh mushrooms, cleaned and sliced
- ¼ cup mushroom soy sauce or regular soy sauce
- ¾ cup daikon, peeled and cut into small cubes, or silken white tofu, cut into small cubes
- Salt
- freshly ground black pepper
- Lemon juice (optional)
- 4 pinches chopped scallion greens, for garnish

Direction

- Place shiitake mushrooms in a small bowl; cover with hot water and set aside. Place porcini mushrooms in a separate bowl; cover with hot water and set aside. Heat oil in a medium saucepan over medium-low heat. Add onion and sauté until translucent. Add garlic and sauté until fragrant, about 1 minute.
- Add Shaoxing wine or sherry, and reduce by half. If planning to use mushroom soy sauce, add 5 cups water. If planning to use regular soy sauce, add 4 2/3 cups water plus 1/3 cup soaking water from porcini mushrooms. Drain

porcini mushrooms of remaining water and add to pan. Add kombu, if using.
- Bring to a full boil, reduce heat to low, and remove and reserve kombu. Drain shiitake mushrooms and discard stems. Slice caps and add to pan. Add fresh mushrooms and soy sauce. Cut kombu into bite-size pieces and return to pan. Add daikon and simmer until softened, 3 to 5 minutes. If using tofu, simmer only until heated, about 30 seconds.
- Season to taste with salt and pepper and, if desired, a touch of lemon juice. To serve, divide among four warmed soup bowls and garnish each with a pinch of scallion greens.

Nutrition Information

- 92: calories;
- 885 milligrams: sodium;
- 4 grams: protein;
- 0 grams: trans fat;
- 3 grams: monounsaturated fat;
- 1 gram: polyunsaturated fat;
- 10 grams: carbohydrates;
- 2 grams: sugars;

---

175.   Noodle Bowl With Mushrooms, Spinach And Salmon

Serving: 4 servings. | Prep: | Cook: | Ready in: 10mins

Ingredients

- 6 cups kombu stock, chicken stock or vegetable stock
- Soy sauce or salt to taste
- 6 ounces Japanese soba noodles, cooked and tossed with 2 teaspoons sesame oil
- 6 fresh shiitake mushrooms, stemmed and thinly sliced (simmer stems in stock for 20 minutes, remove them and discard), or 6 cremini mushrooms, trimmed and thinly sliced

- 12 to 16 ounces salmon fillet without skin, trimmed of fat and cut into 4 equal pieces
- 1 large bunch spinach, stemmed, washed in 2 changes of water and coarsely chopped (about 6 cups) or 1 6-ounce bag baby spinach, rinsed
- 1 bunch scallions, thinly sliced, light and dark green parts kept separateCilantro leaves and sprigs for garnish

Direction

- Bring the stock to a simmer. Taste and adjust seasoning, adding soy sauce or salt if desired. If the noodles have been refrigerated, warm them by placing them in a strainer and dipping the strainer into the simmering broth. Then distribute the noodles among 4 deep soup bowls.
- Add the sliced mushroom caps, the salmon fillets, the spinach and the white and light green parts of the scallions to the simmering stock. Cover and turn off the heat. Allow to sit for 5 minutes without removing the cover. The salmon should be just cooked through. Leave it a little longer if you want it more opaque.
- Place a piece of salmon on top of the noodles in each bowl. Ladle in the soup, taking care to distribute the spinach, mushrooms and scallions evenly. Sprinkle on the dark green parts of the scallions, garnish with cilantro and serve.

176.   Northern Greek Mushroom And Onion Pie

Serving: 8 servings | Prep: | Cook: | Ready in: 2hours

Ingredients

- ¼ cup extra virgin olive oil
- 2 medium or large onions, coarsely chopped
- Salt to taste
- 1 ½ pounds mushrooms, preferably portobellos or a mix of wild mushrooms, portobellos and regular mushrooms, trimmed and coarsely chopped
- 2 large garlic cloves, minced
- 1 teaspoon sweet paprika
- ¼ cup chopped fresh mint
- 2 tablespoons chopped flat-leaf parsley
- 2 ounces feta cheese, crumbled (about 1/3 cup)
- 12 sheets phyllo dough

Direction

- Heat 2 tablespoons of the olive oil in a large, heavy skillet over medium heat and add the onions. Cook, stirring, until they begin to wilt, and add salt to taste. Turn the heat to medium-low and cook the onions, stirring from time to time, until they are very soft and beginning to caramelize, about 15 minutes. Add the mushrooms, turn the heat up to medium-high, and cook until they begin to sweat and soften, about 5 minutes. Add the garlic and stir together until fragrant, about 1 minute, and stir in the paprika. Continue to cook until the mushrooms are tender and most of the liquid in the pan has evaporated, 5 to 10 minutes. Remove from the heat, taste and adjust salt, and stir in the mint, parsley, feta and freshly ground pepper to taste
- Heat the oven to 375 degrees. Brush a 10- or 12-inch tart pan or cake pan with olive oil and layer in 7 sheets of phyllo dough, placing them not quite evenly on top of one another so that the edges overlap the sides of the pan all the way around. Brush each sheet with olive oil (or a mixture of olive oil and melted butter) before adding the next sheet. Fill with the mushroom and onion mixture. Bring the overhanging edges of the phyllo in over the filling, brushing each sheet with more olive oil, then layer 5 more sheets of dough over the top, brushing each sheet with olive oil. Crimp the edges into the sides of the pan. Pierce the top of the pie in several places with a sharp knife. Bake for 40 to 50 minutes, until the top is golden brown. Serve warm or at room

temperature. Recrisp the crust, if necessary, in a low oven for 10 to 20 minutes

Nutrition Information

- 205: calories;
- 2 grams: saturated fat;
- 6 grams: protein;
- 1 gram: polyunsaturated fat;
- 3 grams: dietary fiber;
- 394 milligrams: sodium;
- 10 grams: fat;
- 23 grams: carbohydrates;
- 4 grams: sugars;

177.   Oatmeal And Teff With Cinnamon And Dried Fruit

Serving: Serves 1 | Prep: | Cook: |Ready in: 5mins

Ingredients

- For 1 generous bowl
- ⅓ cup rolled oats
- 1 tablespoon teff
- Salt to taste (I use a generous pinch)
- ⅛ teaspoon ground cinnamon
- 1 tablespoon chopped dried apricots and/or golden raisins (more to taste)
- ⅔ cup water
- 1 teaspoon honey, plus additional to taste for drizzling
- ½ tablespoon chopped toasted skinned hazelnuts or almonds
- Optional toppings: milk, grated apple or pear

Direction

- The night before, stir together rolled oats, teff, salt, cinnamon and chopped apricots or raisins in a medium microwave-safe bowl. Bring water to a boil and pour over mixture. Add honey and stir, then cover bowl with a plate.

- In the morning, microwave mixture for 2 minutes on 100 percent power. Remove bowl from microwave and carefully remove plate (bowl will be hot and steam will rise from cereal). Stir mixture, cover again and return to microwave. Heat for 1 to 2 minutes longer, until mixture is no longer watery.
- Transfer to a serving dish and sprinkle chopped nuts over the top. Add other toppings of your choice and serve.

178.   Oats With Amaranth, Chia Seeds And Blueberries

Serving: Serves 1 | Prep: | Cook: |Ready in: 15mins

Ingredients

- For each bowl
- ¼ cup regular or quick cooking steel-cut oats
- 1 tablespoon amaranth seeds
- 1 teaspoon chia seeds
- Salt to taste (I use a generous pinch)
- 1 heaped tablespoon fresh or frozen blueberries, or more to taste
- ¾ cup water
- 1 teaspoon honey or maple syrup, plus more as desired for drizzling
- Optional toppings: milk, chopped toasted skinned hazelnuts, chopped toasted almonds, grated apple or pear, freeze-dried blueberries

Direction

- The night before, stir together steel-cut oats, amaranth seeds, chia seeds, salt and blueberries in a medium microwave-proof bowl. Bring water to a boil and pour over mixture. Add honey or maple syrup and stir, then cover bowl with a plate.
- In the morning, microwave mixture for 2 minutes on 100 percent power. Remove bowl from microwave and carefully remove plate (bowl will be hot and steam will rise from cereal). Stir mixture, cover again and return to

microwave. Heat for 2 minutes more, or until mixture is no longer watery.
- Transfer to a serving dish and sprinkle on toppings of your choice.

179. Olive Oil Granola With Dried Apricots And Pistachios

Serving: About 9 cups | Prep: | Cook: | Ready in: 45mins

Ingredients

- 3 cups old-fashioned rolled oats
- 1 ½ cups raw pistachios, hulled
- 1 cup raw pumpkin seeds, hulled
- 1 cup coconut chips
- ¾ cup pure maple syrup
- ½ cup extra virgin olive oil
- ½ cup packed light brown sugar
- 1 teaspoon kosher salt
- ½ teaspoon ground cinnamon
- ½ teaspoon ground cardamom
- ¾ cup chopped dried apricots
- Fresh ricotta, for serving (optional)
- Fresh berries, for serving (optional)

Direction

- Preheat oven to 300 degrees. In a large bowl, combine oats, pistachios, pumpkin seeds, coconut chips, maple syrup, olive oil, brown sugar, salt, cinnamon and cardamom. Spread mixture on a rimmed baking sheet in an even layer and bake for 45 minutes, stirring every 10 minutes, until golden brown and well toasted.
- Transfer granola to a large bowl and add apricots, tossing to combine. Serve with ricotta and fruit, if desired.

Nutrition Information

- 293: calories;
- 17 grams: fat;
- 32 grams: carbohydrates;
- 6 grams: protein;
- 111 milligrams: sodium;
- 4 grams: dietary fiber;
- 0 grams: trans fat;
- 8 grams: monounsaturated fat;
- 18 grams: sugars;

180. Omelets With Roasted Vegetables And Feta

Serving: Serves 1 | Prep: | Cook: | Ready in: 2mins

Ingredients

- For each omelet
- 2 eggs
- Salt and freshly ground pepper to taste
- 2 to 3 teaspoons milk
- 2 teaspoons unsalted butter or extra virgin olive oil
- ⅓ cup Roasted Winter Vegetable Medley
- 1 tablespoon crumbled feta

Direction

- Break eggs into a bowl and beat with a fork or a whisk until frothy. Whisk in salt and pepper to taste and 2 to 3 teaspoons milk.
- Heat an 8-inch nonstick omelet pan over medium-high heat. Add 2 teaspoons unsalted butter or olive oil. When butter stops foaming or oil feels hot when you hold your hand above it, pour eggs right into the middle of the pan, scraping every last bit into the pan with a rubber spatula. Swirl pan to distribute eggs evenly over the surface. Shake pan gently, tilting it slightly with one hand while lifting up edges of the omelet with the spatula in your other hand, to let eggs run underneath during first few minutes of cooking.
- As soon as eggs are set on the bottom, spoon roasted vegetables over the middle of the egg "pancake" and sprinkle feta over vegetables. Jerk pan quickly away from you then back

towards you so that the omelet folds over onto itself. If you don't like your omelet runny in the middle, jerk pan again so that omelet folds over once more. Cook for 30 seconds to a minute longer. Tilt pan and roll omelet out onto a plate.

---

181. Onion And Zucchini Frittata To Go

Serving: Serves 2 | Prep: | Cook: | Ready in: 45mins

Ingredients

- 1 tablespoon plus 2 teaspoons extra virgin olive oil
- ¾ cup finely chopped onion
- Salt to taste
- 1 garlic clove, minced
- 1 small zucchini, grated (about 1 cup)
- 4 eggs
- 1 tablespoon milk
- Freshly ground pepper

Direction

- Heat 1 tablespoon of the olive oil over medium heat in a heavy 8-inch nonstick omelet pan and add the onion and a generous pinch of salt. Cook, stirring often, until the onion is very soft and sweet, about 10 minutes. Add the garlic and the zucchini, and cook, stirring often, until the zucchini has wilted, about 3 more minutes. Remove from the heat.
- Beat the eggs in a medium bowl and add the milk and salt and pepper to taste. Stir in the onion and zucchini mixture and mix well. Clean and dry the pan.
- Heat the remaining olive oil over medium-high heat in the omelet pan. Drop a bit of egg into the pan and if it sizzles and cooks at once, the pan is ready. Pour in the egg mixture, scraping in every last bit with a heat-proof rubber spatula. Swirl the pan to distribute the eggs and filling evenly over the surface. Shake the pan gently, tilting it slightly with one hand while lifting up the edges of the frittata with the spatula in your other hand, to let the eggs run underneath during the first few minutes of cooking. Once a few layers of egg have cooked during the first couple of minutes of cooking, turn the heat down to low, cover and cook 7 to 10 minutes, until the frittata is puffed and just about set. From time to time remove the lid and loosen the bottom of the omelet with a wooden or heat-proof rubber spatula, tilting the pan, so that the bottom doesn't burn. It will however turn golden.
- If the frittata is still runny on the top, wearing oven mitts, slide the frittata out onto a plate or even better, a saucepan lid that has a handle, reverse the pan over the plate or lid, and holding the two together, flip the plate or lid so that the frittata goes back into the pan on its not-quite-cooked side. Finish for no longer than a minute, then reverse onto a platter. Allow to cool to room temperature, and serve, or chill. Cut into 4 wedges to serve. The wedges pack well and are very portable.

Nutrition Information

- 262: calories;
- 4 grams: sugars;
- 2 grams: dietary fiber;
- 12 grams: protein;
- 20 grams: fat;
- 0 grams: trans fat;
- 11 grams: monounsaturated fat;
- 3 grams: polyunsaturated fat;
- 9 grams: carbohydrates;
- 496 milligrams: sodium;

---

182. Orecchiette With Basil And Pistachio Pesto And Green And Yellow Beans

Serving: Serves 6 | Prep: | Cook: | Ready in: 30mins

Ingredients

- For the pesto
- 2 cups, tightly packed, basil leaves (2 ounces)
- 2 heaped tablespoons unsalted pistachios (1 ounce)
- Salt to taste
- ⅓ cup extra virgin olive oil
- 2 garlic cloves, peeled, halved, green shoots removed if present
- 2 ounces freshly grated Parmesan (1/2 cup)
- Freshly ground pepper
- For the pasta
- 1 pound orecchiette
- 1 pound mixed green and yellow beans, trimmed and cut in 3/4-inch lengths (you can use all green beans if yellow beans are unavailable)
- Pasta water (about 1/4 cup)

Direction

- Begin heating a large pot of water for the pasta. Meanwhile grind the basil leaves and pistachios in a food processor fitted with the steel blade, or in a mortar and pestle. Add salt to taste and slowly drizzle in the olive oil. Blend or grind until smooth.
- Mash the garlic in a mortar and pestle or through a garlic press and add to the basil mixture. Blend together. Add the cheese and blend together. Taste, adjust salt and add pepper. Transfer to a large pasta bowl.
- When the water comes to a boil, salt generously and add the orecchiette. Set the timer for 10 minutes, and after 5 minutes add the green beans. Boil the orecchiette and beans until the pasta is cooked al dente, another 5 to 6 minutes. Remove 1/2 cup of the cooking water from the pot and add 2 to 4 tablespoons to the pesto. Stir with a fork or a whisk until the pesto is smooth (add more water if desired). Drain the pasta and beans, toss with the pesto and serve.

Nutrition Information

- 495: calories;
- 18 grams: fat;
- 4 grams: saturated fat;
- 3 grams: polyunsaturated fat;
- 68 grams: carbohydrates;
- 5 grams: sugars;
- 17 grams: protein;
- 448 milligrams: sodium;
- 11 grams: monounsaturated fat;

183. Orecchiette With Fresh And Dried Beans And Tomatoes

Serving: Serves 4 | Prep: | Cook: | Ready in: 2hours30mins

Ingredients

- ½ pound (about 1 1/2 cups) Good Mother Stallard Beans, pintos, or borlottis, rinsed and soaked for 4 hours or overnight in 1 quart water
- ½ large onion, or 1 small onion, cut in half or quartered
- 2 to 3 large garlic cloves, minced
- Salt to taste
- 1 cup marinara sauce (using fresh or canned tomatoes), or 1 cup finely chopped fresh tomatoes
- ½ pound orecchiette
- ½ pound green beans, broken into 2- or 3-inch lengths
- Slivered fresh basil leaves (about 2 tablespoons)
- Freshly grated Parmesan for serving

Direction

- To cook dried beans, transfer with their soaking water to a heavy pot. Add more water as necessary to cover the beans with 1 1/2 to 2 inches of water. Over medium-high heat, bring to a gentle boil and skim away foam. Add onion and garlic, cover, reduce heat to low and simmer 30 minutes. Add salt to taste (I use at least a rounded teaspoon), cover and continue to simmer very gently for 1 to 1 1/2 hours, until the beans are tender all the way through and their texture is plush and velvety. Taste the bean broth and add more salt as necessary. Remove from heat. Let beans cool in the broth if not using right away.

- Place a strainer over a bowl and drain beans. Measure out 1 cup of the broth and combine with the tomato sauce or tomatoes in a wide pan or a pasta bowl.
- Bring a large pot of water to a boil, salt generously and add orecchiette. Boil 5 minutes and add green beans. Boil another 5 minutes, until pasta is cooked al dente. Drain and toss green beans and pasta with the cooked beans and tomato sauce or tomatoes. Add half the basil and toss again.
- Serve in wide bowls, garnishing each serving with fresh basil and Parmesan.

Nutrition Information

- 290: calories;
- 2 grams: fat;
- 0 grams: monounsaturated fat;
- 1 gram: polyunsaturated fat;
- 58 grams: carbohydrates;
- 6 grams: dietary fiber;
- 10 grams: sugars;
- 11 grams: protein;
- 603 milligrams: sodium;

---

184. Orecchiette With Raw And Cooked Tomatoes

Serving: Serves four | Prep: | Cook: | Ready in: 50mins

Ingredients

- 2 tablespoons extra virgin olive oil
- 1 small onion, chopped
- 2 large garlic cloves, green shoots removed, minced or thinly sliced, plus 1 small clove, green shoots removed, minced or pureed
- ¼ teaspoon crushed red pepper flakes (optional; more to taste)
- 2 pounds ripe tomatoes
- Pinch of sugar
- A few sprigs of fresh basil
- Salt to taste
- ¾ pound orecchiette
- Parmesan, Pecorino or ricotta salata for serving

Direction

- Set aside 1/2 pound of the tomatoes. Quarter the remaining tomatoes, or cut into wedges if very large. Heat 1 tablespoon of the olive oil in a wide, nonstick frying pan or in a 3-quart saucepan over medium heat. Add the onion. Cook, stirring often, until the onion is tender and golden, about eight minutes. Add the two large garlic cloves. Cook, stirring, until fragrant, 30 seconds to a minute. Add the quartered tomatoes, the sugar, basil sprigs and salt, and bring to a simmer. Simmer, stirring often, until the tomatoes have cooked down and the sauce is thick. Taste and adjust seasonings. Remove the basil sprigs, and put through the medium blade of a food mill. Return to the pan.
- Meanwhile, finely chop the tomatoes you set aside. Add the remaining small clove of garlic, salt to taste, 1 tablespoon extra virgin olive oil and a couple of leaves of basil, chopped or slivered. Allow to sit for 15 minutes.
- Bring a large pot of water to a boil, and salt generously. Add the pasta, and cook al dente, 10 to 12 minutes, following the cooking time suggestion on the package. If desired, stir 1/4 to 1/2 cup of the cooking water into the tomato sauce. Drain the pasta, and toss with both the warm tomato sauce and the uncooked tomato concassée. Serve with Parmesan, Pecorino or ricotta salata.

Nutrition Information

- 427: calories;
- 6 grams: dietary fiber;
- 13 grams: protein;
- 1 gram: polyunsaturated fat;
- 5 grams: monounsaturated fat;
- 789 milligrams: sodium;
- 9 grams: sugars;
- 0 grams: trans fat;
- 75 grams: carbohydrates;

---

185.   Oven Fries

Serving: 4 to 6 servings | Prep: | Cook: |Ready in: 45mins

Ingredients

- 1 pound waxy potatoes, such as red potatoes
- 1 pound sweet potatoes, cut in half crosswise
- 3 tablespoons extra virgin olive oil
- Kosher salt or coarse sea salt

Direction

- Preheat the oven to 500 degrees. Line a sheet pan with aluminum foil, shiny side up. Place in the oven while you prepare the potatoes.
- Cut the potatoes into wedges that are 1/4 inch to 1/2 inch thick at the thickest point and toss with the olive oil and salt.
- Remove the hot pan from the oven, and add the potatoes to the pan in an even layer. They should sizzle. Return to the oven, and lower the heat to 450 degrees. Roast 25 minutes or until tender.
- Remove the pan from the oven, and loosen the potatoes from the foil using an offset spatula. Return to the oven and cook for another five minutes. Serve at once, seasoned with more salt if desired.

Nutrition Information

- 153: calories;
- 7 grams: fat;
- 22 grams: carbohydrates;
- 5 grams: monounsaturated fat;
- 3 grams: dietary fiber;
- 4 grams: sugars;
- 2 grams: protein;
- 286 milligrams: sodium;
- 1 gram: polyunsaturated fat;

---

186.   Oven Baked Millet

Serving: 4 to 6 servings. | Prep: | Cook: |Ready in: 1hours10mins

Ingredients

- 4 cups water (or stock)
- 1 cup millet
- 1 teaspoon salt
- 1 tablespoon butter (more to taste)
- ⅓ cup freshly grated Parmesan
- Freshly ground pepper

Direction

- Preheat the oven to 350 degrees. Heat a 10-inch cast-iron skillet over medium-high heat and add the millet. Toast, stirring or shaking the pan, until the grains begin to pop and smell toasty, sort of like popcorn. Add the water or stock and the salt.
- Transfer the pan to the preheated oven. Set the timer for 25 minutes and give the millet a stir. Bake for another 25 minutes. There should still be some liquid in the pan. Stir in the butter and bake for another 5 to 10 minutes, until the millet is thick and no more water or stock is visible in the pan. Remove from the oven; if desired, stir in the Parmesan. Serve right away, topped with tomato sauce or a stew. Alternatively, allow to cool, either in the pan or spread in a small sheet pan, baking dish or cake pan; when it is solid, cut into squares,

slices or rounds, which you can grill, fry or layer in a gratin.

Nutrition Information

- 169: calories;
- 25 grams: carbohydrates;
- 6 grams: protein;
- 5 grams: fat;
- 2 grams: saturated fat;
- 0 grams: sugars;
- 1 gram: polyunsaturated fat;
- 3 grams: dietary fiber;
- 466 milligrams: sodium;

187. Oven Steamed Cod Or Mahi Mahi In Green Tomatillo Salsa

Serving: Serves 4 | Prep: | Cook: |Ready in: 1hours15mins

Ingredients

- 1 pound fresh tomatillos, husked and rinsed
- 2 or 3 jalapeño or serrano chiles, stemmed, seeded for a milder salsa
- ¼ cup chopped onion, soaked for 5 minutes in cold water, then drained and rinsed
- 2 large garlic cloves, peeled
- Salt to taste
- ⅓ cup coarsely chopped cilantro, plus additional chopped cilantro for garnish
- 1 tablespoon grapeseed or sunflower oil
- 1 cup chicken or vegetable stock
- 1 ½ pounds cod or mahi mahi fillets
- Cilantro sprigs or leaves and lemon or lime wedges for serving

Direction

- Place the tomatillos in a saucepan, fill with water and bring to a simmer. Simmer 10 minutes. Drain and place in a blender. Add the

chiles, chopped onion, garlic, salt and cilantro. Blend until smooth.

- Heat the oil in a large, heavy saucepan or skillet over medium-high heat. Drizzle in a drop of the tomatillo purée to test the heat. If it sizzles and sputters immediately, the oil is hot enough. Add the tomatillo purée, and stir constantly until it thickens and begins to stick to the pan, about 5 minutes. When you run your spoon down the middle of the pan it should leave a canal. Stir in the stock, bring to a simmer, and simmer 15 to 20 minutes, stirring often, until it has reduced by about a quarter and coats the front and the back of a spoon like cream. Keep warm.
- Preheat the oven to 300 degrees. Line a sheet pan with foil and oil the foil. Season the fish fillets with salt and pepper and lay on the foil. Place a pan of just boiled water on the floor of your oven and place the baking sheet with the fish in the oven on the middle rack. Bake 10 to 20 minutes, depending on the thickness of the fillets, until the fish is opaque on the surface and you can pull it apart with a fork. Remove from the heat, transfer to plates or a platter, and spoon on the sauce. Garnish with cilantro and lemon or lime wedges, and serve. You will have some sauce left over.

Nutrition Information

- 242: calories;
- 849 milligrams: sodium;
- 6 grams: sugars;
- 1 gram: saturated fat;
- 2 grams: dietary fiber;
- 11 grams: carbohydrates;
- 34 grams: protein;

188. Pan Fried Broccoli Stems

Serving: Serves 4 | Prep: | Cook: |Ready in: 5mins

Ingredients

- 4 to 8 thick broccoli stems
- About 4 tablespoons grape seed oil or olive oil
- Salt to taste

Direction

- Peel broccoli stems and slice crosswise, very thin, about 1/8 inch. (Don't slice paper-thin because then it's too easy to burn them.)
- Heat a heavy skillet over high heat and add enough oil to coat well (about 1/8 inch of oil in the pan). When oil is hot add broccoli stems in a single layer. (Don't add too many at a time because they will cook quickly and you need to turn them all over before they burn.) Turn heat down to medium-high and cook broccoli stems until edges are lightly brown, then flip over with tongs. Cook for 30 seconds to a minute more and remove from oil. Drain on paper towels, sprinkle with salt, and let cool for about a minute before eating.
- Continue with all of the broccoli stems, adding oil as needed.

Nutrition Information

- 143: calories;
- 185 milligrams: sodium;
- 14 grams: fat;
- 1 gram: sugars;
- 2 grams: protein;
- 10 grams: polyunsaturated fat;
- 4 grams: carbohydrates;

189.   Pasta With Asparagus, Arugula And Ricotta

Serving: Serves four | Prep: | Cook: | Ready in: 15mins

Ingredients

- ¾ pound thin asparagus, woody ends snapped off, cut into 1-inch lengths
- Salt

- ¾ pound penne, fusilli or bow-tie pasta
- ½ cup fresh ricotta
- 2 tablespoons extra virgin olive oil
- A generous handful of baby arugula or wild arugula leaves, rinsed and spun dry (about 1 ounce, or 1 cup tightly packed)
- Freshly ground pepper
- ⅓ cup freshly grated Parmesan

Direction

- Bring a large pot of water to a boil, and add a generous amount of salt. Add the asparagus. Cook pencil-thin asparagus for two minutes, three to four minutes if stems are medium-thick. Transfer to a bowl of ice-cold water. Drain and set aside.
- Place the ricotta in a large pasta bowl.
- Bring the water back to a boil, and add the pasta. Cook al dente, following the directions for timing on the package but checking a minute before the suggested cooking time. Stir 1/3 cup of the pasta cooking water into the ricotta. Drain the pasta and toss at once with the olive oil and ricotta, the arugula, asparagus and Parmesan. Serve hot.

Nutrition Information

- 485: calories;
- 15 grams: fat;
- 4 grams: sugars;
- 513 milligrams: sodium;
- 5 grams: dietary fiber;
- 7 grams: monounsaturated fat;
- 1 gram: polyunsaturated fat;
- 69 grams: carbohydrates;
- 20 grams: protein;

190.   Pasta With Mushrooms And Broccoli

Serving: Serves 4 | Prep: | Cook: | Ready in: 30mins

Ingredients

- 2 large stalks broccoli (stems and crowns)
- 2 tablespoons extra-virgin olive oil
- ½ pound mushrooms, sliced 1/3 to 1/2 inch thick
- 2 garlic cloves, minced
- Salt and freshly ground pepper
- 1 teaspoon fresh thyme leaves (optional)
- 8 ounces spaghetti
- Freshly grated Parmesan

Direction

- Cut broccoli stalks away from crowns and peel stalks. Use a vegetable peeler to shave stalks into thin ribbons. Set aside. Cut crowns into thin slices (about 1/4 inch). Combine with the little flower buds that fall off onto your cutting surface in a bowl.
- Begin heating a large pot of water for the pasta. Heat 1 tablespoon of the oil over medium-high heat in a large, heavy skillet. Add sliced mushrooms and sauté until lightly colored and beginning to sweat, 3 to 5 minutes. Reduce heat to medium, add salt to taste, another tablespoon of oil, and shaved broccoli stems. Continue to sauté until the broccoli stem ribbons are crisp-tender, 3 to 5 minutes. Add garlic and thyme, season to taste with salt and pepper, and cook, stirring, until garlic smells fragrant, 30 seconds to a minute. Remove from heat.
- When water in the pasta pot comes to a boil, add salt to taste and spaghetti. Set timer for 2 minutes less than the cooking time suggested on the package. When it goes off, add thinly sliced broccoli crowns and flower buds, and cook 2 minutes more, or until the pasta is al dente. Using a ladle, transfer 1/2 cup of the pasta cooking water to the pan with the mushrooms and shaved broccoli stems. Drain the pasta and broccoli and toss with the mushroom and stem mixture, either in a large bowl or right in the pan. Serve with Parmesan cheese.

---

191.   Pasta With Mushrooms And Gremolata

Serving: 4 servings | Prep: | Cook: | Ready in: 30mins

Ingredients

- 2 plump garlic cloves, finely minced
- ½ cup finely minced flat-leaf parsley
- 1 tablespoon finely chopped lemon zest
- 2 tablespoons extra virgin olive oil
- 1 pound cultivated or wild mushrooms, like shiitakes, chanterelles or oyster mushrooms, or a combination, trimmed and quartered if small, cut in thick slices if large
- Salt to taste
- 2 tablespoons dry white wine
- Freshly ground black pepper
- 12 ounces fettuccini or farfalle
- ¼ to ½ cup pasta cooking water, to taste
- ¼ to ½ cup freshly grated Parmesan (optional)

Direction

- To make the gremolata, place the minced garlic, parsley and lemon zest in a mound and chop them together with a chef's knife. Set aside.
- Begin heating a large pot of water for the pasta. Meanwhile, heat a large, heavy skillet or wok over medium-high heat. Add 1 tablespoon of the olive oil, and when it's hot, add the mushrooms. Sear the mushrooms, stirring with a wooden spoon or tossing in the pan, until they are lightly browned and begin to sweat. Add the salt and the white wine and continue to cook, stirring or tossing the mushrooms in the pan, until the wine has just about evaporated and the mushrooms are glazed, about 5 minutes.
- Add the remaining tablespoon of oil and the gremolata and pepper. Cook, stirring, until fragrant, about 1 more minute. Taste and adjust salt. Keep the mixture warm while you cook the pasta.

- When the water comes to a rolling boil, salt generously and add the pasta. Cook al dente, following the timing instructions on the package. Before draining, remove 1/2 cup of the pasta cooking water. Add 1/4 cup of it to the mushrooms and stir together.
- Drain the pasta and toss with the mushrooms in a large pasta bowl or in the pan. If it seems dry, add 2 to 4 tablespoons of the reserved cooking water. Serve with Parmesan cheese if desired.

Nutrition Information

- 426: calories;
- 5 grams: monounsaturated fat;
- 72 grams: carbohydrates;
- 4 grams: sugars;
- 15 grams: protein;
- 9 grams: fat;
- 1 gram: polyunsaturated fat;
- 6 grams: dietary fiber;
- 572 milligrams: sodium;

---

192. Pasta With Zucchini And Mint

Serving: Serves four | Prep: | Cook: | Ready in: 30mins

Ingredients

- 2 tablespoons extra virgin olive oil
- 1-1/2 pounds zucchini, scrubbed and sliced very thin
- Salt
- freshly ground pepper to taste
- ¼ teaspoon sugar
- 1 tablespoon plus 1 teaspoon sherry vinegar
- 1 teaspoon finely minced lemon zest
- 1 tablespoon chopped fresh mint
- ¾ pound pasta, such as farfalle or fusilli
- Grated ricotta salata or Pecorino for serving (optional)

Direction

- Bring a large pot of water to a boil for the pasta. Meanwhile, heat the oil over medium heat in a large, heavy nonstick skillet, and add the zucchini. Cook, stirring or shaking the pan, until the zucchini is tender, 10 to 15 minutes. Season generously with salt and pepper. Add the sugar, and stir in the vinegar, lemon zest and mint. Remove from the heat, and keep warm while you cook the pasta.
- When the water comes to a boil, salt generously and add the pasta. Cook al dente, following the timing instructions on the package. Add 1/2 cup of the pasta cooking water to the zucchini, then drain the pasta and toss with the zucchini. Serve, passing the cheese at the table for sprinkling.

Nutrition Information

- 409: calories;
- 628 milligrams: sodium;
- 9 grams: fat;
- 1 gram: polyunsaturated fat;
- 5 grams: dietary fiber;
- 70 grams: carbohydrates;
- 7 grams: sugars;
- 13 grams: protein;

---

193. Pear Clafoutis

Serving: 8 servings | Prep: | Cook: | Ready in: 2hours15mins

Ingredients

- 2 tablespoons pear eau-de-vie or liqueur (optional)
- 2 tablespoons mild-flavored honey, like clover
- 2 pounds ripe but firm pears, like Bartlett or Comice
- 3 large eggs
- 1 vanilla bean, scraped

- ⅓ cup sugar
- ⅔ cup sifted unbleached white flour
- ½ cup plain yogurt
- ½ cup milk
- Pinch of salt

Direction

- Combine the pear eau-de-vie and the honey in a bowl. Peel, core and slice the pears and toss with the mixture. Let sit for 30 minutes.
- Preheat the oven to 375 degrees. Butter a 10-inch ceramic tart pan or baking dish.
- In the bowl of an electric mixer or with a whisk, beat together the eggs, the seeds from the vanilla bean and the sugar. Pour off the marinade from the pears and add to the egg mixture. Gradually beat in the flour, then beat in the yogurt, milk and salt.
- Arrange the pears in the baking dish. Pour on the batter. Place in the oven and bake 40 to 50 minutes, until the top is beginning to brown. Serve hot or warm.

Nutrition Information

- 198: calories;
- 1 gram: polyunsaturated fat;
- 0 grams: trans fat;
- 40 grams: carbohydrates;
- 4 grams: dietary fiber;
- 78 milligrams: sodium;
- 3 grams: fat;
- 25 grams: sugars;
- 5 grams: protein;

194.   Pear Vanilla Sorbet

Serving: Makes about 5 cups, serving 6 to 8 | Prep: |
Cook: | Ready in: 4hours30mins

Ingredients

- 125 grams (1/2 cup) water

- 1 vanilla bean or 1 teaspoon vanilla
- 160 grams (approximately 3/4 cup) sugar
- 1,125 grams (4 large) ripe pears, peeled, quartered and cored
- 30 grams (approximately 1 tablespoon plus 1 teaspoon) clover honey
- 40 grams (approximately 2 tablespoons) corn syrup or agave nectar
- 2 teaspoons fresh lemon juice

Direction

- Place the water in a medium saucepan. Cut the vanilla bean in half lengthwise and, using the tip of a paring knife, scrape the seeds into the water. Add the pods and the sugar. Bring to a simmer and simmer until the sugar dissolves. Add the pears and simmer 10 minutes, or until soft when pierced with a knife and translucent on the surfaces. Remove from the heat and stir in the honey, corn syrup or agave nectar, and lemon juice. Allow to cool. Remove the vanilla bean pods from the saucepan.
- Blend the pears with the syrup in a blender until smooth. Chill for 2 hours or overnight.
- Chill a container in the freezer. Using an immersion blender, blend the pear mixture for 30 seconds. Freeze in an ice cream maker following the manufacturer's directions. Transfer to the container and freeze for at least two hours to pack.

Nutrition Information

- 185: calories;
- 4 grams: dietary fiber;
- 41 grams: sugars;
- 1 gram: protein;
- 6 milligrams: sodium;
- 0 grams: polyunsaturated fat;
- 49 grams: carbohydrates;

195. Pear And Apple Soufflé

Serving: Serves six | Prep: | Cook: | Ready in: 1hours45mins

Ingredients

- Juice of 1/2 lemon
- 1 pound apples, peeled, cored and diced
- 1 ½ pounds ripe, juicy pears, peeled, cored and diced
- ⅓ cup sugar
- 1 teaspoon vanilla extract
- ¼ teaspoon powdered ginger
- Butter for the ramekin (or ramekins)
- 8 large egg whites
- ⅛ teaspoon cream of tartar

Direction

- Fill a bowl with water, and add the juice of 1/2 lemon. Place the fruit in the water as you prepare it. When all of the fruit is prepared, drain and transfer to a large, heavy saucepan. Add 1 tablespoon of the sugar, the vanilla and ginger, and 2 tablespoons water. Bring to a simmer over medium heat. Stir, and then turn the heat down to low, cover and simmer, stirring often, for 20 minutes. Uncover and continue to simmer for another 30 to 40 minutes, stirring often, until the fruit is very soft and beginning to stick to the pan. It may or may not look like applesauce, depending on the texture of the apples and pears that you used (Granny Smith apples, for example, will break down, whereas Galas will not). Remove from the heat, and transfer to a food processor fitted with the steel blade. Puree until smooth. Transfer to a large bowl, and allow to cool.
- Preheat the oven to 425 degrees with the rack adjusted to the lowest position. Butter one 2-quart soufflé dish or six 6-ounce ramekins and dust with sugar (use about 1 1/2 tablespoons of the sugar).
- In the bowl of a standing mixer fitted with the whisk attachment, or in a large bowl with a hand mixer, beat the egg whites on low speed for one minute or until they foam. Add the cream of tartar, and continue to beat on low speed for one minute. Turn the speed to medium, and slowly stream in the remaining sugar while you continue to beat until there are firm, satiny peaks. Be careful not to overbeat.
- Fold one third of the egg whites into the apple-pear puree to lighten it. Fold in the rest. Gently spoon into the ramekins or the soufflé dish, mounding it up over the top. Put the ramekins on a baking sheet, and place in the oven. Bake individual soufflés for about 10 minutes, until puffed and golden. They should still be runny on the inside. Bake a large soufflé for 15 to 20 minutes. Serve at once.

Nutrition Information

- 198: calories;
- 40 grams: carbohydrates;
- 31 grams: sugars;
- 76 milligrams: sodium;
- 3 grams: fat;
- 1 gram: monounsaturated fat;
- 5 grams: protein;
- 2 grams: saturated fat;
- 0 grams: polyunsaturated fat;

196. Pearl Couscous With Sautéed Cherry Tomatoes

Serving: 4 servings | Prep: | Cook: | Ready in: 25mins

Ingredients

- 1 ⅓ cups pearl couscous
- 2 quarts water
- Salt to taste
- 2 tablespoons extra-virgin olive oil
- 2 garlic cloves, minced or puréed
- 1 pound (about 3 cups) cherry tomatoes, the sweetest you can find, cut in half
- ¼ teaspoon sugar
- Salt to taste

- 1 sprig basil
- 2 tablespoons, or more, slivered basil leaves

Direction

- Heat a large saucepan over medium-high heat and add couscous. Toast couscous, shaking pan or stirring often, until it colors very lightly and smells aromatic and toasty, a bit like popcorn. Immediately add 2 quarts water and salt to taste (be generous, as if you are cooking pasta) and boil 10 minutes, until couscous is al dente; it should not be mushy, and there should still be plenty of water in the pot. Drain through a strainer and rinse with cold water. Tap strainer against sink to drain well, then return couscous to the pot, cover pot with a kitchen towel, and return lid. Let sit for 10 minutes while you make the sauce.
- In a wide, heavy skillet, heat olive oil over medium heat and add garlic. As soon as it begins to sizzle and smell fragrant, usually in about 30 seconds, add cherry tomatoes and turn heat up to medium-high. Add sugar, salt and basil sprig and cook, stirring often, until tomatoes collapse and skins shrivel. Some of the tomato pulp will be in the pan, and should thicken and caramelize slightly, but there should still be pulp inside the skins. This should only take about 5 minutes. Turn off heat and remove basil sprig. Taste and adjust seasonings. Add a little fresh pepper if desired.
- Add couscous to the pan along with slivered basil, stir together, and serve.

Nutrition Information

- 301: calories;
- 1 gram: polyunsaturated fat;
- 5 grams: monounsaturated fat;
- 3 grams: sugars;
- 9 grams: protein;
- 7 grams: fat;
- 50 grams: carbohydrates;
- 4 grams: dietary fiber;
- 1522 milligrams: sodium;

197. Peppers Stuffed With Rice, Zucchini And Herbs

Serving: Serves 6 | Prep: | Cook: | Ready in: 2hours

Ingredients

- 6 medium peppers, preferably green
- 2 medium zucchini (about 3/4 pound), shredded
- Salt to taste
- ⅓ cup extra virgin olive oil
- 2 garlic cloves, minced
- ½ cup finely chopped fresh mint
- ¼ cup chopped fresh dill or parsley
- 1 scant cup uncooked medium grain rice
- Freshly ground pepper
- 2 tablespoons tomato paste dissolved in 2/3 cup water
- 2 tablespoons freshly squeezed lemon juice

Direction

- Prepare the peppers. With a sharp paring knife, cut away the tops, then reach in and pull out the membranes and seeds.
- Toss the shredded zucchini with salt and let drain in a colander for 20 minutes. Take up handfuls of zucchini and squeeze out as much liquid as possible. Transfer to a medium bowl and add the garlic, mint, parsley or dill, and rice. Season with salt and pepper. Stir in 1/4 cup of the olive oil and let sit for 10 minutes.
- Meanwhile preheat the oven to 375 degrees. Oil a baking dish large enough to accommodate all of the peppers. Fill the peppers about 3/4 of the way full with the stuffing, and replace the caps. Place in the oiled baking dish. Mix together the tomato paste and water with the remaining olive oil and the lemon juice. Season to taste. Add to the baking dish. Cover the dish with foil. Place in the oven and bake 45 minutes to an hour, until the peppers are soft. Remove from the

heat and allow to cool to room temperature, or serve hot. Remove the tops of the peppers and spoon the sauce in the baking dish over the rice before serving.

Nutrition Information

- 268: calories;
- 13 grams: fat;
- 9 grams: monounsaturated fat;
- 1 gram: polyunsaturated fat;
- 36 grams: carbohydrates;
- 4 grams: protein;
- 558 milligrams: sodium;
- 2 grams: saturated fat;
- 5 grams: sugars;

---

198. Peppers Stuffed With Farro And Smoked Cheese

Serving: 6 servings | Prep: | Cook: | Ready in: 1hours15mins

Ingredients

- 2 cups cooked farro or spelt
- 3 ounces smoked cheese, such as smoked gouda, cut in very small dice
- ¼ cup chopped walnuts (1.5 ounces)
- ½ pound fresh, ripe tomatoes, grated
- 1 teaspoon sweet paprika, and additional for sprinkling
- Salt and freshly ground pepper to taste
- 6 medium-size or smallish bell peppers, any color (1 1/2 to 2 pounds)
- ½ cup water
- 2 tablespoons fresh lemon juice
- 1 tablespoon tomato paste
- 1 tablespoon extra-virgin olive oil

Direction

- Preheat oven to 350 degrees. Oil an oven-proof, lidded casserole or Dutch oven large

enough to accommodate all of the peppers. In a large bowl, mix farro, cheese, walnuts, tomatoes and paprika. Season to taste with salt and pepper.

- Cut tops away from peppers and gently remove seeds and membranes. Season the insides with a little salt, then fill with farro mix. Sprinkle a little paprika over the top and replace tops of peppers. Place upright in the casserole.
- Mix water, lemon juice, salt to taste, tomato paste and olive oil and pour into the casserole. Cover, place in the oven and bake 30 to 40 minutes, until peppers are tender. Remove from the heat and allow to cool slightly in the casserole. Remove tops and spoon liquid from the casserole over the filling. Serve warm or at room temperature.

Nutrition Information

- 245: calories;
- 4 grams: polyunsaturated fat;
- 28 grams: carbohydrates;
- 6 grams: sugars;
- 10 grams: protein;
- 666 milligrams: sodium;
- 12 grams: fat;
- 3 grams: monounsaturated fat;

---

199. Perciatelli With Broccoli, Tomatoes And Anchovies

Serving: Serves 4 | Prep: | Cook: | Ready in: 1hours

Ingredients

- ¼ cup golden raisins or currants (optional)
- 1 pound baby broccoli
- Salt to taste
- 2 tablespoons extra virgin olive oil
- 2 garlic cloves, minced
- 2 anchovy fillets, rinsed and chopped
- 2 teaspoons fresh thyme leaves

- 1 pound tomatoes, grated, or 1 14-ounce can chopped tomatoes, with juice
- 8 imported black olives, pitted and chopped
- Freshly ground pepper to taste
- ¾ pound perciatelli (also sold as bucatini) or spaghetti
- 2 to 4 tablespoons grated pecorino or Parmesan cheese

Direction

- Place the raisins in a small bowl and cover with warm water. Let sit for 20 minutes while you prepare the other ingredients.
- Bring a large pot of water to a boil, salt generously and add the baby broccoli. Blanch for 4 minutes and, using a skimmer or tongs, transfer to a bowl of cold water. Drain and shake out excess water. If the stems are thick and hard, peel. Chop coarsely.
- Heat the olive oil over medium heat in a large, heavy skillet and add the garlic. Cook, stirring, until it smells fragrant, about 30 seconds to a minute, and add the anchovies, thyme and tomatoes. Turn the heat down to medium-low and cook, stirring often, until the tomatoes have cooked down and smell fragrant, about 10 minutes. Stir in the olives. Drain the raisins or currants and add, along with the broccoli and about 1/4 cup of the cooking water from the broccoli. Season to taste with salt and pepper. Cover, turn the heat to low and simmer 5 to 10 minutes, stirring occasionally, until the broccoli is very tender and the sauce is fragrant. Keep warm while you cook the pasta.
- Bring the water back to a boil and cook the pasta al dente, following the timing instructions on the package. Check the sauce and if it seems dry add another 1/4 to 1/2 cup of the pasta cooking water. Drain the pasta and transfer to the pan with the sauce. Toss together and serve, sprinkled with pecorino or Parmesan. If desired, drizzle a little olive oil over each serving.

Nutrition Information

- 490: calories;
- 7 grams: sugars;
- 2 grams: polyunsaturated fat;
- 77 grams: carbohydrates;
- 792 milligrams: sodium;
- 12 grams: fat;
- 3 grams: saturated fat;
- 20 grams: protein;
- 8 grams: dietary fiber;

200. Persimmon Spice Bread

Serving: 1 9x5-inch loaf (12 slices) | Prep: | Cook: | Ready in: 1hours30mins

Ingredients

- 2 to 3 ripe or over-ripe persimmons (enough for 1 cup purée)
- 10 grams (2 teaspoons) baking soda
- 140 grams (approximately 1 cup) whole wheat flour
- 70 grams (approximately 1/2 cup) unbleached all-purpose flour
- 75 grams (approximately 3/4 cup) almond powder (also known as almond flour)
- 1 teaspoon ground cinnamon
- ½ teaspoon ground nutmeg
- ¼ teaspoon ground allspice
- ⅛ teaspoon ground cloves
- ½ teaspoon salt
- 2 large eggs, at room temperature
- 100 grams (approximately 1/2 cup) raw brown sugar or tightly packed light brown sugar
- 75 grams (1/3 cup) melted unsalted butter, grape seed oil or canola oil
- ⅓ cup plain low-fat yogurt or buttermilk
- 1 teaspoon vanilla extract
- ½ cup raisins
- ½ cup chopped walnuts (optional)

Direction

- Preheat the oven to 375 degrees with a rack in the middle. Butter or oil a loaf pan and line with parchment. Oil the parchment. Cut the persimmons in half along the equator, remove any visible seeds and scoop out the pulp, which should be nice and soft. Purée with a hand blender or in a food processor fitted with the steel blade and measure out 1 heaped cup (260 grams). Freeze the remaining pulp.
- Stir 1 teaspoon of the baking soda into the persimmon pulp and set aside. It will stiffen into a gelatinous mass but don't worry about it. Sift together the flours, remaining baking soda, spices, and salt.
- In a standing mixer fitted with the whip, or with a hand beater or whisk, beat together the eggs and sugar until thick and they ribbon when lifted with a spatula, 5 to 8 minutes. Beat in the melted butter or oil, the yogurt, persimmon purée, and vanilla and beat until the persimmon purée has blended into the mixture.
- At low speed, beat in the flour in 3 additions. Fold in the raisins and the optional nuts. Scrape into the loaf pan and bake 50 to 60 minutes, until the bread is firm and a toothpick inserted in the middle comes out clean. Remove from the oven, remove from the pan and allow to cool on a rack.

Nutrition Information

- 217: calories;
- 249 milligrams: sodium;
- 4 grams: saturated fat;
- 0 grams: trans fat;
- 30 grams: carbohydrates;
- 5 grams: protein;
- 10 grams: fat;
- 2 grams: dietary fiber;
- 1 gram: polyunsaturated fat;
- 13 grams: sugars;

201. Pesto Filled Deviled Eggs

Serving: Serves 6 | Prep: | Cook: | Ready in: 30mins

Ingredients

- 6 extra-large eggs
- ⅓ cup pesto, either basil pesto or (preferably) basil-mint (1/2 recipe)
- Salt and freshly ground pepper to taste (optional)

Direction

- To hard-cook eggs, place in a saucepan, fill with water and bring to a rolling boil over high heat. As soon as water is at a roll, cover tightly and turn off heat. Let stand for 12 minutes. Meanwhile, fill a bowl with ice water. Transfer hard-cooked eggs to ice water and leave until completely cooled. Peel off shells and cut eggs in half lengthwise.
- Remove yolks from eggs. Set aside 3 of them for another use (or discard) and mash the other 3 together with the pesto, either in a mortar and pestle or in a food processor. Pipe, scoop or spoon into the egg whites.
- If desired, season exposed egg whites with salt and pepper. Arrange on a plate or small platter and serve.

Nutrition Information

- 80: calories;
- 0 grams: sugars;
- 1 gram: polyunsaturated fat;
- 7 grams: protein;
- 80 milligrams: sodium;
- 5 grams: fat;
- 2 grams: monounsaturated fat;

202. Pickled Asparagus

Serving: 3 or 4 pint jars | Prep: | Cook: | Ready in: 1hours

Ingredients

- About 5 pounds asparagus, thin to medium-thick
- 2 ¼ cups distilled white or white wine vinegar (labeled at least 5 percent acidity)
- 4 tablespoons salt
- 2 garlic cloves, slivered
- 1 teaspoon dill seed (optional)
- ¼ teaspoon hot pepper flakes
- ¼ teaspoon whole allspice (optional)
- ¼ teaspoon cumin seed (optional)
- ¼ teaspoon coriander seed (optional)
- Hard-boiled eggs for serving
- extra virgin olive oil for serving
- freshly ground black pepper, for serving

Direction

- Cut bottoms off asparagus to make them fit upright in a pint jar. Asparagus tips should be at least 1/2 inch below lid. (Reserve bottoms for another use.)
- Pour about 2 inches water into a skillet large enough to hold asparagus lying down; bring to a boil. In batches, blanch asparagus: place in skillet, bring water back to a boil, and then immediately remove and run under very cold water or dunk in ice water. Set aside to drain.
- Combine remaining ingredients in a saucepan with 2 1/4 cups vinegar and bring to a boil. Stir occasionally and cook just until salt dissolves; turn off heat.
- Prepare 4 clean, hot pint jars and bands, and new lids. (Dip in boiling water, or run through dishwasher.) When jars are dry but still hot, pack asparagus into them, wedging spears in tightly. There should be enough for 3 or 4 full jars: do not half-fill jars.
- Pour in vinegar solution, just to barely cover tips of asparagus. Make sure to leave 1/2 inch air space above vinegar solution. Distribute garlic slivers and spices evenly among jars. Wipe rims with a clean paper towel dipped in hot water, place lids on top and screw on bands. (Not too tight, just firmly closed.)
- Prepare a boiling-water bath in a deep pot with a rack. Place jars on rack and pour water over them, making sure water covers jars by 2 to 3 inches. Bring water back to a rolling boil over high heat, start a timer for 10 minutes, then reduce heat and gently boil. When timer goes off, turn off heat and wait 5 minutes before removing jars with jar lifter or tongs. Let cool on counter, untouched, 4 to 6 hours. After 12 to 24 hours, check seals: lift each jar up by the lid, and press the lid to make sure the center is sucked down tightly.
- Store in a cool, dark, dry place (not refrigerator) for 4 weeks before using, or up to 1 year. Refrigerate after opening. To serve, drain off pickling liquid and arrange asparagus on plates. Add hard-boiled egg, drizzle with oil and shower with black pepper.

Nutrition Information

- 140: calories;
- 13 grams: protein;
- 1634 milligrams: sodium;
- 1 gram: fat;
- 0 grams: polyunsaturated fat;
- 23 grams: carbohydrates;
- 12 grams: dietary fiber;
- 11 grams: sugars;

---

203.   Pickled Green Tomatoes

Serving: 4 pints | Prep: | Cook: | Ready in:

Ingredients

- 2 pounds green tomatoes, sliced
- ⅓ cup kosher salt
- 1 ¾ cups cider vinegar
- ⅔ cup raw brown sugar
- 3 tablespoons whole mustard seeds
- ¼ teaspoon celery seeds
- 1 ½ teaspoons turmeric
- 2 large yellow onions, sliced

- 2 large green peppers, seeded and diced
- 1 to 2 hot red or green chiles (such as a Serrano or jalapeño), seeded if desired and minced

Direction

- Discard stem and blossom ends of tomatoes and place on a rack over a baking sheet. Sprinkle evenly with salt and refrigerate for 8 to 10 hours or overnight. Place in a colander and drain for another 30 minutes.
- Combine vinegar, sugar, mustard seeds, celery seeds and turmeric in a large, heavy saucepan and bring to a boil over medium heat, stirring occasionally. Add onions and simmer for 5 minutes. Stir in tomatoes, peppers and chiles, stir together and bring back to a boil. Reduce heat to low and simmer for 5 minutes.
- Pour into hot, sterilized jars. Seal and allow cool. Refrigerate for at least 2 weeks before serving.

Nutrition Information

- 247: calories;
- 1245 milligrams: sodium;
- 2 grams: fat;
- 0 grams: trans fat;
- 1 gram: polyunsaturated fat;
- 51 grams: carbohydrates;
- 6 grams: protein;
- 39 grams: sugars;

204.   Pineapple Avocado Salsa

Serving: 2 1/2 cups | Prep: | Cook: | Ready in: 15mins

Ingredients

- ¼ ripe pineapple, peeled, cored and finely chopped (about 1 1/2 cups)
- 2 tablespoons fresh lime juice
- 1 medium or 1/2 large avocado, cut in small dice (about 1/2 cup)

- ½ medium jicama, cut in small dice (about 1 cup)
- 1 to 2 jalapeño or serrano chiles, to taste (or more, to taste)
- Salt to taste
- ¼ cup chopped cilantro

Direction

- Combine all the ingredients in a bowl and gently toss together, taking care not to mash the avocado. Allow to sit for 15 to 30 minutes before serving, then toss again.

Nutrition Information

- 120: calories;
- 5 grams: monounsaturated fat;
- 14 grams: carbohydrates;
- 4 grams: sugars;
- 2 grams: protein;
- 406 milligrams: sodium;
- 7 grams: dietary fiber;
- 1 gram: polyunsaturated fat;

205.   Pineapple Chia Smoothie With Herbs

Serving: 1 serving | Prep: | Cook: | Ready in:

Ingredients

- ¼ ripe pineapple, cored, skinned and cut into 1-inch pieces (about 1 heaped cup, or/ 7 ounces)
- 1 tablespoon soaked chia seeds (1 teaspoon dry unsoaked)
- 1 tablespoon sunflower seeds, soaked overnight in water and drained
- ½ cup carrot juice
- 1 tablespoon flat-leaf parsley leaves, firmly packed
- 4 to 5 fresh mint leaves
- Ice cubes

Direction

- To soak the chia seeds, place in a jar or bowl and add 4 tablespoons water for every tablespoon of chia seeds. Place in the refrigerator for several hours or overnight. The seeds and water will be become gelatinous.
- Scoop up a tablespoon of seeds with the gooey liquid and place in a blender (don't worry, your smoothie won't have this consistency). Add the remaining ingredients and blend for 1 full minute at high speed.

---

206. Pineapple And Millet Smoothie

Serving: 1 generous serving | Prep: | Cook: | Ready in: 10mins

Ingredients

- ¼ cup, tightly packed, cooked millet
- 1 ½ cups fresh sweet pineapple (7 ounces)
- ½ cup fresh orange juice
- 1 tablespoon fresh lime juice
- 1 teaspoon agave nectar
- 1 tablespoon soaked cashews or almonds (optional) (.5 ounce)
- 2 ice cubes

Direction

- Place all of the ingredients in the jar of a blender and blend at high speed until smooth. Serve right away.

---

207. Pizza Margherita

Serving: | Prep: | Cook: | Ready in: 45mins

Ingredients

- For the garlic olive oil

- ½ cup extra virgin olive oil
- 3 garlic cloves, halved, green shoots removed, and minced
- For the pizza
- ½ batch whole wheat pizza dough
- 2 tablespoons garlic olive oil (above)
- ¾ cup grated mozzarella or crumbled goat cheese
- About 2 pounds ripe tomatoes, sliced about 1/4 inch thick I like to use a mix of mostly red with some yellow and green tomatoes
- Coarse salt
- freshly ground pepper to taste
- Several fresh basil leaves, torn into small pieces

Direction

-
-

Nutrition Information

- 256: calories;
- 5 grams: saturated fat;
- 13 grams: monounsaturated fat;
- 6 grams: protein;
- 380 milligrams: sodium;
- 21 grams: fat;
- 2 grams: dietary fiber;
- 12 grams: carbohydrates;
- 3 grams: sugars;

---

208. Pizza With Spring Onions And Fennel

Serving: One 12- to 14-inch pizza | Prep: | Cook: | Ready in: 45mins

Ingredients

- 2 tablespoons extra virgin olive oil
- 1 medium size sweet spring onion, chopped, about 1 cup

- Salt, preferably kosher salt
- freshly ground pepper
- 1 ¼ pounds trimmed fennel bulbs, tough outer layers removed, cored and chopped
- 2 large garlic cloves, minced
- 2 tablespoons minced fennel fronds
- ½ recipe whole wheat pizza dough (see recipe)
- Parmesan

Direction

- Preheat the oven to 450 degrees, preferably with a baking stone in it. Heat 1 tablespoon of the olive oil over medium heat in a large, heavy skillet, and add the onion and about 1/2 teaspoon salt. Cook, stirring often, until the onion is tender, about five minutes. Add the fennel and garlic, and stir together. Cook, stirring often, until the fennel begins to soften, about five minutes. Turn the heat to low, cover and cook gently, stirring often, until the fennel is very tender and sweet and just beginning to color, about 15 minutes. Season to taste with salt and pepper. Stir in the chopped fennel fronds, and remove from the heat.
- Roll or press out the pizza dough and line a 12- to 14-inch pan. Brush the pizza crust with the remaining tablespoon of olive oil and sprinkle on the Parmesan. Spread the fennel mixture over the crust in an even layer. Place on top of the pizza stone, and bake 15 to 20 minutes, until the edges of the crust are brown and the topping is beginning to brown. Remove from the heat. Serve hot, warm or room temperature.

209. Pizza On The Grill With Cherry Tomatoes, Mozzarella And Arugula

Serving: 3 10-inch pizzas | Prep: | Cook: | Ready in: 30mins

Ingredients

- 3 10-inch pizza crusts (1 recipe)
- Extra virgin olive oil for brushing the pizzas
- 1 1/2½ to 2 boxes cherry tomatoes (12 to 16 tomatoes per pizza)
- 5 to 6 ounces mozzarella, shredded if fresh, sliced if low-moisture
- Coarse salt and freshly ground pepper
- 3 generous handfuls baby arugula

Direction

- Prepare a hot grill. Meanwhile, cut the cherry tomatoes in half along the equator and place near the grill, along with the olive oil, salt and pepper, mozzarella and arugula.
- Oil the hot grill rack with olive oil, either by brushing with a grill brush or by dipping a folded wad of paper towels in olive oil and using tongs to rub the rack with it. Place a round of dough on a lightly dusted baker's peel or rimless baking sheet. Slide the pizza dough from the peel or baking sheet onto the grill rack. If the dough has just come from the freezer and is easy to handle, you can just place it on the rack without bothering with the peel. Close the lid of the grill – the vents should be closed —-- and set the timer for 2 minutes.
- Lift up the grill lid. The surface of the dough should display some big air bubbles. Using tongs, lift the dough to see if it is evenly browning on the bottom. Rotate the dough to assure even browning. Keep it on the grill, moving it around as necessary, until it is nicely browned, with grill marks. Watch closely so that it doesn't burn. When it is nicely browned on the bottom (it may be blackened in spots), use tongs or a spatula to slide the dough onto the baking sheet or peel, and remove from the grill. Cover the grill again.
- Make sure that there is still some flour on the peel or baking sheet and flip the dough over so that the uncooked side is now on the bottom. Brush the surface lightly with oil, then top with cherry tomatoes and shreds or slices of mozzarella. You can place the cherry

tomatoes cut side up or cut side down, or alternate them cut side up, cut side down. Sprinkle with coarse sea salt and freshly ground pepper.

- Slide the pizza back onto the grill. If using a gas grill, reduce the heat to medium-high. Close the lid and cook for 2 to 3 more minutes, until the bottom begins to brown. Open the grill and check the pizza; if the cheese hasn't melted, leave for a few more minutes. If the bottom is getting too dark, move the pizza to a cooler part of the grill and close the top. Use a spatula or tongs to remove the pizza to a cutting board. Scatter the arugula on top, cut into wedges and serve. Repeat with the other two pizza crusts.

| 210. | Polenta Or Grits With Beans And Chard |

Serving: Serves 4 | Prep: | Cook: | Ready in: 2hours

Ingredients

- ½ pound (about 1 1/8 cups) dried pintos, red beans, borlottis or other similar heirloom beans, rinsed and picked over for stones
- 5 cups water
- 1 small onion, halved
- 1 medium or large carrot, diced
- 3 garlic cloves, 2 crushed, 1 minced
- A bouquet garni made with a couple of sprigs each parsley and thyme, a bay leaf and a Parmesan rind
- Salt to taste
- 1 tablespoon extra virgin olive oil
- ½ teaspoon red pepper flakes (more to taste)
- 1 generous bunch Swiss chard (about 3/4 pound), stemmed, leaves washed in 2 changes water, and chopped (7 to 8 cups chopped greens)
- 1 tablespoon tomato paste
- 1 cup Anson Mills polenta or Pencil Cob grits, cooked

- Freshly grated Parmesan or feta for serving

Direction

- Chop 1/2 of the onion and set aside. To cook dried beans, transfer with their soaking water to a heavy pot. If beans are not covered by 1 1/2 to 2 inches of water, add more water as necessary. Over medium-high heat, bring to a gentle boil and skim away foam. Add unchopped halved onion, crushed garlic cloves and bouquet garni, cover, reduce heat to low and simmer 1 hour. Using tongs, removed halved onion and whole garlic cloves.
- Meanwhile, heat olive oil over medium heat in a medium skillet and add chopped onion and carrot. Cook, stirring, until beginning to soften, about 3 minutes, and add chard stems, garlic and pepper flakes. Continue to cook for another couple of minutes, until onion and chard stems are soft. Stir vegetable mixture into beans. Add tomato paste and salt to taste (I use at least 1 1/2 teaspoons), cover and continue to simmer very gently for 1 hour or until beans are tender all the way through and their texture is plush and velvety. Remove and discard bouquet garni.
- Add chard greens (depending on the size of your pot you may have to add a portion at a time, cover for a minute until the first portion wilts, then add the next portion and so on until all of the greens have been added) and continue to simmer for 5 to 10 minutes, until greens are tender but still have some color and life in them. Taste bean broth; it should taste rich, delicious, a little spicy. Add salt as necessary. Keep warm.
- Meanwhile, toward the end of the cooking time for the beans, cook polenta; or wait until beans are done and start polenta or grits. When done, spoon into wide soup bowls and press down in the middle with the back of a spoon. Spoon beans and greens with broth over polenta or grits. Top with a little Parmesan or feta and serve.

149

Nutrition Information

- 229: calories;
- 1214 milligrams: sodium;
- 4 grams: fat;
- 1 gram: polyunsaturated fat;
- 3 grams: monounsaturated fat;
- 43 grams: carbohydrates;
- 6 grams: protein;
- 5 grams: sugars;

211.   Poppy, Lemon And Sunflower Seed Pancakes

Serving: 20 pancakes | Prep: | Cook: | Ready in: 40mins

Ingredients

- 2 cups (280 grams) whole-wheat flour, or 1 cup whole-wheat flour and 1 cup unbleached all-purpose flour
- 2 teaspoons baking powder
- 1 teaspoon baking soda
- 1 tablespoon sugar or raw brown sugar
- ½ teaspoon fine sea salt
- ¼ cup (25 grams) poppy seeds
- ⅓ cup (45 grams) sunflower seeds, toasted until golden brown
- 2 large eggs
- 2 cups buttermilk
- 2 tablespoons canola oil
- 2 teaspoons vanilla extract
- 2 tablespoons finely chopped lemon zest
- 1 box raspberries (optional)

Direction

- Sift together the flour(s), baking powder, baking soda, sugar and salt. Stir in the poppy seeds and sunflower seeds
- In a medium bowl, whisk the eggs. Whisk in the buttermilk, canola oil and vanilla. Quickly stir in the flour mix and lemon zest. Do not overwork the batter

- Heat a griddle or a large skillet, either nonstick or seasoned cast iron, over medium-high heat. Brush with butter or oil. Use a 1/4-cup ladle or cup measure to drop 3 to 4 tablespoons of batter per pancake onto your heated pan or griddle. Place about 6 raspberries, if using, on each pancake. When bubbles break through the pancakes, flip them over and cook for another minute, until they are brown on the other side. Serve right away, or allow to cool and wrap individual servings in plastic, then place in a freezer bag and freeze

Nutrition Information

- 123: calories;
- 18 grams: carbohydrates;
- 5 grams: protein;
- 154 milligrams: sodium;
- 4 grams: fat;
- 1 gram: saturated fat;
- 0 grams: trans fat;
- 2 grams: sugars;

212.   Potato Focaccia With Oyster Mushrooms

Serving: 1 large focaccia, serving 12 | Prep: | Cook: | Ready in: 3hours50mins

Ingredients

- For the sponge
- 1 teaspoon / 4 grams active dry yeast
- ½ cup / 120 ml lukewarm water
- ¾ cup / 90 grams unbleached all-purpose flour
- For the dough
- 8 ounces / 225 g potatoes, such as Yukon gold, peeled and diced
- 1 teaspoon / 4 grams active dry yeast
- 1 cup / 240 ml lukewarm water
- 3 tablespoons extra-virgin olive oil

- ¾ to 1 cup / 100 to 125 grams unbleached all-purpose flour, as needed
- 2 cups / 250 grams whole wheat flour or durum flour
- 1 ¾ teaspoons/ 12 grams fine sea salt
- For the topping
- 2 tablespoons extra-virgin olive oil
- 2 teaspoons finely chopped fresh sage
- 1 to 2 garlic cloves, to taste (optional)
- ½ pound oyster mushrooms
- Salt and freshly ground pepper to taste
- 12 to 24 small sage leaves

Direction

- Make sponge. Combine yeast and water in the bowl of a stand mixer and stir to dissolve. Whisk in flour. Cover with plastic wrap and let rise in a warm place until bubbly and doubled in volume, about 45 minutes.
- While starter is proofing, steam potatoes above 1 inch of boiling water until tender, 15 to 20 minutes. Mash with a potato masher or put through a potato ricer or sieve. Set aside to cool.
- Make dough. Whisk together yeast and water in a small bowl and let stand until creamy, a few minutes. Add to sponge in mixer bowl, along with the olive oil. Add mashed potatoes, flours (using smaller amount of unbleached flour) and salt and mix in with paddle attachment for 1 to 2 minutes, until ingredients are amalgamated. Change to dough hook and knead on medium speed for 8 to 10 minutes, adding more white flour if dough seems impossibly sticky (it will be sticky no matter what). The dough should come together and slap against the sides of the bowl. It will be tacky.
- Cover bowl tightly with plastic wrap and let dough rise in a warm spot until doubled, about 1 1/2 hours.
- Shape the focaccia. Coat a 12-x 17-inch sheet pan (sides and bottom) with olive oil. Line with parchment and flip the parchment over so exposed side is oiled. Turn dough onto the baking sheet. Oil or moisten your hands, as dough is sticky, and press out dough until it just about covers the bottom of the pan. Cover with a towel and allow it to relax for 10 minutes, then continue to press it out until it reaches the edges of the pan. Cover with a damp towel and let rise in a warm spot for 45 minutes to an hour, or until dough is full of air bubbles.
- Preheat oven to 425 degrees after 30 minutes of rising (30 minutes before you wish to bake), preferably with a baking stone in it. Place olive oil, sage and garlic in a small saucepan and heat over medium heat until the ingredients begin to sizzle in the oil. Allow to sizzle for 30 seconds, then remove from heat, swirl the oil in pan and transfer to a measuring cup or small bowl or ramekin. Allow to cool.
- Cut away the tough stems bottoms from the mushrooms and tear large mushrooms into smaller pieces. In a large bowl, toss with salt and pepper and the cooled olive oil mix. With lightly oiled fingertips or with your knuckles, dimple the dough, pressing down hard so you leave indentations. Arrange the mushrooms over the dough. Drizzle on any oil left in the bowl.
- Place pan in oven on baking stone. Spray oven with water 3 times during the first 10 minutes of baking, and bake 20 to 25 minutes, until edges are crisp and the top is golden. If you wish, remove the focaccia from the pan and bake directly on the stone during the last 10 minutes. Remove from oven, remove from pan at once and cool on a rack. Arrange the whole sage leaves over the top. If you want a softer focaccia, cover with a towel when you remove it from the oven. Serve warm or at room temperature.

Nutrition Information

- 216: calories;
- 35 grams: carbohydrates;
- 3 grams: dietary fiber;
- 0 grams: sugars;
- 264 milligrams: sodium;

- 6 grams: fat;
- 1 gram: polyunsaturated fat;
- 4 grams: monounsaturated fat;
- 5 grams: protein;

213. Potato And Collard Green Hash

Serving: Serves four to six | Prep: | Cook: |Ready in: 2hours

Ingredients

- 1 large bunch collard greens, about 1 1/2 pounds, stemmed and washed in 2 changes of water
- Salt to taste
- 3 tablespoons extra virgin olive oil
- 1 onion, sliced very thin in half-moons
- 2 to 4 garlic cloves, green shoots removed, sliced thin
- ¼ to ½ teaspoon crushed red pepper flakes (optional)
- ¾ pound yellow-fleshed potatoes, such as Yukon gold

Direction

- Bring a large pot of water to a boil. Fill a bowl with ice water. When the water comes to a boil, salt generously and add the collard greens. Blanch for four minutes, and transfer to the ice water with a slotted spoon or skimmer. Drain and squeeze out extra water. Chop coarsely. Set aside the cooking water.
- Heat 2 tablespoons of the oil over medium heat in a wide, lidded skillet or Dutch oven, and add the onion. Cook, stirring often, until it begins to soften, about three minutes. Add a generous pinch of salt, the garlic and crushed red pepper flakes. Continue to cook, stirring often, until the onion is tender, about five minutes. Stir in the collard greens. Mix together for a few minutes, and then add 1 cup of the cooking water and salt to taste. Bring to

a simmer, cover partially, and simmer over low heat for 45 minutes to 1 hour, stirring often and adding more cooking water from time to time, so that the greens are always simmering in a small amount of liquid.
- While the greens are cooking, scrub the potatoes and add to the pot with the cooking water. Bring back to a boil, lower the heat and simmer until the potatoes are tender, about 25 minutes. Remove the potatoes from the cooking water, and allow to cool slightly so that you can peel them if you wish. Cut them into large chunks.
- Uncover the greens, and add the potatoes. Using a fork or the back of a wooden spoon, crush the potatoes and stir into the greens. Add a tablespoon of olive oil and salt and pepper to taste, and stir over low heat until the greens and potatoes are well combined. The potatoes should not be like mashed potatoes, just crushed and intermingled with the greens, like hash. Taste, adjust seasonings and serve.

Nutrition Information

- 115: calories;
- 1 gram: sugars;
- 5 grams: monounsaturated fat;
- 13 grams: carbohydrates;
- 2 grams: protein;
- 215 milligrams: sodium;
- 7 grams: fat;

214. Potato, Green Bean And Spinach Salad

Serving: Serves four as a main dish or six as a side dish | Prep: | Cook: |Ready in: 30mins

Ingredients

- 1 pound waxy potatoes, cut in 1-inch dice

- 2 tablespoons finely minced red onion, soaked for five minutes in cold water, then drained, rinsed, and drained on paper towels
- 2 tablespoons sherry vinegar
- 1 tablespoon freshly squeezed lemon juice
- Salt to taste
- 1 small garlic clove, green shoot removed, minced or pureed
- 1 teaspoon Dijon mustard
- ⅓ cup extra virgin olive oil
- 3 tablespoons plain low-fat yogurt
- Freshly ground pepper to taste
- 2 tablespoons finely chopped fresh herbs, such as parsley, tarragon, chives, chervil or dill
- 6 ounces green beans, trimmed and broken in half
- 2 ounces feta cheese, crumbled
- 1 6-ounce bag baby spinach

Direction

- Steam the potatoes above 1 inch boiling water for 10 minutes or until tender. Meanwhile, whisk together the vinegar, lemon juice, salt, garlic, Dijon mustard, olive oil and yogurt.
- When the potatoes are tender, remove from the heat and toss at once with 1/4 cup of the dressing, the onion, herbs, and salt and pepper to taste.
- Add the green beans to the steamer pot, and steam for five minutes. Remove from the heat, refresh briefly with cold water, drain well and toss with the potatoes, 2 more tablespoons of the dressing and the feta. In a separate bowl, toss the spinach with the remaining dressing. Top with the potatoes and beans, and serve.

Nutrition Information

- 322: calories;
- 14 grams: monounsaturated fat;
- 2 grams: polyunsaturated fat;
- 27 grams: carbohydrates;
- 4 grams: sugars;
- 7 grams: protein;
- 22 grams: fat;

- 5 grams: dietary fiber;
- 0 grams: trans fat;
- 611 milligrams: sodium;

---

215. Provençal Artichoke Ragout

Serving: Serves 6 to 8 | Prep: | Cook: | Ready in: 1hours15mins

Ingredients

- 2 pounds baby artichokes or globe artichokes if baby artichokes aren't available, trimmed (see below)
- 1 lemon, cut in half
- 2 tablespoons olive oil
- 1 large sweet onion, such as Vidalia or Maui, chopped, or 1 bunch of spring onions, chopped
- 2 celery stalks, from the inner hart, sliced
- 1 large or 2 small red bell peppers, diced
- 4 large garlic cloves, minced or pressed
- Salt
- 1 28-ounce can chopped tomatoes with juice, peeled, seeded and chopped
- ¾ to 1 cup water, as needed
- Freshly ground pepper
- 1 teaspoon fresh thyme leaves, or 1/2 teaspoon dried thyme
- 1 bay leaf
- 2 to 4 tablespoons chopped fresh basil or parsley
- 2 to 3 teaspoons fresh lemon juice

Direction

- How to trim artichokes: Fill a bowl with water, and add the juice of 1/2 lemon. Cut the stems off the artichokes, and with a sharp knife, cut away the tops — about 1/2 inch from the top for baby artichokes, 1 inch for larger artichokes. Rub the cut parts with the other half of the lemon. Break off the tough outer leaves until you reach the lighter green leaves near the middle. With a paring knife, trim the bottom of the bulb right above the stem by holding the knife at an angle and cutting around the artichoke, until you reach the light flesh beneath the tough bottoms of the leaves. Cut small baby artichokes in half, or large artichokes into quarters, and cut away the chokes if the artichokes are mature. Immediately place in the bowl of acidulated water.

- Heat the oil in a large, heavy nonstick skillet or casserole over medium heat, and add the onion and celery. Cook, stirring, until tender, about three to five minutes. Add the red pepper and about 1/4 teaspoon salt, and stir together for three to five minutes until the pepper begins to soften. Add the garlic, and stir together for another minute, until the garlic is fragrant. Add the tomatoes and a little more salt, and cook, stirring from time to time, for 10 minutes, until the tomatoes have cooked down and smell fragrant. Add the artichokes, thyme, bay leaf and enough water to cover the artichokes halfway, and bring to a simmer. Add salt and pepper, then cover and simmer 30 to 40 minutes, until the artichokes are tender and the sauce fragrant. Check from time to time and add water if necessary. Add the lemon juice, taste and adjust salt and pepper.

Nutrition Information

- 113: calories;
- 4 grams: sugars;
- 1 gram: polyunsaturated fat;
- 3 grams: monounsaturated fat;
- 19 grams: carbohydrates;
- 9 grams: dietary fiber;
- 5 grams: protein;
- 643 milligrams: sodium;

216.	Provençal Onion Pizza

Serving: One 12- to 14 inch pizza | Prep: | Cook: | Ready in: 1hours15mins

Ingredients

- 3 tablespoons olive oil
- 2 pounds sweet onions, finely chopped
- Salt
- freshly ground pepper
- 3 garlic cloves, minced
- ½ bay leaf
- 2 teaspoons fresh thyme leaves, or 1 teaspoon dried thyme
- 1 tablespoon capers, drained, rinsed and mashed in a mortar and pestle or finely chopped
- ½ recipe whole wheat pizza dough (see recipe)
- 12 anchovy fillets, soaked in water for five minutes, drained, rinsed and dried on paper towels
- 12 Niçoise olives

Direction

- Preheat the oven to 450 degrees, preferably with a pizza stone inside. Heat 2 tablespoons of the olive oil in a large, heavy nonstick skillet over medium-low heat. Add the onions and cook, stirring, until they begin to sizzle and soften, about three minutes. Add a generous pinch of salt and the garlic, bay leaf, thyme and pepper. Stir everything together, turn the heat to low, cover and cook slowly for 45 minutes, stirring often. The onions should melt down to a golden brown puree. If they begin to stick, add a few tablespoons of water. Stir in the capers, then taste and adjust seasonings. If there is liquid in the pan, cook over medium heat, uncovered, until it evaporates.
- Roll out the pizza dough and line a 12- to 14-inch pan. Brush the remaining tablespoon of oil over the bottom but not the rim of the crust. Spread the onions over the crust in an even layer. Cut the anchovies in half, and decorate the top of the crust with them, making twelve small X's and placing an olive in the middle of

each X. Place on top of the pizza stone, and bake 15 to 20 minutes, until the edges of the crust are brown and the onions are beginning to brown. Remove from the heat. Serve hot, warm or room temperature.

Nutrition Information

- 189: calories;
- 9 grams: fat;
- 1 gram: polyunsaturated fat;
- 6 grams: monounsaturated fat;
- 23 grams: carbohydrates;
- 5 grams: protein;
- 2 grams: dietary fiber;
- 8 grams: sugars;
- 503 milligrams: sodium;

217. Provençal Tomato And Bean Gratin

Serving: Serves eight to 12 | Prep: | Cook: | Ready in: 3hours45mins

Ingredients

- 1 pound (2 heaped cups) chick peas, borlotti beans or pinto beans, washed, picked over and soaked for six hours or overnight
- 2 onions
- 2 whole cloves
- 4 to 6 large garlic cloves (to taste), 2 crushed, the rest minced
- A bouquet garni made with a couple of sprigs each parsley and thyme, a bay leaf and a Parmesan rind
- Salt to taste
- 2 tablespoons extra virgin olive oil
- 2 28-ounce cans chopped tomatoes, with juice
- 1 tablespoon tomato paste
- ⅛ teaspoon sugar
- ½ teaspoon dried oregano
- Pinch of cayenne
- Freshly ground pepper

- ½ cup freshly grated Gruyère, or a combination of Gruyère and Parmesan (2 ounces)
- ¼ cup fresh breadcrumbs

Direction

- Cut one of the onions in half, and stick a clove into each half. Chop the other onion. Drain the soaked beans and combine with 2 quarts water in a large pot. Bring to a boil and skim off any foam, then add the halved onion, the crushed garlic cloves and the bouquet garni. Reduce the heat, cover and simmer for 1 hour. Add salt to taste, and continue to simmer for another 30 to 60 minutes, until the beans are tender but not mushy. Remove from the heat, remove and discard the onion and the bouquet garni, and drain over a bowl. Measure out 3 cups of the cooking liquid, taste and adjust salt. Set aside.
- Heat 1 tablespoon of the oil over medium heat in a large, heavy soup pot or Dutch oven, and add the chopped onion. Cook, stirring, until tender, about five minutes. Add the remaining garlic, and stir together until fragrant, 30 seconds to a minute. Add the tomatoes, tomato paste, sugar, oregano, cayenne and salt to taste. Cook, stirring often, for 10 to 15 minutes, until the tomatoes have cooked down somewhat and smell very fragrant. Stir in the beans and 3 cups of their cooking broth (refrigerate the rest if you are making this ahead; you may need it for thinning out). Bring to a simmer, cover and cook over low heat for 30 minutes, until the mixture is thick and fragrant. Stir often so that it doesn't stick to the bottom of the pot. Add pepper, taste and adjust salt and garlic.
- Preheat the oven to 375 degrees. Oil a 3-quart gratin or baking dish. Spoon the tomatoes and beans into the baking dish. Combine the breadcrumbs and cheese in a bowl, and toss with the remaining tablespoon of olive oil. Sprinkle in an even layer over the beans. Bake 30 minutes, or until the top is browned and the gratin is bubbling. Serve hot or warm.

Nutrition Information

- 257: calories;
- 2 grams: saturated fat;
- 0 grams: trans fat;
- 1 gram: polyunsaturated fat;
- 11 grams: dietary fiber;
- 3 grams: monounsaturated fat;
- 40 grams: carbohydrates;
- 7 grams: sugars;
- 14 grams: protein;
- 570 milligrams: sodium;
- 5 grams: fat;

218.	Provençal Zucchini And Swiss Chard Tart

Serving: One 10-inch tart, serving eight to ten | Prep: | Cook: | Ready in: 1hours45mins

Ingredients

- 1 recipe whole wheat yeasted olive oil pie pastry
- 1 pound Swiss chard
- Salt to taste
- 2 tablespoons extra virgin olive oil
- 1 medium onion, finely chopped
- 2 pounds zucchini, cut in small dice (1/4 to 1/3 inch)
- 2 to 3 large garlic cloves (to taste), minced
- 1 teaspoon fresh thyme leaves, chopped
- 1 to 2 teaspoons chopped fresh rosemary (to taste)
- 2 ounces Gruyère cheese, grated (1/2 cup, tightly packed)
- 3 large eggs, beaten
- Freshly ground pepper

Direction

- Bring a large pot of water to a boil while you stem the greens, and wash them thoroughly in several rinses of water. If the ribs are wide, wash and dice them, then set aside. Fill a bowl with ice water. When the water reaches a rolling boil, add a generous amount of salt and the chard leaves. Blanch for one minute, until just tender. Using a slotted spoon or deep-fry skimmer, transfer to the ice water, then drain. Squeeze out excess water and chop. Set aside.
- Heat the oil over medium heat in a large nonstick skillet, and add the onion and diced chard stems, if using. Cook, stirring, until tender, about five minutes. Stir in the zucchini. Season to taste with salt, and cook, stirring, until just tender and still bright green, about 10 minutes. Stir in the garlic, thyme and rosemary, and cook with the zucchini and onion until the garlic is fragrant, about one or two minutes. Stir in the greens, toss everything together, and remove from the heat. Taste and season with salt and pepper.
- Beat the eggs in a large bowl. Stir in 1/4 to 1/2 teaspoon salt (to taste), the zucchini mixture, and the Gruyère. Mix everything together, add pepper, taste once more and adjust seasoning.
- Preheat the oven to 375 degrees. Oil a 10-inch tart pan. Roll out two-thirds of the dough and line the pan, with the edges of the dough overhanging. Freeze the remaining dough. Fill the lined pan with the zucchini mixture. Pinch the edges of the dough along the rim of the pan. Place in the oven and bake 50 minutes, until set and beginning to color. Allow to rest for at least 15 minutes before serving (preferably longer). This can also be served at room temperature.

Nutrition Information

- 201: calories;
- 2 grams: dietary fiber;
- 3 grams: sugars;
- 6 grams: protein;
- 447 milligrams: sodium;
- 12 grams: fat;
- 4 grams: saturated fat;
- 0 grams: trans fat;

- 5 grams: monounsaturated fat;
- 18 grams: carbohydrates;

219. Publican Chicken

Serving: 2 servings | Prep: | Cook: | Ready in: 40mins

Ingredients

- ½ cup extra-virgin olive oil
- 2 ½ tablespoons fresh lemon juice
- 1 ½ tablespoons brown sugar
- 1 tablespoon Espelette pepper or Spanish smoked hot paprika
- 1 tablespoon dried oregano
- 2 garlic cloves, sliced
- ½ teaspoon salt
- ¼ teaspoon freshly ground black pepper
- 1 (3-pound) chicken, backbone removed

Direction

- In a large mixing bowl, combine oil, lemon juice, brown sugar, Espelette pepper or hot paprika, oregano, garlic and salt and pepper. Mix well.
- Flatten chicken and add to marinade, turning it until coated. Cover and refrigerate for at least one hour or overnight.
- Prepare a grill, arranging coals or gas flame so it is hot on only one side. Place chicken skin-side down on unheated side of grill (so it will cook by indirect heat). Grill, basting every 5 minutes and turning chicken once about halfway through, until juices run clear when chicken is pierced near joint of thigh, about 30 minutes.
- Remove chicken from grill and allow to rest 5 minutes. Carve as desired, and serve.

220. Pumpkin Caramel Mousse

Serving: 8 servings | Prep: | Cook: | Ready in: 45mins

Ingredients

- ½ cup (125 grams) heavy cream
- 2 tablespoons (25 grams) brown sugar
- ½ teaspoon ground cinnamon
- ¼ teaspoon ground ginger
- ¼ teaspoon freshly grated nutmeg
- 3 tablespoons (45 grams) water
- 1 ½ teaspoons (5 grams) gelatin
- Scant 1/2 cup (100 grams) sugar for the caramel, plus an additional 3 tablespoons (45 grams) sugar for the meringue
- ½ teaspoon lemon juice
- 1 cup (290 grams) plain canned pumpkin (no spices) or puréed roasted winter squash or pumpkin
- 3 egg whites
- ⅛ teaspoon cream of tartar
- ¼ cup (30 grams) toasted hazelnuts, finely chopped or crushed

Direction

- Whip the cream until it forms soft peaks. Chill in the refrigerator until ready to use.
- Combine the brown sugar, cinnamon, ginger and nutmeg in a small bowl.
- Place 2 tablespoons of the water in a small bowl and sprinkle the gelatin over the top. Stir, then let it sit while you make the caramel.
- Find a bowl that is large enough for you to dip the bottom of your saucepan into it; fill it with an inch of ice water and place it on your stove. Place the scant 1/2 cup (125 grams) sugar in a medium saucepan, preferably stainless steel. Add the remaining tablespoon of water and the lemon juice and carefully stir together with a heatproof rubber spatula. Using a wet pastry brush, brush down the sides of the saucepan so that there are no stray sugar crystals that could cause the caramel to seize. Turn the heat on medium-high and heat until the sugar

dissolves and the mixture turns a light caramel color, 4 to 5 minutes. Do not stir, but from time to time carefully brush down the sides of the pan with the wet brush. Do not let the caramel get hotter than 325 degrees. As soon as it reaches this temperature and is golden brown, remove from the heat and dip the bottom of the saucepan into the bowl of cold water to stop the caramel from heating further. Let sit until the bubbles subside.

- Using a heatproof spatula, carefully stir the brown sugar mixture into the hot caramel. It may bubble up, so be careful. Add the softened gelatin and stir to dissolve. Whisk in the canned pumpkin and transfer to a large mixing bowl.
- Place the egg whites in the bowl of a stand mixer (or use a mixing bowl and electric beaters). Beat until they begin to foam, and add the cream of tartar and 1 tablespoon of the sugar. Beat at medium speed and add the remaining sugar in a slow, steady stream. Beat until the egg whites are stiff and shiny, about 2 minutes. Be careful not to overbeat.
- Lighten the warm pumpkin mixture by folding in one-third of the beaten egg whites, using a balloon whisk or a large spatula. Pour the remaining egg whites over the top, and carefully fold them into the pumpkin mixture using a rubber spatula. Fold in the whipped cream.
- It's easiest to do a neat job of filling the glasses if you use a pastry bag fitted with a wide round tip. Pipe or spoon the mousse into 8 glasses; use small tumblers, wine glasses or whiskey glasses. Sprinkle the ground hazelnuts over the top. If desired, make 2 layers of the hazelnuts: Pipe half the amount of the pumpkin mousse you need for each serving into the glasses, then sprinkle on a layer of hazelnuts; then pipe the rest and top with another layer. Cover the glasses and refrigerate for at least 2 hours and preferably overnight.

Nutrition Information

- 164: calories;
- 1 gram: dietary fiber;
- 19 grams: carbohydrates;
- 14 grams: sugars;
- 3 grams: protein;
- 57 milligrams: sodium;
- 9 grams: fat;
- 4 grams: monounsaturated fat;

221. Puree Of Chickpea Soup

Serving: Serves four | Prep: | Cook: | Ready in: 8hours30mins

Ingredients

- ½ pound chickpeas (about 1 1/8 cups), washed and picked over
- 2 tablespoons extra virgin olive oil
- ½ medium size red onion, chopped
- 2 to 3 large garlic cloves, green shoots removed, minced
- 1 teaspoon cumin seeds, ground
- ½ teaspoon coriander seeds, ground
- Salt to taste
- 2 tablespoons freshly squeezed lemon juice, plus additional for drizzling
- Chopped fresh mint for garnish

Direction

- Soak the chickpeas in 1 quart water for six hours or overnight. Drain.
- Heat 1 tablespoon of the olive oil over medium heat in a large, heavy soup pot or Dutch oven. Add the onion. Cook, stirring, until tender, about five minutes. Stir in the garlic, spices and a generous pinch of salt. Cook, stirring, for about a minute, until the mixture is fragrant. Add the chickpeas and 6 cups water. Bring to a boil, reduce the heat and simmer one hour. Add salt to taste (about 1 teaspoon) and continue to simmer for another 30 minutes to an hour. The beans should be very tender.

- Puree the soup in a blender (in small batches, covering the top with a dish towel to avoid hot splashes) or with an immersion blender until smooth. Put through a strainer for a very smooth texture, pushing it through with the bottom of a ladle or a spatula. Return to the pot, and heat through, stirring the bottom and sides of the pot so that the puree doesn't stick. Stir in the remaining tablespoon of olive oil and the lemon juice. Taste and adjust seasonings.
- Serve, garnishing each bowl with a few drops of olive oil or lemon juice if desired and a sprinkle of chopped fresh mint.

Nutrition Information

- 285: calories;
- 1 gram: saturated fat;
- 6 grams: monounsaturated fat;
- 2 grams: polyunsaturated fat;
- 7 grams: sugars;
- 10 grams: fat;
- 38 grams: carbohydrates;
- 12 grams: protein;
- 187 milligrams: sodium;

---

222.   Puree Of Shell Beans And Potato

Serving: Serves 6 | Prep: | Cook: |Ready in: 1hours

Ingredients

- 1 pound shell beans, shelled (about 1 3/4 cups shelled)
- 1 small onion, halved
- 3 to 4 large garlic cloves (to taste), peeled and crushed
- A bouquet garni made with a sprig each parsley and sage, and a bay leaf
- Salt to taste
- 1 russet potato, about 10 ounces, peeled and diced

- About 6 tablespoons plus 1 teaspoon extra virgin olive oil
- About 1/4 cup broth from the beans (more to taste)
- Freshly ground pepper

Direction

- Combine the beans, onion, garlic, bouquet garni and potato in a heavy saucepan or soup pot. Add enough water to cover by two inches. Add salt, and bring to a simmer. Cover and simmer 40 to 45 minutes, or until the beans and potato are tender. Taste and adjust salt. Remove and discard the onion and the bouquet garni. Drain though a strainer or colander set over a bowl.
- Add enough bean broth to get a moist puree, beginning with 1/4 cup and adding more as needed, and stir again to incorporate. Taste, adjust salt and add freshly ground pepper. Heat gently in the pot, stirring, and drizzle a little more olive oil over the top. Serve warm.

Nutrition Information

- 219: calories;
- 15 grams: fat;
- 2 grams: polyunsaturated fat;
- 10 grams: monounsaturated fat;
- 18 grams: carbohydrates;
- 4 grams: dietary fiber;
- 5 grams: protein;
- 1 gram: sugars;
- 376 milligrams: sodium;

---

223.   Pureed Carrot Soup

Serving: Serves 6 | Prep: | Cook: |Ready in: 1hours

Ingredients

- 1 tablespoon unsalted butter
- 1 tablespoon extra virgin olive oil

- 1 large onion, chopped
- 2 pounds sweet carrots, peeled and thinly sliced
- Salt to taste
- ¼ teaspoon sugar
- 2 quarts water, chicken stock, or vegetable stock
- 6 tablespoons rice, preferably Arborio
- Freshly ground pepper to taste
- 2 tablespoons chopped fresh herbs, such as chervil, mint, chives, or parsley, for garnish
- 1 cup toasted croutons for garnish (optional)

Direction

- Heat the butter and olive oil in a large, heavy soup pot over medium-low heat and add the onion. Cook, stirring, until tender, about 5 minutes. Add the carrots and 1/2 teaspoon salt, cover partially and cook for another 10 minutes, stirring often, until the vegetables are tender and fragrant. Add the rice, water or stock, salt (about 1 1/2 teaspoons), and sugar. Bring to a boil, reduce the heat, cover and simmer 30 minutes, or until the carrots are tender and the soup is fragrant.
- Blend the soup either with a hand blender, in batches in a blender (cover the top with a towel and hold it down to avoid hot splashes), or through a food mill fitted with the fine blade. The rice should no longer be recognizable (it thickens the soup). Return to the pot. Stir and taste. Adjust salt, add a generous amount of freshly ground pepper, and heat through. If the sweetness of the carrots needs a boost, add another pinch of sugar.
- Serve, garnishing each bowl with croutons and a sprinkle of herbs.

Nutrition Information

- 157: calories;
- 0 grams: trans fat;
- 28 grams: carbohydrates;
- 3 grams: protein;
- 5 grams: dietary fiber;
- 2 grams: monounsaturated fat;
- 1 gram: polyunsaturated fat;
- 8 grams: sugars;
- 1186 milligrams: sodium;

224. Pureed Potato And Broccoli Soup With Parmesan Croutons

Serving: Serves 6 to 8 | Prep: | Cook: | Ready in: 1hours

Ingredients

- 2 tablespoons extra virgin olive oil
- 1 large onion, chopped
- 2 leeks, white and light green parts only, sliced and cleaned (optional)
- 3 garlic cloves, chopped, plus 1 small clove, cut in half
- Salt, preferably kosher salt, to taste
- 2 pounds starchy potatoes (russets or Yukon golds), peeled and cut in large dice
- A bouquet garni made with a bay leaf and 2 sprigs each parsley and thyme
- 2 quarts water, chicken stock, or vegetable stock
- 1 pound broccoli crowns, coarsely chopped
- Freshly ground pepper to taste
- 12 thin slices baguette or country bread
- ¼ cup freshly grated Parmesan

Direction

- Heat the olive oil in a large, heavy soup pot over medium heat and add the onion and optional leeks. Cook, stirring, until tender, about 5 minutes. Add 1/2 teaspoon salt and the chopped garlic and cook, stirring, for another minute, until fragrant. Add the potatoes, bouquet garni, water, and salt to taste. Bring to a boil, reduce the heat, cover and simmer 30 minutes. Add the broccoli, turn the heat up slightly to bring back to a boil, then reduce the heat again and simmer, uncovered, for 10 minutes, until the broccoli is thoroughly tender but still bright. Remove the bouquet garni.

- Blend the soup either with a hand blender, in batches in a blender (cover the top with a towel and hold it down to avoid hot splashes), or through a food mill fitted with the fine blade. For a silky texture, strain through a medium strainer set over a bowl, using a pestle or the bottom of a ladle to push the soup through. Return to the pot, taste and adjust salt, add a generous amount of freshly ground pepper, and heat through.
- Lightly toast the bread and rub with a cut clove of garlic. Top each slice with a spoonful of Parmesan and heat through in a toaster oven or under a broiler, being careful to watch closely, until the cheese melts. Serve the soup, topping each bowl with 2 croutons.

Nutrition Information

- 183: calories;
- 1029 milligrams: sodium;
- 5 grams: dietary fiber;
- 1 gram: polyunsaturated fat;
- 0 grams: trans fat;
- 3 grams: sugars;
- 31 grams: carbohydrates;
- 6 grams: protein;

---

225.   **Puréed Trahana And Vegetable Soup**

Serving: Serves 6 to 8 | Prep: | Cook: | Ready in: 1hours

Ingredients

- 3 tablespoons extra virgin olive oil
- 1 large red or yellow onion, chopped
- Salt to taste
- 2 garlic cloves, minced
- ¾ pound carrots, diced

- 2 large leeks, white and light green parts only, rinsed of all sand and chopped
- 1 1/2 cups sour bulgur trahana
- 2 quarts vegetable stock, chicken stock or water
- A bouquet garni made with a bay leaf and a couple of sprigs each parsley and thyme or oregano
- Freshly ground pepper
- Additional olive oil and chopped fresh herbs such as dill, parsley or mint, for garnish
- Red pepper flakes or cayenne for garnish (optional)

Direction

- Heat 2 tablespoons of olive oil over medium heat in a heavy soup pot and add onion. Cook, stirring often, until onion is soft, 5 to 8 minutes, and add a generous pinch of salt, garlic, carrots and leeks. Continue to cook, stirring often, until carrots and leeks are beginning to soften, 3 to 5 minutes.
- Add remaining olive oil and stir in trahana. Stir until trahana is coated with oil, about 1 minute, and add stock or water and bouquet garni. Bring to a boil, add salt to taste, reduce heat and simmer 30 minutes, until vegetables are tender and trahana has fallen apart in the soup and is tender. Taste and adjust salt. Remove and discard bouquet garni.
- For a coarse purée, use an immersion blender to purée the soup. For a finer purée, transfer, in batches, to a blender or a food processor. If using a blender do not put the top on tight; leave out the center of the lid and cover tightly with a towel. Purée until smooth and if desired, strain. Return to the pot, taste and adjust salt. Add freshly ground pepper to taste.
- Reheat gently and serve, garnishing each serving with a drizzle of olive oil and a sprinkling of herbs. If you want spice, sprinkle with red pepper flakes or a little bit of cayenne.

Nutrition Information

- 181: calories;
- 4 grams: protein;
- 31 grams: carbohydrates;
- 805 milligrams: sodium;
- 6 grams: dietary fiber;
- 1 gram: polyunsaturated fat;

---

226.   Puréed Winter Squash Soup With Ginger

Serving: 4 to 6 servings | Prep: | Cook: | Ready in: 1hours30mins

Ingredients

- 1 tablespoon canola or rice bran oil
- 1 medium onion, chopped
- 1 carrot, diced
- 2 pounds peeled winter squash, like butternut or kabocha
- 2 garlic cloves, minced
- 1 tablespoon minced ginger
- 6 ½ cups water, chicken stock or vegetable stock
- ⅓ cup rice
- Salt and freshly ground pepper
- ½ teaspoon ginger juice (made by grating a teaspoon of fresh ginger, wrapping in cheesecloth and squeezing the cheesecloth)
- Pinch of freshly grated nutmeg
- ½ lime
- 4 to 6 tablespoons plain yogurt

Direction

- Heat the oil over medium heat in a large, heavy soup pot or Dutch oven and add the onion and carrot. Cook, stirring, until the vegetables are tender, about 5 minutes. Add the winter squash, garlic and minced ginger and cook, stirring, until the mixture smells fragrant, about 1 minute

- Add the water or stock, the rice and salt to taste and bring to a boil. Reduce the heat, cover and simmer 45 minutes to 1 hour, until the squash is very tender
- Using a hand blender, or in batches in a regular blender, purée the soup. If using a regular blender, cover the top with a towel pulled down tight, rather than airtight with the lid. Return to the pot and heat through. Stir in the ginger juice, taste and season with salt and pepper. If desired, thin out with a little more water or stock
- Ladle the soup into bowls and add a tablespoon of yogurt (more to taste), then slowly swirl the yogurt into the soup with a spoon. Squeeze a few drops of lime juice onto each serving and sprinkle with whisper of nutmeg

Nutrition Information

- 154: calories;
- 5 grams: sugars;
- 1094 milligrams: sodium;
- 3 grams: protein;
- 1 gram: polyunsaturated fat;
- 32 grams: carbohydrates;
- 4 grams: dietary fiber;

---

227.   Quiche With Red Peppers And Spinach

Serving: 6 generous servings | Prep: | Cook: | Ready in: 1hours30mins

Ingredients

- 2 tablespoons extra-virgin olive oil
- 1 medium-size onion (yellow or spring onion), chopped
- 2 large garlic cloves, or 1 small bulb green garlic, peeled and minced
- Salt to taste

162

- 2 large red bell peppers (about 3/4 pound), seeded and cut in thin 1-inch strips
- 1 teaspoon chopped fresh thyme leaves
- 1 generous bunch spinach, stemmed, washed in 2 changes of water, and coarsely chopped
- Freshly ground pepper to taste
- 2 egg yolks
- 2 whole eggs
- 1 (9-inch) whole wheat pâte brisée pie crust, fully baked and cooled
- Freshly ground pepper
- ⅔ cup milk
- 2 ounces Gruyère, grated (1/2 cup)
- 1 ounce Parmesan, grated (1/4 cup)

Direction

- Preheat oven to 350 degrees.
- Heat oil over medium heat in a large, heavy skillet and add onion. Cook, stirring, until tender, about 5 minutes, and add a generous pinch of salt, the garlic, peppers and thyme. Cook, stirring often, for 5 minutes, then turn the heat to medium low and continue to cook for 5 to 10 minutes more, until peppers are very tender and sweet.
- Turn up heat to medium-high and, a handful at a time, add spinach and stir until each handful wilts. If there is liquid remaining in the pan turn up the heat and stir while you let it cook off. Remove from heat and transfer to a bowl. If you are making filling a day ahead, refrigerate uncovered.
- Beat together egg yolks and eggs in a medium bowl. Set tart pan on a baking sheet for easy handling. Using a pastry brush, lightly brush bottom of the crust with some of the beaten egg and place in oven for 5 minutes.
- Add salt (I use 1/2 teaspoon), pepper, and milk to the remaining eggs and whisk together.
- Spread pepper and spinach mixture in an even layer in the crust. Stir together cheeses and sprinkle in an even layer on top. Very slowly pour in the egg custard over the filling. If your tart pan has low edges, you may not need all of it to fill the shell, and you want to avoid the

custard spilling over. Place quiche, on baking sheet, in the oven and bake for 30 to 35 minutes, until set and just beginning to color on the top. Remove from oven and allow to sit for at least 10 minutes before serving. Serve hot, warm or room temperature.

Nutrition Information

- 365: calories;
- 9 grams: saturated fat;
- 0 grams: trans fat;
- 10 grams: monounsaturated fat;
- 12 grams: protein;
- 3 grams: polyunsaturated fat;
- 29 grams: carbohydrates;
- 4 grams: dietary fiber;
- 5 grams: sugars;
- 555 milligrams: sodium;
- 23 grams: fat;

---

228. Quick Fresh Tomatillo Salsa

Serving: 2 cups, serving 8 | Prep: | Cook: | Ready in: 45mins

Ingredients

- 1 pound tomatillos, husked and rinsed
- 2 to 4 jalapeño or serrano chiles, seeded for a milder salsa, coarsely chopped
- ¼ cup chopped onion, soaked for 5 minutes in cold water, drained and rinsed
- ¼ to ½ cup coarsely chopped cilantro (to taste)
- Salt to taste (about 1/2 teaspoon)
- ¼ to ½ cup water, as needed

Direction

- Place the tomatillos in a saucepan, cover with water and bring to a boil. Reduce the heat and simmer for 8 to 10 minutes, flipping them over halfway through, until softened and olive green. Remove from the heat. Transfer to a blender. Add the chiles, onion, cilantro, and 1/4 cup water to the blender and blend to a coarse puree. Transfer to a bowl, add salt, and thin out as desired with water. Taste and adjust salt, and set aside for at least 30 minutes before serving, to allow the flavors to develop.

Nutrition Information

- 21: calories;
- 4 grams: carbohydrates;
- 3 grams: sugars;
- 170 milligrams: sodium;
- 1 gram: protein;
- 0 grams: polyunsaturated fat;

229. Quick Grilled Flanken With Chili, Sesame And Ginger

Serving: 3 to 4 servings | Prep: | Cook: | Ready in: 20mins

Ingredients

- 6 garlic cloves, minced
- 1 inch long piece fresh ginger root, peeled and chopped
- 2 tablespoons soy sauce
- 2 tablespoons rice vinegar, more to taste
- 2 tablespoons brown sugar
- 1 teaspoon kosher salt, more to taste
- 3 tablespoons toasted Asian sesame oil, more to taste
- 1 tablespoon Asian chili sauce like sriracha
- 3 pounds flanken
- Arugula or sunflower sprouts, for serving
- 2 tablespoons toasted sesame seeds

Direction

- Put garlic, ginger, soy sauce, vinegar, brown sugar and salt into a blender and blend until

smooth. Add sesame oil and chili sauce and blend well.
- Coat flanken with just enough of the mixture to cover it; there should be some left over. Let it marinate, covered, for at least 30 minutes at room temperature, or up to 24 hours in refrigerator (the longer the better).
- Preheat grill or broiler. Grill or broil meat until done to taste, about 4 minutes a side for rare. Toss greens with a drizzle of sesame oil and rice vinegar and a pinch of salt.
- Slice meat (you can slice it off bones or leave bones in) and serve over greens. Sprinkle everything with sesame seeds and more salt if desired, and drizzle with remaining marinade.

Nutrition Information

- 714: calories;
- 9 grams: carbohydrates;
- 5 grams: sugars;
- 13 grams: saturated fat;
- 41 grams: fat;
- 16 grams: monounsaturated fat;
- 6 grams: polyunsaturated fat;
- 1 gram: dietary fiber;
- 74 grams: protein;
- 901 milligrams: sodium;

230. Quick Quesadilla With Dukkah

Serving: 1 serving | Prep: | Cook: | Ready in: 10mins

Ingredients

- 2 corn tortillas
- 1 ounce melting cheese, like Monterey Jack, mozzarella or Mexican string cheese, shredded
- ½ to 1 teaspoon pumpkin seed dukkah (to taste) (see recipe)

Direction

- Top one of the tortillas with the cheese and the dukkah. Place the other tortilla on top. Zap for 1 minute in the microwave, or heat in a dry skillet, flipping the quesadilla from time to time, until the cheese melts. The tortilla will be crispier using the pan method. Cut into quarters and serve.

Nutrition Information

- 225: calories;
- 1 gram: sugars;
- 23 grams: carbohydrates;
- 10 grams: fat;
- 5 grams: saturated fat;
- 3 grams: dietary fiber;
- 11 grams: protein;
- 41 milligrams: sodium;
- 0 grams: trans fat;

231. Quinoa Bowl With Artichokes, Spring Onions And Peas

Serving: 4 servings | Prep: | Cook: | Ready in: 40mins

Ingredients

- 1 lemon, cut in half, plus more lemon juice for drizzling
- 4 medium or 2 large artichokes
- 1 generous bunch spring onions
- 3 tablespoons extra-virgin olive oil, plus more for drizzling
- Salt and pepper
- 1 ½ pounds peas, shelled
- ¼ cup chopped dill, mint or fennel fronds, or a combination
- 1 to 2 garlic cloves (to taste)
- 1 to 1 ½ cups Greek yogurt or drained yogurt, to taste
- 3 cups cooked quinoa

- Chopped preserved lemon or dukkah, for serving

Direction

- Heat oven to 425 degrees. Line a sheet pan with parchment.
- Fill a bowl with water and add the juice from one of the lemon halves. Trim the artichokes. Then, if using medium artichokes, cut into quarters; if using large ones, cut into sixths or eighths. As you work, rub the cut artichokes with remaining lemon half and place them in the water. When all artichokes are cut, drain and pat dry with paper towels. Place on sheet pan.
- Trim away the dark green part of the onion stems and the hairy root ends, and cut onions in half. Place on sheet pan.
- Toss artichokes and onions with the olive oil and salt and pepper to taste. Take care to coat all of the cut surfaces of the artichokes with olive oil. Place in oven and roast for 20 to 30 minutes (depending on the size of the pieces), turning vegetables with tongs every 10 minutes, until tender and lightly browned. The edges of the artichoke leaves will be charred. Transfer to a bowl.
- Meanwhile, steam or boil peas in salted water for 5 minutes; drain. Transfer to the bowl with onions and artichokes. Add half the chopped fresh herbs and toss together.
- In a mortar and pestle, mash garlic to a paste with a pinch of salt. Stir into yogurt.
- To serve, divide quinoa among four bowls and top with artichokes, onions and peas. Spoon yogurt over vegetables and sprinkle with remaining herbs. Douse with a little lemon juice and drizzle on a little oil if desired. Garnish with dukkah or about 2 teaspoons preserved lemon, or both.

Nutrition Information

- 565: calories;
- 1413 milligrams: sodium;
- 8 grams: monounsaturated fat;

- 3 grams: polyunsaturated fat;
- 78 grams: carbohydrates;
- 16 grams: sugars;
- 28 grams: protein;
- 19 grams: fat;
- 5 grams: saturated fat;
- 23 grams: dietary fiber;

232. Quinoa And Carrot Kugel

Serving: 6 servings | Prep: | Cook: |Ready in: 2hours

Ingredients

- 2 tablespoons extra virgin olive oil
- ½ medium onion, finely chopped
- ½ cup quinoa
- 1 ¼ cups water
- Salt to taste
- 1 pound carrots, peeled and cut into 3-inch-long sticks
- ½ cup low-fat cottage cheese
- 3 eggs
- 1 scant teaspoon caraway seeds, lightly crushed
- Freshly ground pepper

Direction

- Heat 1 tablespoon of the olive oil in a medium saucepan and add the onion. Cook, stirring, until the onion is just about tender, 3 to 5 minutes, and add the quinoa. Cook, stirring, for another 2 to 3 minutes, until the quinoa begins to smell toasty and the onion is tender. Add the water and salt to taste and bring to a boil. Add the carrots, cover, reduce the heat and simmer 15 to 20 minutes, until the quinoa and carrots are tender and the grains display a threadlike spiral. Uncover and use tongs to transfer the carrot sticks to a bowl. If any water remains in the pot, drain the quinoa through a strainer, then return to the pot. Place a dish towel over the pot, then return the lid and let sit undisturbed for 10 to 15 minutes

- Meanwhile, preheat the oven to 375 degrees and oil a 2-quart baking dish or gratin
- In a food processor fitted with the steel blade, purée the cooked carrots. Scrape down the sides of the bowl, add the cottage cheese and purée until the mixture is smooth. Add the eggs, salt (I suggest about 1/2 teaspoon), pepper and caraway, and purée until smooth. Scrape into a large mixing bowl. Add the quinoa and mix together thoroughly. Scrape into the oiled baking dish. Drizzle the remaining oil over the top and place in the oven
- Bake 40 to 45 minutes, until the top is lightly browned. Remove from the oven and allow to cool for at least 15 minutes before serving. Serve warm or at room temperature, cut into squares or wedges

Nutrition Information

- 175: calories;
- 0 grams: trans fat;
- 451 milligrams: sodium;
- 4 grams: dietary fiber;
- 1 gram: polyunsaturated fat;
- 19 grams: carbohydrates;
- 5 grams: sugars;
- 8 grams: protein;
- 2 grams: saturated fat;

233. Rainbow Beef

Serving: 4 servings | Prep: | Cook: |Ready in: 20mins

Ingredients

- ½ pound lean flank steak
- 1 ½ teaspoons cornstarch
- 1 tablespoon plus 1 teaspoon rice wine or dry sherry
- 1 teaspoon low sodium soy sauce
- 2 fat garlic cloves, minced
- Salt and freshly ground pepper

- 1 teaspoon sesame oil
- 2 tablespoons hoisin sauce
- 2 tablespoons peanut oil, rice bran oil or canola oil
- 1 tablespoon minced ginger
- ½ teaspoon red pepper flakes
- 8 ounces shiitake mushrooms, stems removed, caps quartered
- 4 bell peppers of varying colors
- 1 tsp cold water
- 1 anaheim pepper
- Salt to taste

Direction

- Slice the steak first with the grain into 2-inch wide strips. Then cut each strip across the grain into 1/4-inch thick slices. Place in a medium bowl and toss with the cornstarch, 1 teaspoon of the rice wine or sherry, the soy sauce, one of the minced garlic cloves, salt and pepper to taste, 1 teaspoon cold water, and the sesame oil.
- Combine the remaining rice wine or sherry and the hoisin sauce in a small bowl and set aside.
- Heat a 14-inch flat-bottomed wok over high heat until a drop of water evaporates within a second or two when added to the pan. Swirl in 1 tablespoon of the oil and add the beef in a single layer. Let sit in the pan for about 1 minute, until it begins to sear, then stir fry for 1 minute. Transfer to a plate or bowl.
- Swirl in the remaining oil, then add the garlic, ginger and red pepper flakes and stir-fry for no more than 10 seconds. Add the mushrooms and peppers, sprinkle with salt to taste and stir-fry for 1 to 2 minutes. Return the beef and any juices that have accumulated on the plate or bowl to the wok, add the hoisin sauce mixture and stir-fry for another 30 seconds to a minute, until the beef is cooked through. Remove from the heat and serve with rice, grains or noodles.

Nutrition Information

- 258: calories;
- 5 grams: dietary fiber;
- 14 grams: fat;
- 3 grams: polyunsaturated fat;
- 18 grams: carbohydrates;
- 15 grams: protein;
- 632 milligrams: sodium;
- 6 grams: monounsaturated fat;
- 9 grams: sugars;

234. Raw And Cooked Tomato And Herb Salad With Couscous

Serving: Serves 6 to 8 | Prep: | Cook: | Ready in: 1hours45mins

Ingredients

- 1 cup couscous
- Salt to taste
- ¼ cup extra virgin olive oil
- ½ cup Israeli couscous or sorghum, cooked following the package directions, drained and cooled
- ½ pound plum tomatoes
- 1 cup finely diced cucumber
- ½ cup basil leaves, cut in slivers
- 2 tablespoons chopped fresh mint
- 2 tablespoons chopped fresh tarragon
- 1 pound heirloom tomatoes in assorted colors
- 1 tablespoon sherry vinegar (more to taste)
- 1 garlic clove, finely minced or puréed
- Basil leaves and cherry tomatoes, halved if desired, for garnish

Direction

- Preheat the oven to 375 degrees. Line a baking sheet with parchment. Place the couscous in a microwave-safe bowl and add salt to taste (about 1/2 teaspoon) and 2 teaspoons of the olive oil. Toss together. Cover by 1/2 inch with hot or boiling water. Cover the bowl tightly and let sit 30 minutes, or until all of the water has been absorbed. Fluff with forks and transfer to a large bowl. If you want the couscous to be really fluffy, once it has absorbed the water, cover the bowl with a plate and microwave for 3 minutes. Remove the bowl from the microwave carefully (it will be hot) and carefully remove the plate. Allow to cool slightly. Add the cooked Israeli couscous or sorghum.

- Meanwhile, core the plum tomatoes, quarter lengthwise and toss with 1 teaspoon of the olive oil and salt and pepper to taste. Place on the baking sheet in a single layer and place in the oven. Roast 30 minutes and remove from the heat. Allow to cool. Pull off the skins from the wedges (they will be loose and will come off in the salad if you don't do this now) and toss, along with any juice from the baking sheet, with the couscous. The tomatoes will break down and clump with the couscous. Add the chopped herbs.
- Dice the heirloom tomatoes and place in a bowl. Add salt and pepper to taste, the garlic, balsamic vinegar, sherry vinegar, and remaining olive oil and toss together. Add to the couscous and combine well. Mound onto a platter, garnish with basil leaves and cherry tomatoes, and serve.

Nutrition Information

- 202: calories;
- 5 grams: protein;
- 29 grams: carbohydrates;
- 3 grams: dietary fiber;
- 2 grams: sugars;
- 332 milligrams: sodium;
- 7 grams: fat;
- 1 gram: polyunsaturated fat;

235.   Red Cabbage, Carrot And Broccoli Stem Latkes With Caraway And Sesame

Serving: About 30 latkes, serving 6 | Prep: | Cook: | Ready in: 45mins

Ingredients

- 5 cups shredded red cabbage
- ½ pound carrots, shredded (about 1 1/2 cups)
- 1 ½ cups shredded peeled broccoli stems
- 2 tablespoons sesame seeds
- 2 teaspoons caraway seeds
- 1 teaspoon baking powder
- Salt to taste
- 3 tablespoons oat bran
- 3 tablespoons all-purpose flour
- 3 tablespoons cornmeal
- 2 tablespoons buckwheat flour
- 3 eggs, beaten
- About 1/4 cup canola, grape seed or rice bran oil

Direction

- Heat the oven to 300 degrees. Line a sheet pan with parchment and place a rack over another sheet pan.
- In a large bowl mix together the shredded cabbage, carrots, broccoli stems, baking powder, sesame seeds, caraway seeds, salt, oat bran, flour, cornmeal and buckwheat flour. Taste and adjust salt. Add the eggs and stir together. Let the mixture sit for 10 to 15 minutes.
- Begin heating a large heavy skillet over medium heat. Take a 1/4 cup measuring cup and fill with 3 tablespoons of the mixture. Reverse onto the parchment-lined baking sheet. Repeat with the remaining latke mix. You should have enough to make about 30 latkes.
- Add the oil to the pan and heat for 3 minutes or until hot. When it is hot (hold your hand a few inches above – you should feel the heat), slide a spatula under one portion of the latke

mixture and transfer it to the pan. Press down with the spatula to flatten. Repeat with more mounds. In my 10-inch pan I can cook four at a time without crowding; my 12-inch pan will accommodate 4 or 5. Cook on one side until golden brown, about 4 to 5 minutes. Slide the spatula underneath and flip the latkes over. Cook on the other side until golden brown, another 2 to 3 minutes. Transfer to the rack set over a baking sheet and place in the oven to keep warm.

- Serve hot topped with low-fat sour cream, Greek yogurt or crème fraîche.

Nutrition Information

- 217: calories;
- 13 grams: fat;
- 374 milligrams: sodium;
- 21 grams: carbohydrates;
- 4 grams: sugars;
- 7 grams: protein;
- 3 grams: saturated fat;
- 0 grams: trans fat;
- 5 grams: polyunsaturated fat;

---

236. Refrigerator Corn Relish

Serving: 2 pints | Prep: | Cook: | Ready in:

Ingredients

- 3 ears corn
- ⅔ cup apple cider vinegar
- ⅓ cup water
- ⅓ cup raw brown (turbinado) sugar
- 1 tablespoon mustard seeds
- 2 teaspoons cumin seeds
- ½ teaspoon celery seeds
- ½ teaspoon kosher salt
- ½ cup finely diced red onion
- 2 garlic cloves, sliced
- 1 small or medium red bell pepper, finely diced

- 1 small or medium green bell pepper, finely diced
- 1 serrano or jalapeño chile, minced (more to taste)

Direction

- Bring a large pot of water to a boil and add corn. Boil 3 minutes and transfer to a bowl of ice water. When corn is cool enough to handle, pat dry and cut kernels from cobs. Set aside.
- In a medium-size, heavy pot combine vinegar, sugar, water, mustard seeds, cumin seeds, celery seeds and salt and bring to a boil. Stir until sugar has dissolved and add onion. Reduce heat and simmer 5 minutes. Add peppers, garlic and chile and simmer for another 5 minutes. Stir in corn and simmer 1 minute. Remove from heat and pack into hot sterilized pint jars. Seal and allow to cool. Store in the refrigerator.

Nutrition Information

- 356: calories;
- 1 gram: polyunsaturated fat;
- 2 grams: monounsaturated fat;
- 49 grams: sugars;
- 510 milligrams: sodium;
- 4 grams: fat;
- 0 grams: trans fat;
- 76 grams: carbohydrates;
- 7 grams: dietary fiber;
- 8 grams: protein;

---

237. Rice Pilaf With Carrots And Parsley

Serving: 4 to 6 servings | Prep: | Cook: | Ready in: 1hours

Ingredients

- 1 cup basmati rice
- 2 cups water or stock (chicken or vegetable)

- 2 tablespoons extra virgin olive oil
- 1 small onion or 1 medium leek, finely chopped
- ¾ pound carrots (2 large), peeled, cut in half lengthwise if large, and thinly sliced on the diagonal
- Salt to taste
- ½ cup finely chopped flat-leaf parsley

Direction

- Place the rice in a bowl in the sink and rinse several times with water, or soak for 30 minutes, to wash away some of the starch. Drain through a strainer.
- Heat the water or stock to a bare simmer in a saucepan or in a Pyrex measuring cup in the microwave.
- Meanwhile, heat the oil in a wide, heavy skillet or saucepan over medium heat and add the carrots, onion or leek, and salt to taste. Cook, stirring, until the vegetables begin to soften, about 3 minutes, and add the rice. Cook, stirring, until the grains of rice are separate and beginning to crackle. Add the hot water or stock and salt to taste and bring to a boil. Reduce the heat, cover and simmer 15 minutes, until all of the liquid has been absorbed.
- Uncover the rice and place a clean towel over the top of the pan (it should not be touching the rice). Replace the lid and allow the rice to sit for 10 minutes, undisturbed. Add the parsley and gently fluff the rice, then pile the pilaf onto a platter or into a wide bowl and serve.

Nutrition Information

- 182: calories;
- 436 milligrams: sodium;
- 5 grams: fat;
- 1 gram: polyunsaturated fat;
- 3 grams: protein;
- 31 grams: carbohydrates;
- 2 grams: dietary fiber;

238. Rice Pilaf With Pistachios And Almonds

Serving: Serves 4 | Prep: | Cook: | Ready in: 35mins

Ingredients

- 1 cup basmati rice or purple jasmine rice
- 2 cups water or stock (chicken or vegetable)
- 2 tablespoons extra-virgin olive oil, unsalted butter or ghee
- ½ cup finely chopped onion (optional)
- Salt to taste
- 2 teaspoons rose water
- ¼ cup pistachios, coarsely chopped (30 grams)
- ¼ cup almonds, blanched, skinned and coarsely chopped (35 grams)
- ½ teaspoon cumin seeds, lightly toasted and ground
- ¼ teaspoon ground cinnamon
- ¼ teaspoon ground cardamom
- ¼ cup barberries or chopped dried apricots, soaked in warm water for 1/2 hour and drained

Direction

- Place rice in a bowl in the sink and rinse several times with water, or soak for 30 minutes to an hour. Drain.
- Heat water or stock to a bare simmer in a saucepan or in microwave.
- Meanwhile, heat 1 tablespoon of the oil, butter or ghee in a wide, heavy skillet or saucepan over medium heat and add onion and salt to taste. Cook, stirring, until the onion begins to soften, about 3 minutes, and add rice. Cook, stirring, until the grains of rice are separate, dry and beginning to crackle. Add hot water or stock, rose water and salt to taste and bring to a boil. Reduce heat, cover and simmer 15 minutes, until all of the liquid has been absorbed.
- Uncover rice and place a clean towel over the top of the pan (it should not be touching the

rice). Replace lid and allow to sit for 10 minutes, undisturbed.

- Meanwhile, heat remaining tablespoon of oil, butter or ghee over medium heat in a medium frying pan or saucepan and add the nuts. Cook, stirring, until lightly toasted, and add spices and barberries or dried apricots. Continue to cook for another minute, until the spices smell fragrant, and remove from the heat. Immediately scrape over the rice.
- Pile the pilaf onto a platter or into a wide bowl and toss to incorporate the nut and spice mixture. Serve.

Nutrition Information

- 343: calories;
- 3 grams: dietary fiber;
- 46 grams: carbohydrates;
- 5 grams: sugars;
- 463 milligrams: sodium;
- 15 grams: fat;
- 2 grams: saturated fat;
- 10 grams: monounsaturated fat;
- 0 grams: trans fat;
- 7 grams: protein;

---

239.   Risotto With Winter Squash And Collard Greens

Serving: Serves six | Prep: | Cook: | Ready in: 2hours

Ingredients

- 1 ½ pounds winter squash, such as butternut, banana or hubbard, peeled, seeded and cut in 1/2 inch dice (about 2 cups diced squash)
- 2 tablespoons extra virgin olive oil
- Salt
- freshly ground pepper to taste
- 1 bunch collard greens, about 1 pound, stemmed and washed
- 2 quarts chicken or vegetable stock, or 1 quart chicken or vegetable broth and 1 quart water
- 1 small or 1/2 medium onion
- 2 large garlic cloves, green shoots removed, minced
- 1 ½ cups arborio or carnaroli rice
- ½ cup dry white wine, such as pinot grigio or sauvignon blanc
- Pinch of saffron (optional)
- ½ cup freshly grated Parmesan cheese (2 ounces)
- 3 to 4 tablespoons chopped flat-leaf parsley

Direction

- Preheat the oven to 425 degrees. Cover a baking sheet with foil. Toss the squash with 1 tablespoon of the olive oil, season with salt and pepper, and spread on the baking sheet in an even layer. Place in the oven, and roast for 30 to 40 minutes, stirring every 10 minutes until tender and caramelized. Remove from the heat.
- While the squash is roasting, blanch the collard greens. Bring a large pot of water to a boil. Fill a bowl with ice water. When the water comes to a boil, salt generously and add the collard greens. Blanch for four minutes and transfer to the ice water with a slotted spoon or skimmer. Drain and squeeze out extra water. Chop coarsely, or cut in ribbons.
- Bring the stock to a simmer in a saucepan. Heat the remaining oil over medium heat in a large, heavy nonstick frying pan or a wide saucepan, and add the onion. Cook, stirring, until the onion begins to soften, about three minutes, and add the garlic and about 1/2 teaspoon salt. Cook, stirring, until the onion is tender and the garlic fragrant, about one minute, and add the rice. Cook, stirring, until the grains of rice are separate.
- Stir in the wine, and cook over medium heat, stirring constantly. The wine should bubble but not too quickly. When the wine has just about evaporated, add the collard greens, a third of the squash and the saffron. Stir in a ladleful or two of the simmering stock, enough to just cover the rice. The stock should bubble slowly. Cook, stirring often, until it is just

about absorbed. Add another ladleful of the stock, and continue to cook in this fashion -- not too fast and not too slowly, adding more stock when the rice is almost dry -- until the rice is tender all the way through but still chewy, 20 to 25 minutes. Taste and adjust seasonings.

- Add the remaining roasted squash and another 1/2 cup of stock to the rice. Stir in the Parmesan and parsley, and remove from the heat. Add freshly ground pepper, taste one last time and adjust salt. The mixture should be creamy (add more stock if it is not). Serve right away in wide soup bowls or on plates, spreading the risotto in a thin layer rather than a mound.

Nutrition Information

- 506: calories;
- 6 grams: dietary fiber;
- 82 grams: carbohydrates;
- 20 grams: sugars;
- 12 grams: fat;
- 3 grams: saturated fat;
- 1 gram: polyunsaturated fat;
- 17 grams: protein;
- 1639 milligrams: sodium;

240. Risotto With Asparagus And Pesto

Serving: Serves 4 to 6 | Prep: | Cook: | Ready in: 30mins

Ingredients

- 7 cups well-seasoned chicken or vegetable stock
- 2 tablespoons extra-virgin olive oil
- ½ cup minced onion
- Salt to taste
- 1 ½ cups arborio rice
- 1 garlic clove, minced
- ½ cup dry white wine such as pinot grigio or sauvignon blanc
- ¾ pound asparagus, trimmed and cut in 1-inch lengths
- ¼ to ⅓ cup pesto, to taste
- 2 to 4 tablespoons Parmesan, to taste

Direction

- Put well-seasoned stock or broth into a saucepan and bring it to a simmer over low heat, with a ladle nearby or in the pot.
- Heat olive oil over medium heat in a wide, heavy nonstick skillet or a wide, heavy saucepan. Add onion and a generous pinch of salt, and cook gently until it is just tender, about 3 minutes. Do not brown.
- Stir in rice and garlic and stir until the grains separate and begin to crackle. Add wine and stir until it is no longer visible in the pan. Begin adding simmering stock, a couple of ladlefuls (about 1/2 cup) at a time. The stock should just cover rice and should be bubbling, not too slowly but not too quickly. Cook, stirring often, until it is just about absorbed. Add another ladleful or two of the stock and continue to cook in this fashion, adding more stock and stirring when rice is almost dry. You do not have to stir continually, but stir often. After 10 minutes, add asparagus and continue to stir and add stock for another 10 to 15 minutes, until rice is cooked through but still al dente.
- Add another ladleful of stock to the rice. Stir in pesto and additional cheese and remove from heat. Taste and adjust seasoning. Mix should be creamy (add more stock if it isn't). Serve right away in wide soup bowls or on plates, spreading risotto in a thin layer rather than a mound.

Nutrition Information

- 425: calories;
- 55 grams: carbohydrates;
- 15 grams: protein;
- 1035 milligrams: sodium;

- 14 grams: fat;
- 3 grams: dietary fiber;
- 6 grams: sugars;
- 1 gram: polyunsaturated fat;

---

241. Roasted Broccoli With Tahini Garlic Sauce

Serving: Serves 6 | Prep: | Cook: | Ready in: 30mins

Ingredients

- For the tahini sauce
- 1 garlic clove, cut in half, green shoots removed
- Salt to taste
- ⅓ cup sesame tahini
- 2 to 4 tablespoons fresh lemon juice (more to taste)
- ⅓ cup water
- Aleppo pepper or red pepper flakes for sprinkling
- For the broccoli
- 1 to 1 ½ pounds broccoli crowns
- 2 tablespoons extra virgin olive oil
- Salt and freshly ground pepper to taste

Direction

- In a mortar and pestle mash the garlic clove to a purée with a generous pinch of salt. Transfer to a bowl and whisk in the sesame tahini. Whisk in the lemon juice, beginning with the smaller amount. The mixture will stiffen up. Gradually whisk in up to 1/3 cup water, until the sauce has the consistency of thick cream (or runny yogurt). Taste and adjust salt.
- Heat the oven to 450 degrees. Line a baking sheet with parchment paper. Slice the broccoli crowns 1/3 inch thick, letting the flower buds on the edges fall off. Peel any large pieces of stem by gently pulling away the thick skin, then toss the slices and the unattached buds with the olive oil, salt, and pepper. Place on the baking sheet in an even layer. Roast until

the tops are nicely browned, stirring and flipping the large slices over (tongs are a good tool for this) after 8 minutes, roasting about 15 minutes total. Remove from the oven and transfer to a platter or to individual serving plates. Drizzle on the tahini sauce and serve, or serve the tahini sauce in small bowls for dipping.

Nutrition Information

- 155: calories;
- 310 milligrams: sodium;
- 12 grams: fat;
- 2 grams: sugars;
- 6 grams: monounsaturated fat;
- 4 grams: dietary fiber;
- 10 grams: carbohydrates;
- 5 grams: protein;

---

242. Roasted Carrot, Parsnip And Potato Soup

Serving: 6 servings | Prep: | Cook: | Ready in: 1hours

Ingredients

- 1 ½ pounds carrots, peeled and cut in 3/4 inch pieces
- ½ pound (2 large) parsnips, peeled, quartered, cored and cut in 3/4 inch pieces
- 1 medium or large red onion, cut in large dice
- 1 medium (about 6 ounces) Yukon gold potato, quartered
- 2 garlic cloves, in the skin
- 2 tablespoons extra virgin olive oil
- Salt and freshly ground pepper
- 6 cups chicken or vegetable stock or broth
- Chopped fresh herbs, such as parsley, thyme, tarragon or chives, for garnish
- Crème fraîche or yogurt for garnish (optional)

Direction

- Preheat oven to 425 degrees. Line a sheet pan or a baking dish with parchment or foil. Toss vegetables, including garlic cloves, with olive oil and salt and pepper to taste. Spread in baking dish or on sheet pan in an even layer and place in oven. Set timer for 20 minutes.
- After 20 minutes, stir vegetables and turn heat down to 400 degrees. Roast for another 20 to 30 minutes (or longer; I have found every oven I've used to be different, thus the range), or until very tender and caramelized on the edges, stirring every 10 minutes. Remove from the heat. You should have about 4 cups roasted vegetables.
- Hold garlic cloves with a towel so that you don't burn your fingers. Squeeze out the pulp into a blender. Add half the vegetables and 2 cups of the stock. Cover the top of the blender with a towel pulled down tight, rather than airtight with the lid, because hot mixture will jump and push the top off if the blender is closed airtight. Blend until smooth and transfer to a soup pot. Repeat with the second half of the roasted vegetables. Transfer to the pot and whisk in remaining broth. Season to taste with salt and pepper and heat through. Serve each bowl with a sprinkle of chopped fresh herbs and if you wish, a swirl of crème fraîche or yogurt.

Nutrition Information

- 243: calories;
- 1 gram: polyunsaturated fat;
- 5 grams: monounsaturated fat;
- 12 grams: sugars;
- 9 grams: protein;
- 1066 milligrams: sodium;
- 8 grams: fat;
- 36 grams: carbohydrates;
- 7 grams: dietary fiber;

243. Roasted Carrots With Turmeric And Cumin

Serving: Serves 6 | Prep: | Cook: |Ready in: 40mins

Ingredients

- 10 medium carrots, peeled
- 2 tablespoons extra virgin olive oil
- Salt and freshly ground pepper to taste
- 1 tablespoon fresh thyme leaves
- ½ teaspoon cumin seeds, lightly toasted
- ½ teaspoon coriander seeds, lightly toasted
- 2 tablespoons unsalted butter, at room temperature
- ½ teaspoon turmeric
- ½ teaspoon Aleppo pepper or mild chili powder
- 2 tablespoons chopped fresh mint

Direction

- Preheat the oven to 425 degrees. Cut the carrots in half lengthwise and crosswise. If the carrots are fat at one end, cut the fat half in half again lengthwise, so that the pieces are more or less equal in thickness. Place in a large bowl and toss with the olive oil, salt and pepper, and thyme leaves.
- Heat a heavy baking sheet in the oven for 3 to 4 minutes. Remove from the oven and place the carrots on it in one layer. Roast for 20 to 25 minutes, stirring the carrots every 10 minutes. They should be slightly caramelized and tender.
- While the carrots are in the oven place the cumin and coriander seeds in a mortar and pestle and grind. Add the soft butter, turmeric and Aleppo pepper or chili powder and stir with the pestle until well amalgamated. Transfer to a large pan.
- Remove the carrots from the oven when done and add to the pan with the spice butter and the mint. Toss together, taste and adjust salt and pepper. Serve from the pan or transfer to a platter.

Nutrition Information

- 121: calories;
- 9 grams: fat;
- 0 grams: trans fat;
- 4 grams: monounsaturated fat;
- 1 gram: protein;
- 3 grams: dietary fiber;
- 11 grams: carbohydrates;
- 5 grams: sugars;
- 268 milligrams: sodium;

244.   Roasted Carrots And Scallions With Thyme And Hazelnuts

Serving: Serves 4 | Prep: | Cook: | Ready in: 1hours

Ingredients

- 1 ounce hazelnuts (about 1/4 cup)
- 1 pound carrots, preferably young small carrots, any color (but a mix is nice)
- 1 bunch white or purple spring onions or scallions
- Salt and freshly ground pepper
- 2 teaspoons fresh thyme leaves
- 2 tablespoons extra virgin olive oil
- Optional: a drizzle of hazelnut oil or walnut oil for serving

Direction

- Preheat the oven to 325 degrees. Place the hazelnuts on a baking sheet and roast for 8 to 10 minutes, until they smell toasty and they a're golden all the way through (cut one in half to check). Remove from the oven and turn up the heat to 425 degrees.
- Immediately wrap the hazelnuts in a clean, dry dish towel. Rub them in the towel to remove the skins. Then place the skinned hazelnuts in a plastic bag or, if you have one, a disposable pastry bag and set on your work table in one layer. Use a rolling pin to crush the nuts by rolling over them with the pin. Set aside.
- Line a sheet pan with parchment or oil a baking dish large enough to fit all of the vegetables in a single layer. If the carrots are small, just peel and trim the tops and bottoms. If they are medium- sized, peel, cut in half and cut into 4-inch lengths. Quarter large carrots and cut into 4-inch lengths. Trim the root ends and greens from the spring onions or scallions. If they are bulbous, cut them in half. Season with salt and pepper, add the thyme and olive oil and toss well, either directly on the pan or in the dish or in a bowl. Spread in an even layer in the baking dish or on the baking sheet.
- Roast in the oven for 20 to 30 minutes, stirring every 10 minutes. The onions may be done after 10 minutes – they should be soft and lightly browned. Remove them from the pan if they are and hold on a plate. When the carrots and onions are tender and browned in places, remove from the oven. Add the onions back into the mix if you 've removed them and toss together. Sprinkle on the toasted ground hazelnuts, and drizzle on the optional nut oil, and serve.

Nutrition Information

- 170: calories;
- 5 grams: dietary fiber;
- 6 grams: sugars;
- 3 grams: protein;
- 1 gram: saturated fat;
- 2 grams: polyunsaturated fat;
- 15 grams: carbohydrates;
- 367 milligrams: sodium;
- 12 grams: fat;
- 9 grams: monounsaturated fat;

245.　　　Roasted Corn And Tomato Salsa

Serving: Makes a little about 2 1/2 cups | Prep: | Cook: | Ready in: 45mins

Ingredients

- 1 ½ pounds ripe tomatoes, preferably plum tomatoes
- 1 or 2 jalapeños (about 1 ounce)
- 1 ear of corn, shucked
- ½ small white onion, sliced about 1/4 inch thick (about 2 ounces)
- 4 garlic cloves, peeled
- Salt to taste
- 1 ½ teaspoons cider vinegar
- ¼ cup water (optional)
- ⅓ to ½ cup chopped cilantro (to taste)

Direction

- Preheat broiler and set rack 4 inches below. If your broiler and oven are separate, also preheat the oven to 425 degrees. Line 2 baking sheets with foil.
- Place tomatoes and jalapeños on one of the baking sheets and set under broiler, about 4 inches from heat. Broil for about 6 minutes, until skins are charred and blackened in spots. Using tongs, flip over tomatoes and jalapeño and continue to broil for another 6 minutes. The tomatoes and chiles should be softened and cooked through as well as charred. Tip tomatoes and chiles, along with any juices in the pan, into a bowl and allow to cool.
- Place corn on baking sheet and set under the broiler. Broil until you hear the kernels beginning to pop, 2 to 4 minutes. Corn should be nicely browned on one side. Flip over and broil for 2 minutes, or until you hear popping, on the other side. Remove from heat, allow to cool, then cut kernels from cob and set aside.
- If using the same oven to roast the onions, turn heat down to 425 degrees. Break up onions into rings and place on baking sheet in a single layer. Add garlic and place in oven. Roast,

stirring every 5 minutes, until onions have softened and are lightly browned and charred on edges and garlic is soft and browned in spots, about 15 minutes. If some of the smaller pieces of onion begin to char more quickly than others, remove them sooner.
- Stem jalapeños and place with onions and garlic in a food processor fitted with the bowl as necessary. Transfer to a large bowl.
- When tomatoes are cool enough to handle, core and discard skins (hold over bowl to catch juices). Place in food processor with juice and pulse to a coarse purée. Add to bowl with chopped onions, garlic and jalapeño. Add the vinegar, season generously with salt (Rick Bayless recommends a generous teaspoon), and stir in the cilantro and corn. If desired, thin out with water.

Nutrition Information

- 293: calories;
- 14 grams: dietary fiber;
- 12 grams: protein;
- 2132 milligrams: sodium;
- 0 grams: saturated fat;
- 1 gram: polyunsaturated fat;
- 3 grams: fat;
- 67 grams: carbohydrates;
- 26 grams: sugars;

246.　　　Roasted Mushroom Base

Serving: 1 1/4 pounds or about 3 cups | Prep: | Cook: | Ready in: 45mins

Ingredients

- 2 tablespoons extra-virgin olive oil
- 2 pounds mushrooms, sliced or quartered
- Salt to taste
- Freshly ground black pepper to taste

Direction

- Preheat oven to 400 degrees. Line 2 baking sheets with parchment.
- In a large bowl, toss mushrooms with oil, salt and pepper. Spread in an even layer on baking sheets and bake in the middle and lower racks of the oven for 20 minutes, stirring every 5 minutes and switching pans top to bottom halfway through. The mushrooms should be tender and dry when done. Remove from heat and allow to cool.
- Grind in a grinder or pulse in a food processor fitted with steel blade until broken down into small pieces resembling ground meat. What works best in my food processor is to pulse about 10 times, scrape down the sides of the bowl and then pulse another five to 10 times. Taste and adjust seasoning.

Nutrition Information

- 111: calories;
- 1 gram: polyunsaturated fat;
- 5 grams: monounsaturated fat;
- 2 grams: dietary fiber;
- 4 grams: sugars;
- 7 grams: protein;
- 545 milligrams: sodium;
- 8 grams: carbohydrates;

---

247.   Roasted Mushroom And Gruyère Sandwich

Serving: Serves 1 | Prep: | Cook: | Ready in: 30mins

Ingredients

- ½ pound mushrooms (white or cremini), sliced
- 2 tablespoons plus 1/2 teaspoon extra-virgin olive oil
- 1 teaspoon fresh thyme leaves
- Salt and freshly ground pepper
- 2 slices whole-grain bread (3 ounces)
- 1 garlic clove, cut in half (optional)
- 2 teaspoons minced chives

- Handful of arugula
- ¾ ounce grated Gruyère cheese (3 tablespoons)

Direction

- Preheat oven or toaster oven to 400 degrees. Line a baking sheet with parchment. Toss mushrooms with 2 tablespoons of the olive oil and thyme leaves and spread in an even layer on the baking sheet. Place in oven and roast for 15 to 20 minutes, stirring halfway through, or until mushrooms are bubbling and moist. Remove from heat and season with salt and pepper.
- If desired, rub one side of each slice of bread with the cut clove of garlic.
- Sprinkle 2 tablespoons of the cheese over 1 of the slices (on the side you rubbed with garlic). Top with half the mushrooms (use the other half for another sandwich or another recipe). Sprinkle chives over the mushrooms and top with a handful of arugula and remaining cheese. Top with remaining slice of bread (garlic-rubbed side down) and press down firmly. Drizzle remaining olive oil over top slice.
- Toast in toaster oven 3 to 4 minutes, until cheese melts. Remove from heat, press down firmly, cut in half and serve.

Nutrition Information

- 708: calories;
- 47 grams: fat;
- 13 grams: saturated fat;
- 6 grams: polyunsaturated fat;
- 10 grams: sugars;
- 31 grams: protein;
- 920 milligrams: sodium;
- 26 grams: monounsaturated fat;
- 46 grams: carbohydrates;
- 9 grams: dietary fiber;

248. Roasted Sweet Potato Oven Fries

Serving: 4 servings | Prep: | Cook: | Ready in: 1hours

Ingredients

- 2 inches lemon grass stalk, hard papery layers discarded, the rest coarsely chopped
- 1 tablespoon coarsely chopped ginger
- Salt to taste
- ¼ cup extra virgin olive oil
- 2 pounds orange-fleshed sweet potatoes, also sold as yams
- ½ teaspoon cumin seeds, lightly toasted and coarsely ground
- ½ teaspoon coriander seeds, lightly toasted and coarsely ground

Direction

- Place the chopped lemon grass and ginger in a mortar and pestle and add a generous pinch of kosher salt. Pound and grind until you have obtained a coarse paste. Add 1 tablespoon of the olive oil and work the ingredients together with the pestle. Scrape into a small saucepan and add the remaining olive oil. Stir together and bring to a very gentle sizzle over medium-low heat. Sizzle, shaking or swirling the pan often, for 2 minutes and turn off the heat. Allow the mixture to steep for 30 minutes. Strain into a large bowl, pressing the ginger and lemon grass against the strainer to extract all of the oil. You should have 3 tablespoons of oil. Add a little more olive oil if necessary.
- Meanwhile preheat the oven to 400 degrees. Line a baking sheet with parchment and brush the parchment with olive oil. Cut the sweet potatoes in half lengthwise. If they are very long, cut the halves in half crosswise as well. Cut each half into 4 long wedges – smaller sweet potatoes will yield 8 wedges, larger will yield 16.
- Place the sweet potato wedges in the bowl with the oil. Add the ground cumin and coriander, and salt to taste, and toss together until the wedges are thoroughly coated with oil. Place on the baking sheet in a single layer (use 2 baking sheets if necessary). Place in the oven and set the timer for 10 minutes. Turn the wedges over and roast for another 10 minutes. Turn the wedges again and roast for another 5 to 10 minutes, depending on the thickness of the wedges and how fast they are caramelizing. The wedges should be tender when pierced and there should be some caramelized bits, especially at the thin tips. Remove from the heat and allow to cool slightly before eating.

Nutrition Information

- 400: calories;
- 1 gram: sugars;
- 14 grams: fat;
- 2 grams: polyunsaturated fat;
- 10 grams: monounsaturated fat;
- 4 grams: protein;
- 587 milligrams: sodium;
- 66 grams: carbohydrates;
- 9 grams: dietary fiber;

249. Roasted Tomatillo Poblano Avocado Salsa

Serving: About 2 cups, serving 6 to 8 | Prep: | Cook: | Ready in: 30mins

Ingredients

- ½ pound tomatillos, husked and quartered
- 2 poblano or Anaheim chiles, stemmed and quartered (cut in half lengthwise, pull out seeds and membranes, then cut halves in half crosswise)
- 1 to 2 jalapeño or serrano chiles (to taste), stemmed and seeded if desired
- 1 medium white or yellow onion, peeled and quartered
- 2 garlic cloves, peeled

- 2 tablespoons extra virgin olive oil
- Salt to taste
- ½ cup chopped cilantro
- 1 teaspoon ground toasted cumin
- 1 large ripe avocado, halved and pitted
- Juice of 2 limes

Direction

- Preheat oven to 425 degrees. Line a sheet pan with parchment. Place tomatillos, chiles (both types), onion, and garlic on the parchment and drizzle on olive oil. Add salt to taste and toss together with your hands. Place in oven and roast 20 minutes, stirring halfway through, until blistered and softened. Remove from heat.
- Place roasted vegetables, with any juice from the pan, in a food processor fitted with the steel blade. Pulse until well blended but not puréed. Add cilantro, cumin, avocado and lime juice and pulse until blended. Taste and adjust salt. Serve at once or store in a well-sealed container in the refrigerator. Stir well before serving.

Nutrition Information

- 108: calories;
- 6 grams: monounsaturated fat;
- 9 grams: carbohydrates;
- 4 grams: dietary fiber;
- 3 grams: sugars;
- 2 grams: protein;
- 256 milligrams: sodium;
- 8 grams: fat;
- 1 gram: polyunsaturated fat;

250.　　Roasted Winter Vegetable Medley

Serving: Serves 6 | Prep: | Cook: | Ready in: 30mins

Ingredients

- 1 medium butternut squash (about 1 1/2 pounds), peeled, seeds and membranes scraped away, and cut into 3/4 to 1-inch dice
- 2 large carrots, peeled and cut into 3/4-inch pieces (quarter at the fat ends, cut in half at the thin ends, then cut in thick slices)
- 1 large parsnip, quartered, cored, and cut in 3/4-inch pieces
- 1 medium-size fennel bulb, quartered, cored and cut in 3/4 inch pieces
- 1 medium or large red onion, cut in large dice
- 3 tablespoons extra virgin olive oil
- Salt and freshly ground pepper to taste
- Optional: Chopped fresh rosemary, thyme or sage, about 2 teaspoons

Direction

- Preheat oven to 425 degrees. Line 2 baking sheets or roasting pans with parchment or foil. Place squash on one and remaining vegetables on the other, and toss each batch with 1 tablespoon olive oil and salt and pepper to taste. If desired, add fresh herbs such as rosemary, thyme or sage, and toss together. Spread vegetables in an even layer.
- Place in the oven, on the same shelf if both pans will fit, or on the middle and lower shelves, and roast for 20 minutes, stirring halfway through. Switch pans top to bottom halfway through if on separate shelves Turn heat down to 400 degrees and continue to roast for another 10 to 20 minutes (the squash may be ready sooner than the root vegetables), stirring halfway through, until tender and caramelized.
- Remove from oven, combine squash and other vegetables and stir together.

Nutrition Information

- 155: calories;
- 6 grams: dietary fiber;
- 2 grams: protein;
- 545 milligrams: sodium;
- 7 grams: sugars;
- 1 gram: polyunsaturated fat;

- 5 grams: monounsaturated fat;
- 24 grams: carbohydrates;

---

251. Rose Petal And Vanilla Tea

Serving: Serves 2 | Prep: | Cook: | Ready in: 30mins

Ingredients

- 2 tablespoons dried rose petals
- 1 vanilla bean, split and scraped
- 2 ½ cups boiling water
- 1 tablespoon honey

Direction

- Place the dried rose petals and vanilla bean and seeds in a large measuring cup or teapot and pour on the boiling water. Stir in the honey, cover and let steep for 30 minutes. Strain and serve warm, or reheat and serve hot.

Nutrition Information

- 39: calories;
- 0 grams: protein;
- 9 grams: sugars;
- 13 milligrams: sodium;

---

252. Salmon Rillettes

Serving: 1 3/4 cups, serving 8 generously | Prep: | Cook: | Ready in: 20mins

Ingredients

- 1 6-ounce salmon fillet, bones removed
- Salt and freshly ground pepper
- 5 ounces smoked salmon, cut into thin strips, then into 1/4-inch pieces
- 1 tablespoon unsalted butter, at room temperature
- 1 tablespoon extra virgin olive oil
- 4 tablespoons plain Greek yogurt
- 1 tablespoon crème fraîche (or omit and use 5 tablespoons yogurt)
- 1 1-2 to 2 tablespoons fresh lemon juice
- 2 tablespoons chopped chives

Direction

- Lightly oil a steamer basket. Season salmon with salt and pepper and place in steamer basket over 1 inch of boiling water. Cover and steam 5 to 8 minutes, depending on thickness of the salmon. It should be just cooked through and easy to flake apart, but moist. Remove from heat and allow to cool.
- Using a fork or a whisk, cream butter and olive oil together until mixture is smooth and emulsified.
- Flake salmon into a medium-size bowl and add smoked salmon. Using a fork, mash the two together until well combined and salmon has broken down like canned tuna. Add butter and olive oil, yogurt and crème fraîche and work together with a fork until well combined. Add lemon juice to taste and the chives, and mix together well. Add pepper and mix together. Chill for 1 to 2 hours. Allow to come to room temperature before serving.
- Either spoon onto endive leaves or other vegetables, or serve with toasted bread or crackers.

Nutrition Information

- 105: calories;
- 8 grams: protein;
- 2 grams: saturated fat;
- 0 grams: sugars;
- 3 grams: monounsaturated fat;
- 1 gram: carbohydrates;
- 137 milligrams: sodium;

253. Salmon Tacos With Greens And Tomatillo Salsa

Serving: 8 to 10 tacos | Prep: | Cook: | Ready in: 50mins

Ingredients

- 1 pound salmon or arctic char fillets
- Salt and freshly ground pepper
- 1 bunch spinach or chard (about ¾ pound), stemmed and washed well in 2 changes of water
- 1 tablespoon extra virgin olive oil
- 1 to 2 garlic cloves (to taste), minced
- 1 to 3 serrano or jalapeño chiles (to taste), minced
- 1 cup cooked tomatillo salsa (see recipe)
- 2 to 3 ounces crumbled queso fresco or feta (optional)
- Shredded cabbage (optional)
- 8 to 10 corn tortillas
- Chopped cilantro

Direction

- Preheat the oven to 300 degrees. Cover a baking sheet with foil and lightly oil the foil. Place the salmon or arctic char on top. Season with salt and gently rub the salt into the surface of the salmon. Add pepper to taste. Fill a roasting pan or cake pan halfway with boiling water and place it on the oven floor. Place the fish in the oven and bake 10 to 20 minutes (depending on the thickness), until white beads of protein appear on the surface and the fish can be pulled apart with a fork. Remove from the heat and allow to cool until you can handle it. If desired, scrape away the white protein beads, then flake the fish and place in a bowl. Discard the skin. Season the fish well with salt and pepper.
- Steam the spinach or chard just until wilted, about 1 minute for spinach, 2 minutes for chard, or blanch in boiling salted water (20 seconds for spinach, about 1 minute for chard). Transfer to a bowl of cold water, then drain and, taking the greens up by the handful, squeeze out excess water. Chop medium-fine.
- Heat the olive oil over medium heat in a heavy, medium size skillet and add the garlic and chile. Stir until fragrant, 30 seconds to a minute, and add the greens and salt and pepper to taste. Stir and toss in the pan for about a minute, until nicely infused with the oil, garlic and chile. Remove from the heat and add to the fish. Stir in 1/2 cup of the salsa. Taste and adjust seasonings.
- Heat the tortillas: wrap in a kitchen towel and place in a steamer basket over 1 inch of boiling water. Bring to a boil, cover the pot and steam 1 minute. Turn off the heat and allow to sit for 10 to 15 minutes without uncovering. Top the hot tortillas with the fish. Spoon on a little more salsa and if desired, garnish with crumbled cheese and shredded cabbage. Fold the tortillas over and serve.

Nutrition Information

- 191: calories;
- 344 milligrams: sodium;
- 9 grams: fat;
- 2 grams: sugars;
- 3 grams: dietary fiber;
- 15 grams: carbohydrates;
- 13 grams: protein;

254. Salmon And Cucumber Tartare With Wasabi Sauce

Serving: 4 to 6 appetizer servings | Prep: | Cook: | Ready in: 10mins

Ingredients

- 1 pound salmon fillet, skin and small bones removed
- 1 cup (about 5 ounces) finely diced cucumber
- 1 medium size shallot, minced
- 2 tablespoons capers, rinsed and chopped

- 1 to 2 tablespoons minced pickled ginger (available in Japanese markets), to taste, plus additional pickled ginger for garnish
- ½ teaspoon Worcestershire sauce
- Salt and freshly ground pepper to taste
- 2 tablespoons fresh lemon juice
- 2 teaspoons wasabi paste
- 1 tablespoon seasoned rice vinegar
- 1 teaspoon soy sauce
- 2 tablespoons extra virgin olive oil
- Chopped chives for garnish

Direction

- Make sure there are no small pin bones in the salmon. Remove with tweezers if there are, then mince the fish very fine. Combine with the cucumber in a medium bowl.
- Rinse the shallot with cold water and drain on a paper towel. Add to the salmon and cucumber. Add the capers, minced pickled ginger, Worcestershire sauce, salt and pepper, and lemon juice and toss together.
- In a small bowl or measuring cup, whisk together the wasabi or horseradish, vinegar, soy sauce, and olive oil. Toss with the fish and cucumber mixture. Cover and refrigerate until ready to serve.
- To serve, spoon onto cucumber rounds or pita triangles, or mold in plastic wrap-lined ramekins and unmold onto plates as a first course. Sprinkle with chives and garnish with pickled ginger.

Nutrition Information

- 213: calories;
- 16 grams: protein;
- 294 milligrams: sodium;
- 15 grams: fat;
- 3 grams: polyunsaturated fat;
- 6 grams: monounsaturated fat;
- 4 grams: carbohydrates;
- 1 gram: sugars;

---

255. Salmon In Fig Leaves

Serving: 6 servings | Prep: | Cook: | Ready in: 30mins

Ingredients

- 1 2-pound king-salmon fillet, skinned
- Olive oil
- Salt and pepper
- 8 large fig leaves
- Fennel fronds, preferably wild

Direction

- Preheat the oven to 350. Cut the salmon into 6 equal portions. Coat lightly with olive oil, and season with salt and freshly ground pepper.
- Wash the fig leaves, and leave them moistened. Place 4 on a baking sheet, and lay the salmon pieces on top. Scatter small pieces of fennel frond on top of the fish, and cover with the remaining fig leaves. Bake in the upper part of the oven until the fish is just cooked through, 10 to 12 minutes, then transfer the salmon to a serving platter immediately. Serve with blanched new potatoes and green beans, tomatoes, cucumber, hard-cooked eggs and aioli.

---

256. Salsa Fresca With Kohlrabi

Serving: About 2 1/4 cups | Prep: | Cook: | Ready in: 15mins

Ingredients

- ¼ cup finely chopped red or white onion
- ½ medium kohlrabi (about 1/2 pound), cut in small dice (1 cup)
- 1 pound ripe tomatoes, diced (2 cups)
- 1 to 2 serrano or jalepeño chiles (or more, to taste), minced
- ¼ to ½ cup chopped cilantro (to taste)
- 1 to 2 tablespoons fresh lime juice (to taste)

- Salt to taste

Direction

- Place onion in a small bowl and cover with cold water. Let sit for 5 minutes. Drain and rinse with cold water. Drain on paper towels.
- Combine kohlrabi and tomatoes in a medium bowl. Add onions, chiles, cilantro, lime juice and salt to taste and stir together. Let sit for 15 to 30 minutes before serving.

Nutrition Information

- 27: calories;
- 1 gram: protein;
- 294 milligrams: sodium;
- 0 grams: polyunsaturated fat;
- 6 grams: carbohydrates;
- 2 grams: dietary fiber;
- 3 grams: sugars;

---

257.   Sautéed Apple Rings

Serving: 6 servings | Prep: | Cook: | Ready in: 30mins

Ingredients

- 4 large apples
- 1 lemon wedge
- 2 tablespoons unsalted butter
- 1 tablespoon raw brown (turbinado) sugar
- ½ teaspoon cinnamon
- 1 teaspoon vanilla extract
- 2 tablespoons calvados or brandy (optional)

Direction

- Core apples and rub inside with lemon wedge. Peel if desired (I don't). Slice about 1/4 inch thick, or a little bit thicker.
- Melt half the butter over medium-high heat in a large, heavy skillet. When it stops foaming (wait this long so that the apples sear when you add them to the pan) add half the apples,

half the sugar and half the cinnamon. Cook, flipping apple rings often, until apples are caramelized, 10 to 12 minutes. Test, using the tip of a knife or the edge of a spoon, to see if the apples are soft all the way through. Remove to a bowl. Repeat with remaining apples, butter, sugar and cinnamon. When second batch is caramelized return first batch to pan. Add vanilla and brandy if using and continue to cook, flipping apples, until the liquid evaporates. Transfer to a bowl or serving dish. Serve warm.

Nutrition Information

- 122: calories;
- 2 milligrams: sodium;
- 4 grams: dietary fiber;
- 2 grams: saturated fat;
- 0 grams: protein;
- 1 gram: monounsaturated fat;
- 23 grams: carbohydrates;
- 18 grams: sugars;

---

258.   Sautéed Spicy Carrots With Black Quinoa

Serving: Serves 6 to 8 | Prep: | Cook: | Ready in: 15mins

Ingredients

- 2 tablespoons extra virgin olive oil
- 2 garlic cloves, minced
- 1 to 2 serrano or jalapeño chiles, minced
- 2 teaspoons coriander seeds, lightly toasted and coarsely ground or crushed
- 2 teaspoons cumin seeds, lightly toasted and coarsely ground or crushed
- 2 pounds carrots, peeled and sliced on the diagonal, about 1/4 inch thick
- 1 ½ teaspoons sugar
- Salt
- 1 tablespoon unsalted butter (optional)
- ¼ to ⅓ cup cooked black quinoa

- 2 tablespoons chopped fresh mint or cilantro

Direction

- Heat olive oil in a large, heavy skillet over medium-high heat and add garlic and chile. Stir for about 10 seconds and add ground coriander and cumin. Stir for about 10 seconds, until mixture is very fragrant, and add carrots, sugar and salt to taste. Sauté, stirring often or tossing in the pan, for 5 minutes and turn heat down to medium. Continue to cook, stirring often or tossing in the pan, for another 10 minutes, until carrots are tender and lightly colored.
- Add butter, quinoa and mint or cilantro and stir or toss in the pan for another minute or two, until quinoa is warmed through and butter has melted. Taste and adjust seasonings. Serve hot or warm.

Nutrition Information

- 93: calories;
- 3 grams: monounsaturated fat;
- 14 grams: carbohydrates;
- 6 grams: sugars;
- 2 grams: protein;
- 302 milligrams: sodium;
- 4 grams: dietary fiber;
- 1 gram: polyunsaturated fat;

259. Sautéed Winter Squash With Swiss Chard, Red Quinoa And Aleppo Pepper

Serving: Serves 4 | Prep: | Cook: | Ready in: 35mins

Ingredients

- 1 generous bunch Swiss chard (about 3/4 pound), with wide ribs
- Salt
- 1 medium-size butternut squash, about 2 pounds, peeled and cut into small dice (1/2 inch or a little smaller), about 4 cups diced
- 2 tablespoons plus 1 teaspoon extra virgin olive oil
- 1 large or 2 medium garlic cloves, minced
- ¾ teaspoon Aleppo pepper (more to taste)
- ⅓ cup cooked red quinoa

Direction

- Bring a large pot of water to a boil while you strip leaves from chard ribs. Wash leaves in 2 changes of water and cut ribs into 1/4-inch dice. You should have about 1 cup diced chard ribs.
- When water comes to a boil salt generously and add chard leaves. Blanch just until wilted, about 1 minute. Transfer to a bowl of cold water, drain and squeeze out excess water, taking chard up by the handful. Chop medium-fine and set aside. You should have about 1 cup chopped blanched chard.
- In a large, heavy skillet heat 2 tablespoons olive oil over medium-high heat and add diced chard ribs. Sauté for 1 to 2 minutes and add squash. Allow to brown in the pan without stirring for a couple of minutes, then toss in the pan and sauté for 10 minutes, tossing or stirring in the pan occasionally. Season with salt and continue to cook, tossing or stirring in the pan occasionally, for another 8 to 10 minutes, until tender and lightly colored. Add remaining teaspoon of olive oil and garlic, chard and Aleppo pepper and toss together. Cook, stirring often, for another 3 to 4 minutes, until chard is evenly distributed throughout and garlic is fragrant. Add quinoa and toss together until evenly distributed and warmed through. Taste and adjust seasoning. Remove from heat and serve.

Nutrition Information

- 193: calories;
- 9 grams: fat;
- 1 gram: polyunsaturated fat;

- 6 grams: dietary fiber;
- 29 grams: carbohydrates;
- 5 grams: sugars;
- 4 grams: protein;
- 782 milligrams: sodium;

260. Savory Cornbread Stuffing

Serving: 8 to 10 servings | Prep: | Cook: | Ready in: 40mins

Ingredients

- For the cornbread
- 1 cup yellow cornmeal, preferably organic stone ground
- ½ cup all purpose flour or whole wheat flour
- ¾ teaspoon salt
- 1 tablespoon baking powder
- ½ teaspoon baking soda
- 2 eggs
- 1 cup plain low-fat yogurt or buttermilk
- ½ cup milk
- 1 tablespoon mild honey
- 2 to 3 tablespoons unsalted butter (to taste)
- For the cornbread and sage stuffing
- 2 tablespoons extra virgin olive oil, or 1 tablespoon each olive oil and unsalted butter
- 1 large onion, finely chopped
- Salt to taste
- 4 stalks celery, cut in small dice
- 4 garlic cloves, minced
- 2 teaspoons rubbed sage, or 2 tablespoons chopped fresh sage
- 1 tablespoon fresh thyme leaves or 1 1/2 teaspoons dried thyme
- ½ cup finely chopped flat-leaf parsley
- Freshly ground pepper
- A double batch of cornbread (see above), crumbled you can do this in a food processor fitted with the steel blade
- ½ cup milk, or as necessary, for moistening

- 4 tablespoons unsalted butter if baking separately

Direction

- Preheat the oven to 400 degrees. Place a 9-inch cast iron skillet, a heavy 2-quart baking dish or a heavy 9-inch square baking pan in the oven while you prepare the batter.
- Place the cornmeal in a bowl, and sift in the flour, salt, baking powder and baking soda. Stir the mixture with a spoon or whisk to amalgamate. In a separate bowl, beat together the eggs, yogurt (or buttermilk), milk and honey. Whisk the cornmeal mixture into the liquid mixture. Do not overwork the batter.
- Remove the pan from the oven, and add the butter to the pan. Swirl the pan so that the butter melts quickly before it gets too brown, then quickly whisk the butter into the batter. Brush the sides of the pan with any butter remaining in the pan.
- Quickly scrape all of the batter into the hot pan, and place in the oven. Bake 35 to 40 minutes, until golden brown and a toothpick inserted in the center comes out clean. It will be quite brown on the edges. Allow the bread to cool in the pan, or serve warm.
- Heat the olive oil (or oil and butter) over medium heat in a large, heavy, nonstick skillet, and add the onion. Cook, stirring often, until it begins to soften, about three minutes, and add 1/2 teaspoon salt and the celery. Cook together for another few minutes, until the onion is tender. Add the garlic, and stir together for 30 seconds to a minute, until fragrant. Transfer to a large bowl, and add the remaining ingredients. Combine well. Taste and adjust salt. Moisten as desired with milk.
- Stuff the cavity of the turkey, or transfer to a buttered or oiled 2-quart baking dish. Dot with butter. Cover with aluminum foil, and heat through in a 325-degree oven for 30 minutes.

Nutrition Information

- 266: calories;

185

- 6 grams: protein;
- 30 grams: carbohydrates;
- 332 milligrams: sodium;
- 13 grams: fat;
- 0 grams: trans fat;
- 5 grams: monounsaturated fat;
- 1 gram: polyunsaturated fat;
- 2 grams: dietary fiber;

---

261.   Savory Oatmeal Pan Bread

Serving: Serves 8 to 10 | Prep: | Cook: | Ready in: 1hours

Ingredients

- 110 grams (1 1/8 cups) rolled oats
- 70 grams (1/2 cup plus 1 tablespoon) whole wheat pastry flour
- 10 grams (2 1/4 teaspoons) baking powder
- 4 ½ grams (scant 3/4 teaspoon) salt
- 1 gram (1/4 teaspoon) freshly ground pepper
- 150 grams (1/2 cup plus 1 tablespoon) milk
- 110 grams (2 extra large) egg
- ½ cup fresh herbs, such as parsley leaves, sage, marjoram, thyme, dill, chopped (1/3 cup chopped)
- 50 grams (3 tablespoons) grated onion
- 4 tablespoons extra virgin olive oil

Direction

- Preheat the oven to 400 degrees.
- Place the oats in the bowl of a stand mixer or into the bowl of a food processor fitted with the steel blade. Sift together the flour, baking powder, salt, and ground pepper and add to the oats. Add the remaining ingredients except 2 tablespoons of the olive oil and mix at medium speed or pulse together until well blended. Scrape down the sides of the bowl and the beater and mix again for about 30 seconds.
- Add 2 tablespoons of the oil to a 9-inch cast iron skillet and place in the oven for 5 minutes.

Remove from the oven and spread the batter in the pan.
- Place in the oven and bake 30 minutes, until the top is nicely browned and a tester comes out clean when inserted in the middle. Remove from the heat and serve hot, or allow to cool on a rack.

Nutrition Information

- 140: calories;
- 0 grams: trans fat;
- 5 grams: monounsaturated fat;
- 1 gram: sugars;
- 14 grams: carbohydrates;
- 4 grams: protein;
- 130 milligrams: sodium;
- 8 grams: fat;
- 2 grams: dietary fiber;

---

262.   Savory Whole Wheat Buttermilk Scones With Rosemary And Thyme

Serving: 12 small scones | Prep: | Cook: | Ready in: 30mins

Ingredients

- 150 grams (approximately 1 1/4 cups) whole-wheat flour
- 100 grams (approximately 3/4 cup) unbleached all-purpose flour
- 10 grams (2 teaspoons) baking powder
- 5 grams (1/2 teaspoon) baking soda
- 4 grams (approximately 1 teaspoon) brown sugar
- 5 grams (approximately 3/4 teaspoon) salt
- 70 grams (2 1/2 ounces / 5 tablespoons) unsalted butter
- 1 tablespoon finely chopped mixed fresh rosemary and thyme
- 125 grams (approximately 1/2 cup) buttermilk

Direction

- Preheat oven to 400 degrees. Line a baking sheet with parchment.
- Sift together flours, baking powder, baking soda, sugar and salt. Rub in butter, or place in a stand mixer fitted with the paddle and beat at low speed until incorporated. Add chopped rosemary and thyme and buttermilk and mix just until the dough comes together.
- Transfer to a lightly floured work surface and gently shape into a 1/2-inch thick rectangle. Either cut 2-inch circles with a biscuit cutter or cut into 6 squares, then cut each square in half on the diagonal. Transfer to baking sheet. Bake 15 minutes, until browned on the bottom. Flip over, bake 2 more minutes, and remove from the heat. Serve warm or allow to cool.

Nutrition Information

- 121: calories;
- 0 grams: polyunsaturated fat;
- 1 gram: sugars;
- 17 grams: carbohydrates;
- 2 grams: dietary fiber;
- 201 milligrams: sodium;
- 5 grams: fat;
- 3 grams: protein;

---

263.   Scallion And Celery Quiche

Serving: Serves 6 generously | Prep: | Cook: | Ready in: 45mins

Ingredients

- Salt to taste
- 1 to 2 tablespoons extra-virgin olive oil, to taste
- 2 bunches good-size scallions (the kind you get in the farmers market) or 3 bunches thin scallions (the kind you get in the supermarket) (about 10 ounces), trimmed, quartered lengthwise and sliced thin
- 1 cup finely diced celery
- Salt to taste
- 1 to 2 garlic cloves, to taste, minced
- Freshly ground pepper
- 1 teaspoon fresh thyme leaves
- 2 tablespoons minced flat-leaf parsley
- 2 egg yolks
- 2 whole eggs
- 1 (9-inch) whole wheat pâte brisée pie crust, fully baked and cooled
- Freshly ground pepper
- ⅔ cup milk
- 2 ounces Gruyère, grated (1/2 cup)
- 1 ounce Parmesan, grated (1/4 cup)

Direction

- Preheat oven to 350 degrees.
- Heat oil in a medium skillet over medium heat and add scallions and celery. Cook, stirring, until celery is just tender, about 5 minutes. Add a generous pinch of salt, the garlic and thyme, and cook, stirring, until fragrant, about 30 seconds. Stir in the parsley. Season to taste with salt and pepper. Remove from heat.
- Beat together egg yolks and eggs in a medium bowl. Set tart pan on a baking sheet to allow for easy handling. Using a pastry brush, lightly brush bottom of the crust with some of the beaten egg and place in oven for 5 minutes.
- Add salt (I use 1/2 teaspoon), pepper, and milk to remaining eggs and whisk together.
- Spread scallion and celery mixture in an even layer in the crust. Stir together cheeses and sprinkle evenly on top. Very slowly pour the egg custard over the filling. If your tart pan has low edges, you may not need all of it to fill the shell, and you want to avoid the custard spilling over. Place quiche, on baking sheet, in the oven and bake for 30 to 35 minutes, until set and just beginning to color on the top. Remove from oven and allow to sit for at least 10 minutes before serving. Serve hot, warm or at room temperature.

Nutrition Information

- 334: calories;
- 26 grams: carbohydrates;
- 10 grams: protein;
- 8 grams: saturated fat;
- 2 grams: dietary fiber;
- 0 grams: trans fat;
- 9 grams: monounsaturated fat;
- 3 grams: sugars;
- 374 milligrams: sodium;
- 21 grams: fat;

264.   Seared Brussels Sprouts

Serving: Serves four to six | Prep: | Cook: | Ready in: 15mins

Ingredients

- 1 pound brussels sprouts
- 3 to 4 tablespoons olive oil
- Salt and freshly ground pepper

Direction

- Trim the ends off the brussels sprouts, and cut in half lengthwise through the stem end.
- Heat the oil in a large, heavy skillet, preferably cast iron, over medium-high heat. When the skillet is just short of smoking, place the brussels sprouts cut side down in the oil. Turn the heat to medium, and sear on one side until nicely browned, about three minutes. Turn the brussels sprouts over and cook on the other side until nicely browned and tender, three to five minutes. Some of the leaves can be charred dark brown or black. Remove from the heat, season with salt and pepper and serve.

Nutrition Information

- 103: calories;
- 8 grams: fat;
- 1 gram: polyunsaturated fat;
- 6 grams: monounsaturated fat;
- 7 grams: carbohydrates;
- 3 grams: protein;
- 2 grams: sugars;
- 195 milligrams: sodium;

265.   Seared Red Cabbage Wedges

Serving: Serves six to eight | Prep: | Cook: | Ready in: 15mins

Ingredients

- 1 small head of red cabbage, cut in 8 wedges, core intact so that the wedges stay together
- 3 tablespoons extra virgin olive oil (more as needed)
- Salt
- freshly ground pepper

Direction

- Heat the oil over medium-high heat in a heavy cast iron or nonstick frying pan. When it is very hot, place as many cabbage wedges as will fit in one layer in the pan. Cook for three to five minutes until golden brown on one side. Using tongs or a spatula, turn over and cook on the other side until tender, nicely browned and crispy on the edges, about five minutes. Season generously with salt and pepper, and serve hot.

Nutrition Information

- 67: calories;
- 1 gram: protein;
- 4 grams: monounsaturated fat;
- 2 grams: dietary fiber;
- 3 grams: sugars;

- 177 milligrams: sodium;
- 5 grams: carbohydrates;

---

266. Shell Beans And Potato Ragout With Swiss Chard

Serving: Serves six | Prep: | Cook: | Ready in: 1hours

Ingredients

- 1 ½ pounds Swiss chard or red chard (1 large bunch or 2 medium bunches)
- Salt to taste
- 2 tablespoons extra virgin olive oil
- ½ medium onion, sliced in half moons across the grain
- 2 large garlic cloves, minced
- 1 pound shell beans, such as cannelini, borlotti, or purple runners, shelled (about 1 3/4 cups shelled)
- 1 pound potatoes, preferably fingerlings or Yukon golds, cut in 1-inch pieces
- 3 ½ to 4 cups water
- A bouquet garni made with a sprig each thyme and parsley (or basil), a bay leaf and a Parmesan rind
- Freshly ground pepper to taste
- 2 tablespoons chopped flat-leaf parsley
- 1 to 2 teaspoons fresh marjoram leaves (optional)
- Freshly grated Parmesan for serving

Direction

- Bring a large pot of water to a boil. Fill a bowl with ice water. Stem the chard, setting aside the stems, and wash the leaves thoroughly in two changes of water. Wash the stems, trim away the ends and dice. Set aside. When the pot of water comes to a boil, salt generously and add the chard leaves. Blanch for one to two minutes, until tender but still bright, and transfer to the bowl of ice water. Drain, squeeze out excess water and chop coarsely. Set aside.

- Heat the olive oil in a large, heavy casserole or Dutch oven over medium heat. Add the onion. Cook, stirring, until it begins to soften, about two minutes, and add the diced chard stems. Cook, stirring often, for about two minutes, until the stems begin to soften, and add the garlic. Stir together for a minute, and add the beans, potatoes, water (just enough to cover everything) and bouquet garni. Bring to a simmer. Add salt to taste. Cover and simmer 40 to 45 minutes, until the beans are tender. Add the blanched chard, and simmer for another two to three minutes. Add pepper, and then taste and adjust salt. Remove the bouquet garni. Stir in the parsley and marjoram, and serve, passing Parmesan at the table for sprinkling.

Nutrition Information

- 184: calories;
- 1001 milligrams: sodium;
- 5 grams: fat;
- 1 gram: polyunsaturated fat;
- 29 grams: carbohydrates;
- 7 grams: dietary fiber;
- 3 grams: monounsaturated fat;
- 2 grams: sugars;
- 8 grams: protein;

---

267. Shredded Beet And Radish Slaw With Rice Noodles

Serving: Serves 4 to 6 | Prep: | Cook: | Ready in: 30mins

Ingredients

- 2 ounces rice vermicelli (thin rice sticks) or thin rice noodles for stir-fries
- ¼ cup rice vinegar
- 2 teaspoons soy sauce
- 1 large red beet (7 to 8 ounces), peeled and grated
- 1 bunch radishes (5 to ounces), grated

- ½ cup chopped cilantro, plus sprigs for garnish
- 3 tablespoons slivered mint leaves
- 2 tablespoons slivered Thai basil leaves (may substitute regular basil if you can't get the Thai variety)
- 1 to 2 tablespoons minced pickled ginger (to taste)
- 2 teaspoons finely grated or chopped orange zest
- Salt to taste
- Romaine lettuce leaves for serving

Direction

- Place the rice noodles in a large bowl and cover with hot water. Soak for 20 minutes, or until pliable. Meanwhile, bring a large pot of water to a boil. Drain the noodles and add to the boiling water. Boil 1 minute and drain. Rinse with cold water and transfer to a bowl. Using kitchen scissors, cut the noodles into 2-inch lengths. Toss with 2 teaspoons of the rice vinegar and the soy sauce.
- Place the grated beets, radishes and chopped herbs in a large bowl and toss with the remaining rice vinegar and salt to taste. Add the noodles, pickled ginger and orange zest and toss together. Taste and add salt if desired.
- To serve, line plates or a platter with lettuce leaves and top the lettuce with the salad. Garnish with cilantro sprigs and serve.

Nutrition Information

- 54: calories;
- 0 grams: polyunsaturated fat;
- 11 grams: carbohydrates;
- 1 gram: protein;
- 2 grams: sugars;
- 192 milligrams: sodium;

268. Sicilian Cauliflower And Black Olive Gratin

Serving: Serves 6 | Prep: | Cook: | Ready in: 45mins

Ingredients

- 1 generous head green or white cauliflower (2 to 2 1/2 pounds)
- Salt
- 1 small onion, finely chopped
- 3 tablespoons extra virgin olive oil
- 2 garlic cloves, minced
- 16 imported oil-cured black olives, pitted and cut in half
- 2 tablespoons minced fresh parsley
- Freshly ground pepper
- ½ cup freshly grated Pecorino or Parmesan, or a combination

Direction

- Break up the cauliflower into small florets while you bring a large pot of water to a boil. Salt the water generously and drop in the cauliflower. Boil 5 minutes while you fill a bowl with ice and water. Transfer the cauliflower to the ice water, let sit for a couple of minutes, then drain and place on paper towels.
- Preheat the oven to 375 degrees. Oil a 2-quart baking dish or gratin dish. Heat 1 tablespoon of the olive oil over medium heat in a large, heavy skillet and add the onion. Cook, stirring, until tender, about 3 minutes, and add a pinch of salt and the garlic. Cook, stirring, for about 30 seconds, until fragrant and translucent. Remove from the heat and stir in the olives.
- Place the cauliflower in the baking dish and add the onion and olive mixture, the remaining olive oil, the parsley and half the cheese. Season to taste with salt and pepper and stir together well. Spread out in the dish and sprinkle the remaining cheese on top.

- Bake in the preheated oven for 25 to 30 minutes, until the cheese is nicely browned. Serve hot or warm.

Nutrition Information

- 163: calories;
- 491 milligrams: sodium;
- 11 grams: carbohydrates;
- 3 grams: saturated fat;
- 7 grams: protein;
- 1 gram: polyunsaturated fat;
- 4 grams: sugars;

---

269.   Simple Pencil Cob Breakfast Grits

Serving: Serves 4 | Prep: | Cook: | Ready in: 35mins

Ingredients

- 1 cup Anson Mills Colonial Coarse Pencil Cob Grits
- About 4 cups spring or filtered water
- Fine sea salt, to taste (1/2 to 1 teaspoon)
- 2 tablespoons unsalted butter
- ½ teaspoon freshly ground black pepper (or to taste)

Direction

- The night before you wish to serve, place grits in a heavy, medium saucepan (Ms. Rentschler recommends a type called a Windsor saucepan; I used a Le Creuset). Add 2 cups spring or filtered water and stir once. Allow grits to settle a full minute, then tilt the pan and, using a fine tea strainer or fine skimmer, skim off and discard chaff and hulls. Cover and allow the grits to soak overnight at room temperature.
- Heat 2 cups water in a small saucepan to a bare simmer and keep hot. Set saucepan with grits over medium heat. Bring mixture to a simmer, stirring constantly with a wooden spoon, until the first starch takes hold (see above – it means that the mixture will begin to thicken and you will no longer have to stir constantly). Reduce heat to lowest possible setting. The grits should not be bubbling, they should be sighing, or breathing like somebody in a deep, comfortable sleep, rising up lazily in one big bubble, then falling as the bubble bursts. Watch carefully and each time they are thick enough to hold a spoon upright, stir in about 1/4 cup of the hot water. Stir in the salt after the first 10 minutes of gentle cooking. It should take about 25 minutes for the grits to be tender and creamy and by this time you should have added 3/4 to 1 cup water (perhaps a little more) in 3 or 4 additions.
- When the grits are done – tender, creamy but not mushy, and able to hold their shape on a spoon – stir in the butter vigorously, add pepper, taste (carefully – don't burn your tongue after all that care) and adjust salt. Serve immediately.

Nutrition Information

- 196: calories;
- 4 grams: saturated fat;
- 31 grams: carbohydrates;
- 6 grams: fat;
- 0 grams: sugars;
- 2 grams: dietary fiber;
- 1 gram: polyunsaturated fat;
- 3 grams: protein;
- 442 milligrams: sodium;

---

270.   Simple Trahana Soup With Lemon And Olive Oil

Serving: Serves 6 | Prep: | Cook: | Ready in: 25mins

Ingredients

- 3 tablespoons extra virgin olive oil

- 1 1/2 cups sour bulgur trahana
- 8 cups water, vegetable stock, or chicken stock
- Salt and freshly ground pepper
- 3 tablespoons lemon juice, strained
- 6 tablespoons crumbled feta
- Plain Greek yogurt for garnish (optional)
- Chopped fresh herbs for garnish

Direction

- In a medium soup pot heat 2 tablespoons of olive oil over medium heat and add trahana. Stir until coated with oil, about 1 minute. Add water or stock and bring to a boil. Add salt and pepper to taste, reduce the heat and simmer, stirring often, until trahana is tender and nutty tasting and the broth slightly thickened, 15 to 20 minutes if using home-made bulgur trahana (if you use semolina or flour trahana the time will only be 8 to 12 minutes and the mixture will be more like a porridge).
- Remove from heat and stir in lemon juice. Spoon into bowls and top with a drizzle of olive oil and a tablespoon of crumbled feta. Garnish with plain yogurt if desired and chopped fresh herbs such as mint, parsley or dill.

Nutrition Information

- 224: calories;
- 1 gram: sugars;
- 28 grams: carbohydrates;
- 7 grams: protein;
- 11 grams: fat;
- 3 grams: saturated fat;
- 6 grams: monounsaturated fat;
- 5 grams: dietary fiber;
- 887 milligrams: sodium;

271. Skordalia

Serving: Makes about 1 1/2 cups | Prep: | Cook: | Ready in: 15mins

Ingredients

- ½ pound russet or Yukon gold potatoes, peeled
- Salt, preferably kosher salt
- 3 to 4 garlic cloves (to taste), halved, green shoots removed
- 1 cup walnuts
- ½ cup olive oil
- 3 tablespoons fresh lemon juice or 1/4 cup red wine vinegar (to taste)

Direction

- Place the potatoes in a saucepan and cover with water. Add 1/2 teaspoon salt and bring slowly to a boil over medium heat. Cover partially, reduce the heat and simmer until the potatoes are tender all the way through when pierced with a skewer. Drain, return the potatoes to the pot, and cover tightly. Set aside for 5 minutes. Mash the potatoes through a potato ricer, a food mill, or in a standing mixer fitted with the paddle attachment. Do not use a food processor.
- Place the garlic in a mortar and pestle with 1/4 teaspoon salt and mash to a paste. Add the nuts and pound together (you can also do this in a food processor, but do not add the potatoes to the food processor). Stir the ground nuts and garlic into the potatoes. Gradually add the olive oil, stirring all the while with a fork or a pestle. Add the lemon juice or vinegar, and salt to taste. The mixture should be like loose mashed potatoes. Taste and adjust lemon juice, vinegar, and salt. Transfer to a bowl and chill until ready to serve. If the mixture stiffens up, thin out with a little olive oil or water.

Nutrition Information

- 223: calories;
- 4 grams: polyunsaturated fat;
- 1 gram: dietary fiber;
- 0 grams: sugars;
- 162 milligrams: sodium;
- 3 grams: saturated fat;
- 8 grams: carbohydrates;
- 2 grams: protein;
- 21 grams: fat;
- 14 grams: monounsaturated fat;

272.   Small Apricot Galettes

Serving: 8 individual galettes | Prep: | Cook: | Ready in: 1hours30mins

Ingredients

- 5 grams (1 1/2 teaspoons) active dry yeast
- 115 grams (1/2 cup) lukewarm water
- 2 tablespoons plus 1/4 teaspoon sugar
- 1 large egg, at room temperature, beaten
- 135 grams (1 cup) whole-wheat flour
- 155 grams (1 1/4 cups) unbleached flour
- 25 grams (1/4 cup) almond powder (also known as almond flour; optional; substitute whole-wheat flour if not using)
- ½ teaspoon salt
- 60 grams (4 tablespoons) unsalted butter at room temperature
- For the galettes
- 1 ½ pounds apricots, pitted and halved or quartered, depending on the size
- 3 tablespoons lightly toasted slivered almonds
- 1 teaspoon vanilla extract
- ¼ teaspoon freshly grated nutmeg
- 1 teaspoon cinnamon
- 3 tablespoons turbinado or brown sugar
- 25 grams (1/4 cup) almond powder

Direction

-
-

Nutrition Information

- 305: calories;
- 0 grams: trans fat;
- 15 grams: sugars;
- 8 grams: protein;
- 159 milligrams: sodium;
- 11 grams: fat;
- 4 grams: monounsaturated fat;
- 1 gram: polyunsaturated fat;
- 47 grams: carbohydrates;
- 5 grams: dietary fiber;

273.   Smoked Sardines Rillettes

Serving: About 1 cup, serving 6 | Prep: | Cook: | Ready in: 20mins

Ingredients

- 6 ounces (usually 2 cans) smoked sardines in olive oil, drained and filleted
- 2 tablespoons extra virgin olive oil
- 4 tablespoons plain Greek yogurt
- 1 tablespoon crème fraîche (optional; can substitute yogurt or olive oil)
- 1 to 2 tablespoons fresh lemon juice (to taste)
- 1 to 2 tablespoons minced chives (to taste)
- Freshly ground pepper

Direction

- In a medium bowl, break up sardines and mash with fork. Work in olive oil, yogurt and crème fraîche. Work in lemon juice and stir in minced chives and pepper. Refrigerate for 1 hour or longer. Allow to soften for 30 minutes before serving.

Nutrition Information

- 115: calories;
- 8 grams: protein;
- 94 milligrams: sodium;
- 9 grams: fat;

- 2 grams: polyunsaturated fat;
- 5 grams: monounsaturated fat;
- 1 gram: sugars;
- 0 grams: dietary fiber;

---

274. Soba Noodles With Shiitakes, Broccoli And Tofu

Serving: Serves 4 to 6 | Prep: | Cook: | Ready in: 20mins

Ingredients

- ½ cup chicken or vegetable stock
- 1 tablespoon rice wine or dry sherry
- 1 tablespoon soy sauce (more to taste)
- ½ teaspoon sugar
- Salt to taste
- 1 tablespoon minced garlic
- 1 tablespoon minced ginger
- ¼ to ½ teaspoon red pepper flakes, or 1 to 2 serrano or Thai chiles, minced
- 8 ounces soba noodles
- 2 teaspoons sesame oil
- ½ pound baby broccoli
- 2 tablespoons grapeseed oil, peanut oil, sunflower oil or canola oil
- ½ pound tofu, cut in dominoes or small dice
- 6 ounces fresh shiitake mushrooms, stemmed (discard stems or use for stock), caps sliced
- 1 bunch scallions, thinly sliced, dark green parts separated
- ½ cup coarsely chopped cilantro

Direction

- Combine stock, soy sauce, rice wine or sherry, sugar and salt to taste in a small bowl. Stir until sugar and salt dissolve. Combine garlic, ginger, and pepper flakes or minced chile in another bowl.
- Bring a large saucepan or pot of water to a boil, add salt to taste and baby broccoli. As soon as water comes back to a boil (about 1 minute), use a skimmer to remove broccoli and transfer it to a bowl of cold water. Drain

in a colander, then on paper towels. Cut stems away from florets and slice about 1/2 inch thick. Bring water back to a boil and cook soba. Drain and toss with 2 teaspoons sesame oil.
- Place all ingredients within reach of your wok. Heat a 14-inch flat-bottomed wok over high heat until a drop of water evaporates within a second or two when added. Swirl in 1 tablespoon of the oil and add tofu. Stir-fry 1 to 2 minutes, until it begins to color, and remove to a plate. Add remaining oil and garlic, ginger and chile. Stir-fry for no more than 10 seconds and add mushrooms. Stir-fry for 1 minute and add broccoli and the light parts of the scallions. Stir-fry 1 to 2 minutes. Add the noodles, tofu and the stock mixture. Reduce heat to medium and stir-fry 1 to 2 minutes. Add cilantro and the dark green part of the scallions, stir-fry another 30 seconds to a minute, until well combined, and serve.

Nutrition Information

- 252: calories;
- 8 grams: fat;
- 2 grams: monounsaturated fat;
- 3 grams: sugars;
- 11 grams: protein;
- 1 gram: saturated fat;
- 5 grams: polyunsaturated fat;
- 37 grams: carbohydrates;
- 498 milligrams: sodium;

---

275. Soba And Herb Salad With Roasted Eggplant And Pluots

Serving: Serves 6 | Prep: | Cook: | Ready in: 45mins

Ingredients

- 2 long eggplants, about 1 pound, cut in 3/4-inch dice

- Salt to taste
- ⅓ cup sunflower oil
- 9 ounces (1 package) soba noodles
- 1 tablespoon dark sesame oil
- 6 ounces firm tofu, cut in 1/2-inch dice and blotted dry
- 1 tablespoon soy sauce
- 1 to 2 serrano or Thai chiles, minced (to taste)
- 2 firm but ripe plums or pluots, cut in thin slices
- 1 cup basil leaves (preferably Thai basil), chopped, torn or cut in slivers
- 1 cup chopped cilantro
- 2 to 4 tablespoons chopped chives
- ⅓ cup seasoned rice vinegar
- Juice and grated zest of 1 lime
- 1 large garlic clove, minced or pureed

Direction

- Preheat the oven to 450 degrees. Cover a sheet pan with foil. Place the eggplant in a large bowl and season with salt to taste. Add 2 tablespoons of the oil and toss well. Spread on the baking sheet in an even layer. Place in the oven and roast for 20 minutes, or until the eggplant is soft when you pierce it with a fork and beginning to brown on the edges. It will look dry on the outside surfaces. Remove from the oven and very carefully fold over the foil and crimp the edges so that the eggplant is now contained within a foil envelope, where it will steam and become softer. Set aside until the eggplant cools.
- Meanwhile, cook the soba noodles. When they're done, drain, rinse with cold water, shake well in the colander and transfer to a bowl. Add the sesame oil and stir together.
- Heat a wok or a large heavy frying pan over high heat until a drop of water evaporates within a few seconds when added to the pan. Add 1 tablespoon of the sunflower oil and the tofu. Let sit in the pan to sear for 30 seconds, then stir-fry until lightly browned. Add 1 teaspoon of the soy sauce, toss together, then remove from the heat and add to the noodles. Add the roasted eggplant and the minced

chiles, the plums or pluots and all of the chopped herbs if serving right away, half of them if serving later.
- In a small bowl or measuring cup mix together the seasoned wine vinegar, the remaining soy sauce, salt to taste, the lime juice and zest, and the garlic. Whisk in the remaining oil. Taste and adjust seasoning. Toss with the noodle salad and serve.

Nutrition Information

- 382: calories;
- 2 grams: saturated fat;
- 7 grams: dietary fiber;
- 49 grams: carbohydrates;
- 10 grams: sugars;
- 13 grams: protein;
- 784 milligrams: sodium;
- 18 grams: fat;

---

276. Soda Bread With Walnuts And Raisins

Serving: 1 large loaf (about 16 slices) | Prep: | Cook: | Ready in: 1hours

Ingredients

- 375 grams (3 cups) whole wheat flour
- 125 grams (1 cup) unbleached all-purpose flour
- 10 grams (2 teaspoons) baking soda
- 10 grams (1 1/4 teaspoons) fine sea salt
- 60 grams (heaped 1/2 cup) chopped walnuts
- 110 grams (1 cup) golden raisins or regular raisins
- 475 grams (2 cups) buttermilk

Direction

- Preheat the oven to 400 degrees. Line a baking sheet with parchment. Sift together the flours, baking soda and salt and place in a wide bowl

- Make a well in the middle of the flour, add the walnuts and raisins and pour in the buttermilk. Using a wide rubber spatula, a wide wooden spoon or your hands mix in the flour from the sides of the bowl to the center, turning the bowl and sweeping the flour from the sides into the buttermilk. Mix until the buttermilk, raisins and walnuts have been incorporated into the flour, then scrape out onto a lightly floured work surface. The dough should be soft and a bit sticky. Flour your hands so it won't stick to them.
- Gently and quickly knead the dough, only enough to shape it into a ball, then with floured hands gently pat it down to a 2-inch high round. Place it on the parchment-lined baking sheet and cut a 1/2-inch deep cross across the top. You shouldn't let too much time lapse between the time you add the buttermilk to the flour and the moment you put the loaf into the oven.
- Bake 40 to 45 minutes, until the loaf responds with a hollow sound when tapped on the bottom. Remove from the oven, wrap loosely in a cloth or kitchen towel, and cool on a rack.

Nutrition Information

- 165: calories;
- 6 grams: protein;
- 229 milligrams: sodium;
- 3 grams: dietary fiber;
- 1 gram: saturated fat;
- 0 grams: monounsaturated fat;
- 2 grams: polyunsaturated fat;
- 30 grams: carbohydrates;

277. Soft Tacos With Chicken And Tomato Corn Salsa

Serving: Serves four | Prep: | Cook: | Ready in: 15mins

Ingredients

- ½ small red or white onion, finely chopped
- 1 ear of corn, steamed for five minutes
- 1 pound ripe tomatoes, finely chopped
- 1 to 3 jalapeño or serrano peppers (to taste), seeded if desired and minced
- ½ cup chopped fresh cilantro
- 2 tablespoons fresh lime juice
- Salt to taste
- 1 boneless, skinless chicken breast, poached and shredded (about 2 cups)
- 8 corn tortillas
- ½ cup crumbled queso fresco or feta cheese

Direction

- Place the chopped onion in a small bowl, and cover with cold water. Let sit for five minutes, then drain and rinse with cold water. Drain on paper towels. Cut the kernels off the steamed ear of corn.
- Toss together the tomatoes, minced chiles, cilantro, onion and steamed corn. Season to taste with salt, and add up to 1 tablespoon fresh lime juice. Place the shredded chicken in a bowl, and season with 1 tablespoon lime juice and salt to taste.
- Heat the tortillas. Wrap in aluminum foil, and heat through in a 350-degree oven for 10 to 15 minutes; or heat through one at a time in a dry skillet over medium-high heat until flexible. Place one or two on each plate, top with shredded chicken and a generous spoonful of the salsa, and sprinkle some cheese on top. Serve, passing additional salsa if there is any at the table.

Nutrition Information

- 346: calories;
- 36 grams: carbohydrates;
- 812 milligrams: sodium;
- 0 grams: trans fat;
- 8 grams: fat;
- 3 grams: saturated fat;
- 2 grams: polyunsaturated fat;
- 6 grams: sugars;

- 33 grams: protein;

278. Soft Tacos With Scrambled Tofu And Tomatoes

Serving: Serves four | Prep: | Cook: |Ready in: 25mins

Ingredients

- 1 14-ounce can tomatoes, drained
- 2 large garlic cloves, coarsely chopped
- 1 serrano or jalapeño chile, seeded if desired and chopped (more if you like things really hot)
- 1 tablespoon canola oil
- 1 small or 1/2 medium onion, chopped
- 1 teaspoon lightly toasted cumin seeds, ground
- Salt to taste
- 1 12-ounce box medium or firm silken tofu, drained
- Soy sauce to taste
- ¼ cup chopped cilantro
- 8 corn tortillas
- Salsa

Direction

- Combine the tomatoes, garlic and chile in a blender, and blend until smooth.
- Heat the oil in a large nonstick skillet over medium heat, and add the onion. Cook, stirring, until tender, about five minutes. Increase the heat to medium-high, and add the cumin. Stir together, and when the pan is quite hot, pour in the blended tomato mixture. It should sizzle. Cook, stirring, about five minutes, until the sauce is thick, dark and fragrant, and your spoon leaves a canal when you run it down the center of the pan. Add salt to taste.
- Add the tofu to the pan, and mash it into the sauce using the back of your spoon. Add the soy sauce, and continue to cook for another five minutes, stirring and mashing the tofu.

Stir in the cilantro. Taste and adjust seasonings.
- Heat the tortillas and place two on each plate. Top with the tofu mixture and serve, passing salsa on the side.

279. Soufflé Omelet With Apricot Sauce

Serving: Yield: 4 servings. | Prep: | Cook: |Ready in: 25mins

Ingredients

- For the apricot sauce
- ¼ cup sugar
- 1 cup fresh orange juice
- 1 vanilla bean, split and scraped, or 1 teaspoon vanilla extract
- 6 ripe apricots, pitted and quartered
- For the omelet
- 3 eggs, separated
- Small pinch of cream of tartar
- 2 tablespoons sugar
- 1 tablespoon Cointreau
- Small pinch salt
- Small pinch freshly grated nutmeg
- 1 tablespoon unsalted butter
- 3 tablespoons lightly toasted slivered almonds
- Powdered sugar for dusting (optional)

Direction

- For the sauce, in a medium saucepan combine the sugar, orange juice and vanilla bean seeds or vanilla extract and bring to a boil. Reduce by a third. Add the apricots, turn the heat down to medium and simmer 5 to 10 minutes, until the apricots are soft. Remove from the heat and divide among 4 plates or pour the sauce onto a platter and arrange the apricots on the edge.
- Preheat the oven to 425 degrees. Have the platter for your omelet close at hand.

- Whisk the egg whites in a clean dry bowl or in the bowl of a standing mixer fitted with the whisk attachment. When they begin to foam, add the cream of tartar and continue to whisk at medium speed until they form medium peaks. Continue whisking on medium speed while you slowly add the sugar, until the egg whites form stiff, satiny but not dry peaks.
- In another large bowl, beat the egg yolks and add the Cointreau, salt and nutmeg. Stir 1/4 of the egg whites into this mixture, then gently fold in the rest.
- Heat a 10-inch skillet that can go into the oven over medium-high heat. Add the butter to the hot pan, and when the foam subsides and the butter is just beginning to color, gently scrape in the egg mixture, using a rubber spatula. Do not stir. Immediately transfer to the oven for 2 1/2 to 3 minutes, until puffed. Remove from the heat, sprinkle half the toasted almonds over the omelet and slide or turn out onto the platter, folding the puffed omelet in half as you do. Sprinkle with the remaining toasted almonds and dust with powdered sugar if you wish. Spoon onto the plates with the apricot sauce and serve. Note: You can also serve the apricot sauce separately and spoon it over the soufflé.

Nutrition Information

- 238: calories;
- 3 grams: saturated fat;
- 29 grams: sugars;
- 1 gram: polyunsaturated fat;
- 33 grams: carbohydrates;
- 2 grams: dietary fiber;
- 6 grams: protein;
- 9 grams: fat;
- 0 grams: trans fat;
- 4 grams: monounsaturated fat;
- 102 milligrams: sodium;

---

280.   Soy Ginger Chicken With Greens

Serving: 4 servings | Prep: | Cook: |Ready in: 45mins

Ingredients

- 1 tablespoon soy sauce
- ½ teaspoon sugar
- 2 tablespoons fresh lime juice
- 1 tablespoon seasoned rice vinegar
- Salt to taste
- 1 garlic clove, minced or puréed
- 2 teaspoons minced fresh ginger
- ¼ cup plus 2 tablespoons grapeseed oil or sunflower oil
- 1 tablespoon dark sesame oil
- 1 to 2 serrano or Thai green chiles, minced (to taste), or 1/8 to 1/4 teaspoon cayenne
- 2 boneless skinless chicken breasts (most weigh 8 to 10 ounces)
- Salt and freshly ground pepper
- 2 tablespoons all-purpose flour or a gluten-free flour such as rice flour or corn flour
- 2 tablespoons chopped cilantro
- 4 cups wild arugula or salad mix, rinsed and spun dry

Direction

- In a small bowl or measuring cup, whisk together the soy sauce, sugar, 1 tablespoon of the lime juice, the vinegar, salt, garlic, ginger, 1/4 cup of the grapeseed or sunflower oil and the sesame oil. Pour half of this mixture into a bowl large enough to accommodate the chicken breasts and add the remaining tablespoon of lime juice and the chiles or cayenne to the bowl. Cut each chicken breast into 2 equal pieces (3 if 12 ounces or more) and place in the bowl. Stir together and refrigerate for 15 to 30 minutes.
- Remove chicken from marinade and pat dry with paper towels (discard marinade). Place two sheets of plastic wrap (1 large sheet if you have extra-wide wrap) on your work surface, overlapping slightly, to make 1 wide sheet,

and brush lightly with olive oil. Place a piece of chicken in the middle of plastic sheet and brush lightly with oil. Cover the chicken with another wide layer of plastic wrap. Working from the center to the outside, pound chicken breast with the flat side of a meat tenderizer until about 1/4 inch thick. (Don't pound too hard or you'll tear the meat. If that happens it won't be the end of the world, you'll just have a few pieces to cook.) Repeat with the remaining chicken breast pieces.

- Season the pounded chicken breasts with salt and pepper on one side only. Dredge lightly in the flour (you will not use all of it) and tap breasts to remove excess.
- Turn oven on low. . Heat a wide, heavy skillet over high heat and add remaining 2 tablespoons grapeseed or sunflower oil. When oil is hot, place one or two pieces of chicken in the pan – however many will fit without crowding. Cook for 1 1/2 minutes, until bottom is browned is spots. Turn over and brown on the other side, about 1 1/2 minutes. (Do not overcook or chicken will be dry.) Transfer to a platter or sheet pan and sprinkle cilantro over the top. Keep warm in the oven.
- Place arugula or salad mix in a bowl and toss with the remaining dressing. Distribute among plates or arrange on a platter and serve with the chicken.

Nutrition Information

- 414: calories;
- 1 gram: dietary fiber;
- 2 grams: sugars;
- 32 grams: protein;
- 3 grams: saturated fat;
- 6 grams: monounsaturated fat;
- 9 grams: carbohydrates;
- 515 milligrams: sodium;
- 28 grams: fat;
- 0 grams: trans fat;
- 16 grams: polyunsaturated fat;

| 281. | Spaghetti Squash With Garlic, Parsley And Breadcrumbs |

Serving: Serves 4 | Prep: | Cook: | Ready in: 1hours30mins

Ingredients

- 1 spaghetti squash, about 3 pounds
- 2 tablespoons extra virgin olive oil
- 3 to 4 large garlic cloves, green shoots removed, minced
- 2 tablespoons breadcrumbs
- 2 tablespoons finely chopped flat-leaf parsley
- Salt
- freshly ground pepper to taste
- Freshly grated Parmesan

Direction

- Preheat the oven to 375 degrees. Pierce the squash in several places with a sharp knife. Cover a baking sheet with foil, and place the squash on top. Bake for one hour, until the squash is soft and easy to cut with a knife. Remove from the heat, and allow to cool until you can handle it. Cut in half lengthwise, and allow to cool some more. Remove the seeds and discard. Scoop out the flesh from half of the squash, and place in a bowl. Run a fork through the flesh to separate the spaghettilike strands. You should have about 4 cups of squash. (Use some squash from the other half if necessary). Set aside the other half for another dish.
- Heat the oil in a large, heavy nonstick skillet over medium heat, and add the garlic and bread crumbs. When they begin to sizzle and smell fragrant and the breadcrumbs are crisp — that is, after about a minute — stir in the squash and parsley, and season to taste with salt and pepper. Toss together over medium heat until the squash is infused with the garlic and oil and heated through, 6 to 8 minutes.

Remove to a warm serving dish, top with freshly grated Parmesan and serve.

282. Spaghetti With Broccoli And Walnut/Ricotta Pesto

Serving: Serves 6 | Prep: | Cook: | Ready in: 30mins

Ingredients

- 1 garlic clove, cut in half, green shoot removed
- 2 tablespoons shelled walnuts (about 3/4 ounce)
- 1 cup basil leaves
- ¼ cup fresh ricotta
- 2 tablespoons warm water
- ¼ cup freshly grated Parmesan, plus additional for sprinkling (Pecorino can be substituted for some of the Parmesan)
- 2 tablespoons extra virgin olive oil
- 1 tablespoon walnut oil
- Salt to taste
- ½ pound broccoli crowns, broken into small florets
- 1 pound spaghetti
- About 1/4 cup pasta cooking water (more to taste)

Direction

- Turn on a food processor fitted with the steel blade and drop in the garlic. When it is chopped and adhering to the sides of the bowl, turn off and scrape down the bowl. Add the walnuts and basil and process to a paste. Add the ricotta, 2 tablespoons warm water, and Parmesan and pulse until well blended. Add the olive and walnut oils and process until smooth and homogenous. You can also make this in a mortar and pestle. Taste and add salt as desired. Transfer to a wide pasta bowl.
- Bring a large pot of water to a boil. Add the spaghetti and boil 5 minutes. Add the broccoli and continue to boil until the pasta is al dente, about 4 more minutes. Before draining the

pasta, remove 1/2 cup of the pasta cooking water. Add 1/4 cup of it to the ricotta mixture and stir until well blended. The sauce should have a creamy consistency (add more of the pasta water if necessary). Drain the spaghetti and broccoli and toss at once with the sauce. Serve, passing Parmesan or Pecorino on the side.

Nutrition Information

- 414: calories;
- 3 grams: sugars;
- 5 grams: monounsaturated fat;
- 4 grams: dietary fiber;
- 60 grams: carbohydrates;
- 14 grams: protein;
- 368 milligrams: sodium;
- 13 grams: fat;

283. Spaghetti With Cauliflower, Almonds, Tomatoes And Chickpeas

Serving: 4 servings | Prep: | Cook: | Ready in: 30mins

Ingredients

- 24 raw almonds (about 3 tablespoons), blanched, skinned* and chopped
- 1 small or 1/2 large head cauliflower, broken into florets
- 2 tablespoons extra virgin olive oil
- 2 garlic cloves, minced
- 1-14 1/2-ounce can chopped tomatoes in juice
- ¼ teaspoon sugar
- Pinch of cinnamon
- Salt to taste
- ½ to 1 teaspoon dried oregano (to taste)
- Freshly ground pepper to taste
- ½ cup cooked chickpeas (canned or freshly cooked)
- ¾ pound spaghetti

- Crumbled feta or freshly grated Parmesan for serving

Direction

- Fill a large pasta pot with water and bring to a boil. Add salt to taste and cauliflower. Boil 5 minutes, then using a Chinese skimmer, a strainer or a slotted spoon, transfer cauliflower to a bowl of cold water (do not drain the pot; you'll use the water for the pasta). Drain the cauliflower and chop medium-fine. Set aside.
- (You can do this step while you are waiting for the water to come to a boil for the cauliflower). Heat 1 tablespoon of the olive oil over medium heat in a large, heavy skillet or a wide saucepan and add garlic. Cook, stirring, until fragrant, about 30 seconds, and stir in tomatoes with liquid, sugar, cinnamon, salt and oregano. Turn up heat to medium-high and stir often as tomatoes come to a brisk boil. Turn heat down to medium and cook, stirring often, until tomatoes have cooked down and taste very fragrant, about 10 minutes. Add pepper to taste.
- Add cauliflower and almonds to the tomato sauce, along with 1/4 cup cooking water from the cauliflower, and stir together. Stir in chickpeas.
- Bring water in the pot back to a boil and add spaghetti. Cook al dente, following timing instructions on the package but checking for doneness a minute before indicated time on the package. Set aside 1/2 cup of the cooking water from the pasta, in case you want to moisten the sauce more, drain pasta and toss with the tomato and cauliflower sauce and the remaining tablespoon of olive oil. Add water from pasta only if you think the mixture seems dry. Serve, passing crumbled feta or grated Parmesan at the table for sprinkling.

Nutrition Information

- 489: calories;
- 6 grams: monounsaturated fat;
- 84 grams: carbohydrates;
- 9 grams: sugars;
- 896 milligrams: sodium;
- 10 grams: dietary fiber;
- 2 grams: polyunsaturated fat;
- 0 grams: trans fat;
- 18 grams: protein;

---

284. Spaghetti With Roasted Cauliflower, Tomato Sauce And Olives

Serving: Serves 4 | Prep: | Cook: | Ready in: 1hours10mins

Ingredients

- ½ medium head of cauliflower, broken into florets
- 2 tablespoons extra virgin olive oil
- 2 garlic cloves, minced
- ¼ to ½ teaspoon red pepper flakes, to taste
- 1 (14-ounce) can chopped tomatoes, with juice
- Pinch of sugar
- 1 teaspoon fresh thyme leaves, or 1/2 teaspoon dried thyme
- Salt
- freshly ground pepper
- 12 kalamata olives, pitted and cut in half lengthwise
- ¾ pound spaghetti
- 2 ounces either feta (crumbled), ricotta salata, Parmesan, or a mix of Parmesan and Pecorino (grated)

Direction

- Preheat oven to 400 degrees. Bring a large pot of generously salted water to a boil and add the cauliflower. Blanch for two minutes and transfer to a bowl of ice water. Drain and blot dry. Cover the pot; you'll use the water again for the pasta. Quarter the cauliflower florets, toss with 1 tablespoon of olive oil and salt generously. Transfer to a baking sheet, place in the oven and roast 30 minutes, stirring from time to time, until tender and lightly browned. Remove from the oven and set aside.

- Meanwhile, in a wide, nonstick frying pan or a 3-quart saucepan, heat the remaining oil over medium heat and add the garlic and red pepper flakes. Cook, stirring, until fragrant, about one minute. Add the tomatoes, sugar, thyme and salt, and bring to a simmer. Simmer over medium-low heat, stirring often, until thick, 15 to 20 minutes. Stir in the cauliflower and the olives, and simmer a few minutes more. Taste and adjust seasonings.
- Bring the water back to a rolling boil. Add the spaghetti and cook until the pasta is al dente, usually about 10 minutes. Drain and toss with the cauliflower-tomato mixture. Sprinkle the cheese over the top and serve at once.

Nutrition Information

- 482: calories;
- 13 grams: fat;
- 1 gram: polyunsaturated fat;
- 73 grams: carbohydrates;
- 6 grams: sugars;
- 19 grams: protein;
- 677 milligrams: sodium;
- 4 grams: saturated fat;
- 7 grams: dietary fiber;

---

285. Spiced Green Beans And Baby Broccoli Tempura

Serving: 6 to 8 servings | Prep: | Cook: |Ready in: 30mins

Ingredients

- ½ cup plus 1 tablespoon cornstarch
- 2 tablespoons fine polenta or cornmeal
- 3 tablespoons whole wheat flour
- ¼ teaspoon salt, plus more to taste
- ½ teaspoon ground cumin
- ⅔ cup cold sparkling water
- ¼ cup finely chopped cilantro
- 2 tablespoons dukkah (see recipe)
- ½ pound green beans
- ½ pound baby broccoli
- Canola oil or grapeseed oil for frying

Direction

- Make the batter: In a medium bowl, whisk together cornstarch, polenta or cornmeal, whole wheat flour, salt and cumin. Whisk in sparkling water. Stir in cilantro and dukkah.
- Top and tail beans. Cut long stems off broccoli; cut broccoli tops into smaller florets or leave intact.
- Pour oil to a depth of 3 inches into a wok or wide saucepan and heat over medium-high heat to 350 to 375 degrees. Set up a sheet pan with a rack on it next to pan and cover rack with layers of paper towels. Have a deep-fry skimmer handy for removing vegetables from the oil onto the rack.
- Using tongs, dip vegetables into the batter a few at a time, making sure to coat thoroughly. Transfer to hot oil and fry until golden brown, 1 to 2 minutes. Flip over with skimmer to make sure coating is evenly fried. Do not crowd pan. Let oil come back up to temperature between batches.
- Using skimmer, remove vegetables from oil, allowing excess oil to drip back into pan, and drain on towel-covered rack. Sprinkle with salt right away if desired. Cool slightly and serve.

Nutrition Information

- 205: calories;
- 2 grams: protein;
- 1 gram: saturated fat;
- 0 grams: trans fat;
- 9 grams: monounsaturated fat;
- 4 grams: polyunsaturated fat;
- 15 grams: fat;
- 16 grams: carbohydrates;
- 88 milligrams: sodium;

286.   Spiced Roasted Almonds

Serving: 3 cups (about 20 handfuls) | Prep: | Cook: | Ready in: 35mins

Ingredients

- 3 cups (about 400 grams) almonds
- 2 teaspoons extra virgin olive oil
- Salt to taste
- ¼ to ½ teaspoon cayenne, or to taste
- 1 to 2 teaspoons finely chopped fresh thyme or 1/2 to 1 teaspoon crumbled dried thyme (optional)

Direction

- Preheat the oven to 350 degrees. Toss the almonds with olive oil, salt and cayenne, and place on a baking sheet. Roast in the hot oven until they begin to crackle and smell toasty, 15 to 20 minutes. Be careful when you open the oven door because the capsicum in the cayenne is quite volatile, so avoid breathing in, and be careful of your eyes. Remove from the heat and allow to cool. Toss with the thyme.

Nutrition Information

- 240: calories;
- 9 grams: carbohydrates;
- 0 grams: trans fat;
- 5 grams: dietary fiber;
- 8 grams: protein;
- 95 milligrams: sodium;
- 21 grams: fat;
- 2 grams: sugars;
- 13 grams: monounsaturated fat;

287.   Spiced Tomato Ketchup

Serving: Makes 1 2/3 cups | Prep: | Cook: | Ready in: 2hours20mins

Ingredients

- 2 tablespoons extra virgin olive oil
- 1 tablespoon minced ginger
- 2 large garlic cloves, minced
- ¼ cup cider vinegar
- ¼ cup packed brown sugar
- 2 pounds tomatoes, peeled, seeded and diced or pulsed to a coarse purée in a food processor
- 1 teaspoon cumin seeds, lightly toasted and ground
- ½ teaspoon ground cinnamon
- 8 allspice berries, ground (1/2 teaspoon)
- 2 cloves, ground
- ⅛ teaspoon cayenne
- Salt and freshly ground pepper to taste
- 1 tablespoon mild honey, such as clover

Direction

- Heat olive oil over low heat in a heavy-bottom saucepan. Add ginger and garlic cloves and cook, stirring, until fragrant but not browned, about 1 minute. Add vinegar, turn up the heat and reduce volume by half, about 2 to 3 minutes. Add sugar and stir until it has dissolved in the vinegar. Add tomatoes and spices (but not salt), bring to a simmer, reduce heat to very low, cover partly and simmer slowly until mix has reduced to a thick purée and there is little liquid in the pan, about 1 hour 45 minutes. Uncover and continue to simmer until all the liquid has cooked off, about 15 minutes.
- Season to taste with salt and pepper and stir in honey. Continue to simmer, stirring, until mix is shiny, about 5 minutes. Remove from heat and allow to cool. Taste and adjust salt. Transfer to a jar and refrigerate if not using right away. Serve at room temperature as an accompaniment to fish, chicken, meat or vegetables; spread it on bread; or use as a sandwich condiment.
- Optional step: Before or after the mix cools, put through the fine blade of a food mill.

Nutrition Information

- 219: calories;
- 6 grams: monounsaturated fat;
- 763 milligrams: sodium;
- 9 grams: fat;
- 1 gram: polyunsaturated fat;
- 0 grams: trans fat;
- 35 grams: carbohydrates;
- 4 grams: dietary fiber;
- 29 grams: sugars;
- 3 grams: protein;

---

288.   Spiced Wok Popped Popcorn

Serving: About 12 cups popcorn | Prep: | Cook: | Ready in: 5mins

Ingredients

- 2 tablespoons oil – either canola, rice bran, peanut, grape seed, or olive
- 6 tablespoons popcorn
- 2 teaspoons tabil (see below; more to taste)
- Kosher salt to taste
- Tabil
- 2 large garlic cloves, chopped and left out on a piece of paper towel to dry air for 2 days, or 2 teaspoons garlic powder or granulated garlic
- 4 tablespoons coriander seeds
- 1 tablespoon caraway seeds
- 2 teaspoons cayenne

Direction

-
-

---

289.   Spiced Yellow Lentils With Quinoa

Serving: 4 to 6 servings | Prep: | Cook: | Ready in: 1hours30mins

Ingredients

- For the quinoa
- ¾ cup regular blond quinoa
- ¼ cup red quinoa
- 1 ¼ cups water
- ½ to ¾ teaspoon salt, to taste
- For the dal
- 1 cup brown or split yellow lentils (toor dal), rinsed
- 1 teaspoon minced fresh ginger
- 1 ½ teaspoons turmeric
- ½ medium onion (intact), peeled
- Salt to taste
- 1 ½ tablespoons fresh lime juice or 1/4 cup tamarind water (made from soaking 1 tablespoon tamarind paste in warm water for 10 minutes; optional)
- 2 tablespoons grape seed oil, canola oil, safflower oil or sunflower oil
- ½ cup finely minced red bell pepper
- 1 plump garlic clove, minced
- 1 teaspoon cumin seeds
- Cayenne pepper to taste
- 3 tablespoons chopped cilantro

Direction

- Rinse the quinoa thoroughly and combine with the water and salt in a large saucepan. Bring to a boil, cover and reduce the heat to low. Simmer 15 to 20 minutes, until the white quinoa displays a little white spiral. Turn off the heat, remove the lid and place a dish towel over the top of the pot. Return the lid and let sit for 15 minutes. The quinoa will now be fluffy. Keep warm.
- Meanwhile, combine the lentils, ginger, turmeric and onion half (don't chop it) with 1 quart water and salt to taste (about 1 to 1 1/2 teaspoons) and bring to a gentle boil. Stir only

once to make sure there are no lentils sticking to the bottom of the pot. Reduce the heat to medium – the lentils should simmer briskly – and cook uncovered until the lentils are tender, 30 to 40 minutes. Stir in the lime juice or tamarind concentrate and add another 1/2 cup water. Stir together and simmer for another minute. Turn off the heat and using an immersion blender, an Indian mathani (a wooden tool used for mashing dal) or a wooden Mexican hot chocolate mixer, partially pureé the dal. It should be thick but not like a pureed soup.

- Heat the oil over medium-high heat in a small saucepan or small frying pan (such as an 8-inch omelet pan). Add the cumin seeds and allow to sizzle, stirring, for 10 seconds. Add the garlic and cook until lightly colored, about 15 seconds. Add the red pepper and cook until slightly softened, about 1 minute. Remove from the heat and pour over the lentils. Add the cayenne pepper and 1 tablespoon of the cilantro and stir gently. Taste and adjust seasoning.

- Serve the quinoa with the dal spooned on top. Garnish with chopped fresh cilantro.

Nutrition Information

- 270: calories;
- 4 grams: polyunsaturated fat;
- 41 grams: carbohydrates;
- 6 grams: dietary fiber;
- 2 grams: sugars;
- 7 grams: fat;
- 1 gram: monounsaturated fat;
- 0 grams: trans fat;
- 12 grams: protein;
- 324 milligrams: sodium;

290. Spicy Carrot And Spinach Latkes

Serving: Makes 15 to 16, serving 4 | Prep: | Cook: | Ready in: 40mins

Ingredients

- 1 pound carrots, peeled and grated (3 cups, tightly packed, grated carrots)
- 6 ounces baby spinach or stemmed washed spinach, chopped (3 cups tightly packed chopped spinach)
- 1 teaspoon baking powder
- Salt to taste
- 1 tablespoon nigella seeds (more to taste)
- 2 to 3 teaspoons mild chili powder, to taste
- 3 tablespoons oat bran
- 3 tablespoon matzo meal or all-purpose flour
- 2 eggs, beaten
- About 1/4 cup canola, grape seed or rice bran oil

Direction

- Begin heating a large heavy skillet over medium-high heat. Heat the oven to 300 degrees and line a sheet pan with parchment. Place a rack over another sheet pan.
- In a large bowl mix together the carrots, spinach, baking powder, salt, nigella seeds, chili powder, oat bran and matzo meal or flour. Taste and adjust salt. Add the eggs and stir together. If the mixture seems dry add a little more egg.
- Pack about 3 tablespoons of the mixture into a 1/4 cup measuring cup. Reverse onto the parchment-lined baking sheet. Repeat with the remaining latke mix. You should have enough to make 15 or 16 latkes.
- Add the oil to the pan and when it is hot (hold your hand a few inches above – you should feel the heat), use a spatula to transfer one portion of the latke mixture to the pan. Press down with the spatula to flatten. Repeat with more mounds. In my 10-inch pan I can cook three or four at a time without crowding; my

12-inch pan will accommodate four or five. Cook on one side until golden brown, about three minutes. Slide the spatula underneath and flip the latkes over. Cook on the other side until golden brown, another two to three minutes. Transfer to the rack set over a baking sheet and place in the oven to keep warm.

- Serve hot topped with low-fat sour cream, Greek yogurt or crème fraîche, or with other toppings of your choice such as chutney or raita.

Nutrition Information

- 64: calories;
- 4 grams: fat;
- 1 gram: sugars;
- 0 grams: trans fat;
- 2 grams: protein;
- 5 grams: carbohydrates;
- 120 milligrams: sodium;

---

291. Spicy Carrot, Parsnip And Potato Latkes

Serving: Makes 2 to 2 1/2 dozen, serving 6 | Prep: | Cook: | Ready in: 15mins

Ingredients

- 3 cups, tightly packed, mixed grated carrots and parsnips (about 1 pound)
- 3 cups grated potatoes (use a starchy potato like Idaho or Yukon gold)
- 1 teaspoon baking powder
- Salt and freshly ground pepper to taste
- 2 serrano chiles or 1 jalapeño, minced (seeded if desired)
- ½ cup chopped cilantro
- 1 tablespoon nigella seeds
- ¼ cup chopped chives
- ¼ cup all-purpose flour or cornstarch
- 2 eggs, beaten

- About 1/4 cup canola, grape seed or rice bran oil

Direction

- Preheat the oven to 300 degrees. Place a rack over a sheet pan.
- In a large bowl mix together the carrots and parsnips, potatoes, baking powder, salt and pepper, chiles, cilantro, nigella seeds, chives, and flour or cornstarch. Add the eggs and stir together.
- Begin heating a large heavy skillet over medium-high heat. Add 2 to 3 tablespoons of the oil and when it is hot, take up heaped tablespoons of the latke mixture, press the mixture against the spoon to extract liquid (or squeeze in your hands), and place in the pan. Press down with the back of the spatula to flatten. Repeat with more spoonfuls, being careful not to crowd the pan. In my 10-inch pan I can cook 4 at a time without crowding; my 12-inch pan will accommodate 5. Cook on one side until golden brown, about 3 minutes. Slide the spatula underneath and flip the latkes over. Cook on the other side until golden brown, another 2 to 3 minutes. Transfer to the rack set over a baking sheet and place in the oven to keep warm. The mixture will continue to release liquid, which will accumulate in the bottom of the bowl. Stir from time to time, and remember to squeeze the heaped tablespoons of the mix before you add them to the pan.
- Serve hot topped with low-fat sour cream, Greek yogurt or crème fraiche, or other toppings of your choice such as salsa, chutney or yogurt blended with cilantro, mint, and garlic.

Nutrition Information

- 60: calories;
- 2 grams: sugars;
- 128 milligrams: sodium;
- 3 grams: fat;
- 1 gram: protein;

- 0 grams: trans fat;
- 8 grams: carbohydrates;

292. Spicy Egyptian Dukkah With Chickpea Flour

Serving: 1 cup | Prep: | Cook: | Ready in: 15mins

Ingredients

- ½ cup chickpea flour
- ¼ cup lightly toasted unsalted peanuts
- 2 teaspoons coriander seeds
- 2 teaspoons caraway seeds
- 2 teaspoons lightly toasted dill seeds (optional)
- 1 tablespoon lightly toasted sesame seeds
- ½ teaspoon kosher salt or coarse sea salt
- ½ teaspoon cayenne pepper
- 2 teaspoons sumac

Direction

- In a heavy frying pan over medium-high heat, toast the chickpea flour, stirring constantly or shaking the pan, just until it begins to smell toasty and darken slightly. Transfer immediately to a bowl.
- Finely chop the peanuts and add to the bowl with the chickpea flour.
- One at a time, heat the coriander seeds, caraway seeds, dill seeds and sesame seeds in a small skillet over medium-high heat, shaking the pan or stirring constantly, just until each is fragrant and beginning to smell toasty. Remove from the pan and allow to cool completely.
- Working in batches, combine the coriander seeds, caraway seeds and dill seeds in a spice mill and grind to a powder. Transfer to the bowl with the chickpea flour and stir in the sesame seeds, salt, cayenne and sumac.

Nutrition Information

- 119: calories;
- 6 grams: protein;
- 60 milligrams: sodium;
- 7 grams: fat;
- 1 gram: saturated fat;
- 3 grams: dietary fiber;
- 2 grams: sugars;
- 10 grams: carbohydrates;

293. Spicy Lentil And Sweet Potato Stew With Chipotles

Serving: Serves 6 to 8 | Prep: | Cook: | Ready in: 1hours

Ingredients

- 1 tablespoon extra virgin olive oil
- 1 medium onion, chopped
- 2 garlic cloves, minced
- Salt to taste
- 2 teaspoons cumin seeds, lightly toasted and ground
- 2 medium carrots, diced
- 1 ½ cups brown or green lentils, rinsed
- 6 cups water
- 2 medium-size sweet potatoes (aka yams, with dark orange flesh, 1 to 1 1/4 pounds), peeled and cut in large dice
- 1 to 2 chipotles in adobo, seeded and chopped (to taste)
- 2 tablespoons tomato paste
- 1 bay leaf
- ¼ cup chopped fresh cilantro or parsley (to taste)
- Lime wedges for serving

Direction

- Heat the olive oil over medium heat in a large, heavy soup pot or Dutch oven and add the onion. Cook, stirring often, until it softens, about 5 minutes, and add the garlic and a generous pinch of salt. Cook, stirring, until the garlic smells fragrant, about 30 seconds, and add the ground cumin seeds and carrots. Stir together for a minute, then add the lentils, water, sweet potatoes, chipotles, tomato paste, salt to taste and the bay leaf. Bring to a boil, reduce the heat, cover and simmer 40 to 45 minutes, until the lentils and sweet potatoes are tender and the broth fragrant. Taste and adjust seasoning. Stir in the cilantro or parsley, simmer for another minute, and serve, passing lime wedges so diners can season their lentils with a squeeze of lime juice if desired.

Nutrition Information

- 163: calories;
- 1 gram: monounsaturated fat;
- 28 grams: carbohydrates;
- 5 grams: dietary fiber;
- 3 grams: sugars;
- 10 grams: protein;
- 2 grams: fat;
- 0 grams: polyunsaturated fat;
- 614 milligrams: sodium;

---

294. Spicy Quinoa Salad With Broccoli, Cilantro And Lime

Serving: 4 servings | Prep: | Cook: | Ready in: 15mins

Ingredients

- 2 ½ cups cooked quinoa
- 1 ½ cups steamed broccoli florets (about 1/3 of a crown), steamed for 4 to 5 minutes then separated into smaller florets
- ½ cup chopped cilantro
- 1 to 2 tablespoons toasted pumpkin seeds (to taste)
- 1 ½ to 2 teaspoons minced serrano or jalapeño chili (to taste)
- ¼ cup split red lentils, soaked for 2 hours or longer and drained (optional)
- 1 ounce crumbled feta cheese (1/4 cup)
- Freshly ground pepper
- 3 tablespoons fresh lime juice

- Salt to taste
- 1 garlic clove, minced or pureed
- 6 tablespoons extra-virgin olive oil
- 2 hard-boiled eggs
- 1 avocado, sliced

Direction

- In a large bowl, combine quinoa, broccoli, cilantro, pumpkin seeds, minced green chile, red lentils if using, feta and freshly ground pepper. Toss together.
- In a small bowl or measuring cup whisk together lime juice, salt, and garlic. Add olive oil and whisk until amalgamated. Add to salad and toss together well. Taste and adjust seasoning.
- Put hard-boiled eggs through a sieve and sprinkle over salad. Season if desired with salt and pepper. Garnish each serving with a few slices of avocado.

Nutrition Information

- 485: calories;
- 22 grams: monounsaturated fat;
- 5 grams: polyunsaturated fat;
- 33 grams: carbohydrates;
- 7 grams: dietary fiber;
- 2 grams: sugars;
- 36 grams: fat;
- 6 grams: saturated fat;
- 607 milligrams: sodium;
- 0 grams: trans fat;
- 12 grams: protein;

---

295. Spinach Gnocchi

Serving: 60 1-inch gnocchi, serving 6 | Prep: | Cook: | Ready in: 30mins

Ingredients

- 1 ½ pounds bunch spinach, stemmed and thoroughly cleaned, or 3/4 pound baby spinach
- Salt and freshly ground pepper to taste
- 2 tablespoons unsalted butter or extra virgin olive oil
- 8 ounces ricotta (1 cup)
- ⅓ cup all-purpose flour (about 45 grams)
- 2 eggs, beaten
- Freshly grated nutmeg
- 2 ounces Parmesan, grated (1/2 cup)
- Marinara sauce for serving

Direction

- Blanch the spinach for no more than 20 seconds in salted boiling water. Transfer to a bowl of cold water, drain and squeeze out excess water. Chop fine.
- Heat the butter or olive oil over medium heat in a heavy saucepan and add the spinach, salt (remembering that you will be adding Parmesan, which is salty), pepper, ricotta and flour. Stir together and let the mixture sizzle while you stir constantly for 5 minutes. Remove from the heat and beat in the eggs, nutmeg and Parmesan. The mixture should be stiff. Transfer to a bowl, cover well and refrigerate for 2 hours or longer.
- Line a sheet pan with parchment and dust generously with flour. Remove the gnocchi mixture from the refrigerator. There are a few ways to form the gnocchi. You can scoop out small balls by the rounded teaspoon and place on the parchment (they will be sticky so use another spoon to scrape them out of the measuring spoon), or you can divide the dough into 4 pieces and on a floured surface, with lightly floured hands, gently roll each piece into a coil about 3/4 inch wide. Cut into 1-inch pieces and place on parchment-lined baking sheet. Alternatively, place the mixture in a pastry bag fitted with a 5/8 inch round tip and pipe 1-inch blobs onto the parchment. Don't worry if the dough is sticky.
- Bring a large pot of water to a boil and salt generously. Meanwhile heat the tomato sauce

in a saucepan. Adjust the heat under the water so that it is boiling gently and drop in the gnocchi, about 10 at a time. If they stick to the parchment or your hands lightly flour your fingers and sprinkle a little flour over the gnocchi. Once they float to the top simmer for 4 minutes, then move them to the pan of sauce with a slotted spoon. Serve with the sauce and additional Parmesan to taste.

<table>
<tr><td>296.</td><td>Spinach Soup With Coriander, Cinnamon And Allspice</td></tr>
</table>

Serving: 4 to 6 servings. | Prep: | Cook: | Ready in: 1hours

Ingredients

- 1 tablespoon extra virgin olive oil
- 1 medium onion, chopped
- ⅓ cup finely diced celery
- Salt to taste
- 2 garlic cloves, minced
- ½ cup medium-grain rice
- 6 cups chicken stock or vegetable stock
- A bouquet garni made with a bay leaf and a couple of sprigs each thyme and parsley
- 1 ½ pounds fresh spinach, stemmed and washed thoroughly in 2 changes of water
- ¼ teaspoon ground allspice
- ⅛ teaspoon ground clove
- ⅛ teaspoon freshly grated nutmeg
- ¼ teaspoon ground cinnamon
- 1 scant teaspoon coriander seeds, lightly toasted and ground
- Salt and freshly ground pepper
- 1 teaspoon cornstarch
- 2 cups drained yogurt or Greek-style yogurt
- 1 small garlic clove (optional)
- ¼ to ⅓ cup chopped walnuts for garnish

Direction

- Heat the olive oil over medium heat in a large, heavy soup pot or Dutch oven, and add the onion and celery. Cook, stirring, until tender, about 5 minutes. Add a generous pinch of salt and the garlic and cook, stirring, until the garlic smells fragrant, 30 seconds to 1 minute.
- Add the stock, rice, bouquet garni, and salt to taste, and bring to a boil. Reduce the heat, cover and simmer 30 minutes. Remove the bouquet garni. Stir in the spinach and spices, cover and simmer 5 minutes, stirring once or twice. The spinach should wilt but should maintain its bright color.
- Using a hand blender that has a powerful motor, or in batches in a regular blender, purée the soup. If using a regular blender, fill only halfway and cover the top with a towel pulled down tight, rather than the lid, because hot soup will push the top off if the blender is closed airtight. Return to the pot and heat through, stirring. Whisk 1 teaspoon cornstarch into 1 cup of the yogurt, and whisk into the soup. Season to taste with salt and pepper.
- If you want a pungent, garlicky yogurt garnish, mash the remaining garlic to a paste with a pinch of salt in a mortar and pestle. Stir into the remaining yogurt. Serve the soup, garnishing each bowl with a swirl of the yogurt and a sprinkling of chopped walnuts.

Nutrition Information

- 291: calories;
- 8 grams: sugars;
- 18 grams: protein;
- 11 grams: fat;
- 0 grams: trans fat;
- 33 grams: carbohydrates;
- 1 gram: polyunsaturated fat;
- 1152 milligrams: sodium;
- 4 grams: dietary fiber;
- 3 grams: monounsaturated fat;

297.   Spinach With Garlic Yogurt And Walnut Dukkah

Serving: 6 servings | Prep: | Cook: | Ready in: 30mins

Ingredients

- For the dukkah :
- ½ cup broken walnuts, very lightly toasted if desired
- For the dukkah:
- ¼ cup lightly toasted sesame seeds
- 2 tablespoons coriander seeds
- 1 tablespoon cumin seeds
- 2 teaspoons nigella seeds
- 1 teaspoon ground sumac
- ½ to 1 teaspoon mild chili powder or Aleppo pepper (optional)
- ½ teaspoon kosher salt or coarse sea salt (or to taste)
- For the spinach:
- 2 large bunches spinach (1 1/2 to 2 pounds), stemmed and washed in 2 rinses of water
- 1 clove, ground
- 2 allspice berries, lightly toasted and ground
- ½ teaspoon cumin seeds, lightly toasted and ground
- ⅛ teaspoon ground cinnamon
- 1 garlic clove, cut in half, green shoots removed (more to taste)
- Salt to taste
- ⅔ cup drained yogurt or Greek yogurt
- 1 tablespoon extra virgin olive oil
- ¼ to ½ cup pomegranate seeds for garnish (optional)

Direction

- Make the dukkah. Chop the walnuts very fine. Mix with the toasted sesame seeds in a bowl. In a dry skillet lightly toast the coriander seeds just until fragrant and immediately transfer to a spice mill. Allow to cool. In the same skillet toast the cumin seeds just until fragrant and transfer to the spice mill. Allow to cool. When the spices have cooled, grind and add to the nuts and sesame seeds. Add the nigella seeds, sumac, chili powder and salt and mix together. Measure out 2 tablespoons and store the remainder of the dukkah in a jar in the refrigerator or the freezer.

- Steam the spinach over 1 inch of boiling water until wilted, 1 to 2 minutes (or a little longer, depending on how much spinach you have in your steaming basket; you may have to do this in batches). Turn the leaves with tongs about halfway through the steaming. My pot of choice for this is a pasta pot with an insert. Remove from the heat, rinse briefly with cold water and squeeze out excess water. If desired, chop coarsely.
- Combine the ground clove, allspice, cumin and cinnamon for the spinach, and set aside.
- In a mortar and pestle, combine the garlic and a generous pinch of salt and mash to a paste. Stir into the yogurt. Set aside.
- Heat the olive oil over medium heat in a wide, heavy skillet and add the ground clove, allspice, cumin and cinnamon mix. Cook until the mixture begins to sizzle, add the spinach and salt and pepper to taste. Cook, stirring, until the spinach is heated through and coated with the oil, 2 to 3 minutes. Transfer to a serving dish and spoon the yogurt over the top. Sprinkle the dukkah over the yogurt, garnish with pomegranate seeds, if desired, and serve.

Nutrition Information

- 146: calories;
- 2 grams: sugars;
- 4 grams: monounsaturated fat;
- 10 grams: carbohydrates;
- 5 grams: dietary fiber;
- 8 grams: protein;
- 419 milligrams: sodium;
- 0 grams: trans fat;
- 3 grams: polyunsaturated fat;

---

298. Spring Rolls With Spinach, Mushrooms, Sesame, Rice And Herbs

Serving: 8 spring rolls | Prep: | Cook: | Ready in: 30mins

Ingredients

- For the filling
- 1 ¾ cups cooked rice (brown, basmati or jasmine)
- 3 tablespoons rice vinegar
- 2 teaspoons soy sauce
- 1 pound baby spinach or 2 pounds bunch spinach, stemmed and washed
- 2 teaspoons black sesame seeds or lightly toasted regular hulled sesame seeds
- ¼ pound firm tofu, cut into dominoes 1/4 inch thick by 1/2 inch wide and drained on paper towels
- 2 tablespoons peanut sauce
- 2 large carrots (about 1 pound), peeled and grated
- 6 shiitake mushrooms, stems removed, thinly sliced
- ½ cup cilantro, coarsely chopped, plus additional sprigs
- ⅓ cup mint leaves, coarsely chopped, plus additional leaves
- ¼ cup Thai basil leaves, coarsely chopped, plus additional leaves (may substitute regular basil if you can't get the Thai variety)
- Salt to taste
- 8 8 1/2-inch rice flour spring roll wrappers

Direction

- Toss the rice with 1 tablespoon of the rice vinegar and the soy sauce
- Wash the spinach and steam 1 to 2 minutes, tossing halfway through. It should wilt but still have some texture. Rinse with cold water, squeeze dry and coarsely chop. Season with salt to taste
- Spread each tofu domino with about 1/4 teaspoon peanut sauce

- Place the shredded carrots, slivered mushrooms and chopped herbs in a large bowl and toss with the remaining rice vinegar and salt to taste
- Fill a bowl with warm water and place a spring roll in it just until it is pliable, about 30 seconds. Remove from the water and drain briefly on a kitchen towel. Place the wrapper on your work surface in front of you and arrange several cilantro sprigs, whole mint leaves and basil leaves, vein side up, on the wrapper. Leaving a 2-inch margin on the sides, place a handful of the carrot mixture on the wrapper, slightly nearer to the edge closest to you. Top with a handful of rice, then a handful of spinach. Place 3 tofu dominoes down the length of the spinach. Fold the sides in, then roll up the spring rolls tightly, squeezing the filling to get a tight roll. Refrigerate until ready to serve. Serve with a dipping sauce of your choice

Nutrition Information

- 214: calories;
- 2 grams: polyunsaturated fat;
- 39 grams: carbohydrates;
- 6 grams: dietary fiber;
- 5 grams: sugars;
- 9 grams: protein;
- 1 gram: monounsaturated fat;
- 0 grams: trans fat;
- 651 milligrams: sodium;
- 4 grams: fat;

299. Spring Rolls With Tofu, Vegetables, Rice Noodles And Herbs

Serving: 8 substantial spring rolls | Prep: | Cook: | Ready in: 50mins

Ingredients

- 2 ounces rice vermicelli
- ¼ cup rice vinegar
- 2 teaspoons soy sauce
- ¼ pound firm tofu, cut into dominoes 1/4 inch thick by 1/2 inch wide and drained on paper towels
- 2 tablespoons peanut-ginger sauce
- 2 large carrots, peeled and grated
- 2 medium turnips or 1/2 daikon radish, peeled and grated
- 6 shiitake mushrooms, stems removed, cut in thin slices
- ½ cup coarsely chopped cilantro, chopped, plus additional sprigs
- ⅓ cup mint leaves, coarsely chopped, plus additional leaves
- ¼ cup Thai basil leaves, coarsely chopped, plus additional leaves (may substitute regular basil if you can't get the Thai variety)
- Salt to taste
- 8 to 10 inner romaine lettuce leaves, cut in chiffonade (crosswise strips)
- 8 8 1/2-inch rice flour spring roll wrappers
- Peanut-Ginger Sauce
- 3 tablespoons creamy peanut butter, unsalted and unsweetened
- 1 tablespoon rice vinegar
- 2 teaspoons soy sauce
- 1 to 2 teaspoons light brown sugar, to taste
- 1 ½ teaspoon ginger juice (grate 1 tablespoon ginger, wrap in cheesecloth and squeeze)
- Cayenne to taste

Direction

-
-

Nutrition Information

- 189: calories;
- 1 gram: saturated fat;
- 3 grams: dietary fiber;
- 6 grams: fat;
- 0 grams: trans fat;
- 2 grams: polyunsaturated fat;

- 28 grams: carbohydrates;
- 4 grams: sugars;
- 7 grams: protein;
- 331 milligrams: sodium;

---

300. Stir Fried Beans With Tofu And Chiles

Serving: 4 servings | Prep: | Cook: | Ready in: 7mins

Ingredients

- One 14-ounce box firm tofu, drained and cut in 1/4-inch thick, 2-inch by 3/4-inch dominoes
- 1 to 2 tablespoons soy sauce (to taste)
- 1 tablespoon Chinese cooking sherry (Shaoxing rice wine) or dry sherry
- ½ cup vegetable stock, chicken stock, or water
- ¼ to ½ teaspoon salt, to taste
- ¼ to ½ teaspoon sugar, to taste
- 1 teaspoon cornstarch or arrowroot dissolved in 2 tablespoons vegetable stock, chicken stock, or water
- 2 tablespoons peanut, canola, sunflower, or grape seed oil
- 1 tablespoon minced garlic
- 1 tablespoon minced ginger
- 1 or 2 Thai or serrano chiles, minced (to taste)
- 1 pound green beans, or 1/2 pound each yellow and green beans, stem ends trimmed
- 1 bunch scallions, white and green parts separated
- ½ cup chopped cilantro

Direction

- Drain and dry tofu slices on paper towels. In a small bowl or measuring cup combine soy sauce, rice wine or sherry, and stock or water. Combine salt and sugar in another small bowl and cornstarch slurry in another. Have all ingredients within arm's length of your pan.
- Heat a 14-inch flat-bottomed wok or 12-inch steel skillet over high heat until a drop of water evaporates within a second or two when added to the pan. Add 1 tablespoon of the oil to the wok or pan and swirl the pan so that the oil coats the sides, then add tofu and stir-fry until lightly colored, 1 to 2 minutes. Remove to a plate.
- Swirl in remaining oil, add garlic, ginger and chiles and stir-fry for no more than 10 seconds. Add beans and white parts of the scallions, and stir-fry for 2 minutes. Add salt and sugar, toss together and add soy sauce mixture. Stir-fry for 1 to 2 minutes, until vegetables are crisp-tender. Return tofu to the wok along with scallion greens, cilantro and cornstarch slurry. Stir together just until lightly glazed, and remove from heat. Serve with hot grains or noodles.

Nutrition Information

- 264: calories;
- 6 grams: dietary fiber;
- 5 grams: sugars;
- 16 grams: fat;
- 2 grams: saturated fat;
- 19 grams: protein;
- 580 milligrams: sodium;
- 3 grams: monounsaturated fat;
- 10 grams: polyunsaturated fat;
- 17 grams: carbohydrates;

---

301. Stir Fried Rice Noodles With Beets And Beet Greens

Serving: Serves 4 to 5 | Prep: | Cook: | Ready in: 10mins

Ingredients

- 7 ounces rice vermicelli or thin rice stick noodles
- ½ cup chicken stock or vegetable stock
- 1 tablespoon soy sauce (more to taste)
- 1 tablespoon Shao Hsing rice wine or dry sherry
- Salt to taste

- ½ teaspoon sugar
- 1 tablespoon minced garlic
- 1 tablespoon minced ginger
- ¼ to ½ teaspoon red pepper flakes, or 1 to 2 serrano or Thai chiles, minced
- 2 eggs
- 2 tablespoons peanut oil, grapeseed oil, sunflower oil or canola oil
- 4 small or 2 medium beets (1/2 pound), preferably golden or Chioggia beets, peeled and very thinly sliced, then cut into half-moons
- 2 medium-size leeks, white and light green parts only, cut in half, cleaned of sand, and thinly sliced
- 1 generous bunch beet greens, stemmed, washed well in 2 changes of water, and coarsely chopped or cut in ribbons
- ½ cup chopped walnuts
- ½ to 1 cup coarsely chopped cilantro
- 2 teaspoons walnut oil

Direction

- Place noodles in a large bowl and cover with warm water. Soak for 20 – 30 minutes, until soft. Drain in a colander and using kitchen scissors, cut into 6-inch lengths. Set aside within reach of your wok. Combine stock, soy sauce, rice wine or sherry, salt and sugar in a small bowl and stir until salt and sugar dissolve. Combine garlic, ginger, and pepper flakes or minced chile in another bowl. Have all ingredients within reach of your wok.
- Beat eggs in a bowl and season with a little salt. Heat a 14-inch flat-bottomed wok over high heat until a drop of water evaporates within a second or two when added to the pan. Swirl in 2 teaspoons of oil by adding it to the sides of the wok and swirling the wok. Make sure that the bottom of the wok is coated with oil and add beaten eggs, swirling the wok so that the eggs form a thin pancake. Cook 30 seconds to a minute, until set. Using a spatula, turn pancake over and cook for 5 to 10 more seconds, until thoroughly set, then transfer to a plate or cutting board. Roll up or fold in half

and cut into strips using the edge of your spatula or a knife. Set aside.

- Swirl remaining oil into wok and add garlic, ginger, and pepper flakes or chile. Stir-fry no more than 10 seconds and add beets and leeks. Stir-fry 2 minutes, until beets are crisp-tender. Add greens and walnuts and stir-fry until greens wilt, about 1 minute. Add noodles and stock mixture. Reduce heat to medium and stir-fry 1 to 2 minutes, until noodles are just tender. Add cilantro and eggs and stir-fry another 30 seconds to a minute, until well combined. Remove from heat and serve.

Nutrition Information

- 384: calories;
- 0 grams: trans fat;
- 5 grams: dietary fiber;
- 9 grams: protein;
- 48 grams: carbohydrates;
- 7 grams: sugars;
- 548 milligrams: sodium;
- 3 grams: saturated fat;
- 17 grams: fat;

302.   Stir Fried Soba Noodles With Turkey And Cabbage

Serving: Serves 4 to 6 | Prep: | Cook: | Ready in: 20mins

Ingredients

- 1 tablespoon egg white, lightly beaten
- 2 teaspoons cornstarch
- 1 ½ teaspoons plus 1 tablespoon rice wine or dry sherry
- Salt to taste
- 1 ½ teaspoons water
- ½ pound turkey cutlets, cut across the grain in 1/4-inch thick slices
- ½ cup chicken or vegetable stock
- 1 tablespoon soy sauce (more to taste)
- ½ teaspoon sugar

- 1 tablespoon minced garlic
- 1 tablespoon minced ginger
- ¼ to ½ teaspoon red pepper flakes, or 1 to 2 serrano or Thai chiles, minced
- 6 ounces soba noodles (2 bundles)
- 2 teaspoons sesame oil
- 2 tablespoons grapeseed oil, peanut oil, sunflower oil or canola oil
- ½ medium cabbage, shredded (about 4 cups)
- 1 bunch scallions, thinly sliced, dark green parts separated
- ½ cup coarsely chopped cilantro

Direction

- In a large bowl stir together egg white, cornstarch, 1 1/2 teaspoons of rice wine or sherry, salt to taste and 1 1/2 teaspoons water. When you can no longer see any undissolved cornstarch add turkey and stir until coated. Cover bowl and place in refrigerator for 30 minutes.
- Combine stock, soy sauce, remaining rice wine or sherry, salt to taste and sugar in a small bowl and stir until salt and sugar dissolve. Combine garlic, ginger, and pepper flakes or minced chile in another bowl. Have everything within reach of your wok.
- Cook the soba in a large saucepan and toss with 2 teaspoons sesame oil. Do not drain the water. Bring it back to a boil and turn the heat down so that water is at a bare simmer. Carefully add turkey to the water, stirring so that the pieces don't clump. Cook until turkey turns opaque on the surface but is not cooked through, about 1 minute. Drain in a colander, then on paper towels.
- Heat a 14-inch flat-bottomed wok over high heat until a drop of water evaporates within a second or two when added to the wok. Swirl in grapeseed oil, peanut oil, sunflower oil or canola oil and add garlic, ginger and chile mixture. Stir-fry no more than 10 seconds and add turkey, cabbage and the light parts of the scallions. Stir-fry 2 minutes. Add noodles and the broth mixture. Reduce heat to medium and stir-fry 1 to 2 minutes. Add cilantro and dark

green part of the scallions and stir-fry another 30 seconds to a minute, until well combined. Serve, garnished with cilantro sprigs if desired.

Nutrition Information

- 249: calories;
- 28 grams: carbohydrates;
- 14 grams: protein;
- 439 milligrams: sodium;
- 9 grams: fat;
- 2 grams: dietary fiber;
- 3 grams: sugars;
- 5 grams: polyunsaturated fat;

303.   Stir Fried Tofu And Peppers

Serving: 4 servings | Prep: | Cook: | Ready in: 30mins

Ingredients

- ½ pound firm tofu
- 2 tablespoons soy sauce
- 1 ½ teaspoons brown sugar
- 2 tablespoons vegetable, peanut or canola oil
- 2 teaspoons hoisin sauce
- 1 teaspoon sesame oil
- 2 red bell peppers, seeded and cut in 1-inch squares
- 1 green bell pepper, seeded and cut in 1-inch squares
- 1 tablespoon minced fresh ginger
- 2 large garlic cloves, green shoots removed, minced
- ¼ to ½ teaspoon dried red pepper flakes (to taste)
- 2 scallions, white and green parts, cut on the diagonal into 1-inch lengths
- Cooked rice or noodles for serving

Direction

- Optional step for firmer tofu: Blot the tofu dry, wrap in a clean kitchen towel and place a cutting board on top. Let sit for about 15 minutes. Whether weighted or not, slice the tofu about 1/2 inch thick into 1- x 2-inch dominoes.
- Mix together 1 tablespoon of the soy sauce, 1 teaspoon of the brown sugar and 1 tablespoon of the oil in a medium bowl. Toss with the tofu, and stir to make sure all of the pieces are coated. Let sit for five to 10 minutes while you prepare the other ingredients.
- In a small bowl, stir together the remaining soy sauce and sugar, hoisin sauce and sesame oil. Set aside.
- Heat a large nonstick skillet or wok over high heat until a drop of water evaporates on contact. Add the oil, turn the heat to medium-high and add the peppers. Stir-fry for a couple of minutes, until the peppers begin to soften, and add the garlic and ginger. Stir-fry for 20 seconds, until the garlic and ginger begin to smell fragrant, and add the tofu, dried red pepper flakes and green onions. Stir-fry two minutes, give the sauce a stir and add to the pan. Cover and cook for three minutes. Remove the lid, stir the ingredients in the pan, and taste and adjust seasonings. Serve with rice or noodles.

Nutrition Information

- 200: calories;
- 12 grams: carbohydrates;
- 11 grams: protein;
- 496 milligrams: sodium;
- 13 grams: fat;
- 1 gram: saturated fat;
- 0 grams: trans fat;
- 5 grams: sugars;
- 6 grams: monounsaturated fat;
- 3 grams: dietary fiber;

---

304. Stir Fried Turkey Breast With Snap Or Snow Peas And Chard

Serving: Serves 4 | Prep: | Cook: | Ready in: 7mins

Ingredients

- 1 pound turkey cutlets, cut across the grain in thin (1/4 to 1/2-inch) slices
- Salt and freshly ground pepper
- 1 to 2 tablespoons soy sauce (to taste)
- 1 tablespoon Chinese cooking sherry (Shaoxing rice wine) or dry sherry
- ¼ cup vegetable stock or water
- ¼ to ½ teaspoon salt (to taste)
- ¼ to ½ teaspoon sugar (to taste)
- 1 teaspoon cornstarch or arrowroot dissolved in 1/2 cup vegetable stock, chicken stock or water
- 2 tablespoons peanut, canola, sunflower, or grape seed oil
- 1 tablespoon minced garlic
- 1 tablespoon minced ginger
- ¾ pound sugar snap peas or snow peas, strings and stems removed
- 1 bunch scallions, white and green parts separated, minced
- ½ pound Swiss chard, stemmed, leaves washed in 2 changes of water and chopped (about 3 cups), stems diced
- ½ cup chopped cilantro

Direction

- Season sliced turkey cutlets with salt and pepper. In a small bowl or measuring cup combine soy sauce, rice wine or sherry, and stock or water. Put salt and sugar in another container, and place it and the other ingredients near your burner.
- Heat a 14-inch flat-bottomed wok or 12-inch steel skillet over high heat until a drop of water evaporates within a second or two when added to the pan. Add 1 tablespoon of the oil to the wok or pan and swirl to coat the sides, then add sliced turkey cutlets in one layer. Let

sit untouched for about 30 seconds, then stir-fry until lightly colored and no pink is visible, about 2 to 2 1/2 minutes. Remove to a plate.

- Swirl in remaining oil, add garlic and ginger and stir-fry for no more than 10 seconds. Add sugar snap peas and white parts of scallions and stir-fry for 1 minute. Add chard, salt and sugar and stir-fry for about 1 minute, until chard wilts. Return turkey to wok and add soy sauce mixture. Stir-fry for 1 to 2 minutes, until vegetables are crisp-tender and turkey cooked through. Add cilantro, scallion greens, and cornstarch slurry. Stir until mixture is lightly glazed, and remove from the heat. Serve with hot grains or noodles.

Nutrition Information

- 311: calories;
- 4 grams: dietary fiber;
- 5 grams: sugars;
- 3 grams: saturated fat;
- 15 grams: fat;
- 7 grams: polyunsaturated fat;
- 13 grams: carbohydrates;
- 30 grams: protein;
- 749 milligrams: sodium;

---

305.   Stir Fried Rice With Amaranth Or Red Chard And Thai Basil

---

Serving: Serves 4 | Prep: | Cook: | Ready in: 6mins

Ingredients

- 4 to 5 cups cooked rice (white or brown, medium-grain preferred), either chilled or at room temperature
- 3 eggs
- 2 teaspoons plus 2 tablespoons peanut, canola, rice bran or grape seed oil
- 2 to 3 teaspoons minced garlic (to taste)
- 2 to 3 teaspoons minced fresh ginger (to taste)

- 1 bunch amaranth, thick stem ends cut away, the rest coarsely chopped (about 4 cups), or red chard, leaves torn from stalks, stalks diced
- ⅔ cup chopped Thai basil
- 1 bunch scallions, sliced, white and dark green parts separated
- 1 to 2 tablespoons soy sauce, to taste
- 1 tablespoon sriracha sauce (optional)
- ¼ teaspoon ground pepper
- ½ cup chopped cilantro

Direction

- Beat one of the eggs in a bowl and season with a pinch of salt. Prepare remaining ingredients and place in separate bowls within arm's reach of your burner.
- Heat a 14-inch flat-bottomed wok or a 12-inch skillet over high heat until a drop of water evaporates within a second or two when added to the pan. Add 3/4 easpoon of the oil to the wok or pan and swirl to coat the sides. Make sure that bottom wok or pan is coated with oil and add beaten egg, swirling the pan so that egg forms a thin pancake. Cook 30 seconds to a minute, until set. Using a spatula, turn pancake over and cook for 5 to 10 more seconds, until thoroughly set, then transfer to a plate or cutting board. Season to taste. Allow to cool, then roll up or fold in half and cut into strips or just break up with edge of spatula . Repeat with remaining eggs.
- Swirl remaining oil into wok or pan and add garlic and ginger. Stir-fry no more than 10 secods, and add amaranth or chard, and white parts of the scallions. Stir-fry for 2 minutes and add Thai basil; stir together for a few seconds, then add rice. Stir-fry, scooping up the rice with your spatula, then pressing it into the hot wok and scooping it up again, for about 2 minutes. The rice should sear and stick to the sides of the wok. Add soy sauce, sriracha, pepper, green part of the scallions, and eggs and cilantro, stir for about 30 seconds, scraping the rice off the sides of the wok as it sticks. Remove from the heat. Serve hot.

Nutrition Information

- 351: calories;
- 0 grams: trans fat;
- 3 grams: monounsaturated fat;
- 14 grams: protein;
- 626 milligrams: sodium;
- 7 grams: fat;
- 2 grams: sugars;
- 59 grams: carbohydrates;
- 4 grams: dietary fiber;

Nutrition Information

- 238: calories;
- 6 grams: sugars;
- 1038 milligrams: sodium;
- 10 grams: fat;
- 4 grams: monounsaturated fat;
- 0 grams: trans fat;
- 1 gram: dietary fiber;
- 18 grams: protein;

---

306.   Stracciatella With Spinach

Serving: 4 servings | Prep: | Cook: |Ready in: 1hours

Ingredients

- 1 ½ quarts chicken or turkey stock
- Salt
- freshly ground pepper to taste
- 2 large or extra large eggs
- 1 ½ tablespoons semolina
- ⅓ cup freshly grated Parmesan (1 1/2 ounces)
- 1 6-ounce bag baby spinach, or 1 bunch spinach, stemmed, washed, dried and coarsely chopped

Direction

- Place the stock in a large saucepan or soup pot. Remove 1/3 cup and set aside. Bring the rest to a simmer. Season to taste with salt and freshly ground pepper. If there is any visible fat, skim it away.
- Beat the eggs in a bowl, and stir in the 1/3 cup of stock, the semolina and the cheese.
- Stir the spinach into the simmering stock, then drizzle in the egg mixture, scraping all of it in with a rubber spatula. Stir very slowly with the spatula, paddling it back and forth until the little "rags" form. Taste, adjust seasoning and serve at once.

---

307.   Strawberry Smoothie

Serving: One 16-ounce or two 8-ounce servings | Prep: | Cook: |Ready in: 5mins

Ingredients

- 1 medium-size or large, ripe banana
- 1 heaped cup fresh or frozen hulled strawberries
- 1 cup milk
- 1 teaspoon honey
- ½ teaspoon vanilla extract (optional)
- 2 to 3 ice cubes

Direction

- Place all of the ingredients in a blender and blend until smooth. Serve right away.

---

308.   Strawberry Soup

Serving: Serves four | Prep: | Cook: |Ready in: 1hours15mins

Ingredients

- 2 ¼ pounds ripe strawberries (2 very generous pints), hulled
- 2 tablespoons fresh lemon juice
- 1 tablespoon sugar

- 1 tablespoon mild flavored honey, such as clover or acacia (more to taste)
- 1 teaspoon rose water (available in Middle Eastern markets)
- ½ cup freshly squeezed orange juice
- Chopped or slivered fresh mint for garnish

Direction

- Separate out a fourth of the prettiest strawberries. Quarter or slice them and toss in a large bowl with 1 tablespoon of the lemon juice and the sugar. Cover and refrigerate for 1 hour or longer.
- Place the remaining strawberries in the bowl of a standing mixer fitted with the paddle, or in a food processor fitted with the steel blade. If using the mixer, turn on at medium-low speed and crush the berries to a coarse puree. If using a food processor pulse to a coarse puree. Add the remaining lemon juice, the orange juice, the honey and the rose water and beat together. Taste and add more honey if desired. Chill until ready to serve.
- Just before serving, stir the quartered strawberries with the juice that has accumulated in the bowl into the crushed strawberries. Ladle into bowls, top with chopped or slivered mint, and serve.

Nutrition Information

- 125: calories;
- 31 grams: carbohydrates;
- 5 grams: dietary fiber;
- 23 grams: sugars;
- 2 grams: protein;
- 3 milligrams: sodium;
- 1 gram: fat;
- 0 grams: polyunsaturated fat;

309.   Stuffed Peppers With Red Rice, Chard And Feta

Serving: Serves 4 | Prep: | Cook: | Ready in: 1hours

Ingredients

- 4 medium peppers, preferably red
- 1 bunch Swiss chard, 12 ounces to 1 pound, stemmed and washed
- Salt to taste
- 3 tablespoons extra virgin olive oil
- 2 garlic cloves, minced
- 2 cups cooked red rice
- ¼ cup chopped mint
- 2 ounces feta, crumbed
- ½ cup water
- 2 tablespoons fresh lemon juice
- 1 tablespoon tomato paste (optional)

Direction

- Cut the tops away from the peppers and gently remove the seeds and membranes. Set aside.
- Bring a large pot of water to a boil, salt generously and add the chard leaves. Blanch 1 minute, until just tender, and transfer to a bowl of cold water. Drain, squeeze out water and chop medium-fine. You should have about 1 cup.
- Heat 1 tablespoon of the olive oil in a large skillet or saucepan and add the garlic. Cook, stirring, until fragrant, about 30 seconds, and stir in the chard. Stir for about 30 seconds, until coated with oil and garlic, and season with salt and pepper. Stir in the rice, toss, together, and remove from the heat.
- Transfer the rice mixture to a bowl and stir in the mint, feta and 1 tablespoon olive oil. Season to taste with salt and pepper.
- Spoon the rice and chard mixture into the peppers and place the peppers upright in a lidded saucepan or skillet. Mix together the water, lemon juice, salt to taste, optional tomato paste and remaining olive oil and add to the pan. Bring to a simmer, reduce the heat,

cover and simmer 40 minutes, until the peppers are tender. Remove the lid and allow to cool in the pan. Transfer to plates or a platter, spoon any liquid remaining in the pan over the peppers if desired, and serve.

Nutrition Information

- 288: calories;
- 2 grams: polyunsaturated fat;
- 6 grams: dietary fiber;
- 14 grams: fat;
- 4 grams: saturated fat;
- 8 grams: protein;
- 35 grams: carbohydrates;
- 5 grams: sugars;
- 925 milligrams: sodium;

310. Stuffed Roasted Yellow Peppers Or Red Peppers In Tomato Sauce

Serving: Serves 4 | Prep: | Cook: | Ready in: 1hours

Ingredients

- 4 medium-size yellow bell peppers
- 2 tablespoons extra virgin olive oil
- 2 garlic cloves, minced
- ½ cup chopped fresh parsley
- 1 ½ cups cooked quinoa
- 2 ounces Manchego cheese or Parmesan, grated (1/2 cup)
- Salt and freshly ground pepper
- 1 ½ cups marinara sauce

Direction

- Roast the peppers over a flame, under a broiler or on a grill until uniformly charred. Place in a plastic bag or a tightly covered bowl and allow to cool. When cool enough to handle, remove all of the charred skin, rinse briefly and pat dry.

- Carefully cut away the stem from the peppers. Cut a slit down the side of each pepper, from the stem end to the bottom. Gently open out and remove the seeds and membranes; tip out the juice. Try to keep the peppers in one piece. Set aside.
- Heat 2 tablespoons of the olive oil over medium heat in a large, nonstick skillet and add the garlic. Cook, stirring, until fragrant, about 1 minute. Stir in the parsley and quinoa and mix together until the quinoa is coated with oil. Remove from the heat and stir in the cheese. Season to taste with salt and pepper.
- Preheat the oven to 350 degrees. Oil a baking dish large enough to accommodate all of the peppers. One at a time, lay a pepper in the dish and fill with the quinoa mixture. I do this by gently opening up the pepper, mounding the filling onto one half, and folding the other half back over the filling, overlapping the edges slightly. Lay the peppers in the dish. Cover the baking dish with foil or a lid and bake the peppers for 20 minutes. Meanwhile, reheat the tomato sauce.
- Ladle the tomato sauce onto serving plates or a serving platter. Top with the stuffed peppers and serve.

Nutrition Information

- 307: calories;
- 2 grams: polyunsaturated fat;
- 36 grams: carbohydrates;
- 10 grams: protein;
- 0 grams: trans fat;
- 7 grams: monounsaturated fat;
- 896 milligrams: sodium;
- 15 grams: fat;
- 4 grams: saturated fat;
- 6 grams: sugars;

311.   Summer Squash Ribbons With Cherry Tomatoes And Mint/Basil Pesto

Serving: Serves 4 | Prep: | Cook: | Ready in: 10mins

Ingredients

- 2 pounds mixed yellow and green zucchini or other long summer squash
- ½ pound cherry tomatoes, halved (about 1 1/2 cups)
- 2 tablespoons extra-virgin olive oil
- 1 garlic clove, minced
- Salt to taste
- Freshly ground pepper to taste
- ¼ cup pesto (both basil and basil/mint are good), diluted with 2 to 3 tablespoons warm or hot water)
- Freshly grated Parmesan cheese (optional)

Direction

- Using a vegetable peeler, cut squash into lengthwise ribbons. Peel off several ribbons from one side, then turn squash and peel off more ribbons. Continue to turn and peel off ribbons until you get to the seeds at the core of the squash. Discard core. You can also do this on a mandolin, adjusted to a very thin slice.
- Cook squash strips and tomatoes in 2 batches. Heat 1 tablespoon of the oil in a large skillet over medium-high heat and when it is hot, add squash ribbons, half the garlic, tomatoes, and salt to taste. Cook, using tongs to toss and stir squash and cherry tomatoes, for 2 to 3 minutes, until squash has softened and is beginning to become translucent and tomatoes are beginning to shrivel. Adjust salt and add freshly ground pepper to taste, and transfer to a serving dish. Repeat with remaining olive oil, squash, cherry tomatoes and garlic. Return first batch to the pan, stir everything together, heat through and transfer again to the serving bowl or individual plates. Pour any juices in the pan over squash. Top each serving with a spoonful of pesto (about a tablespoon), and

serve, with additional freshly grated Parmesan if desired.

Nutrition Information

- 111: calories;
- 7 grams: sugars;
- 1 gram: polyunsaturated fat;
- 5 grams: monounsaturated fat;
- 11 grams: carbohydrates;
- 4 grams: dietary fiber;
- 3 grams: protein;
- 734 milligrams: sodium;

312.   Summer Tacos With Corn, Green Beans And Tomatillo Salsa

Serving: Serves 4 | Prep: | Cook: | Ready in: 20mins

Ingredients

- ½ pound green beans, topped and tailed
- 4 ears corn
- 2 tablespoons extra-virgin olive oil
- 1 small red or white onion, finely chopped
- Salt to taste
- 1 serrano chile, minced
- ¼ cup chopped cilantro
- 1 recipe fresh tomatillo salsa
- 8 warm corn tortillas
- ¼ to ½ cup crumbled feta, queso fresco or goat cheese

Direction

- Bring a large saucepan full of water to a boil and salt generously. Add green beans and cook for 5 minutes. Transfer to a bowl of cold water, drain and cut in 1-inch lengths.
- Cut the kernels off corncobs. Heat olive oil over medium heat in a large, heavy skillet and add onion. Cook, stirring often, until tender, about 5 minutes. Add a generous pinch of salt,

the corn and chile, and continue to cook for another 4 to 5 minutes, stirring often, until corn is tender. Stir in green beans and cilantro, and about 1/4 cup of the salsa (more to taste). Remove from heat. Taste and adjust seasonings.

- Top warm tortillas with corn and bean mix. Sprinkle cheese over the corn and add more salsa if desired.

Nutrition Information

- 321: calories;
- 13 grams: fat;
- 0 grams: trans fat;
- 6 grams: monounsaturated fat;
- 48 grams: carbohydrates;
- 11 grams: sugars;
- 10 grams: protein;
- 4 grams: saturated fat;
- 2 grams: polyunsaturated fat;
- 7 grams: dietary fiber;
- 613 milligrams: sodium;

---

313. Summer Tomato Gratin

Serving: Serves four | Prep: | Cook: | Ready in: 1hours30mins

Ingredients

- 2 pounds ripe, firm tomatoes, sliced
- Salt
- freshly ground pepper to taste
- ½ teaspoon sugar
- ½ cup fresh or dry bread crumbs, preferably whole wheat
- 2 tablespoons chopped flat-leaf parsley
- 2 tablespoons extra virgin olive oil

Direction

- Preheat the oven to 400 degrees. Oil a 2-quart gratin or baking dish. Layer the tomatoes in

the dish, seasoning each layer with salt, pepper and a small sprinkle of sugar.

- Toss together the bread crumbs, parsley and olive oil. Spread over the tomatoes in an even layer. Place in the oven, and bake for 1 to 1 1/2 hours, until the juices are thick and syrupy and the top is golden. Remove from the oven, and allow to cool for at least 15 minutes before serving.

Nutrition Information

- 175: calories;
- 599 milligrams: sodium;
- 8 grams: fat;
- 1 gram: polyunsaturated fat;
- 6 grams: dietary fiber;
- 5 grams: monounsaturated fat;
- 26 grams: carbohydrates;
- 7 grams: sugars;
- 4 grams: protein;

---

314. Suvir Saran's Palak Ki Tiki (Spinach And Potato Patties)

Serving: Makes 10 substantial burgers (about 3 1/2 inches) | Prep: | Cook: | Ready in: 50mins

Ingredients

- 2 pounds red boiling potatoes, scrubbed and quartered
- 4 firmly packed cups finely chopped, stemmed, washed spinach (about 3/4 pound leaves)
- 1 fresh, hot green chili, finely chopped
- ¼ cup chopped fresh cilantro
- 1 teaspoon garam masala
- ½ teaspoon cayenne pepper
- ½ teaspoon ground black pepper
- Salt to taste (Suvir Saran uses about 1 1/4 teaspoons)

- 2 tablespoons fresh lemon juice
- 1 cup panko or chickpea flour (you will not use all of it)
- 2 tablespoons grape seed oil

Direction

- Steam potatoes over 1 inch of boiling water until tender, about 15 minutes. Transfer to a wide bowl and mash with a fork. Add remaining ingredients except panko or chickpea flour and oil and mix well with your hands, squeezing the ingredients together. There will still be small chunks of potato and potato skin in the mixture. Taste and adjust seasoning.
- Scoop out about 1/2 cup of the spinach-potato mixture, roll it with the palm of your hand to make a ball, and coat with panko or chickpea flour. Then press down to flatten to a 3 to 3 1/2-inch cake. Continue with remaining mixture. Chill for at least 1 hour.
- When you're ready to cook, place a rack over a sheet pan. Heat 2 tablespoons of oil in a large frying pan over high heat. Swirl pan to coat with the hot oil. Lower heat to medium. Place 4 to 5 patties in the pan (do not crowd), and cook until well browned on one side, about 4 minutes. Turn and brown for about 4 more minutes. Remove to the rack. Heat remaining oil in pan and cook remaining patties. Keep patties in a low oven until ready to serve. Serve with a salad and your choice of toppings, such as the usual (ketchup, mustard, relish), or yogurt raita, garlic yogurt, or chutney.

Nutrition Information

- 141: calories;
- 5 grams: protein;
- 337 milligrams: sodium;
- 4 grams: dietary fiber;
- 0 grams: saturated fat;
- 1 gram: monounsaturated fat;
- 2 grams: sugars;
- 23 grams: carbohydrates;

315. Sweet Potato And Apple Latkes With Ginger And Sweet Spices

Serving: About 40 small latkes, serving 6 to 8 | Prep: | Cook: | Ready in: 45mins

Ingredients

- 1 ½ pound red-fleshed sweet potatoes (yams), peeled and grated – about 5 cups grated
- 1 cup grated apple, preferably a slightly tart variety such as Braeburn
- 2 teaspoons fresh lime juice
- 1 to 2 teaspoons grated fresh ginger (to taste)
- 2 teaspoons ground cinnamon
- ½ teaspoon freshly grated nutmeg
- 1 teaspoon baking powder
- Salt to taste
- 3 tablespoons oat bran
- 3 tablespoon matzo meal or all-purpose flour
- 2 eggs, beaten
- About 1/4 cup canola, grape seed or rice bran oil

Direction

- Begin heating a large heavy skillet over medium heat. Heat the oven to 350 degrees. Line a sheet pan with parchment and place a rack over another sheet pan.
- Place the grated sweet potatoes in a large bowl. Toss the grated apple with the lime juice and add to the sweet potatoes, along with the ginger, spices, baking powder, salt, oat bran and matzo meal or flour. Taste and adjust salt. Add the beaten eggs and stir together.
- Take a 1/4 cup measuring cup and fill with 2 tablespoons of the mixture. Reverse onto the parchment-lined baking sheet. Repeat with the remaining latke mix. You should have enough to make about 40 latkes.
- Add the oil to the pan and when it is hot (hold your hand a few inches above – you should

feel the heat), slide a spatula under one portion of the latke mixture and press down with the spatula to flatten. Repeat with more mounds. In my 10-inch pan I can cook four at a time without crowding; my 12-inch pan will accommodate five or six. Cook on one side until golden brown, about three minutes. Slide the spatula underneath and flip the latkes over. Cook on the other side until golden brown, another two to three minutes. Transfer to the rack set over a baking sheet. Try one latke and if it is still a bit chewy in the middle transfer them to the baking sheet and place in the oven for 10 minutes, until golden brown and soft in the center.

- Serve hot topped with applesauce and low-fat sour cream, thick Greek yogurt or crème fraîche if desired.

Nutrition Information

- 175: calories;
- 5 grams: sugars;
- 8 grams: fat;
- 2 grams: saturated fat;
- 3 grams: protein;
- 0 grams: trans fat;
- 24 grams: carbohydrates;
- 4 grams: dietary fiber;
- 289 milligrams: sodium;

316. Sweet Potato, Quinoa, Spinach And Red Lentil Burger

Serving: 10 patties | Prep: | Cook: | Ready in: 1hours

Ingredients

- ⅓ cup quinoa (blond or black), rinsed
- ⅓ cup red lentils, rinsed
- 1 ⅔ cups water
- Salt to taste
- 1 ½ pounds sweet potatoes, baked
- 3 cups, tightly packed, chopped fresh spinach

- 3 ounces feta, crumbled (about 3/4 cup)
- 3 tablespoons chopped fresh mint
- ¼ cup minced chives
- 2 teaspoons fresh lemon juice
- Freshly ground pepper to taste
- 1 cup panko or chickpea flour (you will not use all of it)
- ¼ cup grape seed oil

Direction

- Combine quinoa, red lentils, water and salt to taste (I used a rounded 1/2 teaspoon) in a saucepan and bring to a boil. Reduce heat, cover and simmer 15 to 20 minutes, until quinoa is tender and blond quinoa displays a thread, and lentils are just tender. Drain off any water remaining in the pot through a strainer, tapping strainer against the sink to remove excess water, then return quinoa and lentils to the pot. Cover pot with a towel, then return the lid and let sit undisturbed for 15 minutes.

- Skin sweet potatoes and place in a large bowl. Mash with a fork. Add spinach and mash together (I use my hands for this). Add quinoa and lentils, feta, mint, chives, lemon juice, and salt and pepper to taste. Mix together well. Mixture will be moist.

- Take up about 1/3 cup of the mixture and form into a ball (you can wet your hands to reduce sticking). Roll the ball in the panko or chickpea flour, then gently flatten into a patty. Set on a plate and continue with the rest of the mixture. Refrigerate uncovered for 1 hour or longer (the longer the better).

- When you're ready to cook, place a rack over a sheet pan. Heat 2 tablespoons oil in a 12-inch, heavy nonstick frying pan over high heat. Swirl the pan to coat with the hot oil. Lower heat to medium. Place 4 to 5 patties in the pan (do not crowd), and cook until well browned on one side, about 4 minutes. Turn and brown for about 4 more minutes. Remove to rack. Heat remaining oil in the pan and cook remaining patties. Keep patties warm in a low oven until ready to serve. Serve with a salad and your choice of toppings, such as the usual (ketchup, mustard, relish), or yogurt raita, garlic yogurt, or chutney.

Nutrition Information

- 275: calories;
- 11 grams: fat;
- 3 grams: saturated fat;
- 2 grams: monounsaturated fat;
- 6 grams: sugars;
- 35 grams: carbohydrates;
- 9 grams: protein;
- 462 milligrams: sodium;

---

317. Sweet Whole Wheat Focaccia With Pears And Walnuts

Serving: 1 large focaccia, serving 12 | Prep: | Cook: | Ready in: 3hours50mins

Ingredients

- For the sponge
- 1 teaspoon / 4 grams active dry yeast
- ½ cup / 120 ml lukewarm water
- 1 tablespoon / 15 g sugar
- ¾ cup /90 grams unbleached all-purpose flour
- For the dough
- 1 teaspoon / 4 grams active dry yeast
- 1 cup / 240 ml lukewarm water
- 2 tablespoons / 30 grams sugar
- 3 tablespoons extra-virgin olive oil
- Scant 3/4 cup / 100 grams unbleached all-purpose flour
- ½ cup / 60 grams fine cornmeal
- 2 cups / 250 grams whole wheat flour or durum flour
- 1 ¾ teaspoons/ 12 grams fine sea salt
- For the topping
- 2 teaspoons chopped fresh rosemary
- 2 tablespoons extra-virgin olive oil

- ¼ cup / 35 grams chopped walnuts
- 1 pound ripe but firm pears, peeled, quartered, cored and sliced in wedges (about 1/2 inch thick at thickest point)
- 1 tablespoon / 15 grams sugar
- ⅛ teaspoon ground cinnamon

Direction

- Make the sponge. Combine yeast and water in a large bowl or the bowl of a stand mixer and stir to dissolve. Whisk in sugar and flour. Cover with plastic wrap and let proof in a warm place until bubbly and doubled in volume, about 45 minutes.
- Make the dough. If using a stand mixer, whisk together yeast and water in a small bowl and let stand until creamy, a few minutes. Add to sponge in the mixer bowl with sugar and olive oil. Add flours (including cornmeal) and salt and mix in with the paddle attachment for 1 to 2 minutes, until ingredients are amalgamated. Change to the dough hook and knead on medium speed for 8 to 10 minutes. Dough should come together and slap against the sides of the bowl. It will be slightly tacky. To make dough by hand, combine yeast and water as directed and whisk into the sponge with sugar and olive oil. Whisk in all-purpose flour. Add salt, cornmeal and whole wheat flour, one cup at a time, folding it in with a spatula or a wooden spoon. When you can scrape out the dough, add flour to the work surface, put dough on top and knead for 8 to 10 minutes, until soft and velvety. Return to bowl (coat the bowl lightly with olive oil first).
- Cover bowl tightly with plastic wrap and let dough rise in a warm spot until doubled, about 1 1/2 hours.
- Shape the focaccia. Coat a 12-x 17-inch sheet pan (sides and bottom) with olive oil. Line with parchment and flip the parchment over so exposed side is oiled. Turn dough onto the baking sheet. Oil or moisten your hands, and press out dough until it just about covers the bottom of the pan. Dough may be sticky. Cover with a towel and allow it to relax for 10

minutes, then continue to press it out until it reaches the edges of pan. Cover with a damp towel and let rise in a warm spot for 45 minutes to an hour, or until dough is full of air bubbles.

- Preheat oven to 425 degrees after 15 minutes of rising (30 minutes before you wish to bake), preferably with a baking stone in it. Combine rosemary and olive oil for the topping in a small pan and heat just until herbs begin to sizzle. Wait 30 seconds, swirl the oil in the pan, then pour mix into a ramekin or a small measuring cup. Allow to cool.
- With lightly oiled fingertips or with your knuckles, dimple the dough, pressing down hard so you leave indentations. Place walnut pieces in the indentations. Distribute pears evenly over dough and drizzle on the oil with rosemary (you will have to distribute clumps of rosemary that remain behind in the cup with your fingers). Combine remaining tablespoon of sugar and the cinnamon, and sprinkle evenly over pears and dough.
- Place pan in oven on baking stone. Spray oven 3 times with water during the first 10 minutes of baking, and bake 20 to 25 minutes, until edges are crisp and top is golden. If you wish, remove focaccia from the pan and bake directly on the stone during the last 10 minutes. Remove from oven, remove from pan at once and cool on a rack. If you want a softer focaccia, cover with a towel when you remove it from the oven. Serve warm or at room temperature.

Nutrition Information

- 264: calories;
- 8 grams: fat;
- 1 gram: saturated fat;
- 4 grams: monounsaturated fat;
- 9 grams: sugars;
- 2 grams: polyunsaturated fat;
- 43 grams: carbohydrates;
- 3 grams: dietary fiber;
- 5 grams: protein;

- 288 milligrams: sodium;

---

318. Sweet And Sour Stir Fried Radishes With Their Greens

Serving: Serves 3 to 4 as a side dish | Prep: | Cook: | Ready in: 4mins

Ingredients

- 1 generous bunch large radishes, with greens (about 1 pound total), or 2 smaller bunches
- 1 tablespoon soy sauce
- 1 tablespoon rice vinegar
- 2 teaspoons agave nectar or honey
- 2 tablespoons chicken stock, vegetable stock or water
- Salt and freshly ground pepper to taste
- 1 tablespoon peanut, canola, sunflower, or grape seed oil
- 2 teaspoons minced garlic
- 2 teaspoons minced ginger
- 1 bunch scallions, chopped, white and green parts separated
- ¼ cup chopped cilantro
- 1 teaspoon cornstarch dissolved in 2 tablespoons water

Direction

- Cut away greens from radishes and trim off bottoms of the stems. Wash in 2 changes of water and spin dry. Chop coarsely. Trim away tips of radishes and quarter lengthwise if large, cut in half if small.
- In a small bowl or measuring cup combine soy sauce, vinegar, agave nectar or honey, and stock or water. Have all ingredients within arm's length of your burner.
- Heat a 14-inch flat-bottomed wok over high heat until a drop of water evaporates within a second or two when added to the pan. Add oil to wok or pan and swirl to coat sides, then add garlic and ginger and stir-fry for no more than 10 seconds.   Add white parts of scallions and

stir-fry for 30 seconds to a minute. Add radish greens, salt and pepper and stir-fry for 1 to 2 minutes more, until they wilt, and stir in radishes. Stir-fry for 1/2 minute and add soy sauce mixture. Stir-fry for a minute more, then stir in ilantro and scallion greens, stir together for a few seconds, add cornstarch slurry and stir until vegetables are glazed (less than 30 seconds). Remove from heat and serve.

Nutrition Information

- 67: calories;
- 2 grams: dietary fiber;
- 8 grams: carbohydrates;
- 251 milligrams: sodium;
- 4 grams: sugars;
- 0 grams: saturated fat;
- 1 gram: protein;

319.   Sweet And Sour Winter Squash

Serving: Serves 4 | Prep: | Cook: | Ready in: 40mins

Ingredients

- 1 ¼ pounds winter squash, diced
- 2 tablespoons extra virgin olive oil
- Salt
- freshly ground pepper to taste
- 2 ½ teaspoons sugar
- 3 tablespoons red wine vinegar or sherry vinegar
- 3 garlic cloves, minced
- 2 to 4 tablespoons finely chopped fresh mint, to taste

Direction

- Preheat the oven to 400 degrees. In a baking dish large enough to accommodate the squash in an even layer, toss the squash with 1 tablespoon of the olive oil, and salt and pepper

to taste. Cover and place in the oven. Roast 20 minutes, until not quite tender. Remove from the heat.
- Dissolve the sugar in the vinegar in a small bowl. Heat the remaining olive oil over medium heat in a large, heavy skillet, and add the garlic and the squash. Cook, stirring gently, for a few minutes, until fragrant and the squash is tender but not too soft — about 3 to 5 minutes. Add the sugar and vinegar, and continue to cook, stirring gently, until the liquid is just about gone. Add the mint, cook for another minute, and remove from the heat. Serve hot, warm or room temperature.

Nutrition Information

- 127: calories;
- 16 grams: carbohydrates;
- 6 grams: sugars;
- 3 grams: dietary fiber;
- 2 grams: protein;
- 394 milligrams: sodium;
- 7 grams: fat;
- 1 gram: polyunsaturated fat;
- 5 grams: monounsaturated fat;

320.   Sweet Potato Stew

Serving: | Prep: | Cook: | Ready in: 15mins

Ingredients

- Sweet potatoes
- Apples
- Onions
- Coconut milk
- Chilis (dried or fresh)
- Ginger
- Vegetable stock or water
- Peanuts
- Cilantro

Direction

- Saute 1 pound cubed sweet potatoes, a peeled and cubed apple, chopped onion, minced chili (dried or fresh) and minced ginger, along with a sprinkle of curry powder in a large saucepan until the onion is soft, 5 or 6 minutes.
- Add coconut milk thinned with vegetable stock or water to about halfway up the sides of the mixture; cook until soft, then mash about half of the mixture.
- Garnish with chopped peanuts and cilantro and serve.

321.   Tacos With Summer Squash, Tomatoes And Beans

Serving: 6 servings | Prep: | Cook: | Ready in: 30mins

Ingredients

- 2 tablespoons extra-virgin olive oil
- 1 small red or white onion, finely chopped
- Salt to taste
- 2 garlic cloves, minced
- ¾ pound tomatoes, peeled and diced
- 1 ½ pounds summer squash, cut in small dice (about 4 1/4 cups)
- 1 serrano chile, minced
- 1 ½ cups cooked white beans, pinto beans or black beans (1 can, drained and rinsed)
- ¼ cup chopped cilantro (more to taste)
- 12 to 14 warm corn tortillas
- 2 ounces goat cheese, crumbled (1/2 cup)
- Salsa of your choice

Direction

- Heat olive oil in a large, heavy skillet over medium heat and add chopped onion. Cook, stirring, until tender, about 5 minutes, and add a generous pinch of salt and garlic. Cook, stirring, until garlic is fragrant, about 30 seconds, and add tomatoes. Cook, stirring often, until tomatoes cook down slightly, about 10 minutes (this could take more or less

time, depending on the texture and juiciness of the tomatoes).
- Stir in summer squash, chile, and salt to taste. Cook, stirring, until squash is tender but not mushy, about 8 minutes. Stir in beans and cilantro and heat through. Taste and adjust seasonings.
- Heat tortillas and top with squash mixture and crumbled cheese. Serve with the salsa of your choice.

Nutrition Information

- 295: calories;
- 3 grams: saturated fat;
- 4 grams: monounsaturated fat;
- 12 grams: protein;
- 721 milligrams: sodium;
- 2 grams: polyunsaturated fat;
- 43 grams: carbohydrates;
- 5 grams: sugars;
- 10 grams: dietary fiber;

322.   Tacos With Roasted Potatoes, Squash And Peppers (Rajas)

Serving: Serves 4 | Prep: | Cook: | Ready in: 40mins

Ingredients

- 1 pound potatoes, such as Yukon golds, cut into 1-inch chunks
- Salt to taste
- 1 teaspoon lightly toasted cumin seeds, ground
- 1 teaspoon mild chili powder
- 2 tablespoons extra-virgin olive oil
- ½ pound summer squash, preferably a dense squash like Ronde de Nice, cut into 1-inch chunks
- 1 medium red onion, cut in half lengthwise and sliced in half-moons

- 1 pound mixed sweet and hot peppers (such as a mix of poblanos and bell peppers), roasted, peeled, seeded and cut in thin 2-inch strips
- 8 warm corn tortillas
- 1 recipe salsa ranchera (without chipotles)
- 3 ounces goat cheese (about 3/4 cup crumbled)

Direction

- Preheat oven to 425 degrees. Line 2 baking sheets with parchment. Place potatoes on one baking sheet and toss with salt to taste, 3/4 teaspoon each of the ground cumin and chili powder, and 1 tablespoon of the olive oil. Spread in an even layer.
- Place squash and onion slices on other parchment-covered baking sheet and toss with the remaining olive oil, salt to taste, cumin and chili powder.
- Depending on the size of your oven, roast vegetables together or separately on the middle rack. Roast potatoes for 20 to 25 minutes, stirring after 10 minutes, or until lightly browned and tender all the way through. Remove from oven and transfer to a large bowl. Roast squash and onions for about 15 minutes, stirring after 10 minutes, until tender and lightly colored. Remove from oven and add to bowl with potatoes. Add pepper strips (rajas) and toss together. Season to taste with salt, and add more chili powder if desired. Keep warm.
- Spoon filling onto warm tortillas and add a generous spoonful of salsa. Top with goat cheese and serve.

Nutrition Information

- 395: calories;
- 12 grams: protein;
- 945 milligrams: sodium;
- 4 grams: saturated fat;
- 2 grams: polyunsaturated fat;
- 61 grams: carbohydrates;
- 14 grams: fat;

- 6 grams: monounsaturated fat;
- 9 grams: sugars;

---

323. Tarragon Cucumber Pickles

Serving: 2 quarts | Prep: | Cook: | Ready in: 30mins

Ingredients

- 2 large cucumbers (about 1 1/2 pounds)
- 4 large tarragon sprigs, cut into 2-inch pieces
- 2 tablespoons mustard seeds
- 2 tablespoons whole black peppercorns
- 1 tablespoon coriander seeds
- 2 bay leaves
- 4 cups plain rice wine vinegar
- ¾ cup sugar

Direction

- Slice cucumbers crosswise 1/4 inch thick, and pack into 2 quart-size jars. Divide tarragon, mustard seeds, peppercorns, coriander seeds and bay leaves between 2 double layers of cheesecloth. Tie into bundles with string.
- In a medium saucepan, combine vinegar with sugar and bundles of pickling spices, and bring to a boil, stirring to dissolve sugar. Pour brine over cucumbers, pack bundles of pickling spices on top and let cool. Discard spices, close jars and refrigerate at least 1 hour, preferably 3. Serve cold.

Nutrition Information

- 55: calories;
- 0 grams: polyunsaturated fat;
- 11 grams: carbohydrates;
- 1 gram: protein;
- 9 grams: sugars;
- 3 milligrams: sodium;

324. Teff Polenta Croutons Or Cakes

Serving: Serves 6 | Prep: | Cook: | Ready in: 15mins

Ingredients

- 1 batch teff polenta
- Olive oil as needed (or use a more neutral oil like grapeseed or peanut oil)
- Topping of your choice (optional)

Direction

- Make teff polenta as directed. Line a sheet pan, bread pan or baking dish with plastic wrap and spoon polenta on top. Press out to desired thickness and cover with plastic. Allow to stiffen completely, in the refrigerator if not using within the hour. You can also spread the polenta into a thin layer on the plastic on your work surface, cover with another sheet of plastic and gently roll over it with a rolling pin. Allow to cool and stiffen.
- Use a cookie cutter to cut rounds of polenta, or just cut into squares. Heat a heavy well-seasoned or nonstick frying pan over medium-high heat and add enough oil to coat well. Brown polenta pieces on both sides in oil. This doesn't take more than about a minute on each side. Each side should be crisp and brown. If the pieces are thicker cakes, turn down temperature a little so that they can heat through without burning. Remove to rack to drain. Serve hot or warm, or allow to cool and crumble into salads. They reheat nicely: place on a baking sheet in the oven at 325 degrees for 20 minutes.

Nutrition Information

- 288: calories;
- 3 grams: dietary fiber;
- 5 grams: protein;
- 5 milligrams: sodium;
- 2 grams: fat;
- 0 grams: saturated fat;
- 1 gram: sugars;
- 60 grams: carbohydrates;

325. Teff Pancakes With Chia, Millet And Blueberries

Serving: about 15 pancakes | Prep: | Cook: | Ready in: 15mins

Ingredients

- ½ cup (75 grams) teff flour (I make the flour by grinding the grain in a spice mill)
- 1 cup (125 grams) white whole-wheat flour or regular whole-wheat flour
- 2 teaspoons (10 grams) baking powder
- 1 teaspoon (5 grams) baking soda
- Rounded 1/4 teaspoon salt
- 1 tablespoon sugar, honey or agave syrup
- 2 eggs
- 1 teaspoon (5 grams) vanilla
- 1 ½ cups buttermilk
- 3 tablespoons canola oil
- 1 cup (125 grams) cooked millet
- 3 tablespoons (35 grams) chia seeds
- 1 6-ounce box blueberries tossed with 1/2 teaspoon all-purpose flour

Direction

- Sift together the teff, flour, baking powder, baking soda, salt and sugar (if using sugar). In a medium bowl, beat together the eggs, buttermilk, oil, vanilla, and honey or agave nectar if using. Quickly whisk in the flour mixture and fold in the chia seeds and millet.
- Heat a large skillet or griddle over medium-high heat and brush with butter or oil. Drop the pancakes by the scant 1/4 cup onto the hot pan or griddle. Place 7 or 8 blueberries on each pancake, gently pushing them down into the batter. Cook until bubbles break through and turn the pancakes. Cook for about 1 minute on

the other side, until lightly browned. Remove to a rack. Serve with maple syrup and butter.

Nutrition Information

- 156: calories;
- 0 grams: trans fat;
- 2 grams: sugars;
- 23 grams: carbohydrates;
- 3 grams: dietary fiber;
- 200 milligrams: sodium;
- 5 grams: protein;
- 1 gram: saturated fat;

---

326. Thanksgiving Mixed Bean Chili With Corn And Pumpkin

Serving: Yield: Serves 6 generously | Prep: | Cook: | Ready in: 2hours15mins

Ingredients

- 1 pound mixed dried beans, such as pintos and black beans, pintos and red beans, or heirloom beans such as San Franciscano, Good Mother Stallards, and Sangre de Toros (see note), washed, picked over, and soaked for at least 4 hours or overnight in 2 quart
- 2 onions, 1 halved, 1 finely chopped
- 4 garlic cloves, 2 crushed and peeled, 2 minced
- 1 bay leaf
- 2 tablespoons grapeseed or sunflower oil
- 3 tablespoons mild ground chili (or use hot, or use more)
- 1 tablespoon cumin seeds, ground
- 1 14-ounce can chopped tomatoes
- Pinch of sugar
- 2 tablespoons tomato paste dissolved in 1 cup water
- 2 cups diced winter squash (about 3/4 pound)
- 1 cup corn kernels (fresh or frozen)
- Salt to taste
- ½ cup chopped cilantro
- Grated or crumbled cheese for serving (optional)

Direction

- Place beans and soaking water in a large, heavy pot. Add halved onion and bring to a gentle boil. Skim off any foam that rises, then add crushed garlic and bay leaf, reduce heat, cover and simmer 30 minutes. Add salt and continue to simmer another 45 minutes to an hour. Using tongs or a slotted spoon, remove and discard onion and bay leaf.
- . Meanwhile, heat oil over medium heat in a heavy skillet and add chopped onion. Cook, stirring often, until tender, about 5 minutes. Add a generous pinch of salt, stir in chopped garlic, stir together for 30 seconds to a minute, until fragrant, and add ground chili and cumin. Cook, stirring, for 2 to 3 minutes, until mixture begins to stick to pan. Add chopped tomatoes with juice, pinch of sugar, and salt to taste. Bring to a simmer and cook, stirring often, until tomatoes have cooked down and mixture is beginning to stick to the pan, about 10 minutes. Stir in tomato paste dissolved in water and bring back to a simmer. Simmer, stirring often, for 10 minutes, until mixture is thick and fragrant.
- Stir tomato mixture into beans. Add winter squash and bring to a simmer. Taste and adjust salt. Simmer, stirring often so that the chili mixture doesn't settle and stick to the bottom of the pot, for 45 minutes. Add more water if chili seems too thick. Stir in corn and simmer for another 10 minutes. The beans should be very soft and the chili thick and fragrant. Taste and adjust seasonings.
- Shortly before serving stir in cilantro. Simmer for 5 minutes. Spoon into bowls. If you wish, top with grated cheddar, Monterey jack, or crumbled queso fresco. Serve with biscuits or cornbread.

Nutrition Information

- 155: calories;
- 2 grams: polyunsaturated fat;
- 25 grams: carbohydrates;
- 9 grams: sugars;
- 4 grams: protein;
- 657 milligrams: sodium;
- 6 grams: dietary fiber;
- 1 gram: saturated fat;

327. Three Greens Gratin

Serving: Serves 6 generously | Prep: | Cook: |Ready in: 1hours15mins

Ingredients

- 2 generous bunches Swiss chard (about 2 to 2 1/4 pounds), stemmed and washed in 2 changes of water
- Salt
- 1 pound beet greens or spinach, stemmed and washed in 2 changes of water
- 3 tablespoons extra virgin olive oil, plus additional for oiling baking dish
- 1 onion, chopped
- ½ pound leeks (1 large or 2 smaller), white and light green parts only, cleaned and chopped
- 3 garlic cloves, minced
- 1 teaspoon chopped fresh thyme leaves
- 1 pound cabbage (1/2 medium), cored and chopped
- 4 eggs
- 1 cup cooked rice or farro
- Nutmeg
- Freshly ground pepper
- 2 ounces Gruyère, grated (1/2 cup)
- 1 ounce Parmesan, grated (1/4 cup)
- ¼ cup breadcrumbs (optional)

Direction

- Bring a large pot of water to a boil while you stem and wash the greens. When the water comes to a boil salt generously and add chard. Blanch for 1 minute, until just wilted, and using a skimmer or a slotted spoon, transfer to a bowl of cold water. Drain and squeeze out excess water, taking the chard up by the handful. Chop medium-fine and set aside. You should have about 2 cups.
- Bring the water back to a boil and blanch beet greens for 1 minute; if using spinach, blanch for 20 seconds only. Transfer to a bowl of cold water, drain and squeeze out excess water. Chop medium-fine. You should have about 1 cup (less for spinach).
- Preheat oven to 375 degrees. Oil a 2-quart baking dish with olive oil.
- Heat 2 tablespoons olive oil over medium heat in a large, heavy skillet and add onion. Cook, stirring often, until tender, about 5 minutes, and add leeks. Cook, stirring, until leeks begin to soften, 2 to 3 minutes, and add garlic and a generous pinch of salt. Cook, stirring, until garlic is fragrant, 30 seconds to a minute, and add cabbage and thyme. Cook, stirring often, until cabbage collapses in pan, about 5 minutes, and add another generous pinch of salt. Continue to cook the mixture until the cabbage is tender, sweet, and beginning to color, about 10 minutes. Stir in chopped blanched greens and season to taste with salt and pepper. Stir together for about a minute and remove from the heat.
- Beat eggs in a large bowl and add a pinch of nutmeg and salt and pepper to taste. Stir in rice or farro, vegetable mixture and cheeses. Scrape into prepared baking dish. If using breadcrumbs, toss with remaining tablespoon olive oil and sprinkle over the top. If not using breadcrumbs drizzle remaining oil over the top.
- Bake 40 to 45 minutes, until top is lightly browned. Remove from heat and allow to sit for at least 10 minutes before serving. Serve hot, warm or room temperature.

Nutrition Information

- 302: calories;
- 0 grams: trans fat;

- 8 grams: monounsaturated fat;
- 30 grams: carbohydrates;
- 16 grams: protein;
- 15 grams: fat;
- 5 grams: saturated fat;
- 2 grams: polyunsaturated fat;
- 9 grams: dietary fiber;
- 7 grams: sugars;
- 1049 milligrams: sodium;

328.　　Tomato And Avocado Salsa

Serving: | Prep: | Cook: | Ready in: 20mins

Ingredients

- 1 pound ripe tomatoes, finely diced
- ½ small red onion, finely diced, soaked in cold water for five minutes, drained, rinsed and dried on paper towels
- 1 to 3 serrano or jalapeño peppers, minced
- 1 ripe avocado, peeled, pitted and finely diced
- 2 to 3 teaspoons fresh lime juice (to taste)
- 1 tablespoon extra virgin olive oil
- ¼ cup chopped cilantro (more to taste)
- Salt, preferably kosher salt, to taste

Direction

- Mix together all the ingredients. Let sit for 15 minutes, in or out of the refrigerator, before serving.

Nutrition Information

- 137: calories;
- 435 milligrams: sodium;
- 1 gram: polyunsaturated fat;
- 10 grams: carbohydrates;
- 2 grams: protein;
- 7 grams: monounsaturated fat;
- 5 grams: dietary fiber;
- 4 grams: sugars;

- 11 grams: fat;

329.　　Tostadas With Smashed Black Beans Or Vaqueros

Serving: 8 tostadas, serving 4 to 8 | Prep: | Cook: | Ready in: 45mins

Ingredients

- 1 tablespoon grape seed oil or canola oil
- 2 teaspoons cumin seeds, ground
- 4 cups simmered black beans or vaquero beans, with liquid
- 8 corn tortillas
- ¾ pound ripe tomatoes, finely chopped
- 1 to 2 serrano or jalapeño chiles (to taste), minced
- 2 slices red or white onion, finely chopped and soaked for 5 minutes in water to cover, then drained, rinsed, and drained on paper towels
- ¼ cup chopped cilantro (more to taste)
- 1 teaspoon fresh lime juice (optional)
- 1 small ripe Hass avocado, cut in small dice

Direction

- Heat oil over medium heat in a large, heavy pan (I use a heavy nonstick pan for this) and add cumin. When it is sizzling, add beans with their liquid and turn up heat to medium-high. Cook beans, mashing with the back of your spoon and stirring often, until they are thick but still fairly moist, about 10 to 15 minutes. Remove from heat. Every so often a layer of thick broth should begin to stick to the pan. Stir that into the beans – it has a lot of flavor. The smashed beans will continue to dry even after you remove from the heat.
- Toast the tortillas. For really crisp tortillas, heat one at a time (2 if you have a large enough microwave to fit 2 without the tortillas overlapping) in a microwave for 1 minute on full power. Flip tortilla over and microwave for 30 seconds to a minute more on full power,

until crisp. You can also toast them in a dry pan or directly over the flame, but this will not crisp the tortillas, it will just char them.

- In a medium bowl, combine tomatoes, chiles, onion, and cilantro. Season to taste with salt. Stir in lime juice and the avocado. Let sit for 15 to 30 minutes for the best flavor.
- Spread about 1/2 cup of the refried beans over each tortilla. Top with a generous spoonful of salsa. Place a handful of shredded lettuce or cabbage on top and if desired a little more salsa on the lettuce. Sprinkle on some white cheese, and serve.

Nutrition Information

- 181: calories;
- 9 grams: fat;
- 5 grams: sugars;
- 1 gram: saturated fat;
- 4 grams: protein;
- 3 grams: polyunsaturated fat;
- 25 grams: carbohydrates;
- 7 grams: dietary fiber;
- 25 milligrams: sodium;

---

330. Tuna Ceviche Or Tartare With Avocado

Serving: Serves four to six | Prep: | Cook: |Ready in: 30mins

Ingredients

- For the ceviche
- 1 pound albacore or yellowfin tuna, cut in 1/2 inch dice
- ½ small red onion, cut in small dice
- 1 garlic clove, minced
- 1 to 2 serrano or jalapeño chiles, to taste, seeded and minced
- 1 tablespoon capers, rinsed and drained
- 1 ripe medium avocado, cut in small dice
- Salt, preferably kosher salt

- freshly ground pepper to taste
- ⅓ cup fresh lime juice
- ¼ cup extra virgin olive oil
- ¼ to ½ cup chopped cilantro to taste
- Leaf lettuce, baby spinach or arugula, or radicchio leaves for serving

Direction

- Prepare the tuna and refrigerate while you prepare the remaining ingredients.
- Place the onion in a small bowl, and cover with cold water. Let sit five minutes, then drain, rinse and dry on paper towels.
- In a medium bowl, combine the onion, garlic, chile, capers, avocado, salt, pepper and 2 tablespoons of the lime juice. Toss together gently. Add the tuna to the bowl.
- Stir together the remaining lime juice and the olive oil. Pour over the tuna, and toss the mixture together. Season to taste with salt and pepper. Cover and refrigerate for 15 minutes, stirring gently from time to time.
- Just before serving, add the cilantro and toss together. Taste and adjust seasonings. Line plates with salad greens, spoon the ceviche on top, and serve.

Nutrition Information

- 225: calories;
- 335 milligrams: sodium;
- 2 grams: polyunsaturated fat;
- 10 grams: monounsaturated fat;
- 1 gram: sugars;
- 5 grams: carbohydrates;
- 3 grams: dietary fiber;
- 19 grams: protein;
- 14 grams: fat;
- 0 grams: trans fat;

---

331. Tuna Mushroom Burgers

Serving: Serves 4 | Prep: | Cook: |Ready in: 1hours

Ingredients

- 10 ounces sushi grade or ahi tuna, trimmed of blood lines
- 10 ounces roasted mushroom mix
- 1 to 2 teaspoons wasabi paste (more to taste)
- 2 tablespoons capers, coarsely chopped if desired
- Salt to taste
- black pepper to taste
- 1 small shallot, finely minced
- Oil for the pan (no more than 1 tablespoon)

Direction

- Chop tuna very fine. I find a cleaver works well for this. It should be like ground beef and it is best to do this by hand because a food processor will make the fish pasty.
- In a large bowl mix together all of the ingredients except the oil, and season to taste. Combine well. Shape 4 patties with moistened hands, or shape by setting a 2-1/2- or 3-inch ring on a plate and filling the ring with the mixture. Carefully remove the ring.
- Heat a large, heavy nonstick skillet over medium-high heat and brush lightly with olive oil or add a small amount to the pan and swirl the pan. Carefully add burgers to pan, taking care not to crowd them. Turn heat to medium and either sear for only 30 seconds to a minute on each side, or cook 2 minutes on each side if desired. Remove to a plate and serve, on buns if desired. Chef Pleau serves these with "avocado crema," a blend of avocado, yogurt, lime juice, cilantro and wasabi powder.

Nutrition Information

- 122: calories;
- 3 grams: fat;
- 0 grams: trans fat;
- 1 gram: dietary fiber;
- 5 grams: carbohydrates;
- 2 grams: sugars;
- 20 grams: protein;
- 371 milligrams: sodium;

---

332.   Turkey And Vegetable Burgers

Serving: 6 burgers | Prep: | Cook: | Ready in: 30mins

Ingredients

- 1 tablespoon extra virgin olive oil
- ½ cup finely diced onion
- ½ cup finely diced red bell pepper
- Salt to taste
- 1 large garlic clove, green shoot removed, minced
- ⅔ cup finely grated carrot (1 large carrot)
- 1 ¼ pounds lean ground turkey breast, preferably organic, from humanely raised turkeys
- 1 tablespoon prepared barbecue sauce
- 1 tablespoon ketchup
- Freshly ground pepper to taste
- Canola oil for the skillet
- Whole grain hamburger buns
- condiments of your choice

Direction

- Heat the olive oil over medium heat in a medium skillet and add the onion. Cook, stirring, until it begins to soften, about 3 minutes, and add the diced red pepper and a generous pinch of salt. Cook, stirring often, until the vegetables are tender, about 5 minutes. Stir in the garlic and the grated carrot and cook, stirring, for another minute or two, until the carrots have softened slightly and the mixture is fragrant. Remove from the heat.
- In a large bowl, mash the ground turkey with a fork. Add about ¾ teaspoon kosher salt if desired, and mix in the barbecue sauce, ketchup, and freshly ground pepper to taste. Add the sautéed vegetables and mix together well. Shape into 6 patties, about ¾-inch thick.

- Chill for 1 hour if possible to facilitate handling.
- Heat a nonstick griddle or a large nonstick frying pan over medium-high heat and brush with a small amount of canola oil, or prepare a medium-hot grill. When you can feel the heat when you hold your hand above it, cook the patties for 4 minutes on each side. Serve on whole grain buns, with the condiments of your choice.

333.   Turkish Pumpkin Soup

Serving: Serves 4 to 6 | Prep: | Cook: | Ready in: 1hours

Ingredients

- 2 tablespoons extra virgin olive oil
- 1 large onion, chopped
- 1 large leek, white and light green part only, thinly sliced
- 2 to 4 garlic cloves (to taste), minced
- Salt to taste
- 1 teaspoon ground allspice
- 1 teaspoon ground cinnamon
- 2 pounds peeled, seeded butternut or kabocha squash, diced (about 6 cups)
- 6 cups chicken stock, vegetable stock or water
- 3 tablespoons rice
- 1 teaspoon honey or sugar
- Freshly ground pepper to taste
- ½ cup Greek style yogurt
- Aleppo pepper, Turkish red pepper or mild chili powder for garnish

Direction

- Heat the olive oil over medium heat in a large, heavy soup pot or Dutch oven and add the onion and the sliced leek. Cook, stirring, until tender, about 5 minutes. Do not brown. Add a generous pinch of salt and the garlic and cook, stirring, until the garlic smells fragrant, 30 seconds to 1 minute.
- Add the squash, allspice, cinnamon, stock or water, rice, honey or sugar, and salt, and bring to a boil. Reduce the heat, cover and simmer 45 minutes.
- Using a hand blender, or in batches in a regular blender, purée the soup. If using a regular blender fill only half way and cover the top with a towel pulled down tight, rather than airtight with the lid, because hot soup will jump and push the top off if the blender is closed airtight. Return to the pot and heat through, stirring. Season to taste with salt and pepper.
- Ladle the soup into serving bowls. Swirl a tablespoon or two of yogurt into each bowl and sprinkle with Aleppo pepper, Turkish red pepper or chili powder.

Nutrition Information

- 241: calories;
- 10 grams: protein;
- 9 grams: fat;
- 2 grams: saturated fat;
- 5 grams: monounsaturated fat;
- 1 gram: polyunsaturated fat;
- 32 grams: carbohydrates;
- 3 grams: dietary fiber;
- 1021 milligrams: sodium;

334.   Turkish Tarator Sauce With Beets And Beet Greens

Serving: 6 servings (about 1 1/2 cups of sauce). | Prep: | Cook: | Ready in: 1hours30mins

Ingredients

- 1 large or 2 small bunches beets, with their greens (see note)
- ¾ cup coarsely chopped walnuts (about 2 1/2 ounces)
- 2 garlic cloves, halved, green shoots removed
- ½ teaspoon salt (or to taste)

236

- 2 ounces baguette (about 4 thick slices), crusts removed, soaked briefly in water and squeezed dry
- ¼ cup extra virgin olive oil
- 2 tablespoons walnut oil
- ¼ cup thick plain low-fat yogurt (more to taste)
- 2 tablespoons freshly squeezed lemon juice

Direction

- Roast the beets. Preheat the oven to 425 degrees. Cut the greens off of the beets, leaving about 1/2 inch of the stems attached. Scrub the beets, and place in a baking dish or oven-proof casserole. Add about 1/4 inch water to the pot. Cover tightly with a lid or foil, and bake 35 to 45 minutes, depending on the size of the beets, until tender. Remove from the heat, and allow to cool. If not using right away, refrigerate in a covered bowl.
- While you stem and wash the greens, bring a large pot of water to a boil. Fill a bowl with ice water. When the water comes to a boil, salt generously and add the greens. Blanch one or two minutes, just until tender. Transfer to the ice water, then drain and squeeze out the water. Chop coarsely.
- Combine the garlic and salt in a mortar and pestle, and mash to a paste. Place the walnuts in a food processor fitted with the steel blade, and process until finely ground. Add the bread and mashed garlic, and process to a paste. With the machine running, drizzle in the olive and walnut oils. Add the yogurt and lemon juice, and pulse to thin and smooth out the sauce. It should be thick, like a dip. Allow to sit for at least 30 minutes. If you want a creamier sauce, add more yogurt.
- When the beets are cool enough to handle, trim off the ends, slip off their skins, cut in half and then slice into half-moon shapes or wedges. Arrange the beets and greens on a platter. Spoon the tarator on the side or over the top, and serve.

Nutrition Information

- 230: calories;
- 22 grams: fat;
- 2 grams: dietary fiber;
- 9 grams: polyunsaturated fat;
- 8 grams: carbohydrates;
- 5 grams: sugars;
- 3 grams: protein;
- 246 milligrams: sodium;

---

335. Turkish Yogurt And Spinach Dip

Serving: About 2 cups | Prep: | Cook: | Ready in: 20mins

Ingredients

- 1 6-ounce bag baby spinach
- 2 plump garlic cloves, halved, green shoots removed
- Salt, preferably kosher salt, to taste
- 1 tablespoon freshly squeezed lemon juice (more to taste)
- 2 tablespoons chopped fresh dill
- ½ cup finely chopped parsley
- 2 tablespoons chopped fresh mint, or 1 teaspoon dried mint
- 2 to 3 tablespoons extra virgin olive oil
- 2 cups thickened yogurt or thick Greek style yogurt
- 1 bunch scallions, chopped (optional)

Direction

- Bring a large pot of generously salted water to a boil. Fill a bowl with ice water. When the water comes to a boil, add the spinach and blanch for 10 to 20 seconds. Transfer to the ice water, cool for a minute, then drain and squeeze dry. Chop coarsely.
- Place the garlic in a mortar and pestle with 1/2 teaspoon salt and mash to a paste (alternatively, finely mince). Combine with the

lemon juice and olive oil, and let stand for 10 minutes. Stir in the yogurt.

- In a medium bowl, combine the chopped spinach, dill, parsley and mint. Stir in the yogurt and garlic mixture, and the optional scallions. Add freshly ground pepper to taste and more salt if desired. Serve with bread, pita or raw vegetables.

Nutrition Information

- 218: calories;
- 16 grams: fat;
- 6 grams: monounsaturated fat;
- 1 gram: dietary fiber;
- 8 grams: carbohydrates;
- 5 grams: sugars;
- 12 grams: protein;
- 488 milligrams: sodium;

336. Two Bean And Tuna Salad

Serving: 6 Servings | Prep: | Cook: | Ready in: 15mins

Ingredients

- ¾ pound green beans, trimmed
- 1 small red onion, cut in half and sliced in half-moons (optional)
- 2 5-ounce cans tuna (packed in water or olive oil), drained
- 1 ½ cups cooked Good Mother Stallard, borlotti, pinto or white beans (if using canned beans, rinse)
- 2 tablespoons chopped fresh parsley
- 2 tablespoons chopped chives
- 2 teaspoons chopped fresh marjoram or sage
- 2 tablespoons sherry vinegar or red wine vinegar
- Salt to taste
- 1 garlic clove, minced or puréed
- 1 teaspoon Dijon mustard
- 2 tablespoons bean broth

- 6 tablespoons extra-virgin olive oil

Direction

- Bring a medium-size pot of water to a boil and add salt to taste. Blanch green beans for 4 minutes (5 minutes if beans are thick), until just tender. Transfer to a bowl of cold water and drain. (Alternatively, steam beans for 4 to 5 minutes). Cut or break beans in half if very long.
- Meanwhile, place sliced onion, if using, in a bowl and cover with cold water. Soak 5 minutes. Drain, rinse and drain again on paper towels.
- Drain tuna and place in a salad bowl. Break up with a fork. Add cooked dried beans, green beans, onion and herbs. Toss together.
- In a small bowl or measuring cup, whisk together vinegar, salt, garlic, mustard and bean broth. Whisk in olive oil. Toss with tuna and bean mixture, and serve.

Nutrition Information

- 256: calories;
- 2 grams: sugars;
- 10 grams: monounsaturated fat;
- 18 grams: carbohydrates;
- 5 grams: dietary fiber;
- 15 grams: protein;
- 0 grams: trans fat;
- 457 milligrams: sodium;
- 14 grams: fat;

337. Uncooked Tomato And Mint Sauce With Poached Eggs

Serving: Serves 4 to 6 | Prep: | Cook: | Ready in: 15mins

Ingredients

- For the sauce
- 6 ripe plum tomatoes (about 1 pound)

- 2 plump garlic cloves, peeled, halved, green shoots removed
- Salt and freshly ground pepper to taste
- ½ cup fresh mint leaves, lightly packed.
- 3 tablespoons extra virgin olive oil
- 4 to 6 eggs
- 1 tablespoon vinegar (any type)
- 4 to 6 corn tortillas
- Feta cheese for crumbling (optional)

Direction

- Cut tomatoes in half lengthwise. Place a box grater in a wide bowl, and using the large holes of the grater, grate tomatoes by rubbing the cut side against the grater, with the skin side cupped in your hand. When you feel the holes of the grater against the inside of the tomato skin, you are done.
- Turn on a food processor fitted with a steel blade and drop in the garlic. When it is chopped and adhering to the sides of the bowl, stop the machine and scrape down the sides with a spatula. Add tomatoes, salt, pepper, mint and olive oil. Process in the machine for 1-2 minutes, until sauce is frothy. Taste and adjust seasonings.
- Poach eggs. Fill a lidded frying pan with water and bring to a boil. Set timer for 4 minutes. Add 1 tablespoon vinegar. One at a time, break eggs into a teacup, then tip from teacup into pan (do this 2 at a time). Immediately turn off heat and cover pan tightly. Leave for 4 minutes. Using a slotted spoon or spatula, carefully remove poached eggs. Set on a towel to drain.
- While eggs are poaching, heat tortillas by placing them one at a time directly over the flame, until the edges are charred. If you don't have a gas stove, wrap in foil and heat for 10 minutes in a 350-degree oven. Place a tortilla on each plate and top with a poached egg. Spoon 3 tablespoons of the sauce over the eggs and serve.

Nutrition Information

- 173: calories;
- 11 grams: fat;
- 2 grams: sugars;
- 0 grams: trans fat;
- 7 grams: protein;
- 348 milligrams: sodium;
- 6 grams: monounsaturated fat;
- 13 grams: carbohydrates;
- 3 grams: dietary fiber;

338.   Vegetable Torta

Serving: 8 servings | Prep: | Cook: | Ready in: 1hours

Ingredients

- 1 ounce (about 1 cup) dried portobello mushrooms or 1/2 ounce dried porcinis
- 1 ½ cups boiling water
- 1 ½ cups quick-cooking steel-cut oats
- Salt to taste
- 3 tablespoons extra virgin olive oil
- 1 cup diced onion
- 1 cup coarsely shredded zucchini
- 1 to 2 garlic cloves (to taste), minced
- ½ cup diced sun-dried tomatoes (packed in olive oil, drained)
- ¼ to ½ cup chopped fresh oregano, to taste, or 1/4 cup fresh marjoram
- 6 eggs, at room temperature
- Freshly ground pepper
- 4 ounces Parmesan, grated (1 cup)
- Fresh Tomato Sauce

Direction

- Place the dried mushrooms in a bowl and pour on the boiling water. Let sit for 15 to 20 minutes, until the mushrooms are soft.
- Place the steel-cut oats in a bowl. Add salt to taste. Line a strainer with cheesecloth and place over the bowl. Drain the mushrooms, pouring their soaking liquid through the strainer, and then squeeze liquid out of the mushrooms while holding them over the

strainer. The oatmeal should be submerged in the soaking liquid (add a little water if it is not). Leave the oatmeal to soak for 20 minutes while you prepare your other ingredients.

- Rinse the mushrooms of any sand. Drain them, then squeeze dry and chop medium-fine. Set aside.
- Heat 1 tablespoon of the olive oil in a wide saucepan over medium-high heat and add the soaked steel-cut oats, along with any liquid remaining in the bowl. Stir constantly until all of the liquid has evaporated and the oats are cooked al dente, about 3 minutes. Remove from the heat.
- Heat another tablespoon of the olive oil over medium heat in a heavy 10- or 11-inch nonstick skillet. Add the onion and a pinch of salt. Cook, stirring often, until onion is tender and translucent, about 5 minutes. Add the garlic, zucchini, mushrooms and sun-dried tomatoes and cook, stirring, for another minute, until the zucchini begins to soften. Add the steel-cut oats, stir together until everything is well combined, and remove from the heat.
- In a large bowl, beat the eggs and season to taste with salt and pepper. Add the oregano or marjoram and 3/4 cup of the Parmesan. Stir in the oat mixture and mix well. Clean the pan and wipe dry.
- Return the skillet to medium-high heat and add the remaining tablespoon of olive oil. When the oil is hot, pour in the egg mixture, scraping every last bit out of the bowl with a rubber spatula. Cover the pan tightly and turn the heat to medium. Cook for 10 to 15 minutes, until the eggs are set (insert a knife in the middle; it should come out clean). Remove the lid and remove from the heat. Let sit for a few minutes in the pan, then invert onto a serving plate. Top with the remaining Parmesan. Allow to cool for 10 to 15 minutes and cut in wedges. Serve with a simple marinara sauce.

Nutrition Information

- 231: calories;
- 4 grams: dietary fiber;
- 0 grams: trans fat;
- 6 grams: monounsaturated fat;
- 17 grams: carbohydrates;
- 13 grams: protein;
- 2 grams: polyunsaturated fat;
- 3 grams: sugars;
- 365 milligrams: sodium;

---

339.   Veracruzana Vinegar Bathed Shrimp

Serving: Serves 8 | Prep: | Cook: | Ready in: 45mins

Ingredients

- 2 pounds medium shrimp
- 3 cups water
- 3 tablespoons extra-virgin olive oil
- 1 large white or red onion, thinly sliced
- 2 large carrots, thinly sliced
- Salt to taste
- 4 to 6 garlic cloves, minced or puréed
- 2 fresh or pickled serrano or jalapeño chiles, or chipotle chiles in adobo sauce, minced
- 2 large or 4 small bay leaves
- ⅓ cup seasoned rice vinegar
- ¼ teaspoon freshly ground pepper
- ½ teaspoon ground cloves (more to taste)
- 1 teaspoon dried Mexican oregano or 1 tablespoon chopped fresh mint
- ⅓ cup chopped cilantro
- Lettuce leaves for serving (optional)

Direction

- Peel and devein shrimp, saving the shells.
- Bring water to a boil in a medium saucepan and add shrimp shells. Simmer 30 minutes. Line a strainer with cheesecloth and set over a bowl. Strain broth into bowl and discard shells. You will need only 1/2 cup of the

broth; the rest can be frozen, or used to cook rice if you choose it to accompany the shrimp.

- Heat 2 tablespoons olive oil over medium heat in a large, heavy skillet and add onion, carrots and a generous pinch of salt. Cook, stirring often, until tender, 5 to 8 minutes. Add garlic and shrimp and cook, stirring, until shrimp begins to turn pink, about 3 minutes.
- Add chiles, bay leaves, vinegar, pepper, ground cloves, salt to taste and 1/2 cup shrimp stock and bring to a simmer. Reduce heat to low and simmer for 5 minutes or until the shrimp is cooked through, stirring occasionally. Remove from heat and transfer mix to a bowl. Refrigerate for 30 minutes or longer.
- Stir in remaining tablespoon of olive oil, the oregano or mint and cilantro. Taste and adjust seasonings. If desired, line a platter or plates with lettuce leaves and spoon shrimp mix over the lettuce.

Nutrition Information

- 146: calories;
- 6 grams: fat;
- 2 grams: sugars;
- 16 grams: protein;
- 660 milligrams: sodium;
- 1 gram: dietary fiber;
- 0 grams: trans fat;
- 4 grams: monounsaturated fat;
- 5 grams: carbohydrates;

340. Warm Chickpeas And Greens With Vinaigrette

Serving: Serves four | Prep: | Cook: | Ready in: 1hours30mins

Ingredients

- 1 pound spinach or Swiss chard (1 bunch), stemmed and thoroughly cleaned

- ½ pound (1 1/8 cups) chickpeas, soaked for at least six hours in 2 quarts water
- A bouquet garni made with a bay leaf, a couple of sprigs each of parsley and thyme, and a Parmesan rind
- Salt
- freshly ground pepper
- 2 tablespoons fresh lemon juice
- 1 tablespoon red wine vinegar or sherry vinegar
- 1 garlic clove, minced or pureed
- ⅓ cup extra virgin olive oil
- ¼ cup finely chopped flat-leaf parsley
- 1 small red onion, chopped, soaked in cold water for five minutes and drained (optional)

Direction

- Bring a large pot of water to a boil while you stem and wash the spinach or chard. Fill a bowl with ice water. When the water in the pot comes to a boil, add the greens. Cook spinach no longer than one minute. Cook chard one to two minutes. Remove from the pot with a skimmer, and transfer to the ice water. Do not drain the water. Cool the greens for a couple of minutes in the ice water, and then drain and squeeze out excess water. Chop coarsely and set aside. Allow the pot of water to cool for about 15 minutes.
- Drain the soaked chickpeas, and add to the pot along with the bouquet garni. Bring to a boil, reduce the heat to low, cover and simmer for one hour. Add salt to taste, and continue to simmer until the beans are tender, 30 minutes to an hour.
- Drain the chickpeas through a strainer or colander set over a bowl. Return the broth to the pot if you wish to serve it as a light soup. Whisk together the lemon juice, vinegar, minced garlic, salt and pepper to taste, and the olive oil. Combine the cooked chickpeas, greens, parsley and red onion in a bowl, and toss with the dressing. Serve warm.

Nutrition Information

- 401: calories;
- 3 grams: saturated fat;
- 14 grams: protein;
- 4 grams: polyunsaturated fat;
- 8 grams: sugars;
- 474 milligrams: sodium;
- 22 grams: fat;
- 41 grams: carbohydrates;
- 9 grams: dietary fiber;

341.   Warm Hummus

Serving: 2 cups | Prep: | Cook: |Ready in: 35mins

Ingredients

- 2 garlic cloves
- 2 cups cooked chickpeas (if using canned, rinse thoroughly)
- Salt to taste
- 1 teaspoon cumin seeds, lightly toasted and ground
- ¼ cup extra virgin olive oil
- 3 tablespoons lemon juice (more to taste)
- 3 tablespoons sesame tahini
- 1 tablespoon pine nuts
- ½ teaspoon Turkish red pepper or Aleppo pepper

Direction

- Heat the oven to 400 degrees. Oil a small baking dish or oven-proof bowl. Turn on a food processor fitted with the steel blade and drop in the garlic. Process until the garlic adheres to the sides of the bowls. Turn off the machine and scrape down the sides of the bowl. Add the chickpeas and cumin and turn on the machine.
- Combine 3 tablespoons of the olive oil, the lemon juice, and the tahini, and add to the machine. Process until the mixture is smooth. Season to taste with salt. Scrape into the baking dish or bowl. Drizzle on the remaining

tablespoon of olive oil and sprinkle on the pine nuts and red or Aleppo pepper.
- Bake for 10 to 15 minutes and serve hot with pita bread.

Nutrition Information

- 342: calories;
- 13 grams: monounsaturated fat;
- 6 grams: polyunsaturated fat;
- 27 grams: carbohydrates;
- 7 grams: dietary fiber;
- 4 grams: sugars;
- 10 grams: protein;
- 283 milligrams: sodium;
- 3 grams: saturated fat;
- 23 grams: fat;

342.   West African Peanut Soup With Chicken

Serving: 4 servings | Prep: | Cook: |Ready in: 40mins

Ingredients

- ¾ cup roasted and shelled peanuts
- 2 tablespoons peanut or neutral oil, like grapeseed or corn
- 1 medium red or white onion, chopped
- 1 tablespoon minced fresh ginger
- 1 tablespoon minced garlic
- ½ pound skinless, boneless chicken (about 2 thighs or breasts) cut into chunks
- Pinch of cayenne
- Salt
- freshly ground black pepper
- 6 cups stock or water
- 2 sweet potatoes or yams (about 1 pound), peeled and cut into thick slices
- 8 plum tomatoes, cored and halved (canned are fine; drain and reserve liquid for another use)

- ½ pound collards or kale, washed and cut into wide ribbons
- ¼ to ½ cup peanut butter, chunky or smooth

Direction

- Chop peanuts, or crush them with the side of a knife, or pulse them in a food processor to chop roughly.
- Put oil in a deep skillet or medium saucepan over medium heat; a minute later, add onion, ginger and garlic and cook, stirring occasionally, until onion is soft, 3 to 5 minutes. Add chicken and continue cooking for another 3 or 4 minutes, until just coloring. Add 1/2 cup peanuts and the cayenne and sprinkle with salt and pepper.
- Stir in the stock and the sweet potatoes, bring to a boil, and turn heat down to medium-low so the soup bubbles gently. Stir in tomatoes and collards, then cook, stirring occasionally, until chicken is cooked through, about 10 minutes.
- Stir in 1/4 cup peanut butter. Taste, adjust seasoning (you may want to add more peanut butter at this point) and serve, garnished with remaining peanuts.

Nutrition Information

- 689: calories;
- 11 grams: dietary fiber;
- 53 grams: carbohydrates;
- 40 grams: fat;
- 8 grams: saturated fat;
- 0 grams: trans fat;
- 19 grams: monounsaturated fat;
- 10 grams: polyunsaturated fat;
- 18 grams: sugars;
- 37 grams: protein;
- 1870 milligrams: sodium;

---

343. Wheat Berries With Broccoli

Serving: Serves four | Prep: | Cook: | Ready in: 1hours40mins

Ingredients

- 1 cup wheat berries
- 6 cups water, vegetable stock or chicken stock
- Salt to taste
- 2 broccoli crowns, broken into florets
- 2 tablespoons olive oil
- ½ cup minced onion
- 2 garlic cloves, minced
- 2 teaspoons chopped fresh rosemary
- freshly ground pepper
- 1 to 2 ounces Parmesan cheese, grated (1/4 to 1/2 cup, to taste)
- ¼ cup chopped fresh parsley

Direction

- Place the wheat berries in a bowl, and pour on enough hot water to cover by an inch. Soak for at least one hour, preferably overnight.
- Drain the wheat berries, retaining the soaking water. Add the soaking water to the stock. Add salt to taste. Place in a large saucepan, and bring to a boil. Add the broccoli, blanch for three minutes and transfer to a bowl of ice water. Allow to cool for a few minutes, then drain and set aside.
- Bring the liquid in the pan back to a boil, and add the wheat berries. Reduce the heat, cover and simmer one hour, until the wheat berries are tender. Remove from the heat, allow the grains to swell in the cooking water for 10 minutes and then drain over a bowl. You will need some of the liquid later.
- Heat the oil over medium heat in a large, heavy nonstick skillet, and add the onion. Cook, stirring, until tender, about five minutes, and add the garlic and rosemary. Cook, stirring, until fragrant, about one minute, then stir in the wheat berries and the

broccoli and heat through. Add freshly ground pepper, taste and adjust seasoning.

- Scoop 1/4 of the cooking liquid you set aside from the bottom of the bowl, where the starch has settled. Stir into the wheat berries, along with the Parmesan and parsley. Heat through, stirring until the cheese melts, and serve.

Nutrition Information

- 282: calories;
- 3 grams: saturated fat;
- 1 gram: polyunsaturated fat;
- 40 grams: carbohydrates;
- 8 grams: dietary fiber;
- 1204 milligrams: sodium;
- 11 grams: protein;
- 6 grams: monounsaturated fat;
- 2 grams: sugars;

344. Wheat Berries With Spinach And Spring Onion

Serving: 4 servings | Prep: | Cook: | Ready in: 1hours15mins

Ingredients

- 1 cup spelt, farro or kamut
- 3 cups water
- Salt to taste
- 2 bunches spinach, stemmed and washed well in 2 changes of water
- 2 tablespoons extra virgin olive oil
- 1 medium or large spring onion or 1 bunch smaller spring onions
- 2 garlic cloves, minced
- 1 teaspoon each fresh thyme leaves and chopped fresh rosemary
- Salt and freshly ground pepper to taste
- ¼ cup chopped walnuts (optional)
- 2 ounces crumbled feta for topping

Direction

- Rinse the kamut, farro or spelt and cover with boiling water. Soak for 1 hour and drain (alternatively, soak overnight in water from the tap). Combine with 1 quart water in a saucepan. Bring to a boil, add salt to taste (I use about 3/4 teaspoon), reduce the heat, cover and simmer 50 minutes, or until the grains are tender and just beginning to splay at one end. Drain off excess water (use for stocks if desired) and return the grains to the pot. Cover until ready to serve.
- Wilt the spinach: Blanch for 20 seconds in salted boiling water, steam for 1 to 2 minutes, or wilt in a dry frying pan in the liquid remaining on the leaves after washing. Transfer to a bowl of cold water, drain and squeeze out excess water, taking the spinach up by the handful. Chop coarsely.
- Heat 1 tablespoon of the olive oil over medium heat in a medium-size skillet and add the onion. Cook, stirring often, until onion is tender and aromatic, 5 to 6 minutes, and add a generous pinch of salt and the garlic. Cook, stirring, until fragrant, about 30 seconds to a minute, and add the spinach, thyme and rosemary. Stir together for a minute, just until the spinach is coated with oil and infused with the garlic and herbs. Season to taste with salt and pepper and remove from the heat.
- Spoon about 1/2 cup of kamut or spelt into bowls or onto plates. Top with the spinach and onion. Drizzle on a little olive oil, top with walnuts and crumbled feta, and serve.

Nutrition Information

- 253: calories;
- 38 grams: carbohydrates;
- 4 grams: sugars;
- 941 milligrams: sodium;
- 9 grams: dietary fiber;
- 2 grams: polyunsaturated fat;
- 5 grams: monounsaturated fat;
- 11 grams: protein;
- 1 gram: saturated fat;

345.   White Tepary Bean And Potato Purée

Serving: Yield: Serves 6 to 8 | Prep: | Cook: | Ready in: 2hours15mins

Ingredients

- ½ pound / 1 1/8 cups tepary beans or small white beans, soaked in 1 quart water for at least 4 hours or overnight
- 1 onion, cut in half
- 2 large garlic cloves, crushed
- 1 bay leaf
- 2 sprigs thyme
- Salt to taste
- ¾ pound Yukon gold or other fairly starchy potatoes, peeled and cut in large dice
- Optional garnish
- 2 tablespoons extra virgin olive oil
- ½ teaspoon red pepper flakes (more to taste)
- 2 garlic cloves, minced

Direction

- Drain soaked beans and place in a large saucepan or Dutch oven with 1 quart water, the onion and crushed garlic cloves. Bring to a gentle boil, add bay leaf and thyme, cover, reduce heat and simmer 30 minutes. Add salt to taste and simmer another 30 minutes. Add potato and continue to simmer another 30 minutes to an hour, until beans and potatoes are very tender. Using tongs, remove onion, bay leaf and thyme sprigs.
- Set a large strainer over a bowl and drain beans and potato. Transfer to a food processor, add 1/2 cup of bean broth, and process until smooth and creamy. Taste and adjust salt. Add pepper if desired. Transfer to a wide bowl or an oven-proof serving dish. Thin out as desired with more broth. Serve hot or warm.
- For optional garnish, heat olive oil over medium heat in a small frying pan and add garlic and red pepper flakes. When garlic begins to sizzle and smell fragrant, 30 seconds to a minute, remove from heat and drizzle over beans.

Nutrition Information

- 171: calories;
- 1 gram: polyunsaturated fat;
- 28 grams: carbohydrates;
- 2 grams: sugars;
- 216 milligrams: sodium;
- 4 grams: fat;
- 7 grams: protein;
- 3 grams: monounsaturated fat;
- 6 grams: dietary fiber;

346.   Whole Grain Macaroni And Cheese

Serving: 6 servings | Prep: | Cook: | Ready in: 1hours

Ingredients

- 2 tablespoons plus 2 teaspoons extra virgin olive oil, plus additional for oiling dish
- ½ pound whole grain macaroni shells, elbows, penne, or fusilli
- 1 large broccoli crown, broken into small florets (about 3/4 pound)
- 2 tablespoons finely chopped shallot
- 2 tablespoons flour, sifted
- 3 cups milk (1 percent, 2 percent or whole, to taste)
- Salt and white or black pepper
- Pinch of nutmeg
- 4 ounces Gruyère, grated (1 cup tightly packed)
- 1 ounce freshly grated Parmesan (1/4 cup tightly packed)

Direction

- Heat oven to 350 degrees. Oil a 2-quart baking dish.

- Bring a large pot of water to a boil and salt generously. Add macaroni and cook al dente, a minute short of however long you typically cook pasta if you were serving it right away. Use a skimmer or strainer to lift macaroni from cooking water and transfer it to a large bowl. Toss with 2 teaspoons olive oil and set aside.
- Add broccoli to boiling water and boil 3 minutes. Transfer to a bowl of cold water, drain, and then drain again on paper towels or a kitchen towel.
- To make béchamel, heat remaining 2 tablespoons oil over medium heat in a medium-size heavy saucepan. Add shallot and cook, stirring, until softened, 2 to 3 minutes. Stir in flour and cook, stirring, for about 3 minutes, until smooth and bubbling, but not browned. It should have the texture of wet sand. Whisk in milk all at once and bring to a simmer, whisking constantly until mixture begins to thicken. Turn heat to very low and simmer, whisking often and scraping the bottom and edges of the pan with a rubber spatula, for 15 minutes, until sauce has thickened and lost its raw flour taste. Season with salt, pepper and a pinch of nutmeg. Remove from heat.
- Strain béchamel while hot into the bowl with the pasta. Add cheeses and broccoli and stir together until pasta is nicely coated with sauce. Scrape into prepared baking dish.
- Bake 30 to 40 minutes, until bubbly and the top is lightly browned. Remove from oven and allow to sit for 5 to 10 minutes before serving.

Nutrition Information

- 388: calories;
- 17 grams: protein;
- 586 milligrams: sodium;
- 18 grams: fat;
- 8 grams: sugars;
- 1 gram: polyunsaturated fat;
- 39 grams: carbohydrates;
- 2 grams: dietary fiber;

Serving: 5 dozen smaller cookies (cut across the log) | Prep: | Cook: | Ready in: 2hours

Ingredients

- 250 grams (approximately 2 cups) whole wheat flour
- 60 grams (approximately 2/3 cup) almond flour
- 5 grams (approximately 1 teaspoon) baking powder
- ⅛ teaspoon (pinch) of salt
- 125 grams (approximately 2/3 cup, tightly packed) organic brown sugar
- 165 grams (3 large) eggs
- 5 grams (approximately 1 teaspoon) vanilla extract
- 100 grams almonds, toasted and chopped (approximately 3/4 cup chopped)

Direction

- Preheat the oven to 300 degrees. Line a baking sheet with parchment. Whisk together the flour, almond flour, baking powder and salt in a bowl.
- In the bowl of a stand mixer, or in a large bowl with a whisk or electric beater, beat together the sugar and eggs for 2 minutes. Scrape down the sides of the bowl and beaters. Add the vanilla and beat for another minute. Turn off the mixer, scrape down the bowl and beaters, and add the flour mixture. Mix in at low speed until combined. The batter will be sticky. Add the almonds and mix until well combined.
- Using a spatula or a bowl scraper, scrape out half the batter onto the baking sheet. Moisten your hands so the dough won't stick, and form a log, about 12 inches long by 2 1/2 inches wide. Repeat with the other half of the batter. The logs can be on the same baking sheet but

make sure there is at least two inches of space between them.

- Place in the oven and bake 50 minutes, until lightly browned and dry. Remove from the oven and let sit on a rack for 20 minutes (or longer). Place the logs on a cutting board and slice thin, about 1/3 inch, either straight across the logs (for more, but smaller biscotti) or on the diagonal (for more traditionally shaped biscotti).
- Place the cookies on baking sheets and return one sheet at a time to the middle rack of the oven. Bake 15 minutes. Flip the cookies over and bake for another 10 to 15 minutes, until hard and lightly browned. Remove from the heat and allow to cool.

Nutrition Information

- 42: calories;
- 0 grams: polyunsaturated fat;
- 1 gram: protein;
- 6 grams: carbohydrates;
- 16 milligrams: sodium;
- 2 grams: sugars;

---

348. Whole Wheat Apple Pecan Scones

Serving: 12 scones | Prep: | Cook: | Ready in: 30mins

Ingredients

- 1 apple, grated (145 grams grated apple)
- 1 tablespoon lime or lemon juice
- 2 teaspoons lemon or lime zest
- 1 ¼ cups / 160 grams whole wheat flour,
- ¾ cup / 90 grams unbleached all-purpose flour (or use all whole wheat flour)
- 1 tablespoon / 12 grams baking powder
- ½ teaspoon / 2 grams baking soda
- ¼ teaspoon / 2 grams salt
- ½ cup / 55 grams rolled oats
- 2 tablespoons /30 grams raw brown sugar
- 6 tablespoons / 85 grams unsalted butter
- Up to 1/4 cup / 60 grams buttermilk or yogurt
- ½ cup / 60 grams chopped pecans

Direction

- Preheat oven to 400 degrees. Line a baking sheet with parchment. Toss grated apple with lemon or lime juice and zest in a bowl. Sift together flours, salt, baking powder and baking soda, and stir in oats and sugar. Place in a large bowl or in the bowl of standing mixer fitted with the paddle.
- Add butter and mix in with your hands, rubbing the flour and butter briskly between your fingers; or beat on low speed until butter is distributed throughout the flour and the mixture has a crumbly consistency.
- Add apple with liquid to the large bowl. Add pecans and stir or mix at medium speed until incorporated. Add just enough yogurt or buttermilk to allow dough to come together.
- Scrape out onto a lightly floured surface and gently shape into a rectangle, about 3/4 inch thick. Cut into 6 squares, then cut squares in half on the diagonal to form 12 triangular pieces. Or use a biscuit cutter to cut rounds. Place on baking sheet. Bake 18 to 20 minutes, until lightly browned. Cool on a rack.

Nutrition Information

- 193: calories;
- 139 milligrams: sodium;
- 10 grams: fat;
- 4 grams: protein;
- 0 grams: trans fat;
- 2 grams: polyunsaturated fat;
- 24 grams: carbohydrates;
- 3 grams: dietary fiber;

349. Whole Wheat Focaccia With Cherry Tomatoes And Olives

Serving: 1 large focaccia, serving 12 | Prep: | Cook: | Ready in: 3hours50mins

Ingredients

- For the sponge
- 1 teaspoon / 4 grams active dry yeast
- ½ cup / 120 ml lukewarm water
- ¾ cup /90 grams unbleached all-purpose flour
- For the dough
- 1 teaspoon / 4 grams active dry yeast
- 1 cup / 240 ml lukewarm water
- 3 tablespoons extra-virgin olive oil
- 1 ¼ cups / 155 grams unbleached all-purpose flour
- 2 cups / 250 grams whole wheat flour or durum flour
- 1 ¾ teaspoons/ 12 grams fine sea salt
- For the topping
- 2 tablespoons extra-virgin olive oil
- 2 teaspoons chopped fresh thyme
- ½ pound cherry tomatoes, halved (about 1 1/2 cups)
- 16 imported black olives, halved lengthwise
- Coarse sea salt (optional)
- Several fresh basil leaves, cut in slivers or torn

Direction

- Make the sponge. Combine yeast and water in a large bowl or the bowl of a stand mixer and stir to dissolve. Whisk in flour. Cover with plastic wrap and let proof in a warm place until bubbly and doubled in volume, about 45 minutes.
- Make the dough. If using a stand mixer, whisk together yeast and water in a small bowl and let stand until creamy, a few minutes. Add to sponge in the mixer bowl, along with olive oil. Add flours and salt and mix in with the paddle attachment for 1 to 2 minutes, until ingredients are amalgamated. Change to the dough hook and knead on medium speed for 8 to 10 minutes. Dough should come together and slap against the sides of the bowl. It will be slightly tacky. To make the dough by hand, combine yeast and water as directed and whisk into sponge with the olive oil. Whisk in all-purpose flour. Add salt and remaining flour, one cup at a time, folding it in with a spatula or a wooden spoon. When you can scrape out the dough , add flour to the work surface, put the dough on top and knead for 8 to 10 minutes, until soft and velvety. Return to the bowl (coat bowl lightly with olive oil first).
- Cover bowl tightly with plastic wrap and let dough rise in a warm spot until doubled, about 1 1/2 hours.
- Shape the focaccia. Coat a 12-x 17-inch sheet pan (sides and bottom) with olive oil. Line with parchment and flip the parchment over so exposed side is oiled. Turn dough onto the baking sheet. Oil or moisten your hands, and press out dough until it just about covers the bottom of the pan. Dough may be sticky. Cover with a towel and allow it to relax for 10 minutes, then continue to press it out until it reaches the edges of the pan. Cover with a damp towel and let rise in a warm spot for 45 minutes to an hour, or until dough is full of air bubbles.
- Preheat oven to 425 degrees after 30 minutes of rising (30 minutes before you wish to bake), preferably with a baking stone in it. Place thyme and olive oil for the topping in a small saucepan or skillet and heat until thyme begins to sizzle. Count to 30 and remove from heat. Swirl the oil in the pan, then transfer to a measuring cup or ramekin and allow to cool.
- With lightly oiled fingertips or with your knuckles, dimple the dough, pressing down hard so that you leave indentations. Arrange cherry tomato halves and olives on dough, pressing them into the dimples. Drizzle on olive oil and use your fingers to distribute any thyme that remains in the cup or ramekin over the tomatoes. Sprinkle with a little coarse sea salt if desired.
- Place pan in oven on baking stone. Spray oven 3 times with water during the first 10 minutes

of baking and bake 20 to 25 minutes, until edges are crisp and top is golden. If you wish, remove focaccia from the pan and bake directly on the stone during the last 10 minutes. Remove from oven, remove from pan at once and cool on a rack. If you want a softer focaccia, cover with a towel when you remove it from the oven. Sprinkle torn or slivered basil leaves over the surface of the focaccia. Serve warm or at room temperature.

Nutrition Information

- 211: calories;
- 2 grams: dietary fiber;
- 242 milligrams: sodium;
- 7 grams: fat;
- 1 gram: sugars;
- 5 grams: protein;
- 33 grams: carbohydrates;

---

350. Whole Wheat Focaccia With Peppers And Eggplant

Serving: 1 large focaccia, serving 12 | Prep: | Cook: | Ready in: 3hours50mins

Ingredients

- For the sponge
- 1 teaspoon / 4 grams active dry yeast
- ½ cup / 120 ml lukewarm water
- ¾ cup /90 grams unbleached all-purpose flour
- For the dough
- 1 teaspoon / 4 grams active dry yeast
- 1 cup / 240 ml lukewarm water
- 3 tablespoons extra-virgin olive oil
- 1 ¼ cups / 155 grams unbleached all-purpose flour
- 2 cups / 250 grams whole wheat flour or durum flour
- 1 ¾ teaspoons/ 12 grams fine sea salt
- For the topping

- 1 small Japanese eggplant, sliced about 1/3 inch thick
- 3 tablespoons extra-virgin olive oil
- Salt to taste
- ½ medium onion, chopped
- 1 or 2 garlic cloves (to taste), minced
- 2 medium size bell peppers, preferably 2 different colors (such as red and yellow, or red and green), sliced
- 1 jalapeño or serrano, minced (optional)
- 1 small tomato, grated or peeled, seeded and chopped
- 2 to 3 teaspoons minced fresh marjoram
- Several fresh basil leaves, slivered or torn into small pieces

Direction

- Make the sponge. Combine yeast and water in a large bowl or the bowl of a stand mixer and stir to dissolve. Whisk in flour. Cover with plastic wrap and let proof in a warm place until bubbly and doubled in volume, about 45 minutes.
- Make the dough. If using a stand mixer, whisk together yeast and the water in a small bowl and let stand until creamy, a few minutes. Add to sponge in the mixer bowl, along with olive oil. Add flours and salt and mix in with the paddle attachment for 1 to 2 minutes, until the ingredients are amalgamated. Change to the dough hook and knead on medium speed for 8 to 10 minutes. The dough should come together and slap against the sides of the bowl. It will be slightly tacky. To make the dough by hand, combine yeast and water as directed and whisk into sponge along with olive oil. Whisk in all-purpose flour. Add salt and remaining flour, one cup at a time, folding it in with a spatula or a wooden spoon. When you can scrape out the dough, add flour to the work surface, put the dough on top and knead for 8 to 10 minutes, until soft and velvety. Return to bowl (oil the bowl lightly with olive oil first).

- Cover bowl tightly with plastic wrap and let dough rise in a warm spot until doubled, about 1 1/2 hours.
- Shape the focaccia. Coat a 12-x 17-inch sheet pan (sides and bottom) with olive oil. Line with parchment and flip the parchment over so exposed side is oiled. Turn dough onto the baking sheet. Oil or moisten your hands and press out dough until it just about covers the bottom of the pan. Dough may be sticky. Cover with a towel and allow it to relax for 10 minutes, then continue to press it out until it reaches the edges of the pan. Cover with a damp towel and let rise in a warm spot for 45 minutes to an hour, or until the dough is full of air bubbles.
- While the shaped focaccia is proofing, roast eggplant and prepare peppers. Preheat oven to 425 degrees. Line a sheet pan with foil. On the foil, toss eggplant with 1 tablespoon of the olive oil and salt to taste. Arrange in a single layer and place in the hot oven for 15 minutes. Remove from the oven and, taking care not to burn yourself, fold foil over, then crimp the edges so eggplant steams inside the foil. Keep oven on and place a baking stone in it if using one.
- Heat another tablespoon of olive oil in a large skillet over medium heat and add onion. Cook, stirring, until it begins to soften, about 3 minutes, and add garlic, peppers, and chile pepper if using. Add salt to taste and cook, stirring often, until peppers have softened, about 5 minutes. Add tomato and marjoram and cook, stirring, for another 5 to 10 minutes, until peppers are soft and tomato has cooked down. Taste and adjust seasoning. Remove from the heat.
- With lightly oiled fingertips or with your knuckles, dimple dough, pressing down hard so you leave indentations. Spread peppers over the dough and arrange the eggplant slices here and there. Drizzle on the final tablespoon of oil. Place pan in oven on baking stone. Spray oven 3 times with water during the first 10 minutes of baking, and bake 20 to 25 minutes, until edges are crisp and the top is golden. If you wish, remove focaccia from the pan and bake directly on the stone during the last 10 minutes. Remove from oven, remove from pan at once and cool on a rack. If you want a softer focaccia, cover with a towel when you remove it from the oven. Serve warm or at room temperature. Sprinkle slivered or torn fresh basil leaves over the top before serving.

Nutrition Information

- 234: calories;
- 7 grams: fat;
- 1 gram: polyunsaturated fat;
- 5 grams: protein;
- 37 grams: carbohydrates;
- 3 grams: sugars;
- 365 milligrams: sodium;

---

351.   Whole Wheat Focaccia With Tomatoes And Fontina

Serving: 1 large focaccia, serving 12 generously | Prep: | Cook: | Ready in: 4hours

Ingredients

- For the sponge
- 1 teaspoon/4 grams active dry yeast
- ½ cup/120 ml lukewarm water
- ¾ cup/90 grams unbleached all-purpose flour
- For the dough
- 1 teaspoon/4 grams active dry yeast
- 1 cup/240 ml lukewarm water
- 3 tablespoons extra virgin olive oil
- 1 ¼ cups/155 grams unbleached all-purpose flour
- 2 cups/250 grams whole wheat flour or durum flour
- 1 ¾ teaspoons/12 grams fine sea salt
- For the topping
- 2 tablespoons extra virgin olive oil
- 1 pound/450 grams fresh ripe tomatoes, sliced

- 6 ounces/180 grams/3/4 cup grated or sliced fontina
- Coarse salt to taste (optional)
- Chopped, slivered or torn fresh basil leaves

Direction

- Make the sponge. Combine the yeast and water in a large bowl or the bowl of a stand mixer and stir to dissolve. Whisk in the flour. Cover with plastic wrap and let rise in a warm place until bubbly and doubled in volume, about 45 minutes.
- Make the dough. If using a stand mixer, whisk the yeast and the water in a small bowl and let stand until creamy, a few minutes. Add to the sponge in the mixer bowl, along with the olive oil. Add the flours and salt and mix with the paddle attachment for 1 to 2 minutes, until the ingredients are amalgamated. Change to the dough hook and knead on medium speed for 8 minutes. The dough should come together and slap against the sides of the bowl. It will be slightly tacky. To make the dough by hand, combine yeast and water as directed and whisk into the sponge along with the olive oil. Whisk in the all-purpose flour. Add the salt and remaining flour, one cup at a time, folding it in with a spatula or a wooden spoon. When you can scrape the dough onto a work surface, add flour to the work surface, scrape out the dough and knead for 8 to 10 minutes, until soft and velvety. Return to the bowl (oil the bowl lightly with olive oil first).
- Cover the bowl tightly with plastic wrap and let dough rise in a warm spot until doubled, about 1 1/2 hours.
- Shape the focaccia. Oil a 12-x 17-inch sheet pan (sides and bottom) with olive oil. Line with parchment and oil the parchment. Turn the dough onto the baking sheet. Oil or moisten your hands and press out dough until it just about covers the bottom of the pan. Dough may be sticky. Cover with a towel and let it relax for 10 minutes, then continue to press it out until it reaches the edges of the pan. Cover with a damp towel and let rise in a warm spot

for 45 minutes to an hour, or until dough is full of air bubbles.
- Preheat oven to 425 degrees after 30 minutes of rising (30 minutes before you wish to bake), preferably with a baking stone in it. With lightly oiled fingertips or with your knuckles, dimple the dough, pressing down hard enough to leave indentations. Drizzle on the olive oil for the topping and arrange cheese over the surface. Top cheese with the sliced tomatoes and sprinkle tomatoes with coarse sea salt if desired.
- Place pan in oven on baking stone. Spray oven 3 times with water during the first 10 minutes of baking, and bake 20 to 25 minutes, until edges are crisp and the top is golden. If you wish, remove the focaccia from the pan and bake directly on the stone during the last 10 minutes of baking. Remove from oven and from pan and cool on a rack. Sprinkle basil over the top. If you want a softer focaccia, cover with a towel when you remove it from the oven. Serve warm or at room temperature.

Nutrition Information

- 264: calories;
- 11 grams: fat;
- 5 grams: monounsaturated fat;
- 8 grams: protein;
- 301 milligrams: sodium;
- 4 grams: saturated fat;
- 1 gram: sugars;
- 33 grams: carbohydrates;
- 2 grams: dietary fiber;

---

352.   Whole Wheat Mediterranean Pie Crust

Serving: Enough for two 9- or 10-inch tarts | Prep: | Cook: | Ready in: 1hours15mins

Ingredients

- 200 grams (approximately 1 3/4 cups) whole wheat flour or whole wheat pastry flour
- 115 grams (approximately 1 cup) unbleached all purpose flour
- 5 grams (approximately 3/4 teaspoon) salt
- 50 grams (1/4 cup) extra virgin olive oil
- 165 grams (3/4 cup) water
- 10 grams (2 teaspoons) red wine vinegar or strained lemon juice

Direction

- In a large bowl or in the bowl of a standing mixer fitted with the paddle or a food processor fitted with the steel blade, combine the flours and salt and mix together. If using a bowl, make a well in the center, add the olive oil and mix in with a fork. If using a mixer or food processor, turn on and add the olive oil. When it is evenly distributed through the flour combine the water and vinegar or lemon juice and add it to the flour mixture with the machine running. The dough should come together in a ball.
- Turn out the dough onto a lightly floured work surface, flour your hands and work the dough just until smooth and easy to shape into a ball. Do not overwork it or you will develop the gluten in the flour and the dough will be tough. Divide the dough in half, shape each half into a ball and press into a 1/2-inch thick circle. Wrap in plastic and let rest for 1 hour.
- Roll out the dough as needed for savory tarts, dusting your work surface and the top of the dough with flour to prevent it from sticking. Pre-bake and bake as directed in recipes calling for the crust.

Nutrition Information

- 771: calories;
- 28 grams: fat;
- 4 grams: polyunsaturated fat;
- 19 grams: protein;
- 116 grams: carbohydrates;
- 12 grams: dietary fiber;
- 1 gram: sugars;
- 628 milligrams: sodium;

353. Whole Grain Blueberry Buckle

Serving: 1 8-inch cake, serving 9 to 12 | Prep: | Cook: | Ready in: 1hours30mins

Ingredients

- For the topping
- 20 grams rolled oats (about 3 tablespoons, approximately)
- 60 grams quinoa flour (1/2 cup, approximately; grind quinoa in a spice mill to make the flour)
- ½ teaspoon freshly grated nutmeg
- 50 grams unrefined turbinado sugar (1/4 cup, approximately)
- ⅛ teaspoon salt (to taste)
- 60 grams cold unsalted butter, cut into 1/2-inch pieces (4 tablespoons/2 ounces)
- For the cake
- 125 grams whole- wheat flour (1 cup, approximately)
- 65 grams unbleached all-purpose flour (1/2 cup, approximately)
- 5 grams baking powder (1 teaspoon, approximately)
- 1 gram baking soda (1/4 teaspoon, approximately)
- 3 grams fine sea salt (scant 1/2 teaspoon, approximately)
- 90 grams unsalted butter, preferably French-style such as Plugrà, at room temperature (6 tablespoons/3 ounces)
- 120 grams sugar, preferably organic (scant 1/2 cup, approximately)
- 1 teaspoon finely grated lemon zest
- 2 eggs, at room temperature
- 130 grams buttermilk or kefir (1/2 cup)
- 350 grams blueberries (2 1/4 cups, approximately/ 2 boxes), divided

Direction

- Preheat oven to 350 degrees. Butter a 9-inch square baking pan and cover bottom with parchment. Butter parchment.
- Make the crumble topping. Place oats, quinoa flour, turbinado sugar, salt, and nutmeg in a food processor fitted with the steel blade and pulse several times to combine. Add cold butter and pulse until butter is evenly distributed in throughoutthroughout the grain mix. The mixture should have a crumbly consistency. Place in freezer while you make the ix up cake batter.
- Sift together flours, baking powder, baking soda and salt. In a standing mixer fitted with the paddle attachment, or in a bowl with electric beaters, cream butter, sugar, and lemon zest on medium speed for 3 to 5 minutes, until fluffy. Add eggs, one at a time, scraping down bowl between each addition.
- On low speed, add flour mixture in 3 batchesadditions, adding buttermilk or kefir between each addition. Scrape down bowl between each addition. Remove beaters and gently fold in half the blueberries.
- Scrape batter into prepared pan and spread evenly. Distribute remaining blueberries over the top. Sprinkle crumble topping over the blueberries.
- Bake 50 to 55 minutes, until golden and firm when pressed gently in the middle.

Nutrition Information

- 257: calories;
- 210 milligrams: sodium;
- 3 grams: dietary fiber;
- 0 grams: trans fat;
- 1 gram: polyunsaturated fat;
- 35 grams: carbohydrates;
- 18 grams: sugars;
- 4 grams: protein;
- 12 grams: fat;
- 7 grams: saturated fat;

---

354.   Whole Grain Pasta With Mushrooms, Asparagus And Favas

Serving: 4 to 6 servings | Prep: | Cook: | Ready in: 40mins

Ingredients

- 2 pounds fava beans, shelled
- 1 pound asparagus
- 2 tablespoons extra virgin olive oil
- 1 shallot, minced
- ½ pound wild mushrooms, quartered or sliced, or creminis, quartered if small, sliced if large
- 2 garlic cloves or 1 small bulb green garlic, minced
- Salt to taste
- 4 large basil leaves, torn into small pieces or cut in slivers
- ¾ pound whole-wheat pasta, such as penne or fusilli
- Freshly grated Parmesan for serving

Direction

- Begin heating a large pot of water while you shell the favas. Fill a bowl with cold water. When the water comes to a boil, salt generously and add the asparagus. Blanch thin stalks for 3 minutes, thicker ones for 4 to 5. Transfer to the cold water, drain and cut into 1-inch pieces. Set aside.
- Bring the water back to a boil and add the favas. Boil 3 to 5 minutes, depending on the size of the beans. Drain and transfer immediately to the cold water. Allow the beans to cool for several minutes, then slip off their skins by pinching off the eye of the skin and squeezing gently.
- Heat 1 tablespoon of the olive oil over medium heat in a large, heavy skillet and add the shallot. Cook, stirring, until translucent, 2 to 3 minutes, and add the mushrooms. Cook,

stirring often, until the mushrooms have begun to soften and sweat, about 3 minutes, and add the garlic. Cook, stirring, until fragrant, 30 seconds to a minute, and add salt and pepper to taste. Continue to cook, stirring, until the mushrooms are tender, fragrant and juicy, another 2 to 3 minutes. Stir in the asparagus and favas and remove from the heat but keep warm.

- Bring the water in the pot back to a boil and add the pasta. Cook al dente, using the timing instructions on the package as a guide but checking the pasta a minute before the time indicated is up. When the pasta is ready, use a ladle to transfer 1/2 cup of the pasta cooking water to the pan with the vegetables and another 1/2 cup to a bowl, in case you want more to moisten the mixture. Drain the pasta and toss at once with the vegetables and basil. Add more of the cooking water if desired. Serve hot, passing the Parmesan at the table.

Nutrition Information

- 438: calories;
- 80 grams: carbohydrates;
- 17 grams: dietary fiber;
- 23 grams: protein;
- 1 gram: polyunsaturated fat;
- 7 grams: fat;
- 4 grams: monounsaturated fat;
- 18 grams: sugars;
- 811 milligrams: sodium;

---

355. Whole Wheat Buttermilk Scones With Raisins And Oatmeal

Serving: 12 small scones | Prep: | Cook: | Ready in: 30mins

Ingredients

- 150 grams (approximately 1 1/4 cups) whole-wheat flour
- 62 grams (approximately 1/2 scant cup) unbleached all-purpose flour
- 40 grams (approximately 1/3 cup) oatmeal
- 10 grams (2 teaspoons) baking powder
- 5 grams (1/2 teaspoon) baking soda
- 25 grams (approximately 2 tablespoons) raw brown sugar (turbinado)
- 3 grams (approximately scant 1/2 teaspoon) salt
- 70 grams (2 1/2 ounces / 5 tablespoons) unsalted butter
- 125 grams (approximately 1/2 cup) buttermilk
- 75 grams (approximately 1/2 cup) raisins

Direction

- Preheat oven to 400 degrees. Line a baking sheet with parchment.
- Sift together flours, baking powder, baking soda, sugar and salt. Stir in oatmeal. Rub in butter, or place in a stand mixer fitted with the paddle and beat at low speed, or pulse in a food processor, until incorporated. Add buttermilk and raisins and mix just until dough comes together.
- Transfer to a lightly floured work surface and gently shape into a 1/2-inch thick rectangle. Cut either into 2-inch circles with a biscuit cutter or into 6 squares, then cut each square in half on the diagonal. Transfer to baking sheet. Bake 15 minutes, until browned on the bottom. Flip over, bake 2 more minutes, and remove from the heat. Serve warm or allow to cool.

Nutrition Information

- 147: calories;
- 23 grams: carbohydrates;
- 7 grams: sugars;
- 216 milligrams: sodium;
- 5 grams: fat;
- 3 grams: protein;
- 1 gram: monounsaturated fat;

- 0 grams: polyunsaturated fat;
- 2 grams: dietary fiber;

---

356. Whole Wheat Focaccia

Serving: 1 large focaccia or 2 smaller focacce, 12 to 15 pieces | Prep: | Cook: | Ready in: 4hours

Ingredients

- 2 teaspoons (8 grams) active dry yeast
- 1 teaspoon (5 grams) sugar
- 1 ½ cups (340 grams) lukewarm water
- 2 tablespoons (25 grams) olive oil, plus 1 to 2 tablespoons (25 grams) for drizzling
- 250 grams (approximately 2 cups) whole-wheat flour
- 200 to 220 grams (approximately 1 2/3 to 1 3/4 cups) unbleached all-purpose flour or bread flour, plus additional as needed for kneading
- 1 ¾ teaspoons (13 grams) salt
- Simple Toppings
- Coarse sea salt
- 2 to 4 tablespoons chopped fresh rosemary, thyme or sage
- Pitted black olives
- Roasted red peppers, diced or sliced

Direction

-
-
-

---

357. Whole Wheat Seeded Loaves

Serving: | Prep: | Cook: | Ready in: 5hours15mins

Ingredients

- 25 grams sunflower seeds (approximately 2 tablespoons plus 1 teaspoon)
- 25 grams sesame seeds (approximately 2 1/2 tablespoons)
- 25 grams flax seeds (approximately 2 1/2 tablespoons)
- 25 grams rolled oats (approximately 1/4 cup)
- 25 grams pumpkin seeds (approximately 2 tablespoons)
- 180 grams water (approximately 3/4 cup) plus about 60 grams additional water
- 170 grams bread flour or unbleached all-purpose flour (approximately 1 1/3 cups)
- 170 grams lukewarm water (approximately 3/4 cup less 2 teaspoons)
- 4 grams dry yeast (approximately 1 teaspoon)
- 250 grams whole-wheat flour (approximately 2 cups) or 125 grams bread flour and 125 grams whole-wheat flour
- 12 grams sea salt (approximately 1 1/2 teaspoons)

Direction

- Mix seeds and oats together with 180 grams of water in a medium mixing bowl; cover with plastic wrap and and let soak overnight in the refrigerator.
- Combine 170 grams bread flour or all-purpose flour, 170 grams lukewarm water, and yeast in bowl of a standing mixer and mix together until well combined. Cover with plastic and leave to ferment at room temperature for two hours or until it doubles in volume. Meanwhile, remove bowl with nuts and seeds from the refrigerator, drain   and bring to room temperature.
- Add drained seeds, 250 grams   whole-wheat flour and sea salt to the starter.   Start mixing on medium speed. The dough should come together in the first minute. If it does not and you see dry ingredients in the bottom of the bowl, add about 1/4 cup of water. Mix dough for 5 minutes on medium speed, then turn the speed up to medium-high and mix   5 to 7 minutes more, or until dough is elastic.
- Cover bowl with plastic wrap and set in a warm spot to rise for 1 hour.

- Dust work surface lightly with flour and scrape out dough. Weigh dough and divide into 2 equal pieces. Shape each piece into a ball or into oblong pointed loaves. (For oblong loaves, first shape into balls, cover with a towel or lightly with plastic and let rest for 15 minutes. Then press the dough out to a rectangle about 3/4 inch thick. Take the side closest to you and fold lengthwise halfway to the center of the loaf. Lightly press down to seal. Take the top flap and bring it toward you over the first fold to the middle of the loaf and lightly press down to seal. Flip over so seam is on the bottom and roll back and forth with both hands to form an oblong loaf with pointy ends. Place on a sheet pan lined with parchment paper and repeat with the remaining dough. Cover with a towel and place in a warm spot for one hour.)
- Preheat oven to 450 degrees with a pizza stone on the middle rack and a small sheet pan on bottom of the oven for 30 to 45 minutes. Have 1 cup water ready in a small cup or a glass. (If you have a large pizza stone, you can bake both loaves at once. If you have a standard home pizza stone, bake one loaf at a time and place the other loaf in the refrigerator to slow down the fermentation.) Dust a pizza peel or flat baking sheet lightly with flour, semolina or cornmeal and   place one loaf on top. Using a razor blade or a moistened bread knife, make a 1/2-inch deep horizontal cut down the middle of loaf from one end to the other, or if the loaves are round make 2 slashes across top. Slide loaf onto pizza stone and close oven door. Wait 30 seconds, then open oven door quickly and pour water onto the sheet pan on the bottom of the oven to create steam. After 5 minutes take the sheet pan out of the oven. Bake for a total of 30 to 35 minutes, until loaf is dark brown and sounds hollow when you tap the bottom. Transfer loaf to a wire rack to cool completely for 45 minutes.   Repeat with other loaf.

Nutrition Information

- 266: calories;
- 4 grams: polyunsaturated fat;
- 43 grams: carbohydrates;
- 6 grams: dietary fiber;
- 10 grams: protein;
- 7 grams: fat;
- 1 gram: saturated fat;
- 0 grams: sugars;
- 2 grams: monounsaturated fat;
- 279 milligrams: sodium;

---

358.   Winter Squash Puree With Tahini

Serving: About 3 1/2 cups | Prep: | Cook: | Ready in: 1hours

Ingredients

- 2 ½ pounds winter squash, like butternut
- ⅓ cup sesame tahini, stirred if the oil has separated out
- 2 large garlic cloves, halved, with green shoots removed
- Salt to taste
- 2 to 4 tablespoons freshly squeezed lemon juice, to taste
- ½ teaspoon cumin seeds, lightly toasted and ground
- Pomegranate seeds for garnish
- extra virgin olive oil for garnish

Direction

- Preheat the oven to 425 degrees. Cover a baking sheet with foil and brush lightly with olive oil. If using butternut squash, cut the squash in half, scoop out the seeds and stringy membranes, and lay cut-side down on the foil-covered baking sheet. If using a thick slice of squash, scrape off any membranes. Bake 45 minutes to one hour, or until very soft. A knife should cut through it without resistance, and the skin should be wrinkled. Remove from the heat and allow to cool, then peel and transfer to a food processor fitted with the steel blade. Add the tahini, and puree until smooth and creamy.

- Combine the garlic and 1/2 teaspoon salt in a mortar and pestle, and mash to a paste. Add to the food processor along with the lemon juice and cumin, and blend together. Add salt to taste.
- Mound the puree in a wide bowl or on a plate. Drizzle a little olive oil over the top, and garnish with pomegranate seeds. Serve with warm pita bread.

Nutrition Information

- 169: calories;
- 5 grams: dietary fiber;
- 4 grams: protein;
- 491 milligrams: sodium;
- 7 grams: fat;
- 1 gram: saturated fat;
- 3 grams: polyunsaturated fat;
- 26 grams: carbohydrates;

---

359. Winter Squash And Potato Gratin

Serving: Serves 6 | Prep: | Cook: | Ready in: 2hours

Ingredients

- 1 large garlic clove, cut in half
- 1 ¼ pounds russet potatoes or Yukon golds (or add purple potatoes to the mix), scrubbed, peeled if desired and sliced about 1/4 inch thick
- 1 ¼ pounds winter squash, such as butternut, peeled and sliced about 1/4 inch thick
- 1 teaspoon fresh thyme leaves
- 1 teaspoon chopped fresh rosemary
- 1 cup, tightly packed, grated Gruyère cheese (4 ounces)
- Salt to taste
- Freshly ground pepper

- 2-1/2 cups low-fat milk

Direction

- Preheat the oven to 375 degrees. Rub the inside of a 2-quart gratin dish or baking dish with the cut side of the garlic, and lightly oil with olive oil or butter. Slice any garlic that remains and toss with the potatoes, squash, thyme, rosemary, half the cheese and a generous amount of salt and pepper. Arrange in an even layer in the gratin dish.
- Pour the milk over the potatoes and squash, and press the vegetables down into the milk. Place in the oven, and bake one hour. Every 20 minutes, remove the gratin dish and press the potatoes and squash down into the liquid with the back of a large spoon. After one hour, sprinkle on the remaining cheese and bake for another 30 minutes, until the top is golden and the sides crusty. Remove from the oven, and allow to sit for 10 to 15 minutes before serving. Serve hot or warm.

Nutrition Information

- 242: calories;
- 7 grams: fat;
- 0 grams: polyunsaturated fat;
- 12 grams: protein;
- 725 milligrams: sodium;
- 4 grams: saturated fat;
- 2 grams: monounsaturated fat;
- 34 grams: carbohydrates;
- 3 grams: dietary fiber;
- 8 grams: sugars;

---

360. Winter Squash, Leek And Farro Gratin With Feta And Mint

Serving: Serves 6 | Prep: | Cook: | Ready in: 1hours20mins

Ingredients

- 2 pounds winter squash, peeled and cut in small dice (about 1/2 inch)
- Salt and freshly ground pepper
- 4 tablespoons extra virgin olive oil
- 1 pound leeks (2 large), white and light green parts only, cleaned and chopped
- 2 garlic cloves, minced
- 3 to 4 tablespoons chopped fresh mint, or 1 to 2 tablespoons dried mint (to taste)
- 3 eggs
- 3 ounces feta, crumbled
- ¾ cup cooked faro

Direction

- Heat oven to 425 degrees. Oil a 2-quart baking dish or gratin. Line a sheet pan with parchment. Place squash on baking sheet, season with salt and pepper, and add 2 tablespoons olive oil. Toss squash until evenly coated with oil. Place in oven and roast until tender and lightly colored, about 25 to 30 minutes, stirring every 10 minutes. Remove from oven and set aside. Turn heat down to 375 degrees.
- Heat another tablespoon of olive oil over medium heat in a large, heavy skillet and add leeks. Cook, stirring, until they begin to soften, about 2 minutes. Add a generous pinch of salt and continue to cook, stirring often, until tender, another 3 to 4 minutes. Stir in garlic and cook, stirring, until fragrant, 30 seconds to a minute. Add squash and mint to pan and toss together. Remove from heat.
- In a large bowl beat eggs. Add salt to taste (remembering that feta is very salty) and feta, and beat together until feta has broken up into eggs. Stir in squash and leek mixture and farro. Scrape into oiled baking dish. Drizzle remaining oil over top.
- Bake 35 minutes, or until lightly browned. Remove from heat. Serve hot, warm or room temperature.

Nutrition Information

- 325: calories;
- 2 grams: polyunsaturated fat;
- 41 grams: carbohydrates;
- 6 grams: dietary fiber;
- 15 grams: fat;
- 4 grams: saturated fat;
- 0 grams: trans fat;
- 8 grams: sugars;
- 11 grams: protein;
- 688 milligrams: sodium;

361.   Winter Tomato Quiche

Serving: Serves 6 to 8 | Prep: | Cook: | Ready in: 1hours40mins

Ingredients

- 1 9- or 10-inch whole wheat Mediterranean pie crust, (or gluten-free version)
- 1 tablespoon extra virgin olive oil
- ½ medium onion, finely chopped
- 2 to 3 garlic cloves (to taste), minced
- 1-14 1/2-ounce can chopped tomatoes in juice (no salt added), with juice
- 1 tablespoon tomato paste
- Pinch of sugar
- Salt to taste
- 1 sprig fresh basil or rosemary
- 1 teaspoon fresh thyme leaves or 1/2 teaspoon dried thyme
- Freshly ground pepper
- 2 eggs
- 2 egg yolks
- ¾ cup low-fat (2 percent) milk
- 2 ounces Gruyère cheese, grated (1/2 cup, tightly packed)
- 1 ounce Parmesan cheese, grated (1/4 cup, tightly packed)

Direction

- Roll out the crust and line a 9- or 10-inch tart pan. Refrigerate uncovered (place in freezer if using the yeasted crust) while you make the filling.

- Heat the olive oil over medium heat in a wide, heavy saucepan and add the onion. Cook, stirring, until it begins to soften, 2 to 3 minutes. Add a pinch of salt and continue to cook, stirring often, until tender, about 5 minutes. Meanwhile pulse the tomatoes in a food processor fitted with the steel blade or in a mini-processor.
- Add the garlic to the onions and cook, stirring, until fragrant, about 30 seconds. Add to the canned tomatoes and turn up the heat slightly. Add the tomato paste, sugar, salt, basil or rosemary spring and thyme and simmer briskly, stirring often, until the tomatoes have cooked down and smell fragrant, about 15 minutes. Taste and adjust salt, and add pepper. Remove from the heat. Remove the basil or rosemary sprig and, if you used rosemary, remove any rosemary needles that may have detached from the sprig. Allow to cool slightly. You should have about 1 cup of the sauce.
- Preheat the oven to 350 degrees. Beat the eggs and egg yolks in a large bowl. Brush the bottom of the crust with a small amount of the beaten egg and pre-bake for 10 minutes. Remove from the oven and allow to cool for 5 minutes.
- Beat the milk into the eggs. Add 1/2 teaspoon salt, freshly ground pepper to taste and beat together. Stir in the cheeses and the tomato sauce and combine well. Scrape into the crust, using a rubber spatula to scrape out every last bit from the bowl. Place the tart on a sheet pan for easier handling and place in the oven. Bake for 30 to 35 minutes, until set. Remove from the heat and allow to sit for at least 15 minutes before cutting.

Nutrition Information

- 235: calories;
- 2 grams: polyunsaturated fat;
- 19 grams: carbohydrates;

- 3 grams: sugars;
- 7 grams: protein;
- 292 milligrams: sodium;
- 15 grams: fat;
- 6 grams: monounsaturated fat;
- 0 grams: trans fat;
- 1 gram: dietary fiber;

362. Yogurt And Bean Dressing With Cilantro And Lime

Serving: 1 cup, about (about 6 to 8 servings) | Prep: | Cook: | Ready in: 5mins

Ingredients

- 1 small garlic clove, halved, green shoot removed
- ½ cup cooked white beans, drained and rinsed if using canned beans
- ½ cup whole milk or 2 percent Greek yogurt or regular yogurt
- 1 ice cube, if using Greek yogurt
- 1 tablespoon extra-virgin olive oil
- 3 tablespoons chopped cilantro
- Optional: 1 small serrano or jalapeño, minced
- 1 to 2 tablespoons fresh lime juice (to taste)

Direction

- Process garlic in a food processor fitted with the steel blade until minced garlic is adhering to sides. Stop processor and scrape down. Add beans, yogurt, and ice cube and process until smooth. Add remaining ingredients and process until mixture is smooth. Taste and adjust seasoning.

Nutrition Information

- 65: calories;
- 0 grams: polyunsaturated fat;
- 5 grams: carbohydrates;

- 2 grams: sugars;
- 3 grams: protein;
- 22 milligrams: sodium;
- 4 grams: fat;
- 1 gram: dietary fiber;

- 67: calories;
- 6 grams: carbohydrates;
- 2 grams: sugars;
- 3 grams: protein;
- 150 milligrams: sodium;
- 4 grams: fat;
- 1 gram: dietary fiber;

363. Yogurt And Bean Dressing With Thai Flavors

Serving: 1 cup, about (about 6 to 8 servings) | Prep: | Cook: | Ready in: 5mins

Ingredients

- 1 small garlic clove, halved, green shoot removed
- ½ cup cooked white beans, drained and rinsed if using canned beans
- ½ cup whole milk or 2 percent Greek yogurt or regular yogurt
- 1 ice cube, if using Greek yogurt
- 1 teaspoon minced fresh ginger
- 1-2 teaspoons soy sauce, to taste
- 1 teaspoon sriracha (more to taste)
- 1 teaspoon brown sugar
- 1 ½ tablespoons fresh lime juice
- Salt to taste
- 1 tablespoon chopped cilantro
- 1 tablespoon grape seed oil

Direction

- Process garlic in a food processor fitted with a steel blade until minced garlic is adhering to sides. Stop processor and scrape down. Add beans, yogurt, and ice cube and process until smooth. Add remaining ingredients and process until mixture is smooth. Taste and adjust seasoning.
- Scrape into a bowl. Serve as a dip or use with grains or crisp salads (it's a bit too thick for delicate lettuces like spring mixes).

Nutrition Information

364. Yogurt Or Buttermilk Soup With Spinach And Grains

Serving: 6 to 8 servings | Prep: | Cook: | Ready in: 1hours30mins

Ingredients

- ¾ pound (1 generous bunch) spinach, stemmed and washed in 2 changes of water, or 6 ounces baby spinach, rinsed
- 1 ½ cups finely diced cucumber (2 Persian cucumbers)
- Salt to taste
- 5 cups plain low-fat yogurt (free of gums and stabilizers) or buttermilk, or a mixture of the two
- 1 cup finely diced celery
- 1 to 2 garlic cloves (to taste), finely minced or puréed with a little salt in a mortar and pestle
- 2 tablespoons freshly squeezed lemon juice (more to taste)
- 1 cup cooked barley, spelt, kamut or farro
- ⅔ cup diced radishes
- Freshly ground pepper to taste (optional)
- ½ teaspoon sumac (more to taste)
- 2 tablespoons chopped cilantro
- Optional
- 1 ripe Hass avocado, cut in small dice

Direction

- Place the cucumber in a bowl and sprinkle with salt. Toss and place in a strainer set over the bowl. Allow to drain for 15 minutes. Rinse if desired and drain on paper towels.

- Meanwhile, steam the spinach above 1 inch of boiling water until wilted, 1 to 2 minutes, moving the leaves around with tongs once to ensure that they steam evenly. Rinse with cold water and squeeze out excess moisture. Chop medium-fine.
- Combine all the ingredients in a bowl. Thin out with ice water if desired. Season to taste with salt and pepper. Chill for one hour or longer.

Nutrition Information

- 179: calories;
- 6 grams: fat;
- 3 grams: monounsaturated fat;
- 11 grams: protein;
- 668 milligrams: sodium;
- 2 grams: saturated fat;
- 1 gram: polyunsaturated fat;
- 22 grams: carbohydrates;
- 4 grams: dietary fiber;
- 12 grams: sugars;

---

365.   Yogurt Or Buttermilk Soup With Toasted Barley

Serving: Serves six | Prep: | Cook: | Ready in: 2hours20mins

Ingredients

- For the yogurt or buttermilk soup with toasted barley
- ⅓ cup pearl barley
- About 2 cups water
- Salt to taste
- 1 cup finely diced cucumber
- 1 quart plain low-fat yogurt (free of gums and stabilizers) or buttermilk, or a mixture of the two
- 2 ripe but firm tomatoes, cut in small dice
- 1 stalk celery, cut in small dice

- 1 garlic clove, finely minced or pureed with a little salt in a mortar and pestle
- 2 tablespoons freshly squeezed lemon juice
- 2 tablespoons snipped chives
- 2 teaspoons cumin seeds, lightly toasted and ground
- Freshly ground pepper to taste (optional)
- 2 tablespoons slivered fresh mint leaves

Direction

- Heat a heavy, medium-size saucepan over medium-high heat, and add the barley. Stir or shake in the pan until it begins to smell toasty, about five minutes. Add the water and salt (to taste, about 1/2 teaspoon), and bring to a boil. Reduce the heat, and simmer until tender, about 45 minutes. Remove from the heat, drain and set aside.
- While the barley is cooking, place the cucumber in a bowl and sprinkle with salt. Toss and place in a strainer set over the bowl. Allow to drain for 30 minutes. Rinse well and drain on paper towels.
- Combine all the ingredients except the mint. Season to taste with salt and pepper. Chill for one hour or longer. Serve, garnishing each bowl with the mint.

Nutrition Information

- 156: calories;
- 0 grams: polyunsaturated fat;
- 13 grams: sugars;
- 3 grams: dietary fiber;
- 2 grams: saturated fat;
- 1 gram: monounsaturated fat;
- 22 grams: carbohydrates;
- 11 grams: protein;
- 759 milligrams: sodium;

Index

A

Ale 6,51,104,173,174,184,210,236,242

Allspice 7,209

Almond 3,4,5,6,7,8,14,25,89,123,170,200,203,246

Amaranth 3,5,7,10,11,129,217

Anchovies 6,142

Apple 3,4,6,7,8,10,12,13,14,52,59,71,76,88,89,140,183,223,227,247

Apricot 3,4,5,7,14,55,130,193,197

Artichoke 3,6,44,153,165

Asparagus 3,4,5,6,8,17,26,80,136,144,145,172,253

Avocado 3,4,6,8,17,56,58,59,146,178,233,234

B

Banana 3,4,24,25,90

Barley 3,8,26,27,39,261

Basil 5,7,131,167,217,221

Beans 3,4,5,6,7,8,9,15,17,18,39,66,84,131,132,149,159,189,202,213,221,228,233

Beef 3,5,6,31,126,166

Berry 3,32

Biscotti 4,8,91,95,246

Black pepper 27,100

Blackberry 3,34

Blini 3,28

Blueberry 3,4,8,25,36,64,91,252

Bread 3,5,6,7,40,106,143,186,195,199

Broccoli 3,4,5,6,7,8,16,37,95,116,119,135,136,142,160,168,173,194,200,202,208,243

Broth 5,108

Brussels sprouts 81

Buckwheat 3,4,5,41,64,91,108

Burger 3,5,7,8,31,123,126,224,234,235

Butter 3,4,5,7,8,32,41,46,47,56,84,89,106,114,115,139,140,144,186,253,254,260,261

C

Cabbage 3,4,5,6,7,48,49,58,117,168,188,214

Cake 8,230

Caramel 6,157

Carrot 3,4,5,6,7,28,35,38,48,50,52,115,159,166,168,169,173,174,175,183,205,206

Cashew 3,5,34,99

Cauliflower 3,4,5,7,50,51,65,82,115,190,200,201

Cayenne pepper 204

Celeriac 4,52,54

Celery 3,4,7,27,32,35,52,53,187

Chard 4,6,7,54,55,78,79,149,156,184,189,216,217,219

Chayote 5,100

Cheese 3,4,5,6,8,50,76,102,142,245

Cherry 3,4,6,7,8,14,55,56,140,148,221,248

Chicken 4,5,6,7,8,56,110,118,157,196,198,242

Chickpea 3,4,5,6,7,8,12,44,54,57,65,75,120,158,200,207,241

Chipotle 3,4,7,18,58,207

Chives 5,125

Chocolate 4,90,91

Cinnamon 5,7,129,209

Coconut 227

Cod 3,4,5,10,60,135

Collar 3,4,6,34,61,62,152,171

Coriander 7,209

Couscous 4,6,65,66,140,167

Crab 4,76

Cranberry 4,88

Cream 4,68

Crumble 4,62,80,88,201

Cucumber 3,4,5,6,8,35,69,70,99,181,229

Cumin 3,4,5,6,9,70,99,174

D

Daikon 5,127

Dijon mustard 9,14,15,23,30,45,52,59,76,77,123,153,238

Dill 4,70

E

Egg 3,4,5,6,7,8,48,73,74,75,101,120,144,194,238,249

F

Fat 4,79

Fennel 3,4,6,32,80,147,182

Feta 4,5,7,8,79,85,102,104,112,130,219,239,257

Fettuccine 4,81

Fig 4,6,93,182

Fish 4,72

Flank 6,164

Flour 7,196,207

Focaccia 4,6,7,8,82,150,225,248,249,250,255

Fruit 3,4,5,43,71,87,129

G

Garlic 4,5,6,7,69,71,86,87,110,173,199,210

Gin 4,5,6,7,69,87,103,162,164,198,212,223,227

Gnocchi 7,208

Grain 8,245,252,253,260

Grapefruit 3,4,35,78

Gratin 3,5,6,7,8,29,50,121,155,190,222,232,257

H

Halibut 3,19

Ham 126

Hazelnut 4,6,53,175

Herbs 6,7,141,146,211,212

Honey 5,106

Hummus 8,242

J

Jus 51,80,83,105,118,219,234

K

Kale 4,5,65,110,124

Ketchup 7,203

Kirsch 55,56

Kohlrabi 6,182

L

Leek 3,4,5,8,38,52,54,110,257

Lemon 4,5,6,7,26,73,81,110,127,150,191

Lentils 3,5,7,39,113,204

Lettuce 3,4,14,59,240

Lime 3,4,5,7,8,34,56,97,114,207,208,259

M

Macaroni 8,245

Mackerel 5,114

Manchego 220

Mango 5,114

Marjoram 4,67

Meat 5,107

Millet 5,6,8,119,120,121,122,134,147,230

Mince 76

Mint 3,5,7,8,21,115,138,221,238,257

Molasses 4,92

Mozzarella 6,148

Muesli 3,24

Muffins 4,5,64,90,91,92,93,96

Mushroom 3,4,5,6,7,8,16,27,31,42,95,109,119,123,124,125,126,127,12 8,136,137,150,176,177,211,234,253

N

Noodles 3,4,5,7,48,60,108,118,189,194,212,213,214

Nut
3,9,10,11,12,13,14,15,16,17,18,19,20,21,22,23,24,25,26,27,
28,29,30,31,32,33,34,35,36,37,38,39,40,41,42,43,44,45,46,
47,48,49,50,51,52,53,54,55,56,57,58,59,60,61,62,63,64,65,
66,67,68,69,70,71,72,73,74,75,76,77,78,79,80,81,82,83,84,
85,86,87,88,89,90,91,92,93,94,95,96,97,98,99,100,101,102,
103,104,105,106,107,108,109,110,111,112,113,114,115,11
6,117,118,119,120,121,122,123,124,125,126,127,129,130,1
31,132,133,134,135,136,138,139,140,141,142,143,144,145,
146,147,150,151,152,153,154,155,156,158,159,160,161,16
2,163,164,165,166,167,168,169,170,171,172,173,174,175,1
76,177,178,179,180,181,182,183,184,185,186,187,188,189,
190,191,192,193,194,195,196,198,199,200,201,202,203,20
4,205,206,207,208,210,211,212,213,214,215,216,217,218,2
19,220,221,222,223,224,225,226,227,228,229,230,231,232,
233,234,235,236,237,238,239,240,241,242,243,244,245,24
6,247,249,250,251,252,253,254,256,257,258,259,260,261

O

Oatmeal 3,4,5,6,8,25,64,129,186,254

Oats 3,5,40,129

Oil
3,5,7,18,20,22,29,50,62,64,74,75,90,91,92,93,96,103,122,1
30,141,142,144,148,151,155,156,190,191,220,222,225,232,
235,242,245,248,250,251,258

Olive
4,5,7,8,11,28,31,65,74,116,123,130,182,190,191,201,230,2
48

Onion 3,4,5,6,8,49,56,102,128,131,147,154,165,227,244

Orange 3,4,26,35,93

Oyster 6,150

P

Pancakes 3,5,6,8,11,30,40,115,116,117,150,230

Papaya 4,59

Parmesan
4,6,11,15,20,23,28,29,49,64,68,74,80,81,82,87,94,96,97,10
9,116,117,119,120,121,122,123,132,133,134,136,137,138,1
43,148,149,155,160,161,163,171,172,187,189,190,199,200,
201,209,218,220,221,232,239,240,241,243,244,245,253,25
4,258

Parsley 4,5,6,7,67,124,169,199

Parsnip 3,6,7,50,173,206

Pasta 3,5,8,16,132,136,137,138,253

Pastry 4,93

Peanuts 227

Pear 4,5,6,7,71,88,138,139,140,225

Peas 3,4,5,6,7,34,79,85,86,94,114,165,216

Pecan 4,5,8,88,115,247

Pecorino 133,138,190,200,201

Peel 18,30,36,50,88,122,136,139,144,173,183,221,240

Penne 4,94

Pepper
3,4,5,6,7,8,10,15,20,35,60,65,66,85,102,112,122,123,141,1
42,162,184,215,219,220,228,249

Pesto 3,5,6,7,22,124,131,144,172,200,221

Pickle 6,8,144,145,229

Pie 4,5,8,23,74,128,199,251

Pineapple 5,6,99,103,146,147

Pistachio 4,5,6,95,130,131,170

Pizza 5,6,102,147,148,154

Polenta 4,5,6,8,64,69,119,120,122,149,230

Pomegranate 3,35,37,256

Popcorn 7,204

Porcini 4,72

Potato
3,4,5,6,7,8,17,18,46,50,51,52,110,116,117,150,152,159,160
,173,178,189,206,207,222,223,224,227,228,245,257

Pulse 68,121,179

Pumpkin 6,8,157,231,236

Q

Quinoa
3,4,5,6,7,32,37,51,61,85,97,165,166,183,184,204,208,224

R

Radish 4,7,70,189,226

Raisins 7,8,195,254

Rice
3,4,5,6,7,23,28,29,38,39,40,80,83,85,118,141,169,170,189,
211,212,213,217,219

Ricotta 3,4,5,7,11,21,28,81,94,136,200

Risotto 4,6,67,171,172

Roast potatoes 229

Roquefort 76

Rosemary 4,7,82,186

S

Sage 3,4,47,82

Salad
3,4,5,6,7,8,9,14,15,23,26,27,30,32,33,37,39,44,45,59,69,70,
76,78,80,97,104,112,152,167,194,208,238

Salmon 5,6,127,180,181,182

Salsa
3,4,5,6,7,8,17,55,56,59,63,99,100,135,146,163,176,178,181
,182,196,197,221,228,233

Salt
9,10,11,12,14,15,17,18,19,20,21,22,23,26,28,29,30,31,32,3
3,34,35,37,38,39,41,42,44,45,46,47,48,49,50,52,53,54,55,5
7,58,59,60,61,62,63,64,65,66,68,69,70,71,72,73,74,75,76,7
7,78,79,80,81,82,85,86,87,94,97,98,100,102,104,107,108,1
09,110,111,112,113,114,116,117,118,119,120,121,124,125,
126,127,128,129,130,131,132,133,135,136,137,138,140,14
1,142,144,146,148,149,151,152,153,154,155,156,158,159,1
60,161,162,163,165,166,167,168,170,171,172,173,174,175,
176,177,178,179,180,181,182,183,184,185,187,188,189,19
0,192,194,195,196,197,198,199,200,201,203,204,205,206,2
07,208,209,210,211,212,213,214,216,218,219,220,221,222,
223,224,226,227,228,231,232,233,234,235,236,237,238,23

9,240,241,242,243,244,245,249,253,256,257,258,260,261

Sardine 7,193

Savory 6,7,185,186

Seeds 3,5,25,34,88,129

Soda 3,7,40,195

Sorbet 5,6,114,139

Soup
3,4,5,6,7,8,12,52,54,56,70,73,87,111,127,158,159,160,161,
162,173,191,209,218,236,242,260,261

Soy sauce 108,127,197

Spaghetti 3,4,7,22,95,199,200,201

Spices 4,7,60,223

Spinach
3,4,5,6,7,8,12,22,40,42,57,87,109,110,118,123,127,152,162
,205,208,209,210,211,218,222,224,237,244,260

Squash
3,4,5,6,7,8,18,21,22,23,46,47,66,97,162,171,184,199,221,2
27,228,256,257

Stew 4,7,72,207,227

Strawberry 7,218

Stuffing 6,185

Sweet potato 227

Swiss chard
44,54,55,78,79,149,156,184,189,216,219,232,241

Syrup 3,10,18

T

Taco 4,6,7,8,55,181,196,197,221,228

Tahini 4,6,8,54,173,256

Tarragon 4,8,94,229

Tea 3,6,26,180

Tempura 7,202

Thai basil 190,195,211,212,217

Thyme 6,7,175,186

Tofu 3,7,16,194,197,212,213,215

Tomatillo 3,4,5,6,7,17,63,135,163,178,181,221

Tomato

3,4,5,6,7,8,19,20,22,28,64,65,66,74,75,82,99,101,120,132,1
33,140,142,145,148,155,167,176,196,197,200,201,203,220,
221,222,228,233,238,239,248,250,258

Trout 5,113

Turkey 4,7,8,61,73,214,216,235

Turmeric 6,174

V

Vegetable stock 227

Vegetables 5,7,42,130,212

Vinegar 8,60,240

W

Walnut 3,4,7,13,18,46,53,59,95,195,200,210,225

Wasabi 6,181

Watermelon 5,104

Worcestershire sauce 126,182

Y

Yeast 74

L

lasagna 109

Conclusion

Thank you again for downloading this book!

I hope you enjoyed reading about my book!

If you enjoyed this book, please take the time to share your thoughts and post a review on Amazon. It'd be greatly appreciated!

Write me an honest review about the book – I truly value your opinion and thoughts and I will incorporate them into my next book, which is already underway.

Thank you!

If you have any questions, **feel free to contact at:** *author@thymerecipes.com*

Doris Naquin

thymerecipes.com

Made in the USA
Las Vegas, NV
11 December 2021